continued . . .

"A dizzying mishmash of social history, personal narrative, and rock-solid sports journalism. As raw with emotion as it is informative, *Pacific Rims* can make you both laugh out loud and tear up—sometimes in the span of a single sentence."

> —Bethlehem Shoals, author of *FreeDarko Presents:*
> *The Undisputed Guide to Pro Basketball History* and
> *The Macrophenomenal Pro Basketball Almanac*

"A kind of gonzo basketball journey filled with laughs and pathos . . . a ride worth taking."

> —Alex Kotlowitz, author of *There Are No Children Here*
> and *The Other Side of the River*

PACIFIC RiMS

Beermen Ballin' in Flip-Flops
and the Philippines' Unlikely Love Affair
with Basketball

Rafe Bartholomew

NEW AMERICAN LIBRARY

NEW AMERICAN LIBRARY
Published by New American Library, a division of
Penguin Group (USA) Inc., 375 Hudson Street,
New York, New York 10014, USA
Penguin Group (Canada), 90 Eglinton Avenue East, Suite 700, Toronto,
Ontario M4P 2Y3, Canada (a division of Pearson Penguin Canada Inc.)
Penguin Books Ltd., 80 Strand, London WC2R 0RL, England
Penguin Ireland, 25 St. Stephen's Green, Dublin 2,
Ireland (a division of Penguin Books Ltd.)
Penguin Group (Australia), 250 Camberwell Road, Camberwell, Victoria 3124,
Australia (a division of Pearson Australia Group Pty. Ltd.)
Penguin Books India Pvt. Ltd., 11 Community Centre, Panchsheel Park,
New Delhi - 110 017, India
Penguin Group (NZ), 67 Apollo Drive, Rosedale, Auckland 0632,
New Zealand (a division of Pearson New Zealand Ltd.)
Penguin Books (South Africa) (Pty.) Ltd., 24 Sturdee Avenue,
Rosebank, Johannesburg 2196, South Africa

Penguin Books Ltd., Registered Offices:
80 Strand, London WC2R 0RL, England

Published by New American Library, a division of Penguin Group (USA) Inc. Previously published in a
New American Library hardcover edition.

First New American Library Trade Paperback Printing, June 2011

REGISTERED TRADEMARK—MARCA REGISTRADA

LIBRARY OF CONGRESS CATALOGING-IN-PUBLICATION DATA:

New American Library Trade Paperback ISBN: 978-0-451-23322-6

The Library of Congress has catalogued the hardcover edition of this title as follows:

Bartholomew, Rafe.
    Pacific rims: beermen ballin' in flip-flops and the Philippines'
unlikely love affair with basketball/Rafe Bartholomew.
        p. cm.
    ISBN 978-0-451-22999-1
    1. Basketball—Philippines—History.   2. Basketball—Social aspects—Philippines.
    3. Filipinos—Social life and customs.   I. Title.
    GV8838.P5B37   2010
    796.32309559—dc22   2010003851

Set in Minion
Designed by Ginger Legato

PUBLISHER'S NOTE
While the author has made every effort to provide accurate telephone numbers and Internet addresses at the time
of publication, neither the publisher nor the author assumes any responsibility for errors, or for changes that occur
after publication. Further, publisher does not have any control over and does not assume any responsibility for
author or third-party Web sites or their content.

146119709

For my parents, Patricia and Geoffrey Bartholomew

ACKNOWLEDGMENTS

Hundreds of people deserve thanks and credit for bringing this book into existence. To those whom I can't mention in this short space, I'm grateful for your help and sorry for the omission.

I never would have made it to Manila without help from Chris Hager, Sara Anson Vaux and Rick Gaber from the Fellowships Office at Northwestern University. Also at NU, Richard Roth, Bob McClory, Alex Kotlowitz and Charles Whitaker at the Medill School of Journalism prepared me to report and write this book. Every page contains something I've learned from them.

The Philippine American Educational Foundation in Makati City supported me throughout my time in the Philippines, and I owe a large debt of gratitude to their helpful and professional staff: Dr. Esmeralda Cunanan, Con Valdecañas, Marj Tolentino, Gigi Dizon and Yolly Casas.

Thanks to Mollie Glick at Foundry and Mark Chait at NAL, who have done more than anyone else to make this dream a reality. To all the editors I've worked with over the years: Tom Jolly at the *New York Times*, Mike Seely at *Seattle Weekly*, Josh Levin at Slate and Alison True at the *Chicago Reader*. Thank you for believing in the story of Philippine basketball.

To the journalists who made my research possible: Sev Sarmenta, Bill Velasco, Quinito Henson, Jaemark Tordecilla, Ronnie Nathanielsz,

Reuel Vidal, Peter Atencio, Beth Celis, Boyet Sison and Jinno Rufino; and to the professors at Ateneo de Manila University and UP Diliman who taught me so much about Philippine history and society: Michael Tan, Benjie Tolosa, Jojo Hofileña, Aries Arugay, Danton Remoto, Lou Antolihao and many more.

Of course, I'm most thankful to the Philippine Basketball Association and the Alaska Aces for granting me access to the league and the team. In the PBA, commissioners Noli Eala and then Sonny Barrios, as well as Rickie Santos, Fidel Mangonon and Botong Chavez opened many doors for me. I cannot thank the Alaska Milk Corporation and the Aces franchise enough, from Sir Wilfred Steven Uytengsu, Jr., and Joaqui Trillo, to Coach Tim Cone and all of the players, assistant coaches and team staff. You are the biggest part of this book. Thanks to Rosell Ellis for being so generous with his time and basketball wisdom.

To the hundred-plus players, coaches and others I interviewed over the past four years, thanks for sharing your stories with me.

To all the people I played basketball with in the Philippines: Coach Ronnie Magsanoc and the SMC All-Star pickup crew; the regulars at the Xavierville Phase II clubhouse and Loyola Heights barangay hall; Jutes Templo and his Wednesday night group; and especially the La Salle Greenhills group—Ravi Chulani, Matt Makalintal, Darvin Tuason, Chris Tan, Coach Norman, Banjo Albano and Sarah Meier Albano, Aki Aquino, Renz, Sam and Sherwin Dona, Chris Viardo and so many more.

My friends and loved ones on both sides of the Pacific—Lauren Manalang, whose work on this book I will always appreciate; Ricardo Bernard, Pat Michels, Birju Shah, Brian Fuchs, Josh Centor, Mike Paulson, Michael and Kathy Huang, Charlene Dy, Chris Lanning, Ryan Guzman, Becca Dizon, Alex Compton, Kelly Williams, *mga kabarkada ko* from LP TODA (Drew's terminal), and many others—I couldn't have done this without you.

At sa mga mambabasang Pilipino, sana'y matutuwa kayo sa sinulat ko. Ibinuhos ko ang lahat dito. Maraming maraming salamat.

CONTENTS

PACIFIC RiMS

Introduction

Back in the summer of 2005, when I was preparing to move to the Philippines for a year on a government-funded academic grant, I heard a lot of unwelcome advice. At the time, I was filling in as a bartender at McSorley's Old Ale House, the landmark New York pub where my father had been a barman my entire life. During slow shifts, customers from McSorley's curious demographic mix would sidle up to the 151-year-old bar to chat. Sooner or later I'd divulge my Philippine plans, and people's sundry responses painted a discomforting picture of my future home. Japanese tourists, mindful of the Muslim insurgency in the country's far south, said it was better to be blown up in a terrorist attack than kidnapped and beheaded. A genial, red-cheeked midwestern retiree shared, with great joy, that he'd met his twenty-something wife there. A group of Filipino-Americans advised me to hire a private driver and beware razor-toting pickpockets who would slash open my backpack and bolt with its contents. A U.S. Marine who'd recently returned from a mission in the island nation bragged that he'd parlayed a hot hand at a craps table into an "eight-some," and said I shouldn't board my Manila-bound flight without first packing a suitcase full of rubbers.

When I explained that I was going to the Philippines to study the country's devotion to basketball, most of the time the customers' faces just went blank. The idea that I'd travel from New York, a self-proclaimed mecca of hoops, to Southeast Asia in order to learn something about the sport was usually met by a few seconds of confused silence and then the dubious rejoinder: "They play basketball there?" When I answered, "Yes," typical follow-up questions ranged from "Aren't they too short?" to "Do they play on ten-foot rims?" I wanted to feel pissed-off, but even I wasn't sure that the country's reputed passion for hoops could live up to the hype. By then, however, it didn't matter. I was locked in—I'd convinced a panel of academic judges that Philippine hoops was worth studying, received a grant, and bought my plane ticket. And on November 5, 2005, I was flying to Manila to find out for myself if Filipinos did indeed love basketball more than any other people on the planet.

Still half asleep when the twenty-two-hour flight touched down at Manila's Ninoy Aquino International Airport, I trudged through immigration and into the hectic baggage claim area. As passengers filtered into the room's fluorescent yellow light, they began staking out territory around the carousel. A siren let out a long, plaintive note that set people scrambling for the final spots in front of the conveyor belt. The crowd was three deep at the coveted spaces close to the hatch where bags emerged from the basement, and weary travelers jostled for the best positions. There was something oddly familiar about their movements. When a tall American woman tried to squeeze into a gap between the two people in front of her, one of the guys with inside position bent his knees, spread his legs, pushed his butt out and made it impossible for her to get around. She backed off and began maneuvering through the tangle to find another sliver of open space. Again, she was denied.

In the back of my mind I heard my father, who set a rebounding record on his high school basketball team in early 1960s Ohio, barking commands from the sidelines at my own high school games: "Box out, Rafe! Box out!" I thought back to the one-on-one games we'd played when I was still half his size and I could feel his powerful forearm pressing against my back while the ball was on the rim, forcing me to crouch and stay balanced while pushing the heavier man away from the basket. I looked again at the airline passengers using their bodies to seal off space in front of the conveyor, performing the same rugged waltz, sliding from side to side and shuffling backward. No way, I thought. It can't be.

It was. The Filipino passengers were boxing out for position in front of the baggage carousel. I kept waiting for the American woman to execute a spin move around one of the guys' backs to steal his position, but it never happened. No one was manhandling the female passenger, and this was a more civilized form of boxing out than what takes place beneath the backboards, but all the fundamentals were there. When it dawned on the woman that her attempts to worm her way to the front stood little chance against the other passengers' exquisite defensive positioning, she rolled her eyes in frustration and settled into the second row. I, on the other hand, was all smiles. This was an auspicious sign. I'd been in the Philippines less than an hour and already I'd found what I was looking for.

This Is probably a good time for me to come clean about a dirty little secret: I, Rafe Bartholomew, am a basketball fanatic. Phew, that felt so good I almost want to say it again: Hello, my name is Rafe Bartholomew. I'm a twenty-eight-year-old former Fulbright scholar, and I am a basketball freak. Growing up in downtown New York City, I spent every weekday afternoon playing at the Carmine Street Recreation Center in Greenwich Village. Years passed during my teens when I wore basketball shorts at all times except in the shower. I slept in them, wore them around my family's apartment, and kept them on under my jeans to be prepared anytime a game broke out. In college I built the reputation of some kind of hoops zealot, someone more interested in playing solid defense against a varsity player in a pickup game than finding a decent party, and someone who once played ninety-five consecutive days at the university gym.

I know that my strange behavior is beyond my control. You see, basketball is in my genes. Sired by a former college player who passed along his lanky build and passion for the game, basketball called to me from an early age. In fact, even before I picked up a ball there were signs of my future calling. A year before I was born, the Episcopal church in my neighborhood nearly burned down, so I was baptized next door in a school gymnasium. I grew up playing against my father. He was gracious enough to let me beat him one-on-one, but he always saw to it that I had a fresh collection of bruises by the time I pumped my fists in victory. My father's aim wasn't to win those games but to toughen me up. He instilled in me the hard-nosed basketball ethics he'd developed during his scrappy upbringing in a steel town on the outskirts of Cleveland. To my father, defense was next to godliness, and there was nothing more shameful than letting your man score.

When I was nine years old, I finally got my first chance to put these principles into play when my father deposited me at the Carmine Street gym. There, I learned to combine my father's gritty approach with the flash of the city game. Soon, I was playing on youth teams alongside New York playground legend William "Smush" Parker, who started at point guard for the Los Angeles Lakers in the 2005 and 2006 NBA seasons, as well as a crop of other young dynamos whose careers never amounted to much but whose daring forays to the hoop remained in my mind as the Platonic ideal of how the game should be played—with generous helpings of derring-do.

By the time I finished high school I had developed enough skill and versatility to draw the attention of small college teams—but I wasn't big enough to play at the Big Ten university I attended, where six-foot-three white boys like me were more suited to playing Ultimate Frisbee. Instead, I joined a club team and became a dedicated gym rat. I spent so much time playing pickup games at the university gym that I could deliver scouting reports on the ballhandling tendencies of business school yuppies, favorite post-up spots of football linemen, and defensive liabilities of Taiwanese Ph.D. candidates. And I'm proud to say that I can count on one hand the number of times I threw a Frisbee. During those years, when I wasn't playing ball, I was studying the game. Earlier in life, basketball books about New York like Darcy Frey's *The Last Shot* and Rick Telander's *Heaven Is a Playground* were the first books I bothered reading for a reason besides class. Since then I've had a soft spot for hoops lit, and during college I ran across a pair of hardcovers that introduced me to some mind-blowing stories about Philippine basketball.

The first of these was *The Breaks of the Game*, David Halberstam's chronicle of the 1979-80 Portland Trail Blazers' season. The book never mentions the Philippines, but its last forty pages are dominated by a player named Billy Ray Bates, an amalgamation of every long-shot, hard-luck, Cinderella story in the inspirational-but-ultimately-tragic sports handbook. After finishing the book, I looked Bates up on the Internet and read that he became a brief sensation in the Philippine pro league after he washed out of the NBA. Intriguing. That planted the seed in my mind. The second book was *Big Game, Small World* by Alexander Wolff, a hardwood travelogue filled with dispatches from almost twenty countries. The chapter on Wolff's trip to Manila stirred something inside me. Apparently, in this country halfway around the world, basketball was the only team sport that registered in the populace's hearts and minds; baseball and football were afterthoughts. In this overwhelmingly Christian country, basketball was a cultural force on par with the Catholic Church. This was a world where the local dedication to roundball would give my own fanaticism a run for its money. The Philippines.

The truth is, before I boarded my flight to Manila, I knew very little about Philippine basketball. Sure, I'd studied the country's history and politics—but no one on either side of the Pacific offered any real insights into basketball's role in the nation, and online editions of Philippine newspapers offered little more than game recaps from the local pro league and occasional gossip columns about players cheating on their celebrity wives. Aside from Wolff's chapter and the assurances of Sev Sarmenta, a Filipino broadcaster I had contacted via e-mail, I had found little hard evidence that the hoops mania I planned to study actually existed.

The dearth of confirmable facts about Philippine basketball gave my imagination space to run wild, and in the months before I left for Manila, I marveled about the twists of fate and historical anomalies that could have caused Filipinos to fall so hard for a sport that—on the surface, at least—didn't seem to suit them. With an average height of five-foot-five, Filipino men are some of the shortest in the world, giving them a natural disadvantage in the sport's most non-negotiable requirement. Of their Asian neighbors, only the Chinese have any international reputation for basketball, and that notoriety is based mostly on Yao Ming. The Philippines, meanwhile, hasn't sent a basketball team to the Olympics since 1972, and the country's last significant achievement in world basketball was a bronze medal in the 1998 Asian Games. Compared to the Olympics, that's like being runner-up in the Greater Mongolia Shuffleboard Classic.

But still, I had heard some amazing stories.

Supposedly, basketball fever in the Philippines ran so hot that the government once rescheduled a voter registration drive after learning that it conflicted with the telecast of an NBA finals game. According to roundball legend, Filipinos were so dedicated to basketball that the wealthy alumni of a Manila university bought the floor used in a past NBA All-Star game, had it shipped to Manila in pieces, and installed it in the school gym. And apparently, Filipinos' devotion to the game was so absolute that fans once dressed a wooden Santo Niño statue of the boy Christ in a local superstar's uniform during a Christmas procession.

These tall tales were too much to resist. Here was a nation full of basketball freaks just like me! So somehow I managed to convince the Fulbright board to give me their blessing (and the American taxpayers' money) to fund a year in Manila to document the phenomenon. The hoops culture I found there was so deeply embedded in Philippine society and so inspiring to me that I ended up staying for three years.

1

Hoop Epiphanies

On my second day in Manila, I took a taxi to Quezon City to look for an apartment and found myself mired in gridlock. The diesel fumes were so thick that motorcyclists wore asbestos masks to filter the air, and I covered my face with a washcloth as I watched the jeepneys crawl past. A jeepney is a mode of public transportation taken from U.S. military vehicles that once carried GIs around the American naval and air force bases that were located on Philippine soil until the early 1990s. It's an elongated jeep with two benches facing each other and each side seating about ten uncomfortably intimate passengers. But Filipinos have adapted the military designs to suit their own aesthetic. Today, jeepneys are adorned with longhorned bull skulls, imitation Mercedes hood ornaments, and giant bugles mounted on chrome grills. The horns don't beep, they belch "La Cucaracha" and emit *Star Trek* phaser sounds, and—this is creepy—some blare talking doll voices that repeat "I love you" over and over again. The sides of jeepneys are home to a semiotic buffet of logos and decals that provide a window into the cluttered psyches of their operators. The symbols represent a mash-up of familial, religious, and pop culture references with no obvious organizing principle.

On my way to Quezon City, I saw jeepneys painted with nativity scenes and portraits of Jesus over hot pink and neon green backgrounds. I saw cartoonish renderings of professional wrestlers, the Confederate flag, bikini-clad actresses, the Little Mermaid, Shrek, and Alfred E. Neuman. And there wasn't a jeepney on the road that day that didn't somehow pay homage to basketball. Many of them displayed the silhouette of Jerry West dribbling over the NBA's logo or Michael Jordan spread-eagled in mid-air with a ball in his outstretched hand. NBA team decals were scattered on the vehicles' sides like constellations: the New Jersey Nets, the Los Angeles Lakers, even defunct franchises like the Vancouver Grizzlies. Still other jeepneys featured portraits of a beaming Magic Johnson or a stern Larry Bird just inches away from similar paintings of the drivers' daughters, the Virgin Mary, and the Mighty Morphin Power Rangers.

After the two-hour crawl to Quezon City, I viewed an apartment in a twenty-story condominium building along Katipunan Avenue, near some of the country's top universities. My potential landlord's nephew showed me through the dim, narrow hallways with flickering fluorescent lights. He opened the door to a gloomy studio furnished with a bed so short that I could lay on it, bend my legs over the end and rest my feet on the floor. Then I followed him to his family's apartment, where he explained the terms of the lease. Although I had no intention of renting the place, I listened. While he held forth on security deposits and condo association dues, my attention wandered to a collection of 1990s-era basketball action figures hanging on the wall behind him.

The plastic NBA players, kept in their original packaging like something a person dressed as Chewbacca might carry into a Star Wars convention, covered the wall from floor to ceiling. The assortment included not just superstars like Michael Jordan and Charles Barkley, but also several role players who only a true hoops enthusiast would recognize. The collection displayed an obvious Portland Trail Blazers theme.

Clyde Drexler, Terry Porter, Jerome Kersey, Buck Williams, and Kevin Duckworth—the core of the Blazers' NBA finals runner-up squads from the early Nineties—dangled from pushpins. I never would have guessed that toy versions of the late, beefy Duckworth or the rugged, goggle-clad Williams were ever produced, let alone collected and displayed in living rooms. More recent Trail Blazers like the soft-shooting, hard-punching forward Zach Randolph (now with the Memphis Grizzlies, although while in Portland he famously scuffled with Ruben Patterson and broke Patterson's eye socket) also found their way onto the wall. By the time my host asked, "Any questions?" I was too busy cataloging the players to hear him.

"Any questions?" he said again with an emphatic cough.

I snapped out of it: "Yeah, whose action figures are those?" This wasn't the kind of question he was expecting. With a whiff of annoyance, he explained that they belonged to his younger brother, a diehard Portland fan, and then he asked if I was ready to sign a lease.

Although I fancied the idea of watching Blazers games with my prospective landlord's brother, I didn't take the apartment. Instead, I moved in with another Fulbright student who had found a small town house a ten minute walk from the condo building. My first night there, while my roommate was at a renewable energy conference in Beijing, I managed to knock out the electricity by plugging a 110-volt appliance into a 220-volt socket. For hours, I lay in the dark, balmy night, sweating buckets into my new sheets and cursing my unplanned crash course in tropical heat, until my landlady was able to send someone to knock

---

* A couple years later, Clyde the Glide's mien appeared in mall advertisements for a Chinese sporting goods company bearing the uninspired name Athletic. I can't speculate on the marketing campaign's success in other Asian locales, but the posters of a fleshy, middle-aged Drexler posing in an Athletic tank top were a hit in Manila, with families occasionally stopping to take photographs next to his image.

the life back into my circuit breaker with a few expert cracks from a wrench.

Over the next few days, I learned to suffer through Manila's sweltering climate, and eventually I felt brave enough to explore my new surroundings. As I walked through the better neighborhoods, I saw the beautiful hardwood courts that had been installed in tony housing developments, but I also watched several street corner games played under far more rudimentary conditions. I hadn't yet checked in with Sev Sarmenta at Ateneo de Manila University, where he taught in the communications department when he wasn't calling basketball games on local television, but the pull of the courts was too strong to resist. It was time for me to play some basketball. The game was everywhere in Manila. Full- and half-courts awaited me at every turn, and at certain times of day I could listen for the hollow thud of bouncing balls and echolocate to the nearest game. That afternoon, a few hours before dusk, I laced up my sneakers and hit the streets of my new neighborhood, Loyola Heights.

Walking past the town house complexes and airy family homes of a fairly wealthy subdivision, I followed the gentle sound of dribbling. As I drew closer I heard the siren clank of ball on rim. It was late enough in the day that the sun merely tingled on my skin instead of searing it. On the blacktop, I found a motley bunch of guys lofting casual shots and waiting for enough players to arrive for a game of five-on-five.

The locals checked me out: at six-foot-three and almost two hundred pounds I stood six inches to a foot taller and twenty to fifty pounds heavier than everyone else on the court. In my early twenties and wearing an old jersey from a New York summer tournament, I looked like a real player; and it's quite possible that I was the whitest person some of them had ever seen face-to-face. Pastiness aside, I must have looked like a basketball vision, because a giddy tug-of-war broke out over whose team I would join. The players seemed to reflect the neighborhood's social makeup. Relative to the abject poverty that half of the Philippines' 90 million people endure, the local residents were wealthy, but as privileged folk go, they were the working rich. Even the biggest houses in the area looked like sties next to the opulent mansions of Forbes Park and Dasmariñas Village, where business and government oligarchs retained retinues of household cooks, launderers, and drivers, not to mention small militias to guard their property. By comparison, my new neighbors and their single-servant households seemed austere.

The players that day were a mix of teenagers and college students who lived in the neighborhood, and older men who worked there as drivers, gardeners, and handymen. The teams didn't break down exactly according to social group, but the leader of the brat squad was definitely Dean, a lanky fifteen-year-old who was already over six feet tall and who dunked with preternatural ease. I soon found out that a local college basketball powerhouse was eyeing him for its varsity team, but even though the other well-off kids didn't have Dean's natural ability, their Nikes were newer than mine and they had clearly been coached since they were young. They snapped their wrists on jump shots and held their shooting hands high to display the proper duck's neck follow-through. They threw crisp chest passes and their footwork on layups and box-outs smacked of organized basketball.

In contrast, Team Hired Hand looked like the Filipino answer to the Bad News Bears. Half of them were playing in flip-flops, sandals, or bare feet. The oldest of them—a longtime driver for the family who owned the house next to the court—looked like he was pushing eighty, and he played in a pair of Converse Chuck Taylor high-tops without any hint of retro irony. Roger, the caretaker of a nearby pool, was conscripted to play point guard. Joseph, the youngest of the bunch, wore a pair of white Adidas shell-toes that looked suspiciously large on his four-foot-eleven frame. But the most flamboyant player was a toothless fifty-something driver with a buzz cut whose patent leather Air Jordans were of seriously dubious origin. He trotted up and down the court with his gums flapping and a lit cigarette dangling from his lips, smacking his palms together and grunting loudly whenever he wanted to call for the ball and launch a two-handed set shot.

The ragtag crew didn't inspire much confidence, but once we started playing, I was surprised to see that despite the young guys' advantages in training and equipment, the teams were evenly matched. A few times, Dean caught passes on the fast break, took one dribble and then launched into the stratosphere, gliding toward the hoop with the ball raised in one hand and then dropping it through the net. But other times, a swarm of small, pudgy opponents would block Dean's path to the basket and strip the ball away before he could jump. Roger the caretaker turned out to be a clever playmaker who could jump into a crowd of taller defenders, sense where his open teammates were, and squeeze passes to them through the human morass. Tiny Joseph started the game poorly. A few times he beat everyone downcourt and received long passes, but his layups ricocheted off the bottom of the rim. After a few embarrassing moments like this, he threw up his arms in disgust and kicked his shoes to the side. Was he quitting? No. Joseph walked to his pile of belongings in the court's grass perimeter, stepped into a pair of flip-flops, and returned to the game. He wouldn't miss another shot all day.

As I watched my teammates sprint, slide, leap, and land in their thong sandals, with nothing between their feet and the ground but a thin rubber pancake, I felt like I was watching people drive blindfolded. Thinking back on the broken bones and torn ligaments I had suffered in both ankles during my college career—injuries I'd sustained despite strapping my feet into a succession of increasingly cumbersome braces—I saw imminent doom in every one of their jump stops. But there were no flip-flop-related injuries that day. Thongs, not Jordans or Lebrons, are the most common basketball shoes in the Philippines, and many players like Joseph, who have played in them their whole lives, feel more comfortable and play better without sneakers.

Playing in flip-flops had become such an iconic feature of the Philippine game that it had been enshrined in song by the Tagalog rappers Legit Misfitz, who recorded "Air *Tsinelas*."* To many Filipinos, playing basketball in skimpy sandals and bare feet wasn't a remarkable feat; it was just natural. Still, I couldn't help feeling inspired by the sight of guys executing crossovers and spin moves without wearing shoes. If I didn't own sneakers I probably would have ended up a hacky sack buff. When my teammates soared to rebound the ball or lay it in, I saw love and devotion in every injury-defying leap.

Throughout that first game, I deferred to my teammates. On defense, they stuck me in the middle of a two-three zone and told me to guard the rim. Whenever someone drove the lane, I was there to block or challenge his shot. A few times guys drove straight at me and served up soft floaters. Blocking them was like hitting a ball off a tee. I was punching shots into the grass, which, like most of what I did, sent players on both sides into hysterics. The shooter would turn around, shrug and offer his excuse: "*Laki!*" Big! Since they weren't used to competing against someone my height, they were testing out the kinds of shots they could make over me.

At one point in the game my teammate rushed ahead with the ball and missed on a wild drive. The other team rebounded and threw a long outlet pass to a guard who was breaking toward the basket for a layup. I was the last line of defense. The guard charged into the lane, saw me waiting, and took flight. I jumped at the same time, floating backward to avoid committing a foul and holding my arms high in the

---

* *Tsinelas* is the Tagalog word for flip-flops, and the song celebrates a nation of slipper-clad streetball warriors by likening their moves to a roster of legendary professional players. The refrain promises that in their *tsinelas*, the players will never slip. I found that sure-footedness astounding, since on multiple occasions I had trouble simply walking in flip-flops, especially during the rainy season, when I often found myself hydroplaning along slick sidewalks and once tumbled down a flight of stairs on a wet overpass.

air. He adjusted. Instead of approaching directly, he turned in midair so his back was facing me and the basket. I figured I had him. I wouldn't be able to block the shot with him using his body to shield the ball, but it would take a miracle for him to score from that position. He tossed the ball over his shoulder with one hand, without even looking at the rim, and it bounced off the backboard and in. Lucky shot, I thought. But a few possessions later, in a similar situation, another player spun 360 degrees in the air and then spun the ball into the basket on a reverse layup. Later in the game, it happened again. Three different players made once- or twice-in-a-lifetime shots on me in one game. These were guys who weren't all that adept at basics like dribbling with their off-hands or shooting from beyond ten feet, but they were dropping in highlight-reel layups like it was nothing. What was going on?

It was my introduction to the Philippine circus layup. In the States these are the shots that you toss up when you drive into the heart of the defense, get stuck in the air between taller defenders and have to get rid of the ball before you land. You close your eyes and hope for the best, and if the shot goes in, someone congratulates you by saying, "You really pulled that one out of your ass." Well, Filipinos have turned the circus layup into an art form. While many Filipino players are graceful leapers with hang time to spare, when they're five-foot-six, even great hops aren't enough to dunk. So the body-twisting, triple-clutching, no-look, seemingly impossible layup has replaced the dunk as the measuring stick of basketball artistry. Even in semipro and professional games, players will execute these tricky moves when there are no defenders around, just to please the crowd.

While my team was on defense, a player on the opposing side tried to throw a lob pass over me. I tipped it out of bounds and the ball rolled fifty feet down a hill. I trotted through the grass, tiptoeing around the lizards that were sunning themselves in my path. Along the way, I passed several rubber footprints that had peeled off of sneakers after thousands of trips up and down the asphalt. It was like a graveyard for the sneakers' soles. Once detached, they had been kicked to the sidelines, to their final resting place in the blacktop's weedy outskirts. There, they lingered, mementos to all the hard fouls and fast breaks they survived. I paused to look at the black treads and the big white Swoosh, grass poking through the rubber, and thought that if I were a basketball shoe, this is how I'd want to live and die—on the feet of someone who treasured me so much that he wore me until I fell to pieces, then spending eternity with front row seats to the game that was my *raison d'être*. Standing there marveling at the rubber scraps, I felt like those people who claimed to see Jesus in their Cheetos. I was realizing that there was no way to exaggerate the depth of Filipinos' connection to hoops. Everywhere I went I stumbled into some testament to this national obsession. After I stood spellbound in the grass for a couple minutes, the other players reminded me I was holding up the game.

"*Ano ba? Ahas?*" What is it? A snake?

"Nothing," I answered.

"*Sige na! Bilisan mo!*" Come on, then! Hurry up!

Whoops. I inbounded the ball, ran up court and streaked across the baseline, calling for the rock. It was my most practical lesson so far in the ways of Philippine hoops: don't hold up the game.

The next day, I walked to the post office. I wasn't sure exactly where it was, but I had studied a map before setting out and had a decent idea where I was going. The hour-long walk was, according to some of my neighbors, proof of my insanity. In a city as hot and polluted as Manila, anyone who could afford to avoid walking did so. Walking long distances suggested that you couldn't afford a car, a taxi, or even seven-and-a-half pesos (about twenty cents) to ride a jeepney. But as a native New Yorker, I was used to learning my way around by walking, and I was eager to get my bearings in Quezon City. It also seemed like a good way to beef up my Tagalog, the regional tongue that served as a basis for the national language. I had already found a tutor to teach me grammar and structure, but without some real-life practice, I'd end up like every other clueless foreigner in Manila who claimed to understand the language but really knew nothing.

I walked along one of the area's main east-west byways, Kamias Road, passing gas stations, streetside restaurants with counters full of bubbling pots containing rice and various stews, a row of suspicious-looking massage parlors with names like Pick-a-Boo and Mr. Body Physique, junk shops buying and selling scrap metal, and, of course, basketball courts. Down almost every alley and side street half-courts were set up with games of three-on-three in progress. Junk shops had backboards and rims hanging from their streetfront signage, where the owners killed time between shipments by shooting around and telling jokes. On signs and billboards, basketball imagery was used to promote everything from beer and sneakers to vitamin syrup and margarine. I used my own basketball to sell myself and make friends. On nearly every block somebody stopped me for a game of impromptu one-on-one or beckoned for the ball to show me his best ball-handling trick, and no matter how old, how out-of-shape, or how sloshed they appeared, I shared the rock.

When I reached EDSA, the giant highway that cuts north-south through most of Metro Manila, I turned right and headed toward the post office. It was on NIA Road, fronting a sizable squatter community that was tucked behind EDSA's government office buildings. The plywood and corrugated iron shanties piled on top of each other resembled a human hive, with its residents overflowing into the street. Children rolled tires down the street with sticks. Women hawked fish set up on plastic tables, waving minimops over the catch to shoo away flies. Competing karaoke machines contributed to an unharmonious din, punctuated by the horns of cars nudging through the chaos. More kids set fire to a pile of trash on one corner. Young men on bicycles zigged and zagged in every direction. Another corner was hosting a wake,* and the mourners played cards on plastic tables set up next to the coffin. The area was teeming with basketball courts that revealed themselves like a set of Chinese boxes. The *barangay* court was the largest and best-equipped. It was a full-court with ten-foot rims and stanchions made of metal. The longer I scanned the neighborhood, the more courts I noticed. A succession of smaller, jerry-rigged hoops claimed almost every pocket of free space: a portable, nine-foot hoop and backboard made from salvaged two-by-fours and moved from corner to corner to avoid traffic; some rebar twisted into a rim and nailed to a board, then tied to a gasping, leafless tree; a toy rim and backboard stuck on the side of a dilapidated bus with suction cups.

I went to the post office, mailed my letters, and when I emerged, the portable hoop had been moved right across the street from me. "Hey Joe, you wanna play?" a guy about my age called out. "Joe," as in GI Joe, is the standard, if anachronistic name many Filipinos use to refer to American or American-looking men. I was wearing cargo shorts, running sneakers, and a polo shirt, but this Joe couldn't say no to a game of three-on-three.

We played on the southbound side of NIA Road, and moments after one of my teammates shouted "Game *na!*" to start play, a crowd of a couple dozen people materialized in the street and behind the basket. Three guys sat on the base of the hoop to keep the structure from keeling over. We used a striped, black and blue miniball that barely fit through an equally tiny hoop. This made shooting pretty difficult, but with a baby ball and a rim hanging just nine feet above the ground, I could suddenly dunk like Shawn Kemp. As soon as a teammate passed me the ball, someone shouted "Dunk! Dunk!" Instead, I fumbled the

---

* Nearby signs explained that the coffin and burial had been paid for with help from a generous, if opportunistic, local politician.

undersized ball, which was slippery smooth from the wear of thousands of bounces. My first shot squirted out of my hands and flew up one side of the backboard and off the other without hitting the rim. The delighted mob let out a roar of laughter and more chants advising me to dunk. Before I could stuff the ball, however, we had to pause and let some taxis pass.

When we reclaimed the street as our half-court, I rebounded a teammate's miss and jammed it back through the hoop. The crowd erupted. One boy shouted the Jerry Maguire catchphrase: "Show me the money!" A cluster of kids formed an impromptu Soul Train line while the boy in the middle performed the Harlem Shake, a high-octane gyration that went out of style about eight years ago. I seized the moment with some pop culture mimicry of my own, running through the throng and pumping my fist like Michael Jordan while high-fiving everyone within reach. The game turned out to be close. A pint-sized guard on the other team, who played in a powder blue jersey and a snow-white, faux-fur bucket hat, proved to be the only player capable of making long-range shots. Our team kept pace by waiting for me to rebound misses and slam putbacks through the hoop. With the score tied and both teams a point away from victory, I had the ball about ten feet from the basket and a chance to win the game. Perhaps I was enjoying the star treatment a little too much, because I really wanted to end with a flourish. I faked my man to the right, then blew by him with one dribble to the left. After that, I was airborne.

In that moment, I lost awareness of my surroundings. As a player who could never put down more than the simplest one-hand stuff—and even that only happened a couple times—the change in the basket's dimensions had an intoxicating effect on me. I was no longer an exchange student playing with squatters on an undersized, homemade hoop. I was a big-time college player, competing for a Final Four berth, and I was about to stuff my way to victory. Two defenders jumped to stop me, but I went over them and slammed the ball so hard that I almost brought the backboard down with me. The splintered two-by-fours let out a desperate creak and I felt the structure give under my weight as I released the rim. As I returned to the ground, the faces of a thousand pissed-off locals flashed in my mind. Luckily, the shrieking wood was just a warning and the basket survived; the people watching didn't want to tear me limb-from-limb for destroying their hoop, they only wanted to share high-fives and a postgame snack of Skyflakes crackers and RC Cola poured into plastic bags and sipped through straws. I sheepishly accepted the hugs of a few dozen children and thanked God that I hadn't destroyed their rim.

Later that week, when I checked out the *barangay* basketball court in my neighborhood, I discovered that it wasn't unusual for pickup games in Manila to draw crowds of onlookers. The *barangay* is the Philippines' smallest unit of government, and all over the country you will find basketball courts standing side-by-side with *barangay* halls.

The first time I strolled, ball in hand, to the Loyola Heights court for a morning shootaround, I could hardly believe my eyes: this wasn't some playground hoop. It was the Taj Mahal of public courts. Of course, it wasn't Madison Square Garden—the floor was cement and one of the rims was tilted an inch off-center. But back in New York going to a public court usually meant shooting on a half-court blacktop with an aluminum backboard wired to a chain-link fence. The court in Loyola Heights offered much more than rims with nets. A pavilion-style roof sheltered the court from the elements. The backboards were made of fiberglass, an upgrade from wood or metal, and lights dangled from the ceiling for night games. The rims were spring-loaded, breakaway models built to withstand powerful dunks, so that 230-pound athletes could hang on the rims without tearing them down or shattering backboards. Never mind that here in Quezon City they were being used mostly by 140-pound guys who played without sneakers and rejoiced on the rare occasions that they jumped high enough to tap the backboard.

My first thought after laying eyes on my humble neighborhood arena was: Jackpot! I saw myself spending hour after hour working on pull-up jumpers and spin moves in the weeks and months ahead. And, on the off-chance I could find a magic elixir that would add six inches to my vertical leap and turn me into a rim-rattling dunk artist, I knew the breakaways had me covered. I started working out. It was around ten in the morning, already too hot for sane players to want to run, so I had the court to myself. I began a practice routine I developed in college, tossing the ball to spots around the basket, then stepping into these simulated passes and shooting jumpers or driving to the hoop. Sweat came easily as I pushed through the sodden tropical air. The rims were soft and broken-in from the volume of shots (millions, I guessed) hoisted at them. The ball never clanked off the hoop; rather, it met the iron, embraced it for a split second, and if I had the right touch, it rolled in. Man, it felt good.

But then I saw the kids. A group of street kids clung to the fence next to the court, cheering "*Kuya* Raphael! Dunk! Dunk!" It was the first time I had seen them do something other than put their fingers to their lips and moan the words "hungry" or "coins." Although I'd only been in the neighborhood a week, they already knew me. They'd seen me scouting restaurants on Katipunan Avenue and lugging groceries back from the store, and they milked me for loose change and leftover grub. They called me *kuya*, which means "big brother" in Tagalog but is widely used as a friendly title in the street, like "man" or "bro." I obliged the dunk request, or at least I tried. When I got up in the air, the ball slipped out of my hand and I just grabbed the rim and hung for a moment instead of dunking. It was a sad attempt, but the kids applauded anyway. Eight-year-olds didn't make a very demanding audience.

But when I thought back on the crowd who'd watched me play outside the shantytown earlier that week, I wondered if it wasn't just kids who could be awed and pacified by basketball, but whole communities. There I was, in a poor, developing nation, standing on a public basketball court that put most outdoor courts in New York to shame. If I walked a few minutes from my neighborhood, with its beautiful court and solid apartment complexes, I could find myself in any of three different squatter settlements, where people's roofs were built with scrapped sheets of corrugated iron and patched with newspaper. In these communities, access to clean water, consistent electricity, and affordable medicine was a distant fantasy. The kids' parents were the neighborhood denizens who drove motorcycle-sidecar taxis called tricycles, or sold single cigarettes and sticks of gum outside of coffee shops, or collected five-peso (about twelve cents) tips to guard parked cars. They earned enough each day to buy rice and canned sardines for the family, and maybe a bottle of dirt-cheap gin for themselves, only to wake up and start over the next day.

My young fans were tiny, not only because Filipinos tend to be short, but because years of poor nutrition had stunted their growth. When I asked their age, kids who looked six said they were ten. The smallest girl, due to a birth defect, had one arm that ended in a nub at her elbow and another that ended in a three-fingered claw. When it rained and the water of Diliman Creek ran high, I saw these kids toss their mealy clothes into the bushes and dive into the gray slurry, gleefully dodging plastic bags and broken bottles floating in the current. At night the creek smelled like pestilence, yet it was the kids' favorite bathing hole.

In a community as impoverished as this one—and there were many other places far worse off—how did public money end up being poured into a basketball court? It was too early for me to understand how Filipino politicians used hoops to appease constituents without providing urgently needed public services. I hadn't been around long enough to know if the spending on basketball courts was a symptom or cause of the problems facing the Philippines' notoriously corrupt and irresponsible government. But the upside-down priorities were plain to see. You can't drink fiberglass backboards. Breakaway rims don't cure ear infections. Instead of medicine, instead of drinking water, the people got basketball.

But even if there was a dark side to the basketball fanaticism I'd encountered on the streets of Manila, the sport obviously brought people joy. I was amazed by how many games I'd encountered in my first week—and I hadn't even attended a professional match yet.

As soon as I got settled, I reconnected with Sev Sarmenta, the broadcaster who promised to guide me through Manila's elite basketball world. He turned out to be short and a little chubby, with a wide, welcoming face and a wave of black hair. In addition to calling basketball at all levels of the Philippine game, Sev had covered the Olympics and boxing hero Manny Pacquiao's bouts. He had been a male cheerleader while attending Ateneo de Manila University in the 1970s, and he still carried himself with the jovial intensity of a pep squad captain. Sev never seemed to be off the air. His voice was deep and bold and, depending on the situation, it could sound bawdy and gregarious or grave and authoritative. When I met him for the first time, at a mall in Quezon City, he made the words "Do you like Taco Bell?" sound like "Havlicek stole the ball!"

Two beef soft tacos later, Sev took me to a doubleheader of the Philippine Basketball League, a minor league that served as a feeder for the more prestigious PBA. The first game pitted the snack-food sponsored Granny Goose Tortillos against the Complete Protectors, a team named not for its defensive prowess but for the first-rate cavity protection of Hapee toothpaste. This was my first encounter with the bizarre, corporate-themed nomenclature of Philippine basketball teams.

The PBL gym was dark and stuffy and the action was rough— players shoved and scratched each other and the referees allowed all but the most vicious hacking. During that first game I met Alex Compton, a blue-eyed, blond-haired American who had been playing in the

Philippines for eight years. Although Compton had no Filipino blood, he was born in Manila and returned to play in 1998 at the invitation of an upstart professional league with loose eligibility requirements. That league folded after five years, but by then Compton couldn't leave the country behind. He had become fluent in Tagalog and was now an A-list celebrity. He appeared in Nestlé Coffee-Mate commercials and modeled men's underwear on billboards—and apparently Manileños thought he resembled Leonardo DiCaprio so strongly that a local magazine once included Compton and the *Titanic* actor in a separated-at-birth spread. Compton was so popular that even though PBA rules specified that players couldn't participate in the league unless they had Philippine lineage, the minor league PBL made an exception to keep Compton on the court.

During a lull in my conversation with Alex, I glanced at the court and saw a defender send his man crashing into the scorer's table with a double forearm shiver. I just shook my head. I couldn't believe this no-stitches, no-foul style of basketball could attract enough spectators to fill the bleachers. And the games were televised! Compton told me that anything hoops-related could draw an audience here. And apparently the commissioner, a former PBA broadcaster named Chino Trinidad, preferred this brutal style because the fans got an extra thrill out of the flagrant fouls, angry stare-downs, and chest-to-chest confrontations. The PBA, with its higher talent level, could afford to play it straight, but here in the lower tiers of Philippine basketball, stirring up some bad blood—and occasionally some actual blood—was a good way to keep crowds engaged. Compton laughed as he told me that he'd learned to run up and down the court with his abdominal muscles clenched, because he never knew when an opponent might chop him in the gut.

Between games Sev introduced me to Trinidad, whose bubbly enthusiasm and pointy, waxed hair reminded me of a Filipino Pee-Wee Herman who spent a lot of time in the weight room. Trinidad small-talked circles around me, suggesting a roll call of people that I ought to meet and inviting me to games in places I didn't know existed. Had I seen Ginebra play in the PBA yet? No, but I had heard of them. Would I be able to join his PBL teams for their games in Cavite next weekend? Uh, sure. Where's Cavite? Had I met his dad, award-winning poet and sportswriter, Recah Trinidad? Sorry, not yet. I'd been feeling pretty proud of myself for finding a place to live, a grocery store, and a few pickup games my first week in the country, but Commissioner Trinidad had bigger plans for me.

When Trinidad's cell phone rang I was granted a respite long enough to catch my breath, and when I heard the ring tone, I couldn't help but smile. It was the old NBA on NBC playoff jingle. While Trinidad gabbed in Tagalog, images of the Knicks' John Starks fearlessly dunking over Michael Jordan and Charles Barkley releasing a game-winning shot over David Robinson flashed in my mind. It may have been the first and only time that a John Tesh song was ever taken as a good omen, but since I had barely been in the country a week and had already witnessed acts of hoops devotion I never before imagined, I felt confident that these basketball revelations would continue as long as I remained in the Philippines. Hearing that NBA melody, I sensed that I'd stepped into a country where people held hoops as close to their hearts as I did, and it felt like home.

2

Alaska in the Philippines

The Philippine Basketball League was the training ground for the Philippine Basketball Association, and by my second week in Manila, I was ready for the big league. The PBA is the world's second-oldest professional basketball league, after the NBA. It opened in 1975 and has been a prime mover in Philippine pop culture ever since. The league's all-time greats have gone on to become senators, mayors, and city councilors, while other stars retired and settled into television and movie careers. Franchise owners are among the Philippines' most powerful businessmen, and they use their teams not only to promote their commercial interests, but also to compete with each other for bragging rights as the owners of championship squads and all-star players. The athletes and coaches who have devoted their lives to the sport have seen how basketball touches all levels of Philippine society, from their tycoon bosses to the urban poor who wait in parking lots after games to squeeze players' hands and pose for grainy cell phone pictures. I was eager to see these fanatics—who made my own basketball obsession look reasonable by comparison—in action, so on the Friday of my second week in Manila I spent the peso equivalent of eight dollars (fifteen bucks would have gotten me courtside) to check out a PBA doubleheader.

The games were held at the Araneta Coliseum, the same arena that hosted Muhammad Ali and Joe Frazier for the Thrilla in Manila in 1975. The Big Dome, in local parlance, is the country's largest arena, with seating for more than 14,000 people, although during big games the coliseum has been known to accommodate thousands more spectators sitting in the aisles and packed in the hallways. Araneta also has the most reliable air-conditioning of any venue in the capital. A beefy security guard in a commando beret frisked me at the gate, and I wandered past Wendy's, Taco Bell, Dairy Queen, and a local chain called Café Bola on the way to my seat, which was about a dozen rows back from the hardwood. The imitation leather seats were worn and a little rickety, but thanks to a 1999 renovation, the court was state-of-the-art. The starters from each team were lining up around half-court for the jump ball, and the game was about to begin.

What I saw on the court looked like a miniature NBA. Watching power forwards who were my height (as opposed to the American standard of six-foot-ten) was strangely empowering. I hadn't watched a Knicks game and thought, I could play with those guys! since I was ten years old. Physically, at least, I matched up pretty evenly with PBA players. The game, between the brewery-sponsored San Miguel Beermen and the Air 21 Express, started off at a manic pace. San Miguel won the tip and within five seconds one of their guards launched a line-drive three-pointer that ricocheted off the backboard without coming close to the rim. Meanwhile, tinny synthesizer music—it sounded like the unfortunate coupling of European trance and a circus jingle—was piped into the arena. A rebound fell to an Air 21 guard who went coast-to-coast, skittering downcourt with blinding speed and passing most of the Beermen on the way, only to flub his layup on the other end. A San Mig guard scooped up the ball and pushed the action in the other direction, but he ran so fast that he kneed the ball into a teammate's back and out of bounds.

The on-court action looked more like human pinball than professional basketball, and I wondered if I'd traveled 8,000 miles to observe a glorified version of high school hoops. Thankfully, after a few possessions the frenzy wore off, players started to sink their shots, and it became clear that the PBA's level of play was competitive with other foreign professional leagues. Relieved, I was able to let my guard down and take a look at the scene away from the court. The arena was papered with banners and jerseys for teams like the Santa Lucia Realtors, the Talk 'N Text Phone Pals, and the Purefoods Chunkee Giants. PBA teams, including the Beermen and the Express, were marketing vehicles for their owners' primary businesses and were named accordingly, even when they sounded absurd.

The courtside entertainment provided similar commercial thrills. Smaller businesses that couldn't afford their own teams bought the right to have company mascots wander the aisles, where they posed for photographs, danced as much as their cumbersome costumes allowed, and further blurred the line between professional basketball and a Lewis Carroll acid trip. The PBA's in-house mascot—an orange wookie in shorts and a jersey—owned the most traditional costume. He was joined by a rotating cast that included a seven-foot walking waffle;* the Welcoat paint company's person-sized paint can, which required seeing-eye people to lead it through the crowd; and a representative of the Xtreme Magic Sing home karaoke set, dressed as a caped superhero with a microphone head. The most outlandish getup was an anthropomorphized lactobacillus bacterium that was meant to promote the digestive benefits of Yakult yogurt drink, but really looked like a giant white condom. A scarlet L painted on the megamicrobe's chest only confused things further, as the letter could be mistakenly thought to stand for *libog*, Tagalog for "horny." At halftime, human-sized bottles

---

* Araneta patrons called this mascot "Manny Ramos," after a center on the Coca-Cola team whose elongated head and expressionless face resembled the waffle suit.

of Casino brand rubbing alcohol and Omega liniment joined the fray. The brown liniment bottle, wearing khaki safari shorts and a big cartoon smile, danced in a way that made the most of his rectangular body's capacity for lightning-quick pelvic thrusts. When he approached a gang of ecstatic toddlers in the front row and started jackhammering away, I could hardly bear to watch, but the children giggled and squealed in delight.

The PBA was pretty weird, and I liked it. Plus, during the moments when I could pull my attention away from the mascot sideshow, I saw a striking cross section of Manila's population seated in the crowd. At courtside, wealthy families, dressed in matching polo shirts and yellow Livestrong bracelets, took in the game. The teams' die-hard fans sat immediately behind both hoops. Sometimes these PBA lifers harassed the referees and players with high-frequency banshee shrieks and Tagalog epithets vicious enough to make their well-heeled neighbors blush, and sometimes they joyously waved homemade banners with the players' names sewn on them. Nuns shared aisles with television starlets, and the nosebleeds were almost entirely given over to sinewy young men who watched intently from their crow's nest viewpoint. It was hard to imagine an NBA crowd representing such a wide spectrum of Americans, although I couldn't say so with empirical certainty, since I hadn't watched a live NBA game in more than five years. But that was the point: PBA games were affordable—the cheapest tickets sometimes cost less than jeepney fare to the coliseum. Everyone watched, not just suits and celebrities. It seemed that the Philippine relationship with basketball remained so intimate because people communed with the sport daily by playing their own games, following the professional league or even just glancing at the images adorning jeepneys in traffic.

In the double bill's second game, I watched Quemont Greer, a player who'd starred for DePaul while I studied at nearby Northwestern University, rack up almost 50 points against the PBA's most popular team, the Barangay Ginebra Gin-Kings. (Yes, they sell gin.) One of the things that first fascinated me about the PBA was that each team in the league was allowed to hire one American player to reinforce its local lineup. These players had been coming to Manila since the league's founding. Some found fame and small fortunes, while others, who couldn't cut it on the court or who rubbed their coaches the wrong way, were shipped back to the States in less than a week. Over the years, the PBA experimented with different height regulations to limit imports' dominance over local players. Sometimes the league capped the Americans' heights as low as six-foot-four and other times it allowed seven-footers to compete. This season, Greer stood a hair below the current six-foot-six ceiling. No matter the height limit, however, PBA imports were expected to play like stars. I wondered how a player like Greer, who nearly made it to the NBA after college, dealt with life in the center of the PBA's two-rim circus. Was there a sense of being better than it all? Did he just roll with the punches, no matter how bizarre things got? Was the PBA—along with other international leagues—where NCAA stars' hoop dreams went to die?

I had arrived in the middle of the PBA season, so it was too late to observe how Greer's attitude shifted throughout the year, but I knew after watching my first game that to really understand the PBA, I would have to get to know one of the imports. A few days later I got in touch with the league's front office, and they agreed to help me find a team to follow through the next season. After talks with several general managers, a team called the Alaska Aces agreed to open its doors to me. I would go to practices, sit through strategy sessions, eat with the players, travel with the team, and follow the Aces from inside the locker room. I couldn't believe my luck. I'd finally be part of a big league team! Sort of.

I'd watched Alaska play on television a few times, so I was familiar with their roster, but it took a little research to figure out the story behind the team's name. The Alaska Milk Corporation, which owned the PBA franchise, was one of the country's largest retailers of canned and powdered dairy products. But what did milk have to do with the state of Alaska? Nothing, actually, although in the tropical heat, I could see how allusions to an arctic breeze might be an attractive marketing ploy. "Alaska," it turned out, was a Tagalog contraction of the words *alas* and *ka* that means "You're an Ace!" It was also the grammatical root of the Tagalog verb *alaskahan*, which means to joke around or banter with friends. Both meanings fit the dairy empire's family-friendly image, and their team full of tall, robust star athletes was a further extension of that brand identity. Before 2000 the team had gone by a more straight-forward name: the Milkmen.

Within the PBA, people often compared Alaska to the Chicago Bulls. The team ran former Chicago coach Phil Jackson's triangle offense, and, like the Bulls, Alaska was the dominant team of the 1990s, when the franchise won nine league championships. But as the Alaska players of the Nineties aged, the team was forced to rebuild—and apparently they'd never found the right mix of new players. They'd been near the bottom of the league for the past few seasons. But maybe getting assigned to a losing team wasn't such a bad thing. I called Alaska's American-born head coach Tim Cone to introduce myself, and he sounded almost as excited to have a writer nosing around his team as I felt about becoming a PBA insider. In the casual, authoritative tone that he'd developed over eighteen years of coaching, Cone told me to be at practice the next morning. In a few hours he'd be picking up Alaska's import, Rosell Ellis, at the airport. It had been more than five years since Alaska's last title, and Cone hinted that his chances of picking up another championship would depend on Ellis.

Rosell Ellis cleared customs at the Manila airport on a sweaty pre-dawn morning in March. Despite his exhaustion, he was due at practice in less than eight hours. A veteran of international leagues from South America to Australia, Ellis would be joining the Aces as the team's lone American star. Across the street from the terminal, Tim Cone was waiting for Ellis in an outdoor holding pen. Ellis didn't know that Cone couldn't come inside the airport to meet him, so he grabbed his black duffel bags and found a seat near a hallway full of travel agents and money changers. Before long the other passengers collected their bags and headed for the exits, leaving Ellis alone with the airport security guards and porters, who quickly recognized him as a player and asked for autographs. Ellis's twenty-hour flight from Seattle had come only five days after an even longer jaunt to the Pacific Northwest from Melbourne after he'd finished a six-month stint in the Australian league, and he was drained from his travels. Still, he managed to stay fairly cheerful while discussing his prospects for the upcoming season with his newfound fans.

Cone suspected that Ellis was waiting for him inside, but he'd have to talk his way past a succession of security guards to get to him. Cone easily disarmed any suspicion by introducing himself as a PBA coach, although this created its own problems, as the guards were so thrilled to meet the Philippine answer to Phil Jackson that they stopped Cone and insisted on talking hoops. Eventually, Cone sweet-talked his way to the baggage area, where he found Ellis holding court amid a swarm of eager PBA followers.

Cone drove Ellis to his apartment, a luxurious one-bedroom in Makati City, the business center of Metro Manila. Ellis would have preferred to hit the sack immediately, but Cone, riding a caffeine wave from a nearby Starbucks, was eager to bond with his new hire. Ellis was about to become Alaska's most important player—the one expected to set a standard of hard work and competitiveness for his teammates to follow, and to lead the team in most statistical categories from the moment he stepped on the court for his first practice. Cone was determined to start off on the right foot with Ellis, even if it meant waylaying the woozy player at the tail end of a twenty-four-hour transcontinental slog.

While Ellis unpacked, Cone brought him up to speed on the Aces' team dynamic. Alaska lacked a true point guard and played the same triangle offense that NBA coaches Tex Winter and Phil Jackson used as the engine for nine championships with the Bulls and Lakers. Ellis, who knew he needed to win his new coach's trust, patiently endured Cone's description of the role the coach envisioned for him. Cone was particularly excited about the possibility of using Ellis, an adept ballhandler, as an occasional point-forward to plug the aforementioned absence of a lead guard.

Ellis wasn't a rookie import—in fact, he'd played four seasons in the PBA from 2001 to 2004—so he knew that developing a rapport with his coach could mean the difference between staying on the team for a whole season and being replaced by another import. And, at Ellis's salary of around $20,000 per month, the longer he lasted with Alaska, the more money he would earn. Not to mention it was worth losing a bit of sleep if it helped him and Cone achieve the kind of mutually beneficial relationship that could lead to a title. Still, by the time Ellis finally went to bed, it was almost three in the morning and he was due at his first practice by seven. It was going to be a rough day.

Even after a full night's sleep, I was dragging when I walked into the gym the next morning. The journey from my town house in Quezon City had taken an hour and a half, most of which was spent packed inside a train so crowded that it forced passengers into a sort of low-grade hyperventilation. There wasn't enough space in the car to take a deep breath and expand one's rib cage, so instead everyone stood around panting like dogs. I felt fortunate to be a head taller than my fellow straphangers. The passengers around me, especially the guys with their heads nestled in my armpits, weren't so lucky. The trip sounds revolting, but I fancied the hardcore commuting aspect of Manila's train system. I always figured that the six years I spent riding New York's subway during middle and high school had prepared me for anything in the world of light rail, and this was the ultimate test.

PBA teams scheduled practices in the early morning to avoid Manila's debilitating midday heat, but in March, the beginning of Southeast Asia's blistering summer, trying to plan around the temperature was wishful thinking. Well before noon, the tropical air was sticky with the city's humid, particulate miasma, which was known to sometimes leave people sneezing soot at day's end. That morning, instead of reflecting off the gymnasium's sheet-metal roof, the sun beamed through the high windows and the temperature inside climbed to triple digits.

Alaska's owners had agreed to let me write a chronicle of the team during the 2007 Fiesta Conference. For the next four and a half months, I would spend nearly every day with Alaska's players and coaches, observing practice, occasionally stepping in as an auxiliary passer in drills, and sitting behind the bench at games. But before all that could happen, I had to survive my first three-hour practice without collapsing in a puddle of sweat. Shortly after I took a seat on the benches next to the court, Alaska's players shuffled into this hardwood sauna, looking drowsy and dragging large red shoulder bags bearing the Aces logo, a big, stylized A with a basketball peeking out from behind. About six weeks before Ellis joined the team, the Aces lost in the first round of the All-Filipino conference playoffs.* Since then, the players had settled into a tedious practice routine, but when they stepped onto the floor and caught a glimpse of their new import shooting at the far end of the court, the sleepwalking athletes were jarred into alertness.

Ellis, a six-foot-five, 230-pound human muscle gleaming with sweat, was launching casual jumpers from the right side of the court. Outfitted in Alaska's red and white reversible practice uniform, his upper body

---

* PBA seasons are divided into two miniseasons called conferences. The season begins in September with the All-Filipino conference, when teams are not permitted to hire imports like Ellis. That conference usually ends in February, in time for the import conference to run from March through most of July. Both conferences include a sixteen- to twenty-game regular season, plus playoffs. So every year there are two separate PBA champions. If this sounds confusing, imagine what the league must have been like before 2004, when the PBA schedule was split into three conferences and ran eleven months out of the year.

displayed the kind of definition usually seen in comic books. His shoulder muscles were heaped on top of each other like boulders, and the ropy veins in his arms demanded as much attention as the tattoos spread across his upper body. Ellis wore his hair in a two-inch puff—the embryonic stage of an Afro or braids—with a red headband under his hairline. His Filipino teammates watched intently as the thirty-two-year-old forward worked out. They weren't just sizing up their new teammate. They were calculating their own chances for a successful season.

This wasn't the most promising first impression. Ellis was the walking antithesis to the hoops adage that all left-handers possessed textbook shooting form and a sweet stroke. His unconventional shot was riddled with the kind of wasted movements that make coaches cringe. Ellis's shot began normally, with his feet square to the basket and his shooting elbow straight under the ball. From there things got loopy. Once Ellis was airborne, his left elbow jerked out to the side; with the ball still cocked in his hands, he turned his wrist and rotated the ball about ninety degrees to the left before releasing it. When the shot ricocheted off the rim with a harsh thud, the players winced, but they kept watching. Maybe it was a slip. Ellis shot over and over with similar results. It was the basketball equivalent of a knuckleball. Without the slow, even backspin of a proper jumper, his shot spun in a different direction every time he launched it. It always reached the rim, but after that there was no telling where it might bounce.

Ellis missed a steady stream of eighteen-footers. The ball struck the near side of the rim—*clang*! The next one banged off the backboard to the rim and hit the floor. With each shot, the ball boy tasked to chase down Ellis's rebounds had to scramble to a different corner of the gym, and before long he was winded and sweating harder than Ellis. Watching Ellis hurl his barrage of broken shots, I suspected that Alaska was in for a difficult season, but when I asked what they thought, Alaska's players and coaching staff said they saw things differently. The fact that

Ellis dragged himself out of bed early enough to be first at practice impressed them. His character meant more than his shooting touch. It was a wonder that Ellis's travels hadn't sapped his strength; under the circumstances, he could be forgiven for the lack of precision in his outside shot. On top of that, many Alaska veterans had played with and against Ellis during his earlier tours in the PBA. They knew what kind of player he was—that he used athleticism and cleverness, rather than a finely tuned offensive skill set, to dominate games. Before Ellis arrived, the biggest question in their minds was: "Would he be in shape?" One look at his physique convinced the Aces that their import was ready to run.

Cone agreed. "He's got a lot of negatives to his game," he told me before practice. "He can't shoot. He can't make free throws." But those weren't the skills the Aces were looking for in an import. "Generally, the guys we get are right at the cusp of making the NBA," Cone explained. "These guys are as good as any athlete in the NBA, but they've got character issues. Coaches just won't touch them in the States. Or we get the guys that don't really have the skills, but have the great character. It's rare you get a guy who's got good skills and good character, because usually those guys are in the NBA.

"You'd be surprised about a lot of imports. They come in and they don't want to practice, or they'll play a game one night and want the next two nights off. They'll sit on the sidelines with a little ache or pain. You'll never, ever see that with Rosell. He's a workhorse. He just takes everything up to another level. He's gonna bring so much to the game in terms of rebounding, getting out on the floor, hustling for loose balls, and the ability to play as a teammate."

Since starting his overseas career in Argentina in 1998, Rosell Ellis had built a reputation as one of the most versatile and selfless imports on the market. He had earned nicknames like "Mr. Everything" and banked enough money to make himself a millionaire a couple times over, with a handful of luxury cars and snazzy motorcycles sitting in his

Seattle garage. But despite Ellis's success in international basketball, his career had always felt like a bit of a letdown. Like Cone says, no player chooses the PBA over the NBA.

For many players, signing a deal with an international team means giving up their NBA aspirations. Players who can't shake the NBA ambition toil in domestic minor leagues like the CBA and NBDL, while those who accept the fact that they'll probably never play for the Lakers or Celtics become journeymen—literally. The ones who can deal with culture shock, bouts of loneliness, and Shaquille O'Neal–sized communications barriers become imports for international teams, where the pay is better and they can be franchise players. Occasionally, an NBA veteran who's been out of the league for a year or two will wash up on Philippine shores, hoping to play his way into shape and enjoy a paid vacation before making one last run at an NBA line-up. The most recent pedigreed pro to take a walk of shame along the Pacific Rim was Darvin Ham, last seen in the 2005 Finals with the Detroit Pistons. He joined a PBA team for three games in January 2006. Cedric Ceballos, who won the NBA's slam dunk competition in 1992, endured a short PBA stint in 2003. Dickey Simpkins and Scott Burrell, who played for the Bulls' championship squads in the nineties, are also members of the NBA-to-PBA fraternity.

Because basketball strategy in the Philippines was unconventional, a player like Ellis, who might seem small-time compared to these former big leaguers, could outperform his more celebrated colleagues on the court. And Cone seemed quite pleased with his choice of an unconventional import. Watching his highest paid player botch shot after shot, he just smiled and folded his arms in front of his chest. "Right now, I'm stress free," he mused. "I was able to get the guy I wanted."

"Let's go! Four lines!" Cone barked, and the players assembled on the baseline in groups of four. Cone's four-lines drill served as an extended warm-up that let his players find their shooting touch before they moved into full-speed scrimmages. Aside from helping the team break a sweat, the drill also reinforced the foundations of Cone's triangle offense. The triangle relied on options and choices rather than set plays. Instead of dribbling the ball downcourt and calling a play designed to set up the shooting guard by having him run his defender off staggered screens set by the big men, Alaska's players learned a pattern of movements organized around three offensive players at a time. They don't know what they're going to do until they "read" how the defense is playing them. Playing the triangle well depended on split-second decision-making in which the players watched their defenders' reactions and moved to counter them.

Ellis was teamed with other starters Willie Miller, Jeffrey Cariaso and Nic Belasco, while six-foot-seven center Sonny Thoss waited near the far basket. As the players darted up and down the court, Cone called out instructions. "One down!" he bellowed, and Cariaso and Belasco ran in opposite directions off Thoss's screen in the post. The play ended with Ellis dashing toward the basket on the weak side and Thoss shoveling him the ball for a feral two-handed dunk. "Blind pig!" Cone shouted, and the players scrambled into a new series of cuts that ended with Cariaso curling around a screen in the post, catching a pass near the foul line, and draining a pull-up jumper. "Dribble entry! Two-front! Power out!" Cone called out, and each time the players would begin in four lines, then zigzag off to different spots on the floor to execute the play.

Ellis was earning twice as much as his highest-paid teammates, but he threw himself into drills with the enthusiasm of a walk-on desperate to be selected for the last spot on the bench. While Alaska's locals trotted to their spots, Ellis was four or five steps ahead of them, charging forward in a full sprint and leaving trails of sweat in his wake. Every time he received the ball within five feet of the basket, he planted his right foot in front of him and pushed into midair, then cocked the ball with both hands behind his head before banging it through the rim. Still, because this was his first practice and his first time running the triangle in years, he was usually out of position. Sometimes he played catch-up, watching where his teammates were headed and then filling the remaining open area of the floor by process of elimination.

At one point Ellis cut across the baseline too early and crashed into Cariaso, who was streaking in from the wing. Later, Ellis received the ball in the corner and kicked it to Miller at the top, except Miller had already dashed into the lane and the ball sailed into the bleachers. After these initial gaffes, Ellis came up with a new strategy: when in doubt, dunk. But he also strived to learn the offense. After each mistake, he consulted team captain Cariaso, who started running the triangle when he joined Alaska as a rookie in 1995. Ellis rested one hand around Cariaso's shoulder and jabbed a finger into Cariaso's palm, tracing hypothetical cuts and screens. "Don't beat up on yourself," Cariaso told him. "We've been running this for years and we're always making mistakes."

The four-lines drill embedded the triangle's basic movements in the players' minds, so that during games they would read defenses automatically instead of worrying about where they were supposed to run next. In fact, when the offense really got rolling, the players didn't even think about what to do next. They just reacted. Their decisions to pass, drive, or shoot were made on a level beneath conscious thought. The result was a fast-moving offense that appeared artful and creative because of the players' responses to situations on the floor, but such deep understanding of the triangle could only be attained through endless repetition. And indeed, after running through fifteen or twenty minor variations of the offense in a half hour, the players could probably run the offense blindfolded.

Cone taught himself the triangle in the same rote manner. The coach moved to the Philippines from Oregon when he was nine years old. His father was a reforestation expert who came to the country to work in logging. The Philippines introduced Cone to basketball; in his American childhood, he only played football and baseball. He first fell in love with hoops while playing in flip-flops on a provincial dirt court that had a massive coconut tree at halfcourt. He earned the Alaska coaching position on a dare, while watching one of the team's games in the late eighties with Wifred Steven Uytengsu Jr., whose family owned the Alaska Milk Corporation. Cone opined that he could do a better job coaching the team, and Uytengsu called his bluff, inserting him as coach in 1989.

In those early years, Cone groped for his coaching identity. He found it in the early nineties Chicago Bulls teams. Back then NBA games weren't televised regularly in the Philippines, so Cone had to buy a pair of enormous bunny-ear antennae to intercept broadcasts from the U.S. military bases north of Manila. He taped grainy Bulls games and watched them over and over, charting the team's offensive patterns in his mind and then on paper. He didn't even know that the offense had a name. Cone just knew that he wanted it for Alaska. I could see the sleepless nights he spent rewinding and replaying footage of Jordan, Pippen, Bill Cartwright, and Horace Grant in the purple half-moons under the coach's eyes. Deep inside, I hoped the Philippines could in-spire another young American to similar feats of hoops devotion. Of course, that American was me.

Just from watching the team run four lines, I was feeling ready to step in and run a few blind pigs myself. In fact, there were moments during that practice and every subsequent one when I yearned to be out of street clothes, in shorts and on the court. Part of me was curious to see how I'd fare against the Aces. I had already played with Nic Belasco and Alaska's injured point guard Mike Cortez in off-season pickup games, but I still had no proof that I could hang with the pros when it counted. Here's my honest projection of how my imaginary Filipino doppelganger would stack up in the PBA: I had the size and tenacity and court awareness to be a nice complementary piece. I might have been a role player, a seventh man, a glue-guy type who could bother the other team's scorers and make some nice passes. I never would have been a star. The league's best talents were flashy guards like Miller, who could have been undersized stars at mid-major NCAA Division One schools.* The rest of the league was mostly Division Two quality, and in that kind of mixed company, I could blend in and help a team. Proving myself and being able to brag half truths about playing with pros, however, weren't why I pined to join the Aces during practice. It was just that I had never been around basketball so often without playing. No matter how much I learned from watching Cone conduct the offense, I preferred the sweaty realities of hoops: elbows, bruises, gasping for breath, fighting for offensive rebounds, passing the ball out for a teammate's three, and watching it splash through the hoop.

A few ticks before 10:00 a.m. the temperature inside the gym had passed sweltering and was headed to scorching. The players dragged themselves through the heavy air and frequently checked the wall clock hanging above the doorway. I managed to sweat through my shirt just by sitting and scribbling in my notebook. The last of the bananas and apple slices that Alaska's trainers brought to practice had been devoured more than an hour ago, and now only browning peels, Tupperware bins, and empty Gatorade bottles were left roasting on the sideline.

Finally, Cone blew an extended note on his whistle, signaling that practice had ended. The entire team walked toward center court, first

---

* At any given time in the PBA there is a rumor circulating about a local player who could make it in the States. The first and probably only player of Filipino heritage to play in the NBA was half-Filipino Raymond Townsend, who played two full seasons with the Golden State Warriors in the late seventies. In the nineties, Alaska point guard Johnny Abarrientos was supposedly scouted by NBA teams. Virtually any member of Manila's basketball cognoscenti can cite secondhand knowledge of teams like the Warriors or Los Angeles Clippers, which are based in Filipino-American population hubs, sending out feelers for a player who might be good enough to sit on the bench as a twelfth-man marketing tool. Until it happens, the rumors must be considered wives' tales.

clapping together slowly like a steady heartbeat and then speeding up to a frantic pace. At halfcourt, they bowed their heads and held their hands behind their backs. Poch Juinio, a veteran big man, gently put his arm around the waist of fellow forward John Ferriols. Cariaso bent over, held his knees and said a team prayer, while Ellis dropped to one knee and nestled his forehead in his outstretched palm. "Thank you, Lord, for waking us up this morning," Cariaso began, then continued to ask for divine guidance through the upcoming season and protection from injury. He promised that the team would give its all on the court and remain grateful for their charmed lives, whether they won or lost. "Amen," they said in unison, and as the huddle broke, Poch slipped his hand down below Ferriols's ass and goosed him. Ferriols jumped and took a swipe at Juinio's nipple. He missed, squeezing nothing but sweat molecules and putrid midday air. But the season was young, and Ferriols would have plenty more opportunities to seek revenge. As a matter of fact, Alaska's next practice was scheduled to begin a few hours later, at three that afternoon.

3

A Career Reborn

Having adjusted somewhat to the staccato rhythm of Manila life, I was eager to get Ellis's take on the expat experience, but for the first few days practice took up most of his time. He did, however, find a moment to instruct me and everyone else on the team to call him "Roe." Later that week I finally got to know him better, when Roe invited me to see the apartment the team had rented for him.

Since moving to Manila, I'd often bragged to friends in the States that my shared town house was nicer than any apartment I'd lived in since college, but Roe's pad in Makati City put my digs to shame. Makati is Metro Manila's business center and richest municipality. Ayala Avenue, Makati's main drag, feels like a steamier version of Chicago's Miracle Mile with its spotless malls and skyscrapers. Many expatriates live and work in the neighborhood, and the area allows them to avoid the more squalid realities of the teeming, third-world megacity. By no stretch of the imagination could my neighborhood be called a slum, but it offered the more typical Philippine patchwork of privilege and destitution. In Loyola Heights, gated subdivisions sat side by side with labyrinthine shantytowns, and when I glanced out my back window I could see into a neighbor's yard full of fighting cocks. In contrast, Roe's apartment came with daily cleaning and laundry services, air-conditioning in every room and a home entertainment system that could be a showcase item on *The Price Is Right*. Sitting pretty on top of a white leather couch, watching muted CNN on the flat screen, and listening to Marvin Gaye classics, Roe seemed right at home. He sunk into a leather cushion, rested a foot on the coffee table, and began to unravel the basketball wisdom he had accumulated in his ten-year career as an import.

As Roe saw it, being the most talented player wasn't all that important in international ball. Versatility was what really mattered, and throughout his career, his ability to succeed in vastly different on-court situations had served him better than a picture-perfect jump shot ever could. Most teams already had a dead-eye shooter and a go-to scorer among their local talents. Instead, foreign teams needed a guy who was strong enough to wrestle with inside players and fast enough to stay in front of guards; they needed a guy who could post up in the lane as well as face up on the perimeter. They needed a guy who was comfortable handling the ball, who could see the court and pass to streaking teammates for open shots.

According to Roe, if you could be that kind of player, you'd always have a job. But that job might take you to some pretty far-flung places. Roe had played in Venezuela, Argentina, China, Indonesia, and Australia. He'd put up with some pretty shoddy playing conditions. The courts in Chinese gyms looked pristine, but the franchises neglected their playing surfaces—like a "Made in China" knockoff purse that looks fabulous until the zippers fall off. The floors felt more like ice-skating rinks than parquet, and you could forget about sudden stops or turns. Roe, playing at full-tilt, was wiping out all over the court, but he wasn't at a competitive disadvantage because the other players were also skidding to and fro.

Argentine hardwood was similarly afflicted, but ingenious team managers there came up with a solution. Hours before each game, ballboys poured Coca-Cola onto the playing floor. By game time the soda would be dry and sap sticky, causing a different set of traction problems for players to endure. Alas, soft drinks were powerless against the other major problem with Argentina's courts—dead spots. Roe knew the spots to avoid on his team's home court, but on the road, scouring the floor for cracks and stomping up and down the court to listen for the hollow thud of warped wood became a vital part of his pregame routine. The space above players' heads was equally perilous. In some drafty Argentine gyms players dodged fluttering insects and swooping bats.* There were times Roe started a drive to the hoop and was stopped dead in his tracks, not by his defender but by a bat diving to snatch a bug.

And then there were the Argentine fans. Even though Argentina won a gold medal in basketball in the 2004 Olympics and they've sent players like Manu Ginobili and Andres Nocioni to the NBA, Argentina remains a soccer country at heart, and basketball fans there bring a bit of *futbol*-inspired hooliganism to games. It was the only place where Roe, a relentless hustler throughout his career, hesitated to chase loose balls into the crowd. "If you go out of bounds you gonna get up quick," he said, leaning forward and looking urgently into my eyes. "You don't wanna lie down too long or you don't want to get too close to the rail, 'cause they trying to spit on you, grab you, everything. Man, if you fall close to that wall, they are trying to literally kill you."

Roe considered Manila one of the best places for an import to ply his trade. In other countries, basketball played second fiddle to soccer, rugby, and even cricket, but the Philippine infatuation with hoops ensured that imports gained instant celebrity status. Still, this time around, Roe didn't jump at the opportunity to return to the Philippines. He had a competing offer in Venezuela, and although the money there wasn't as good, he was tempted to accept. The PBA had its drawbacks. The same passion for basketball that made the Philippines an

---

* This might help explain the ease with which the San Antonio Spurs' Manu Ginobili swatted a bat out of the air in an early season game in 2008.

ideal place to play could also lead to headaches. Teams were desperate to succeed and could be irrationally demanding of their imports. The media devoted a lot of attention to professional basketball, and a cameraman catching an import at a nightclub in mid-grind with a half-naked groupie (or even worse, a transvestite) would teach an American player a quick lesson about the dark side of fame. With other options and a fat savings account, Roe wondered if another PBA campaign would be worth the hassle. Eventually, however, the money and his desire to prove that he could still handle the PBA led him to sign with Alaska.

I understood why Roe would choose the Philippines, but it took me a while to work up to the question I really wanted to ask: How had he wound up playing overseas in the first place? When I finally asked, his answer caught me off guard.

"You know I choked a ref, right?"

He spoke in the same matter-of-fact tone that he might use to say: "You know I'm from Seattle, right?" I bolted upright in my seat like someone had jolted me with a cattle prod. "Only half the story," I bluffed, while somewhere inside my brain the scandal lobe was doing somersaults. "What happened?"

Roe's career started out on track. He was a bona fide superstar at Seattle's Rainier Beach High School—the same school that produced NBA guards Doug Christie, Jamal Crawford, and Nate Robinson. Roe was Washington's state player of the year as a senior in 1993, when he was also named an honorable mention McDonald's All-American, an accolade that serves as a reliable predictor of NBA potential. But Roe's career veered off course after high school. He didn't meet the academic requirements to receive a basketball scholarship from an NCAA Division One university, so he spent two years at the College of Eastern Utah. Junior colleges like Eastern Utah serve as athletic purgatory for classroom underachievers. They give players a second chance at a scholarship, but at the same time claim two of the athletes' four years of eligibility and tarnish the reputations of once-coveted blue-chip recruits. After toiling at unknown Eastern Utah, Roe moved up to the relative obscurity of McNeese State University in Lake Charles, Louisiana, which competes in the Southland Conference against other no-name schools like Stephen F. Austin University and the University of Texas at Arlington. Even so, he was among the national leaders in field goal percentage, making more than two-thirds of his shots in his senior season. His performance was good enough to win the conference's player of the year award in 1997, but despite his achievements, he didn't attract much NBA attention. McNeese State's basketball program just couldn't compete with major conference schools like Duke and Kansas University.

Another factor in Roe's low profile among NBA prospects was that he wasn't the type of player scouts covet. At only six-foot-five, he was a classic 'tweener, a player whose size and skills left him stuck between positions in the NBA. With his he-man physique and knack for scoring close to the basket, Roe played like a slashing power forward. He was a savvy ballhandler and passer, but his height was closer to that of a shooting guard, and his awkward jump shot ruled out any chance of him playing that position. Roe's reputation as an undersized forward who might not be able to outleap and overpower the NBA's seven-foot centers dropped him off most teams' radars. He was passed over in the 1997 NBA draft.

Roe wasn't about to give up on the NBA dream. After college he joined the Des Moines Dragons in the now-defunct minor league International Basketball Association and played his way back to relevance. Midway through the season he was a lightning quick swingman close to fulfilling the NBA potential he showed back in high school. He was averaging 22 points per game and ranked fifth in the league in scoring. In the post, Roe was strong enough to create space against taller players and release an almost automatic baby hook. His perimeter moves weren't slick, but combined with his powder-keg first step and his battering ram shoulder, they were enough to get into the paint, where he rarely missed. At that point he started attracting the attention of NBA scouts. He was at the height of his basketball powers: capable of beating defenders off the dribble, scoring on powerful dunks or graceful flip shots at the rim, and connecting on occasional long-range bombs.

Then, on January 17, 1998—a Saturday night in Des Moines—Roe's NBA aspirations derailed. The Dragons were playing the Wisconsin Blast for the second night in a row. The previous night's game, which Des Moines won by a close margin, had been hotly contested and very physical. Before the second leg of the back-to-back, referee crew chief Bob Schoewe brought the officials together and told them to call the game closely to keep any lingering tensions from boiling over. "We know it's gonna be interesting out there," Schoewe told the other referees. "Let's keep it under control."

Wisconsin took a double-digit lead early in the first quarter. The Dragons' players blamed the referees. Roe was particularly steamed because Schoewe whistled him twice for fouls in the opening minutes. After Des Moines committed a foul and a Wisconsin player went to the free-throw line, Roe lined up on the block and loudly voiced his grievances to a teammate on the opposite side of the lane. Schoewe was standing under the basket, between the two players. "This is bullshit," Roe said. "We're getting fucked." From the referee's perspective, Roe wasn't just discussing the game with a teammate—he was shouting across the key, and his comments were directed at the official.

"Knock it off or one of you is gonna get hit with a technical foul," Schoewe warned. After the first free throw, Des Moines called time out. Roe continued. "This is some fucking bullshit, man," he yelled. "We're getting jobbed." Schoewe, true to his word, hit Roe with a technical foul.

Roe remembered it differently. According to him, the trouble started when the players took their spots on the line and Schoewe began "talking shit" for no reason. "You guys aren't gonna be shit," the ref said. "You guys are just gonna be in this league—you won't make any money. This is all your careers are gonna amount to." Schoewe, whose twenty-five-year career as a referee included work in NCAA Divisions One, Two, and Three, several semiprofessional leagues, and the NBA during the 1999 lockout-shortened season, said that he had seen the best and that neither Roe nor any of the other players on the court came close.

Roe couldn't believe his ears: "I'm standing there, and I'm thinking, damn, did you guys hear this shit? This is the ref. Not the crowd. This is the ref talking shit." So Roe tried to set Schoewe straight. "Don't talk to me like that," he said to him. "I don't make enough money to sit here and listen to you talk like that." That's when Schoewe called the technical foul.

Schoewe has always denied insulting Roe and the other players. Late that night, after I talked to Roe, I called Schoewe in Minnesota, where he still refereed small college basketball, and he explained that he had no reason to deride the players, since insulting the IBA would insult his own role in it. "Why would I demean where they are?" he asked me. "If you're working in that league, you're doing it for the love of the game."

Although Roe and Schoewe remember the precipitating events differently, no one disputes what happened next. After the first technical foul, Roe became more aggravated and the Des Moines coach called another time-out to calm his player. It was too late. Roe kept cursing at Schoewe on his way to the bench. The referee decided he'd heard enough and gave Roe a second technical foul, ejecting him from the game. Schoewe turned his back to Roe and walked to the scorer's table to report the ejection. Roe followed. Roe only planned to get in Schoewe's face and yell at him, but while he stalked behind Schoewe, a teammate grabbed him in an attempt to defuse the situation. Instead, Roe snapped. He shoved his teammate out of the way, ran to the scorer's table, leaped on Schoewe's back and put him in a sleeper hold. After just a few seconds he realized his mistake and released the referee before a mob of teammates, coaches, and security guards dragged him away. Schoewe never saw Roe coming, but he wasn't hurt as much as bewildered by the attack. The main thought running through the referee's mind was, What the hell is he going to do now? When Schoewe felt Roe's grasp loosen, he figured the player must have come to his senses, and just as fast as the attack had started, it ended. Security shepherded Roe into the locker room.

Afterward, Roe stood in the shower for half an hour, replaying the altercation and pondering the consequences of his attack. The same NBA scouts who had been watching his physical game blossom had just seen his mental game crumble. He made a public apology immediately after the game and Des Moines suspended him indefinitely, with hopes that the scandal would die down and he could eventually return to the team. But Roe's fate was determined the moment he pounced on Schoewe. Within days footage of him choking the ref was on Sports-Center. The IBA banned him for a year, and his reputation in American basketball was ruined.

There is no such thing as a good time to strangle a referee, but Roe probably couldn't have picked a worse one. Less than two months earlier, in December 1997, Latrell Sprewell had beaten Roe to the choke. Sprewell, a standout guard for the Golden State Warriors, tried to strangle then-coach P. J. Carlesimo after a dispute in practice. Sprewell left the gym but returned later to take another swing at Carlesimo. The initial assault on Carlesimo's windpipe and Sprewell's premeditated repeat attack—both unprecedented for the NBA—earned the all-star a one-year suspension without pay and stoked public outrage.

In the basketbrawl canon, Sprewell's attack rests alongside Kermit Washington's spinning punch that nearly killed Rudy Tomjanovich in 1977 (Tomjanovich said he thought the scoreboard fell on him), and the 2004 carnage unleashed on Detroit Pistons fans in Auburn Hills, Michigan, when Ron Artest, Stephen Jackson, and other Indiana Pacers bum-rushed a courtside section after an onlooker tossed a cup of beer at Artest. On the heels of Sprewell's rampage, Roe's misstep was enough to shatter his chances of reaching the NBA. Being branded a ref-throttling headcase became Roe's scarlet letter and thrust him into basketball exile.

How good were Roe's chances of actually making the NBA? He was never a lock, but Mike Bethea, who coached Roe at Rainier Beach (and whose other players, Jamal Crawford and Nate Robinson, made it to the league), thought he had a shot. Although Roe was a couple inches too short and his jumper was rife with kinks, he played the game with a rare and valuable mind-set: like a madman. Roe's obsession with winning every contest and besting every challenge was the kind of trait that, found outside of an elite athlete, might qualify him for a personality disorder. On the court, however, it was priceless. His work ethic had become legendary at Rainier Beach, and Bethea still invited him to team practices to spread the gospel of lunch pail basketball. Roe's manic competitiveness could lead to steals, offensive rebounds, and extra possessions—the kind of unheralded statistics that add up to wins at all levels of the game. If not for bad timing, Bethea thought Roe's relentless style of play would have earned him an NBA roster spot.

After the detonation in Des Moines, Roe became baller non grata in the United States and was forced to look for work abroad. Although it quashed his NBA hopes, his misstep didn't prevent him from making a living in professional basketball. Depending on his base salary and performance incentives, Roe made between $15,000 and $20,000 per month as an import on foreign teams. He could play in Australia from October to February, then in the Philippines from March to July to almost double his earnings. Although Roe's intense nature had led to some volcanic tantrums, there didn't seem to be a coach in the world who wouldn't choose him over a less fiery import who watched practice from the sideline while scheduling dates for later in the evening.

Over the years, Roe developed a reputation as one of the most reliable forwards on the world basketball market, a consistent 20-point scorer who played tireless defense and often outworked his local teammates. The image of Roe clinging to a referee's back with his arms around the official's neck faded and was replaced by that of one of international basketball's most energetic hustlers. Occasionally, though, Roe still thought about his actions in 1998 and wondered what could have been. "It was the biggest mistake of my life," he told me, staring at the bare white wall in his apartment. "If I had never done that to him, there's no telling where I might be."

Roe laid his head back on top of the couch and closed his eyes. I thought of the persistence and determination it must have taken to carry the stigma of his attack on Schoewe while restarting his career. The moment passed and we realized it was already midnight. He walked me to a nearby Starbucks. I left him there and headed toward EDSA, Manila's perpetually congested—even in the dead of the night—thoroughfare, where I could catch a bus to Quezon City.

On my way home I looked out the window at the steady procession of McDonald's franchises, KFCs, and 7-Elevens. Many foreign visitors to the Philippines saw Manila's ubiquitous chain restaurants as a sign of the country's extreme Americanization, but there was another side to the city. For every American restaurant, there were a dozen roadside barbecue stalls selling grilled skewers of *isaw* (pork intestines), *helmet* (chicken heads), and *betamax* (cubes of coagulated pork blood that resemble the ancient video format's tapes). The hard wooden benches of buses were crammed with breast-feeding mothers and construction workers who had washcloths tucked into the backs of their shirts to soak up sweat. This wasn't a country where one foreign culture simply dominated its native counterpart, but a place where Spanish and American colonial influences mixed with the imprints of Chinese and Malay merchants who had been trading in the Philippines since before the archipelago even existed in the eyes of the West. A dizzying array of ingredients made up the Philippines' cultural brew, and they blended over time to form something uniquely Filipino.

Roe, with his swank apartment and team-provided driver, would barely get to see this side of Manila. But on the basketball court he'd encounter a similar mishmash of cultures. Although the PBA was modeled after the NBA, any American who served in the league would tell you that playing here felt vastly different from playing back home. Filipinos have been playing basketball almost as long as Americans have. The game has been the country's dominant team sport since the 1930s, when most Americans were still more interested in baseball and football. Philippine hoops had developed its own styles and idiosyncrasies, and if an import didn't adapt to the PBA's quirks, he'd probably get sent home early—swapped for a more malleable ringer. Roe had endured four seasons in the Philippines, but this time he questioned whether he'd have the patience to make it through another year. Could he earn a full season's worth of salary and hopefully win a championship without garroting anyone along the way? This time, even he wasn't sure.

4

A Head Start Becomes Destiny

The PBA was a symptom of the Philippines' basketball obsession, not the cause. I was thrilled to be witnessing the professional game from inside Alaska's locker room, but that wasn't what brought me to Manila in the first place. I was inspired by the idea that a Southeast Asian nation populated by five-foot-five men and mostly forgotten by America except for its political corruption, widespread prostitution, and violent Muslim separatist movement could be devoted to hoops with a passion unequaled by any other country. It was a nationwide tale of unrequited love. Forty million short men obsessed with basketball—they might as well have been a nation of blind art historians. I followed that alluring and, let's face it, somewhat bizarre fact across the globe. I considered myself an amateur historian-slash-detective, maybe not the most qualified man to discover why basketball became a prime mover in Philippine culture, but the only guy willing to battle tropical cockroaches and fight off a few bouts of hookworm to understand the sport's grip on the Filipino soul.

The Alaska Aces and professional basketball are parts of that story, but they are too modern to reveal the roots of basketball's role in the

Philippines, which date back to the dawn of the twentieth century and the beginning of American colonial rule. I spent the months before Alaska's season buried in the stacks of the American Historical Collection at Ateneo de Manila University's Rizal Library. Ateneo was a fifteen-minute walk from my house, but since the PBA off-season coincided with the Philippine rainy season—a four-month period between June and September when the weather bebops and scats from relative peace to hurricane bedlam—I typically arrived at the library sopping wet and squished up the stairs to the American collection in waterlogged shoes.

The library research I knew as a college student tended to be a solitary pursuit—historians scouring card catalogs (or these days, online databases) for potential sources, then pulling volumes from the stacks and sifting through them in their carrels. My research in the Philippines, however, was much more collaborative. This was because the materials at the American Historical Collection were in a perennial state of reorganization, and the existing catalog was incomplete. There was an index of articles and publications related to sports and basketball, but if I had relied solely on that list of documents, I probably would have missed two-thirds of the relevant material.

I should mention that Ateneo was definitely not starved for resources. The university is one of the Philippines' most elite private institutions, with an alumni list that includes the names of dozens of past and present leaders of government and business. Yet even at this bastion of the upper class, the library lacked a reliable card catalog. It reminded me of the inconsistencies of wealth in the Philippines; many Ateneo students could afford drivers to take them to school in BMWs, but their riches couldn't make up for unreliable infrastructure. Despite its minor inefficiencies, however, the American collection was a gold mine of information about the origins of basketball in the Philippines, and the librarian, Waldette Cueto, was brimming with enough institutional knowledge to fill in the catalog's gaps. When I first sloshed into her domain, I planned to be the solitary historian and wandered toward the drawers filled with index cards. She cut me off midway. "Maybe you should tell me what you're looking for," she suggested not too delicately, and I was on my way.

She took me to the archive's back room. From the door to the back wall, the room was about the length of a shot from the top of the key. With high ceilings and tall shelves in the middle of the room, every inch of space was occupied by books. Thick, dark green volumes of magazines like *Philippine Graphic* and the *Philippines Free Press* that dated back to the 1920s and 1930s lined the outside walls of the room. The shelves in the center housed pamphlets and bound volumes of official documents from the United States colonial government, which ruled the Philippines until the Japanese invasion during World War II. Cueto handed me a stack of books on physical education in the early years of American rule. "Start with this."

In 1898, the United States annexed the Philippines following the Spanish-American War. Over the next four years, American forces held the islands during the Philippine-American War, a brutal conflict to suppress the Filipino independence movement that fought the Spanish and resisted control by yet another foreign power. The United States justified colonizing the Philippines by touting its desire to civilize the natives, who were supposedly incapable of self-rule. There were, of course, less altruistic motives, like gaining a military and commercial foothold in Asia and providing American industrialists access to commodities like sugarcane and lumber.

This early American attempt at nation-building included a broad effort to increase access to education for a local population that had been largely excluded from schooling during the three hundred years of Spanish rule. Education was also used to indoctrinate Filipinos with American values, and sports, in particular, were believed to promote discipline and cooperation. The United States developed a comprehensive physical education curriculum for use in public schools throughout the country; in Manila, Americans built recreational facilities like playgrounds and a YMCA. American teachers in the Philippines began using basketball in gym classes in 1910. The sport was introduced as an activity for girls, who were deemed unfit for the more strenuous track and field exercises taught to boys.

The oldest book Cueto gave me was a 1911 Athletic Handbook for the Philippine Public Schools distributed by the Bureau of Education. The book contained descriptions of about fifty activities that could be taught in gym classes. Basketball received no special attention; it occupied just a page with the heading BASKETBALL FOR GIRLS and a description of how to modify the rules to make the game easier for female players. Longer sections were devoted to baseball and volleyball, while basketball's word count seemed to place it in league with some of the handbook's more offbeat suggestions, like wand wrestling, a competition in which two boys sat facing one another with the soles of their feet touching while they grasped opposite ends of a stick and tried to wrench it away from the other.

Two postcard-size black and white reproductions of photographs of the girls basketball exhibition at the 1911 Carnival Meet, an interscholastic field day event, were printed in the back of the handbook. Elwood S. Brown, the athletic director of the Manila YMCA and a physical education true believer who lobbied the American colonial government to build playgrounds in Manila schools, took the photos. In the top photograph, six girls from the Philippine Normal School stared blankly into Brown's lens. Their baggy V-neck jerseys all had a large letter N printed on the front, with three girls standing behind their teammates, who sat cross-legged in the foreground, the girl in the center holding an old, brownish leather ball. Below that a second photo showed these girls playing against the ladies of Tondo Intermediate School. The girls were pictured running in transition, with their billowing white skirts trailing behind them to reveal black stockings underneath.[*] The court was just a grass field with a hoop at each end. The backboards were constructed from planks of wood and the rims were actual baskets, which seemed appropriate since the Carnival Meet took place just twenty years after James Naismith invented the sport and used peach baskets for goals. It was hard to imagine how those expressionless girls chasing each other through the grass in ankle length skirts evolved into the bruising, flamboyant stars of the PBA. There was one noticeable similarity between Philippine basketball in its embryonic stage and its fully developed form: Even in 1911 the sport could draw a crowd. In Brown's photo, the bleachers next to the field were packed with onlookers, just like the stands at Araneta Coliseum would be teeming with fans when I watched Alaska play against crowd-favorite Ginebra.

With the support of Manila's Catholic colleges, it didn't take long for basketball to grow from a curiosity to a national pastime. Catholic educators shared the colonial government's zeal for teaching values through sport and formed a Philippine NCAA in 1924. The schools built gyms and hired American coaches, who taught players the skills of early twentieth century basketball—set shots, layups, chest and bounce passes, and defensive slides. Basketball didn't dominate the sports landscape back then like it does today; baseball was also popular. But because college hoops was played indoors, it thrived as a spectator sport. Almost every day in the Philippines is either stifling hot and humid or wetter than Noah's flood. Neither was ideal for watching nine-inning baseball

---

[*] The days of fluttering skirts on a basketball court are long gone, as basketball steadily transformed into a man's game. Women have remained engaged with the sport as devoted fans and respected commentators, but relatively few actually play basketball these days. Colleges still field women's teams, but volleyball is considered more feminine and garners more media attention. Philippine gender ideals can be rigid and traditional, so when men adopted basketball as their own, the sport became too macho for the delicate maidens who first played it. Many women who are drawn to the game as journalists or fans say they once dreamed of playing basketball, but their grandmothers or aunties or mothers forbade the sport on the grounds that it would turn them into lesbians.

games. Instead, fans packed themselves and all their school spirit into gymnasiums to watch basketball, and the sport became the preferred pastime of Manila's wealthy, college-educated elite. Along with that social caché came headlines and attention, and that popularity attracted more young athletes to the sport.

In 1933 the news magazine *Philippine Graphic* published an account of basketball's burgeoning popularity. The author was Ambrosio Padilla, who had been a high-scoring forward at Ateneo and would soon be named captain of the Philippine national team. Padilla became the country's first real basketball star; he also went on to earn a law degree from the University of the Philippines and eventually spent time as a senator, solicitor general, and a vice president of FIBA, the governing body for international basketball. His article was another document I never would have found without the librarian. There was no trace of it in the archive's electronic database, and Cueto simply slid it onto the table while I leafed through a bound volume of *Philippines Free Press* issues from the forties. "You should look at this," she said, "but you can't touch the pages." She handled the brittle, seventy-five-year-old newsprint like it might crumble between her fingers. The deteriorating corners of some pages looked like they'd been nibbled off by mice. She held the pages between her fingernails and turned them delicately so I could read Ambrosio's antiquated prose:

> If you want to know where little Pedro is at the sizzling hour of two in the afternoon, amble to the nearest basketball court and there you will find him judiciously throwing a bouncing ball into a hoop. The ambition of every healthy boy now is to be a basketball player. His hero is no longer the baseballer but the basketballer.

The hammy writing had the ring of newsreel patter, but the image of a Filipino youth standing beneath a rim and slinging two-handed shots over his shoulder because he wasn't quite grown enough to shoot a proper shot resonated with me. I felt like I'd already seen hundreds of iterations of it: at the covered cement court in my neighborhood, on dirt courts throughout the countryside, where the backboard was nothing more than a couple sheets of plywood nailed to a coconut tree, and now in the fragile pages of history. The kids I saw in 2007 weren't much different from Padilla's "little Pedro." Philippine basketball's roots ran that deep.

Padilla, as a member of the national team, was a biased commentator. For many Filipinos, baseball wasn't the afterthought Padilla portrayed it as, and throughout the American occupation of the islands, the United States promoted baseball more vigorously than basketball. In 1910, Governor General Cameron Forbes sponsored a nationwide baseball tournament and promised the winning team in each provincial division a set of new uniforms. By the twenties there were more than 1,500 of these school teams. The emphasis that American governors placed on baseball reflected the sport's importance in the pre-WWII United States. Those were the halcyon days of America's national pastime, with players like Babe Ruth, Joe DiMaggio, and Ted Williams rewriting the record books. Basketball, which had only been around since 1891, was still mired in the era of half-court weaves and 19-18 final scores, with innovations like the twenty-four-second shot clock, slam dunk, and three-pointer still decades in the making.

One undeniable factor in basketball's successful conquest of Filipinos' hearts and minds was accessibility. The sport required fewer players, less space, and less equipment than baseball. More of the playgrounds built in Manila contained full-courts than baseball diamonds. And, as I had already seen all over Manila, people didn't need to live near a public court to play basketball; they simply built their own hoops. But there had to be something deeper, some cause behind Filipinos' emotional bond with basketball. I didn't understand yet where that affinity came from, but I knew I felt it too. I had been a decent

Little League pitcher—a lefty—and I had even thrown a no-hitter in a playoff game. I wasn't a serious prospect, but you could have made the argument at the time I quit baseball, at age thirteen, that I was more talented with a bat and a glove than I was with a basketball. It didn't matter. I knew by then that my heart was with hoops.

The early years of basketball history coincided with a golden age in Philippine hoops, at least in terms of international competition. Because the United States had introduced basketball to the islands at such an early point in the sport's history, Filipinos learned to play before the rest of the world. The Philippine national team was fine-tuning its game while players in other countries were still studying the rulebook. Filipino teams used their head start to become one of the most successful countries in early international tournaments. In the 1936 Berlin Olympics, the first games to include basketball as a medal event, a Philippine team captained by Padilla beat every team it faced except for the United States. A scheduling quirk, however, kept the team from earning a medal. The Philippines won their first two games against Mexico and Estonia, but their loss to the Americans in the next game bounced them into a consolation bracket. They ended the tournament with wins over Italy and Uruguay and having defeated bronze medalist Mexico in their opening match, but finished in a disappointing fifth place.* Still, the team's strong performance meant that the Philippines was among international basketball's elite.

As the Philippine team was showing that it could hold its own

---

* Nowadays, with the Philippine national team barely edging out Cape Verde and Bulgaria for 53rd place in FIBA's official rankings, simply qualifying for another Olympic Games seems like a distant fantasy, and hoops old-timers rue the near-miss in 1936 as the country's best shot to earn a medal in the sport that Filipinos love most.

against the world's best, it was also proving itself the cream of Asian basketball. Padilla's Olympic squad cruised to championships in the 1930 and 1934 Far Eastern Games, a precursor to today's Asian Games. In fact, the Philippines won nine of the first ten Far Eastern Games basketball titles. These achievements coincided with an emerging sense of Filipino nationalism and the desire for true self-rule. Just two years before the Philippines' strong Olympic showing, the United States passed the Philippine Independence Act, putting the islands on a ten-year track to full-fledged sovereignty for the first time since 1565, when Miguel Lopez de Legazpi established the first Spanish settlement in Cebu. In the years before the Second World War, Filipinos searched for unifying forces that could forge a national identity out of the scattershot archipelago populated by dozens of regional ethnic groups who spoke disparate languages and followed a mishmash of Christian, Muslim, and animist faiths. Most of their shared experiences came from being under the dominion of Spain and the United States. Catholicism, brought by Spain, was the most common religion. Americans made English the language of instruction in public schools, and it remains an official language, although Filipino, a tongue based on the Manila region's Tagalog language, is more widely spoken. Basketball was also introduced by a colonial power, but Filipinos seemed to embrace it as their own, and as their national team dominated Asian tournaments and delivered gutsy performances on the world stage, basketball became a major source of Philippine pride and a binding agent for the whole archipelago.

I found an account of the country's crowning achievement in international competition during one of my last visits to the American Historical Collection, the same morning that a typhoon arrived in Manila. The storm was merely sideswiping the city while slicing toward the northern Philippines and Taiwan, but even this glancing blow caused enough mayhem to shut the college down. The rain was intermittent that day, but powerful gusts of wind had knocked down trees and sent palm branches swirling through the air. The normally bustling campus had turned desolate, and I tiptoed around the floral detritus and mini-mudslides along the flooded walkways leading to the library. I worried that the building would be closed, but since I had already decided to brave the storm, I felt honor bound to complete the trek. I lucked out. Thanks to a few librarians—probably those who received late notification of the closing and continued to work out of the same stubborn fatefulness that carried me through the storm—Rizal was the only open building on campus.

The librarians were in, but the lights were out. The tempest had knocked out the building's electricity, which made my solo trek between dark, looming bookshelves and up a pitch-black stairway seem even more like a last-man-on-Earth zombie film. But when I arrived at the American archive, Cueto was there and she had set up a table with two lit candles and a volume of *Philippines Free Press* from 1956. I found an article about Caloy Loyzaga, a six-foot-four center of partially Spanish descent who is still considered the best player in Philippine history. Loyzaga led the Philippine team to a bronze medal at the 1954 basketball world championship in Brazil, the hoops version of the World Cup. It is still the best finish of any Asian team in an international hoops competition, and a moment that brought Philippine pride in basketball to its pinnacle while solidifying the sport's monolithic role in society.

Reading by candlelight, with some additional help from my cell phone's built-in flashlight, I imagined Loyzaga. Although he was the team's big man, he was remembered as the best defender, scorer, ball-handler, and playmaker of his era, and his well-rounded skills earned him a majestic nickname: the Great Difference. The article included Loyzaga's recollection of the 1954 triumph, which alluded to the young nation's identity crisis. Although Loyzaga felt Filipinos unite behind the national team, he remained aware of the Philippines' persistent class, ethnic, and regional divisions:

> My most unforgettable experience occurred in 1954 upon our return from the World Cage Tournament in Brazil, where we placed number three. We were lionized at the airport and given a rousing welcome which I will never forget to my dying day. In this connection my only gripe is that whenever I play for the national team, I am hailed as a full-blooded Filipino. But when I play for other teams, I am sneered at as a mestizo.

As I flipped through these volumes under the candle's warm glow, I came across dozens of tangential and offhand references to basketball. Gossip columns tallied the socialites and government ministers who were spotted courtside at NCAA jousts. I unearthed a two-hundred-word brief recounting a visit from Taylor University's basketball team. Players from the Indiana evangelical college sang Gospel tunes with an accordion accompaniment before exhibition games during a 1955 Philippine tour. I felt pangs of postcolonial guilt while looking at print ads featuring drawings of rosy-cheeked, wavy-haired white boys playing hoops, but hand-wringing aside, I was astounded by the variety of businesses that channeled their sales pitches through basketball. The nonslip, rubber-soled sneakers were obvious, but basketball was featured just as prominently in ads for products with weaker connections to the sport. Sloan's Balm ran images of a painter and a baller atop a slogan promoting a good rubdown. A 7UP ad contained the following copy: "So pure, so good, so wholesome for everyone! That's why Seven-Up is the favorite 'Fresh-Up' drink of basketball players." The same way I saw hoops reflected practically everywhere in Manila's street life, I found the sport embedded in publications stretching back almost eighty years. The basketball Nirvana of my imagination was turning out to be a reality.

Aside from Cueto's lesson in teamwork, the time I spent bunkered in the library gave me a skeletal view of the history of Philippine basketball. To put some meat on those bones, I tried to reach some of the game's sage old-timers. An obvious first stop, because of my connection with Alaska, was Kurt Bachmann, whose son Dickie played for Alaska in the nineties and remained with the team as an assistant coach. When I asked Dickie to introduce me to his father, he laughed. "Set aside a full day," he said, "because he's not going to stop talking."

Kurt Bachmann was one of Caloy Loyzaga's contemporaries and also a former Olympian. He joined the national team a few years after the 1954 bronze medal and played in the 1960 games. Bachmann's father was German, but his mother was Filipina and he was raised in Manila. At six-foot-five, he was one of the tallest players of his generation and a star in the Manila Industrial and Commercial Athletic Association (MICAA) during the sixties. Back then, he was known as Mr. Hook Shot, a nickname that spares me the work of describing his offensive arsenal. At the end of his playing career, Bachmann parlayed the business and political connections he'd made into a successful career in selling imported goods. By the time I met him, he was the president and CEO of Mantrade Development Corporation, named for a transportation hub in the southern area of Metro Manila. Under the Mantrade umbrella, Bachmann owned a Nissan dealership, the local rights to distribute And 1 sneakers and apparel, and a host of other consumer items.

I took the train down to Bachmann's Nissan storefront one morning when Alaska had an off day. When I arrived, Bachmann was seated at a table in the corner overlooking the deadlocked traffic on Chino Roces Avenue. His assistant had two piles of checks, outgoing and incoming, and he was pushing them one by one across the table for Bachmann to sign or endorse. As I walked toward the table, Bachmann stood to greet me. He wore dark slacks and a sky blue *barong tagalog*, a short-sleeve dress shirt embroidered with tiny floral patterns. He used his arms to pull each of his long legs from under the table, then unfolded them as he rose to his full height. Seventy-plus years had put a hunch in his back and shaved an inch or two off his standing height, but Bachmann was still about six-foot-four and had giraffe legs, with hips that reached as high as my sternum. He had a grayish complexion and loose, heavy jowls hanging below large, mischievous eyes.

"*Hoy! Puta!* Get him Coke Zero!" Bachmann barked at one of his employees, who returned moments later with a soda can and a glass of ice. Bachmann's crotchetiness evoked some of Walter Matthau's better moments. He greeted everyone with a curse, often in Spanish. Between that first Coke Zero and lunch, I heard "*Puta!*" and "*Coño!*" at least a dozen times, as well as several outbursts of the Spanish-Tagalog hybrid "*Putang ina!*" (meaning, more or less, "son of a bitch") and an occasional "Fuck!" While I'm sure that Bachmann had offended and startled his share of people with his gruff manner, nobody in the dealership seemed upset when he called them "son of a whore," or some near multilingual equivalent. For Bachmann, "shithead" truly seemed to be a term of endearment. It reminded me of the private vernacular I'd developed with my father, where his decades tending bar at McSorley's have inspired a slew of esoteric slurs—"bunghead," "knobber," "scummer," and "skel" to name a few—that have become common adornments in our conversations.

I noticed an odd, tender kind of symbiosis between Bachmann and his assistant, Angel de Leon. Throughout our interview, de Leon would prod Bachmann to recount the proudest moments of his career while beaming with admiration. When the boss flung insults and epithets at his employees in ways that wouldn't be hard to mistake for verbal abuse, the soft-spoken de Leon smiled warmly at the subordinates, soothing their frayed nerves with a gentle touch on the back of the hand or a moment of eye contact and a shrug to remind them it was all part of Bachmann's bombast. Despite his immense frame and put-on fury, Bachmann was becoming weak. After decades of smoking, he had developed emphysema. His tirades were punctuated by wet, guttural coughs and violent gurgling, and it was de Leon, prim and fey with his black pompadour and pencil-thin mustache, who rushed to Bachmann's side and whacked him on the back to clear the mucus from his lungs and airway. "It's okay, boss," de Leon would say. "It's okay."

"Puta," Bachmann would mutter in between wheezes, while de Leon eased his thwacking and massaged circles into the boss's back.

Bachmann was not a shy storyteller. His most grandiose yarn involved an encounter with the young Kareem Abdul-Jabbar—then Lew Alcindor—at UCLA in the early 1960s when the Philippine team swung through California on a training trip before an upcoming tournament. They scrimmaged against Alcindor's Bruins, and Bachmann, as his team's starting center, was matched up with the legendary pivot man. According to Bachmann, Alcindor wasn't able to block his shots despite towering almost nine inches above the Filipino center. That's because Bachmann used his hook to create the distance that kept Alcindor from swatting his shots across the gym. Alcindor was inspired to perfect his own unblockable shot, and the sky hook was born. Or so Bachmann would have you believe. Having a legitimate claim on the genesis of one of basketball's iconic moves would be a feather in the cap of Philippine basketball, so it's with a heavy heart that I admit Bachmann's claim is pure bunk. Bachmann was always hazy about the precise year he played Alcindor, but since Mr. Hook Shot retired due to a knee injury in 1963, when Alcindor was sixteen years old and playing high school basketball at Power Memorial Academy in New York, Bachmann's story can't be true.

Although Bachmann had invented the myth about teaching Abdul-Jabbar the Sky Hook, the old coot was similar to Kareem in that he was his country's last true master of the hook shot, an art that in today's PBA and NBA only survives in diluted forms like the half hook, baby hook, and jump hook. Bachmann taught himself the shot by tying his right arm to an eight-foot ladder and lofting lefty hooks over it. He passed this draconian method on to Dickie, who told me that he spent time strapped to the ladder almost every day until he was thirteen. Dickie also remembered his father calling Alaska coach Tim Cone when the younger Bachmann was a backup forward in the mid-nineties to complain that Dickie wasn't getting enough playing time. Cone called the conversation with Bachmann "terrifying." The coach said it was like hearing Bill Russell tell him he couldn't coach his way out of a paper bag and then call him an asshole in six different ways.

Bachmann's other immortal tale, which is actually true, says more about overprotective Filipino parenting than basketball. When he played for De La Salle University in the late fifties, during a game against the Mapua Institute of Technology, a Mapua player waited until Bachmann wasn't looking and then socked him in the solar plexus. The chop knocked the wind out of Bachmann, who doubled over and began rolling on the floor while La Salle fans in the crowd screamed bloody murder and stood up to point at the perpetrator.* Watching her son writhe in pain, Bachmann's mother snapped. She bum-rushed the court and started swinging her umbrella at the nearest Mapua player. It wasn't the guy who hit her son, but that detail didn't stop her from exacting revenge on Bachmann's behalf. Bachmann went on to a storied career with the national team and in the commercial leagues that preceded the PBA, but in many basketball circles the first story that comes to mind

---

* The pissed-off point, still in use in today's PBA, may be the gravest nonviolent gesture of fan anger in Philippine basketball. When a grim-faced spectator stands up and points at a referee, coach, or player, he or she is beaming shame directly onto the accused. On those occasions when assault by pointing is not enough to calm the crowd's fury, violence sometimes follows in the form of flying peso coins.

when Kurt Bachmann is mentioned is his umbrella-wielding mother and her notion of hardwood vigilante justice.

Bachmann played during the period in Philippine history when basketball was most closely associated with Filipino patriotism and identity. This was partly due to the national team's myriad successes in the 1950s and 1960s—they were regular participants in international competitions like the Olympics and world championships, and perennial champions of regional tournaments—but it also had to do with healing the nation's psychic wounds after World War II. Filipinos suffered greatly in the war. Japanese invaders seized control of the islands in 1942. The Japanese despised Filipinos, whom they considered lesser Asians for submitting to centuries of Western rule, and their wartime conduct was marked by the wanton murder of civilians and the kidnapping of young Filipinas to become "comfort women" for Japanese soldiers to rape. When the United States drove out the Japanese in 1945, Filipino civilians suffered as much as any soldier in the final battle for Manila, a gruesome house-to-house campaign that leveled much of the city. The Japanese, facing sure defeat, chose to fight to the death rather than dishonor the Emperor by surrendering. They set fires in Manila's port area that quickly spread to people's flimsy bamboo homes. They shot fleeing civilians and invaded homes to kill and mutilate their inhabitants. Between the Japanese massacres and the American bombing and artillery campaign that blew the Japanese out of hiding, nearly all of Manila's prewar architecture was destroyed and more than 100,000 Filipino civilians were killed.

Bachmann, born in 1936, lived through the atrocities of wartime Manila. It left him with a mind packed with horrific childhood memories and an enduring hatred of the Japanese. He told me about his uncle, a former basketball player for Letran College. Watching his older relative from the sidelines at NCAA games inspired the five-year-old Bachmann's love for the sport. A few years later Japanese soldiers shot and killed that uncle. During the American siege of Manila, he remembered walking from his family's home in the city proper to Santa Mesa, a safer area on the eastern outskirts of Manila, and seeing the dead bodies of hundreds of Filipino civilians, murdered by the Japanese or caught in American artillery blasts, piled along the sides of the roads. Bachmann still experienced flashbacks of the war's gore and destruction, and he still blamed the Japanese.

For players of Bachmann's generation, basketball in the postwar years became a way to reassert the Philippines' worthiness as a nation. The United States relinquished colonial rule of the Philippines after the war, and, although American military and commercial interests remained unduly powerful in the Philippines for decades (many Filipinos would argue that the United States is still an unequal partner in the countries' relationship today), the Philippines could finally call itself an independent nation. Similar to the virulent heckling in postwar soccer matches between European nations and West Germany, the Philippine national basketball team offered the country a chance to exact cathartic revenge on Japanese athletes.

When Bachmann told me stories about competing against the Japanese, he always called them "Japs." He remembered one occasion, at a tournament during his first year on the national team, when he and Loyzaga found themselves alone in an elevator with Takashi Itoyama, the Japanese center.

"Hey Itoyama, you remember me?" Loyzaga smiled and patted him on the back. Then he pointed his elbow at the Japanese player's Adam's apple. "You remember last time we played? I hit you here; you couldn't breathe?" Then Loyzaga pointed to Bachmann and continued: "New player. Philippine team. Bachmann. Meet Mr. Itoyama. I hit him in the throat the last time." Loyzaga turned again to Itoyama and said, "Be careful. He plays hook shot, but when he plays hook shot, he also stands like this." Loyzaga stood sideways like he was getting ready to release a hook and aimed the elbow of his nonshooting arm at Itoyama's neck. When the teams played the next day, Loyzaga and Bachmann found that the Japanese defenders gave them plenty of room to operate in the low post. As in Bachmann's other tales, I sensed a veneer of revisionism, but the pride underlying his narration wasn't self-aggrandizing swagger, but fierce patriotism as sharp and real as an elbow to the esophagus.

The honor that players like Loyzaga and Bachmann brought to the national team was reflected in the Filipino population and played a major role in cementing the game's hegemonic status in the country's sports scene. The Philippines' success in international play inspired athletes to take up basketball and fans to follow the sport, and college and semipro commercial leagues thrived off the ever-growing interest in hoops. Back in Ateneo's American Historical Collection, articles from the *Philippines Free Press* showed how basketball had metastasized into the country's preeminent sport. One story, written by F. V. Tutay in 1949, asked if basketball was too pervasive in the athletics scene, a question that still consumes reams of newsprint today. The writer mentioned a talented swimmer, on track to become an Olympian, who left the pool for good and decided to shoot hoops instead. "Perhaps the boy believes that there is not as much glamour in being an aquatic star as in being a basketball hero," Tutay wrote, although it's more likely the talented young athlete saw the MICAA players earning salaries to play for local corporations and recognized that basketball offered more opportunities to make a living. "Basketball has ceased to be a mere athletic contest," Tutay continued, citing that the wife of Senator Claro Recto paid twenty-five times face value for a pair of scalped tickets to the opening day games of the 1948 NCAA season. "It has become a full-fledged social affair, where socialites go to see and be seen."

The post–World War II generation of Filipinos came of age in the same basketball-saturated environment I witnessed all over the country sixty years later. Of course, people knew about volleyball, baseball, and soccer, but the country was already fixated on hoops. The country's prowess on the international stage stoked Philippine patriotism, while the social caché of college and semiprofessional leagues put the sport on radio airwaves and the front pages of newspapers. The government built courts in the central plazas of towns throughout Manila and the rest of the country, so that everywhere you visited, you could expect to find a municipal hall, church, public market, and basketball court within steps of each other. Playing and watching the sport became one of the cornerstones of Philippine social life.

At the University of the Philippines Diliman campus, just fifteen minutes from Ateneo and my town house, I met Michael Tan, chairman of the anthropology department and a newspaper columnist whose twice-weekly *"Pinoy Kasi"*[*] examined Philippine culture. U.P. Diliman is known for being not only the most prestigious, but also the most grueling academic institution in the country, and much of this reputation comes from its professors, who are infamous for writing tests with the expectation that half of their students will fail. U.P. Diliman's approach to higher education sounded like the complete opposite of the way American universities prepared students. Most of my college professors seemed primarily concerned with transferring knowledge to students, and I imagine they felt a sense of achievement when their students aced exams. U.P. professors appeared to treat their relationship with students in a more adversarial manner. They were like gatekeepers of intellectual achievement, presenting students with ever more difficult academic trials to ensure that whoever passed the class truly earned it.

The professors' fearsome reputation always put me on guard when I visited the campus. Basketball, despite its oversize role in Philippine society, had been almost completely ignored by local scholars. I once spent an afternoon flipping through Ateneo's entire collection of

---

[*] Loose translation: "Because you're Filipino." And while we're at it, *"pinoy"* is shorthand for "Filipino."

the journal *Philippine Studies,* hoping I'd stumble upon a basketball-related article that somehow didn't make it into the electronic card catalog. It never happened. I found several articles on native dance and even one about spider wrestling, but nothing about basketball. Before meeting a U.P. intellectual, I always feared the worst—that I would explain my interest in basketball and he or she would first frown, then laugh at my banal research and banish me to a campus dungeon, where I'd be forced to read his or her thousand-page magnum opus on pre-Spanish agriculture on Marinduque island. My worries, however, never amounted to much. No matter the school, whenever I met professors to discuss Philippine basketball from an academic perspective, they were helpful and enthusiastic, and Michael Tan was no exception.

Tan's research focuses on gender, sexuality, and public health in the Philippines, so although our plan was to talk about basketball and Filipino identity, he led me on several detours through the labyrinthine world of transgender and homosexual culture. Other than Tan, few academics had made an effort to understand the lives of Philippine homosexuals, and he'd made discoveries that, although fascinating, put me in place as the prude I truly am. After Tan had introduced me to terms like *tsupit*—a Tagalog contraction of *tsupa,* "to suck," and *gupit,* a "haircut," which referred to the practice among poor teenage boys of getting a free haircut from a gay barber in exchange for allowing the haircutter to perform oral sex on the teen—I was grateful when the conversation turned finally to basketball.

The sport had become not just a pastime for young Filipino men, Tan explained, but a rite of passage. When boys reach adolescence, they receive privileges. Their mothers begin to allow them to roam their neighborhoods freely, getting into trouble but also learning how to carry themselves as men. Inevitably, these boys end up playing basketball, first in their own neighborhood, but then branching out to compete against kids from other areas. These early trials teach them masculine virtues like teamwork, aggression, and machismo. "That's the male entry into a larger public sphere," Tan told me. "And it's part of Filipino masculinity. The wider your sphere of influence, the better. So basketball is there to make friends, build alliances. It even crosses class barriers."* This sounded a lot like my adolescence, in which my father first brought me to the local recreation center, then I started going on my own to play three-on-three after school, until finally I was chosen for a traveling team that played all over New York City. The majority of my cherished early memories come from basketball courts, and those experiences formed the foundation of my love for the sport, which led me across two oceans to Manila.

Basketball had become more than just a pastime for Filipinos; it was a social norm, something that young boys were expected to do. As subsequent generations came of age playing and watching hoops, the sport's grasp on society strengthened to the point where it is now impossible for many Filipinos to imagine their lives without basketball. This process continued during the reign of Ferdinand Marcos, which started when he was elected president in 1965 and ended in the 1986 People Power revolution, when millions of Filipinos gathered in the streets and forced the Marcos family into exile. The Marcos regime is best known for its plunder of billions of dollars in public funds and international

---

* Basketball even played a role in the lives of adolescent gay Filipinos, who were sent out into the streets to play ball and become men. Many of them reported to Tan that they had been avid players as teenagers, not necessarily because they loved the game, but because it gave them an opportunity to engage in something called "chancing." Basketball, of course, is a contact sport that leads to a lot of incidental rubbing and brushing. Chancing was the premeditated act of "accidentally" touching another player's butt or balls during the course of play. I realized I had been the victim of chancing a few times on the commuter train, most memorably by a brazen passenger wearing a yellow shirt with HOT STUFF COMING THROUGH printed on it. Yes, to the average hetero dude this practice must sound disturbing, but Tan's sources reported that chancing actually played an important role in helping them experiment and come to terms with their sexuality under the safe guise of "unintentional" touching.

aid money, first lady Imelda Marcos's expansive shoe collection, and a bloodcurdling record of human rights abuses. But the dictator's policies gave a huge boost to basketball's already powerful place in Philippine culture. Under martial law, Marcos exercised strict control over the nation's broadcast and print media. There were only a handful of television channels, and Marcos cronies controlled nearly all of them. Any channel that wasn't an outright propaganda mouthpiece for the regime was cowed into submission by the threat of government takeover. Open political debate and dissident messages were strictly forbidden, so instead broadcasters flooded the airwaves with syndicated American schlock like *Charlie's Angels* and *Donnie & Marie*. The few local productions that weren't banned tended to be corny variety shows, musicals filled with saccharine love songs, and the nascent PBA.

Many middle-age Filipinos can remember walking down the street in the late seventies during PBA broadcasts and not missing a single moment of the games because they could hear the play-by-play emanating from their neighbors' windows. It's tempting for me, as a hoops lover, to romanticize this image as some kind of earthly basketball paradise; that's when I need a kick in the shin (or the temple) to remind me that under martial law, after the game ended I wouldn't have been allowed outside because of curfew, and that if I publicly criticized a government that embezzled funds like it was a biological imperative, I could end up salvaged, a Marcos-era euphemism for being killed by authorities and dumped in the Pasig River. Nevertheless, hoops penetrated ever more deeply into the fabric of Philippine society during the 1970s and 1980s because people had hardly any choice but to watch the PBA, which broadcast games three times a week.

The government's de facto imposition of basketball on the Philippine masses ensured that the sport penetrated every level of society, to the point that a 1997 survey conducted by the Manila-based Social Weather Stations found that 83 percent of men and 64 percent of women named basketball their favorite sport to watch, and 58 percent of men also called it their favorite sport to play. Even people who might not be expected to follow hoops ended up being impacted by the game. Danton Remoto, a poet and gay rights activist, told me he learned to count by keeping a score sheet during televised games for his father, a diehard fan of the Toyota Tamaraws. Three nights a week the family watched PBA doubleheaders. "Basketball was like dessert," Remoto explained. "We would eat at 6:00 p.m. They showed basketball at seven. By then the dishes were cleaned and we would all gather around this black-and-white TV set. Imagine that replicated in many—I'm sure all—Philippine households in the seventies and you can see the effect of basketball. There is a national obsession with a sport that was the only thing you could watch other than a musical."

There was one last wrinkle of the basketball mystery that needed to be explored: soccer. Why hadn't the Philippines fallen under soccer's spell, like most of the rest of the world? Japan developed a deep love for baseball in the early twentieth century, at the same time as basketball was sweeping the Philippines, but soccer eventually gained a foothold and became popular in Japan while it remained an afterthought in the Philippines. Yet soccer seems to fit Filipinos so well—their diminutive stature wouldn't be a disadvantage, and the country's top athletes have the speed, creativity, and agility that make it easy to imagine them playing the "Beautiful Game."

This might sound put-on and corny, but I actually lost sleep over this question. I perused the libraries and asked everyone from sports journalists to my neighbors why soccer never caught on in the country. The conventional wisdom was that soccer was too slow for Filipinos, who love the high scores, seesaw lead changes, and sheer unpredictability of basketball. The idea that a soccer match could end in a tie appalled many Filipinos, whose primary sporting passion besides basketball was cockfighting, a contest in which there is always a winner and the loser gets killed and eaten. This explanation was tempting but too simple. Deep in the night, I'd still find myself tossing and turning, watching palm branches blow against my bedroom window, and listening to the fighting cocks crow in my neighbor's backyard. The slow game theory was weak. Countries throughout Central and South America adored soccer, and they shared a similar cultural heritage with the Philippines. Latin Americans had also been colonized by Spanish and Portuguese conquistadors and converted to Catholicism; their cities were sweaty, fast-paced, and chaotic, like Manila; they too relished telenovelas and beauty pageants. I had never been to Rio de Janeiro, but Brazilians certainly didn't seem dull, and they didn't find soccer boring. *Favelas*, the dense slums whose claustrophobic alleys inspired some of Brazil's best footballers' most creative moves, shot down the idea that there was not enough open space in Philippine cities to play soccer. The ingenuity Filipinos employed to jerry-rig hoops in what seemed like every nook and cranny of Manila proved that if people cared about soccer, they would have found ways to play the sport.

One morning I tracked down Emilio "Jun" Bernardino* and Mauricio "Moying" Martelino at the Century Park Hotel in Pasay City. They were sharing an early lunch of cold, shiny Hainanese chicken before heading to a pair of NCAA games at a nearby stadium. Between the two of them, these elder statesmen of Philippine basketball had held most of the major positions in the sport. Bernardino was serving as the NCAA's commissioner at the time, but had previously been the PBA commissioner from 1994 to 2002. Martelino had been commissioner of the semipro Philippine Basketball League and the secretary general of the Asian Basketball Federation. Yet for all their combined experience and wisdom, when I asked why soccer had never challenged basketball's

---

* Bernardino died of a heart attack in the first month of Roe's season with Alaska, and Cone insisted that the team attend his wake to honor the former commissioner.

dominance in Philippine sports, they couldn't muster any answers besides bewildered shrugs and Zenlike koans.

"Somehow, basketball caught the eye of the Filipino," Martelino said, turning up his palms in surrender. "Why, for heaven's sake, even I cannot understand it."

Bernardino, with a Buddhalike smile, chimed in: "Filipinos took to basketball like a fish takes to water."

I never found a solution to the soccer dilemma. The best explanation doesn't come in the form of an eloquent quip, but wrapped inside history, where basketball and national identity have become intertwined like strands in the double helix of Philippine DNA and passed down through multiple generations. The lack of a precise answer regarding Filipinos' devotion to basketball might be the strongest indicator of how deeply embedded it is in their lives. People have always struggled to define their essence, their soul, or whatever one wishes to call it. For Filipinos, basketball is part of that evanescent core. The Filipino novelist and cultural critic Nick Joaquin, in an essay about Spanish influences on Philippine culture, made a similar argument about food:

> If you tell the Pinoy-on-the-street that *adobo* and *pan de sal* are but a thin veneer of Westernization, the removal of which will reveal the "true" Filipino . . . the Pinoy may retort that, as far as he is concerned, adobo and pan de sal are as Filipino as his very own guts; and indeed one could travel the world and nowhere find . . . anything quite like Philippine adobo and pan de sal.

Basketball, another colonial import, has also become as Filipino as the Pinoy's guts. By following Alaska through a PBA season, I wouldn't merely be learning about the overseas game or investigating a quirky professional league, but watching an essential part of the Philippine national character reveal itself through sport.

5

From Savior to Lemon, in 48 Minutes

The next morning I tagged along with Roe to PBA headquarters to watch the league's technical committee measure his height. The PBA complex was situated on a spacious lot behind two banks in Libis, one of Quezon City's business enclaves. The league had recently moved from its longtime office next to the Philippine Department of Education, and the new location reminded me of office parks in suburban Illinois. I entered the lobby with Roe and two Alaska team representatives, Tomas "Mang Tom" Urbano,* the team's sixty-seven-year-old practice referee and scorekeeper, and Monch Gavieres, the assistant team manager. While Monch and Mang Tom checked in with the receptionist, I inspected the lobby centerpiece, a nearly life-size bronze statue of a player charging to the hoop with a ball cradled in his huge hands and one knee raised almost to his chest. Even though the sculpture bore an odd resemblance to Johnny Carson, I assumed it was meant to be Robert Jaworski, the most famous player in PBA history. A security guard told me it wasn't Jaworski, but a former Alaska player, five-foot-seven point guard Johnny Abarrientos, the shortest MVP in

---

* *Mang,* short for *manong,* is an honorary title used for elder males.

league history and one of the vital cogs in Alaska's late nineties dynasty. The statue's contorted face and rusty color reminded me of *Star Wars* and Han Solo's carbonite tomb, especially with regards to Abarrientos and Alaska; the franchise seemed frozen in time since it traded the point guard in 2000. The security guard must have noticed me beholding the statue with a little too much reverence, because he tiptoed next to it and rapped Abarrientos's leg with his fist. The hollow thud confirmed that the sculpture was not majestic bronze but papier-mâché.

League officials led us through the broad low-rise compound and down a long, pristine hallway, empty except for photographs of former commissioners and the PBA's twenty-five greatest players. We turned into a room with bright fluorescent lighting and a crowd of men waiting for us. They were the technical staff, who would measure Roe and certify that his height was below the league's limit for imports, which was set this season at six-foot-six. Representatives of the other nine teams were also present to make sure that every part of his measurement seemed aboveboard, and also just to size up a rival team's top player.

Roe, who came directly from practice and hardly had time to change out of his sweaty uniform, shivered in the air-conditioned room and bent over to remove his socks and sneakers. The crowd of men closed in around him as he unfolded his muscular frame and lay flat on his back against the linoleum floor. If the witnesses from other teams arrived at the measurement hoping that Alaska's import had come to the country overweight and out of shape, the sight of Roe's bulging muscles and trim waist surely disappointed them. Two men knelt beside Roe and pressed his knees down to the floor to make sure his joints remained locked and his legs fully extended. Three more league employees pinned his upper body to the ground, one pressing down on each shoulder and another gently holding his forehead against the cold floor. Roe shivered again but didn't struggle. His demeanor was that of a patient being examined by a team of doctors—quiet acceptance of the unfamiliar people handling his body in unfamiliar ways. Finally, one last PBA worker placed a wooden board flush against the soles of Roe's feet and hooked a tape measure to the plank. He walked to Roe's head, squatted, and held the tape to the top of the player's skull. Roe was exactly six feet, four and five-eighths inches tall, a little more than an inch below the league's height limit.

There was something unseemly about a dozen middle-age Filipino men pacing circles around a prone, half-naked black man, then holding him against the floor while studiously recording his physical attributes. The size disparity, with Roe being almost a foot taller and about seventy pounds heavier than his assessors, reminded me of Gulliver being tied down by the Lilliputians. There was a racial aspect to it, but it didn't match up to the black-white paradigm that dominated my American frame of reference. The sight of many men surrounding one and holding him down was ominous and primal, like Roe might be sent to the coliseum to wrestle a crocodile after the measurement, but then again · everyone seemed comfortable with the proceedings. For Roe, of course, this was nothing new. This was his fifth season in Philippine basketball, and he had submitted to similar examinations before each of those campaigns. Also, for a professional athlete like Roe, there was nothing disconcerting about the notion that his body could be treated like a commodity. It was a fact of life.

Although he had already been measured by the PBA on several occasions, the league hadn't always found Roe to be this tall. Before his first season in 2001, he was measured at six-foot-two and a half. Now, at thirty-two years old, Roe certainly hadn't grown two inches in the years since his original measurement, nor did he undergo any bizarre bone-lengthening procedure. Back then he had simply taken part in the PBA's long-held tradition of shrinking imports, an act of subterfuge that had been part of the league for as long as teams had been hiring imports.

The PBA set height limits for foreign reinforcements to offset Filipinos' paucity in that most elemental trait of basketball players. The tallest full-blooded Filipino in the league, the Santa Lucia Realtors' Marlou Aquino, crested at six-foot-nine,* and only a handful of other locals, most of whom were of mixed Caucasian or black ancestry, stood six-foot-seven or taller. Several Filipino "big men" were barely taller than six-three, the standard height for NBA point guards. Many coaches and commentators—Manila's basketball intelligentsia—remained skeptical of local big men taller than six-foot-five. They considered these players awkward and too slow to keep up with the manic pace of the Philippine game. According to a common saying, any baller over six-five was abnormal. Supposedly, any Filipino that tall was probably a pituitary case more suited for provincial freak shows than the Araneta Coliseum. Yet the league still wanted to create an entertaining product that would attract fans and advertisers, and fans wanted dunks. Slams, however, were so rarely executed by local players that the league had toyed with the idea of making them worth three points.† Imports were employed to add a dash of high-wire athleticism to PBA games, but the league limited their dominance by banning foreign players over certain heights.

The rule works. PBA imports have always been a versatile bunch:

---

* Aquino always struck me as a man burdened by his height, like he might have preferred to be a chef, but because he was extremely tall and fairly athletic in a country full of hoops addicts, he had no choice but to become a basketball player. I had never seen someone look so glum on a basketball court. Aquino plodded from baseline to baseline, grimacing whenever a smaller player bumped him or swiped at the ball while he operated in the low post. For more than a decade he held one of no more than 150 roster spots in a country of 90 million people; it was a dream job, but Aquino seemed like a captive of his nation's passion, and he went to work with the same energy and vigor as a 7-Eleven cashier.

† Most coaches thought this to be a terrible idea that would make a mockery of the game. They're probably right, but I would have loved to see the PBA try this because then every player who could sometimes dunk in practice would start trying to jam the ball in games. The inevitable parade of missed dunks would have catapulted the PBA to the top of the list of the world's funniest leagues.

workhorses like Roe who did a little of everything, pure scorers with velvet smooth inside-outside games, and burly inside operators who bulldozed their way to the hoop. But while the foreigners provided highlights and team leadership, they still left room for the best Filipino players—guards like Alaska's Willie Miller, who whirled through defenses to score on twisting layups spun off the backboard at every conceivable angle—to do what they do best. In a competitive league, however, setting a height limit created an incentive to cheat. If a team could somehow temporarily shrink its import just before the league measured him, that team would have an advantage over its rivals. In the PBA, as in many Philippine institutions (like provincial municipalities that reported zero crime over the course of a year), the objective reality was often different from the more malleable official reality, data that could be massaged through gamesmanship or bribery.

PBA teams managed to shave inches off their imports without greasing any palms. Instead, the league permitted a form of unspoken collusion between teams, wherein everyone played the same tricks and usually got away with them. The most effective shrinking technique was also the simplest. Until 2005 the league made imports stand against a wall during measurements. To appear shorter, players would just hunch over and bend their knees. In most cases the players were only an inch or two taller than the limit, so it didn't take much crouching. All they needed was a slight bend in the neck and a pair of billowing shorts to conceal the crimp in their knees. This is how Roe got down to six-foot-two-and-a-half in 2001, when the ceiling was set at six-foot-four. It was Roe's first season in the Philippines, and he was worried that he'd come in over height and be sent home before collecting his first paycheck. The idea of pretending to be shorter than his actual height ran contrary to the career-long habit for Roe and most other imports of overestimating height to appeal to NBA scouts. Since college, he had been listed as six-foot-seven. The assistant coach who accompanied him to his 2001 measurement reassured him that he'd make the cut and told him to get as low as possible, within reasonable limits. Roe did precisely that. He backed up against the wall, tucked his head down to the base of his neck and locked his knees. When the PBA's knee-pushing henchmen arrived and did their darnedest to straighten his legs, Roe held the position and claimed it was his natural posture. Like so many imports who preceded him, this world-class athlete shriveled into the frame of a septuagenarian and shrunk by more than two inches. Behold, the amazing adjustable-height basketball player!

When I asked Alaska's players and coaches about the finer points of height manipulation they became giddy, as if this cheating was just one of the league's lovable peculiarities, the PBA equivalent of a white lie. Nic Belasco, Alaska's starting power forward and a ten-year PBA veteran, gleefully reenacted the bent-knees, tucked-chin stance for me after practice one afternoon, and when Cone saw Belasco he chortled, "Is he doing the import position? That's not it!" After the players left, when Cone was less concerned about looking authoritative, he took me into his office and demonstrated the proper form: Belasco's joints were properly crooked, but he wasn't leaning against the wall at a severe enough angle. If an import got his legs out in front of him an extra inch or two, he could shrink more.

The basketball elite's happy-go-lucky approach to height manipulation reminded me of many Filipinos' bemused fatalism toward the country's famously corrupt politicians. They couldn't stop the cheating, so they just laughed at it. Throughout his reign as PBA commissioner during the 1990s and early 2000s, Jun Bernardino invited teams to send witnesses to the measuring sessions, so they could see that the measurement process was fair and accurate. Instead, coaches found themselves schlepping to the league office to helplessly watch imports slouch their way below the height limit. If a team protested, the league would reappraise the player's height and invariably determine that the original measurement was correct, since admitting an error would embarrass the PBA more than allowing the mistake to go uncorrected. Rather than demand an accurate system of measuring imports, PBA teams formed an unspoken agreement that allowed everyone to save face: as long as players remained reasonably close to the height limit, there would be no complaints.

Over the years, teams developed a battery of other height-reduction methods based on grooming and pseudoscience that coaches and team managers still believed to be effective. The league's original height-altering technique was a trip to the barber. In the 1970s and 1980s teams tried to shave off inches by shaving players' heads, but the practice had lapsed in recent years as large hairstyles like afros, shags, and flat tops went out of style. Also, the technique wasn't foolproof. As many teams discovered, it was not big hair but pointy skulls that disqualified their imports.

In terms of sheer lunacy, however, bald-faced cheating and goofy hairdos had nothing on the PBA's musculoskeletal means of shrinking imports. Coaches throughout the league swore that intense exercise in the hours before a measurement would knock as much as an inch off a player's everyday height. Shoulder presses and squats could compress a player's bone structure, while running in the tropical heat would shrink him via dehydration. These techniques had more in common with folk remedies sold in the market outside Manila's Quiapo church—magic potions and voodoo candles that served every cause from making some-one fall in love to inducing abortion—than with medical science. There is no known way to shrink a person, although NYU orthopedic surgeons told me that weightlifting could compress the soft, fluid-filled disks between the vertebrae, and aerobic exercise might cause dehydration-related shrinkage in the disks. The resulting loss in height, however, would be in millimeters, not inches.

Despite PBA teams' widespread adoption of modern training meth-ods like plyometric and core-strengthening exercises, the false notion that draining workouts could shrink imports persisted. Coaches and trainers vowed that these techniques were effective and claimed to have seen them work dozens of times. It was more likely that they saw the players shrink by means of drooping posture and attributed the change in height to spine-compacting workouts. I also wondered if coaches' willful ignorance regarding the quack methods helped them avoid whatever pangs of guilt they might have felt over their mild dishonesty. Clinging to the myth that players could be shrunk through training preserved the illusion of fair play and let coaches off the hook. They didn't recruit an over height player and then encourage him to break the rules; they found a competitive advantage. Or so they told themselves.

The shift after the 2005 season to measuring players while they lay flat on their backs was rooted not in a desire to improve league policy, but a simple changing of the guards. That year, the league's technical committee, which oversees officiating, was put in charge of measuring imports. Previously, the task had been outsourced to private doctors. The new committee thought heights would be more accurate if the players were measured lying down, so that became the standard operating procedure. As of yet, no team has figured out how to cheat the new system, and although there have been no official complaints about the stricter rules, there have been unintended consequences. The magical, shrinking imports of yore stopped shrinking. Some, like Roe, actually grew, as players who passed the measurement in previous seasons failed to make the same height under the new regime.

Alaska was one of the first teams to be stung by the measurement change. The previous season, the team replaced import Artemus Mc-Clary late in the regular season. Cone brought in Victor Thomas, a gifted offensive player who won the league's best import award in 2004. He arrived in Manila and immediately joined Alaska's practices. Thomas could score from all over the floor and appeared to be a competent and willing passer; he looked like a perfect fit for Cone's triangle offense. Management thought another championship might be on the way. The night before Thomas's first game, he went to get measured. Because he had already played under the six-foot-six height limit, Cone assumed

Thomas would pass. But in earlier seasons he had been measured while standing, and this time he had to lie down. An hour later Cone's phone rang with the news that Thomas had sprouted and was now over height. Alaska was forced to hire a less experienced import and the team was swept from the playoffs.

The week of Roe's measurement, the lying-down system claimed its second victim. Jaws dropped in the Alaska players' lounge when Mang Tom returned from witnessing the measurement of the San Miguel Beermen's intended import, former Seton Hall standout Kelly Whitney. San Miguel was one of the PBA's flagship teams. It was almost unfathomable that the import they had flown out for the upcoming season would get the boot for being too tall. But there was no leeway in the new scheme, so when Whitney lay down and measured less than half an inch over six-foot-six, he had to go. When the news passed from the lounge into the coaches' room, Cone smiled; it was the kind of grin you see on a cartoon cat who just scarfed a bird. He knew San Miguel would have to scramble to find a replacement for Whitney, and whoever they hired would likely be a downgrade. A major rival was likely to get off to a slow start that season; Alaska's window for success just got a little wider.

Getting stretched out on the floor and measured was just the first of many potential hurdles Roe would face in the PBA, which was known as one of the trickiest and most unforgiving leagues in the world for visiting imports. The Philippines' outsize passion for hoops cut both ways on the lives of imports. In Manila the PBA was the only game in town, and imports were feted as kings of the local league. That is, if they could remain on their teams long enough to enjoy the royal treatment. As long as imports satisfied the expectations of coaches, teammates, and the media, Beatlemania could be theirs: awestruck teens would screech and point at them in malls; earnest, lifelong basketball fans would approach them to shake hands and say "You're my idol"; and mothers would ask them to hold their babies and pose for cell phone pictures. The catch, however, was that satisfying a PBA team could require Herculean efforts, and about half of the imports who arrived in the Philippines in any given season ended up being shipped home before the playoffs even began.

The international pro leagues where basketball hired guns like Roe played were known as results-oriented businesses, but even in this unforgiving universe, PBA teams were known for being among the most cutthroat employers. The expectations heaped on imports were limitless. With few exceptions, Philippine teams demanded that their imports put up gaudy statistics every night. An acceptable game might include at least 25 points, around 12 rebounds, and a smattering of assists, blocked shots, and steals, depending on a player's talents. For most players that would be a career game, a dominant performance that occurred maybe five times before retirement. For PBA imports that was an average. And although numbers mattered, they alone were not enough. Ideally, they would be accompanied by wins. Nothing pleased owners more than topping the standings. It attracted more press for the franchise and associated the team's corporate backer—whether it be a canned meat company or real estate developer—with success.

The only imports with a measure of job security were those who filled up stat sheets and delivered winning records; achieving one or the other was not enough. An underperforming import on a winning team might be swapped for a new reinforcement who could make the team even better. An impressive import on a losing team would be branded a talented loner who didn't know how to win. Stats and wins were the absolute requirements, but a second tier of expectations also burdened imports. They were expected to play tirelessly for forty-five minutes every game, and some nights they wouldn't rest at all. They had to play through injuries and set an example by outworking their teammates in practice. Teams wanted imports to be clutch scorers who could will their teams to victory in tight games.

There was no reasonable boundary to the responsibilities heaped on PBA imports; anything short of Michael Jordan was not quite good enough. Of course, the PBA had neither the money nor the prestige to lure a player like His Airness, or even most NBA twelfth men, to Manila, so they settled for lesser talents and poorer pedigrees. But PBA teams were constantly on the lookout for upgrades, and no import was ever totally safe. The failure to satisfy any of his team's myriad expectations could buy him a seat on the next plane back to the States.

To ratchet the pressure up even further, PBA teams made it clear to imports during preseason meetings that they had to produce these results immediately. Learning curves and gradual success were the luxuries of NBA teams, with their eighty-two-game seasons. In the PBA, where the import conference lasted only eighteen games before playoffs, it was score and win or go home. It wasn't uncommon for a team to lose faith in an import and send him packing after just one performance, and during some seasons a third of the imports hired by PBA teams were gone after three games or less. A mid-season replacement might face the daunting prospect of flying to Manila from the United States or wherever he'd been playing in Europe, then having twenty-four hours to acclimate to Manila's heat, meet his teammates, learn a couple of plays, and sleep as many hours as his frazzled circadian rhythms would permit before suiting up for his first game. And if this dehydrated, jet-lagged, somewhat bewildered substitute turned in a lackluster debut, chances weren't bad that he would be sliding his passport through an immigration window on his way out of the Philippines at week's end.

PBA teams had split personalities when it came to their imports. As long as the club was winning and the import looked great on the court, he would be heralded as a savior. But the moment his game sputtered or the team dropped a few close games, team managers reoriented themselves and began treating the import like a flat tire that needed to be changed immediately. Around the PBA, disappointing imports were

referred to as "lemons," a term usually reserved for broken-down washing machines and used cars.

The season before I started following Alaska, I watched another import, Quemont Greer, go through the PBA wringer. Greer was the De-
Paul star I watched pour in almost 50 points in the first PBA game I
attended. Greer scored almost every time he caught the ball, using slippery stutter-steps and crossover dribbles that had the big men who tried
to guard him stumbling over their own feet. When smaller, more agile
defenders were assigned to stay in front of him, Greer set up in the low
post, where his bulk was too much for them to handle. His shooting
touch was feathery; Greer converted three-point shots, pull-up jumpers in the lane, a tricky bank shot on the run, and several point-blank
layups, tip-ins, and dunks off offensive rebounds. On the few occasions
when Greer broke down his initial defender and a second line of opponents swarmed him, he was able to shovel the ball to open teammates
for easier baskets. It was a masterful performance, and I was not surprised to find out after the game that Greer was leading the league in
scoring while his team, Red Bull, was near the top of the standings.

A few games before the end of the regular season, I talked my way
into a Red Bull practice to get a closer look at Greer. The team worked
out in a cavernous gym with two adjacent full-courts, each showing a
lot of wear and tear. I could hear the thud of dead spots in the hardwood as players dribbled through warm-up exercises, and the far court
was only used for shooting around because one of its rims was slightly
off-kilter. I thought the spacious interior might make this gym cooler
than some of the stuffy bandboxes other teams used.* Instead, however,

---

* The most infamous of these hellholes had to be the subterranean Dumlao
Gym on Shaw Boulevard, which was housed in the basement of a dilapidated
apartment tower. I had never wondered what it might feel like to run wind sprints
on a New York subway platform on the hottest day in July, but thanks to Dumlao,
I now have a pretty good idea.

there seemed to be too much space in Red Bull's gym to get the heavy air moving. The breeze from four wheezing electric fans on the sidelines couldn't reach the players at center court. In between drills the players walked to the bleachers and wrung pools of sweat from the bottom of their shorts, then crowded around the fans and lifted up their jerseys.

No one seemed more bummed about the facility than Greer, who had spent the previous four years practicing in DePaul's state-of-the-art field house. During individual drills, coaches asked Greer and Red Bull's big men to fake running to the corner, then change directions and sprint to the free throw line for a catch-and-shoot. Greer moved through this sequence like he was caught in a glue trap. His body language while waiting his turn alternated between two langorous poses—hands on his hips with head lolling, or bent over with hands on his knees—that seemed like comic exaggerations of off-the-charts laziness. After some cajoling from the Red Bull coaching staff, Greer straightened out and trotted gingerly through the exercises, an improvement over his previous effort but still not exactly inspired basketball. Minutes later he walked off the court without saying anything to his coaches. He took a folding chair and sat on the sidelines. An assistant coach looked at Greer and raised his eyebrows to get his attention. Greer pointed to his hamstring. It was tight. He spent the next half hour or so watching practice from the chair while two ball boys massaged his calves and thighs. I got the feeling Greer, as the temporary face of the Red Bull franchise, wasn't the ideal spokesman for an energy drink.

Red Bull scrimmaged during the final half hour of practice, and the opportunity to compete roused Greer. He stepped into the game and immediately took over. He scored on his typical array of pull-up jumpers, powerful drives, and a couple emphatic dunks. It looked like a reminder to the coaching staff: "I may dog it in practice from time to time, but I'm also really good."

When practice ended I walked over to Red Bull Coach Yeng Guiao to chat about how the season had been going and how he felt about his import. Since Greer was averaging more than 27 points a game and Red Bull was in contention for a top seed in the playoffs, I expected Guiao to repeat a few old basketball saws about Greer's talent, pepper it with a couple caveats about his inconsistent effort, then sum things up with a generally positive and confident outlook heading toward the postseason. And that's pretty much how it started.

"You know, I think Quemont is probably just one notch below the NBA," Guiao said. "He definitely has the talent of an NBA player." Then Guiao used his own change-of-direction move to turn the conversation. "But actually, he's not the right import for us. Please don't tell Quemont, because he doesn't know yet, but there's another player arriving later this week who could be his replacement."

If Guiao had told me he saw Imelda Marcos's face in a bowl of mangoes that morning and it asked him for a Bulgari watch, I would have been less confused. The fact that Guiao had plans to dump the league's leading scorer, who'd carried Red Bull to a winning record throughout the season, was shocking. Plus, the nonchalant way the coach described his plan took my breath away. The team concepts that had been drilled into me throughout my own paltry basketball career and reinforced by countless sports broadcasters—togetherness and loyalty, win or lose, to the end—didn't seem to apply in the PBA, at least not for imports. Guiao thought there was a better player available, and he wasn't going to stick with Greer based on fealty alone. "We're reaching a point," he told me, "where it's better to make a wrong decision than not make one at all."

Guiao's problem with Greer had little to do with his talent or production on the court. In fact, Guiao's only quibble with Greer's game was that he was a volume shooter and a possession killer, a player who often attempted twenty or more shots per game and who sometimes dribbled away half of the twenty-four-second shot clock instead of passing to his teammates. When Greer was hot, he'd score 45 and Red Bull won. When he was cold, he'd score 17 and they lost. Guiao didn't want to hang his team's playoff fate on Greer's streak shooting. These seemed like valid critiques—at the NBA level. Aside from his lack of height (six-foot-six is dreadfully short for NBA forwards), Greer's affinity for one-on-one basketball and low percentage shots probably played a role in his not being selected in the 2005 NBA draft. But in the PBA, so-called "black hole" players like Greer—the ball goes into them and doesn't come out—had once been the prototypical imports. In fact, when Guiao was coaching the Swift Mighty Meaties hot dog franchise in 1992, one of his most celebrated past imports, Tony Harris, set the PBA single-game scoring record with 105 points. Guiao and Harris won a championship that season, and even though the league had grown to embrace a more team-oriented style in recent years, imports were still expected to play with a ball-hog streak. Besides, in a league where imports were expected to average close to 30 points per game, jacking up shots was a way to keep your job.

The rift between Greer and his coach was rooted in personality differences and Greer's reluctance to embrace the role of team leader. I met up with Greer later that week to hear his thoughts about the season. Red Bull was putting him up in a Holiday Inn not far from the team's practice facility. Greer said that Guiao had challenged him to act like Red Bull's captain, but as a twenty-four-year-old in his first job, Greer wasn't comfortable giving orders when he was the most recent addition to the roster. He had teammates who'd been playing pro ball for ten years. Why weren't they leading the team? Guiao countered that Greer's talent trumped the locals' experience. They would follow his cues on the court, and sitting down at practice to enjoy a thirty-minute rubdown while the rest of the team panted their way through suicides certainly wasn't inspirational leadership. Again, Greer defended himself. Guiao rarely gave him a breather during games, and Greer didn't want to wear himself out or exacerbate his nagging injuries by going all-out in practice: "I felt that I'm out here doing a lot of the work, and I need a break too. They was looking at it like, he's the import. He don't need no breaks."

Greer's mild-mannered ways seemed to irk Guiao, one of the PBA's most volatile coaches. PBA lore had it that years ago Guiao, in a fit of Napoleonic rage, waved a pistol at his players during practice to motivate them. It was a tale that everyone seemed to have heard but no one could ever confirm. Even if the story was pure fantasia, it reinforced Guiao's fiery reputation and lent credence to the conventional wisdom that Guiao's players worked so hard because they were scared of him. One indisputable display of Guiao's wrath occurred a month before Roe arrived for the import conference, when Red Bull was playing the San Miguel Beermen in the semifinals of the previous all-Filipino conference. During the second quarter of game six, San Miguel guard Dondon Hontiveros hit a jump shot in front of Red Bull's bench, then turned to head back on defense and ran into a hybrid clothesline-forearm shiver from Guiao. The blow struck Hontiveros in the Adam's apple, and he collapsed to the ground clutching his neck. Guiao was ejected from the game but not suspended. It may come as a surprise, then, to learn that Guiao was also a statesman. When he wasn't coaching, Guiao moonlighted as the vice governor of Pampanga province north of Manila, but Guiao's coaching colleagues believed that his combative nature originated from his experience in the vicious world of local politics, which made the PBA look like Romper Room.

With his players, Guiao's only rule was that they remain confident and aggressive and never back down from challenges. If a player passed up an open shot or let an opponent continually get the best of him, he was likely to end up planted on the bench with Guiao howling in his face. Greer, on the other hand, was calm and docile to the point of seeming passionless. Even when he dominated games, he did so with the air of someone who drank a pregame cocktail of Sleepytime Tea and Quaaludes.

Guiao thought this sent mixed messages to Greer's teammates—play lazy but score 40. Greer's easygoing style contradicted his coach's kill or be killed hoops philosophy. So when Red Bull lost, Guiao blamed Greer's blasé air, and even when they won, Guiao couldn't feel the satisfaction of winning his way because Greer didn't buy into his confrontational ethic.

When we spoke, Greer was always polite and responsive, but the blank expression on his face never wavered. If he felt any emotion while discussing his dashed NBA ambitions and PBA difficulties, it remained hidden behind his hooded eyes. Even the threat of being sent home before season's end failed to rouse more than mild frustration. "If they don't like me being myself, so be it," he told me. "If they decide to replace me, that's on them. It's really not in my control."

I returned to Red Bull practice later in the week to see Greer play against his potential replacement, James Penny. Penny had arrived the night before—not long after Red Bull management finally informed Greer they were hiring a second import—and he looked drained and frazzled at practice. Penny, twenty-nine, had played at Texas Christian University and possessed a significant edge on Greer in experience. He had suited up in U.S. minor leagues, Canada, Argentina, the Dominican Republic, China, and Lebanon. Red Bull planned to conduct an extended tryout between Greer and Penny over the last two weeks of the regular season. Since Greer was clearly a serviceable import, the team would let him finish out the schedule and give Penny time to settle in, get over his jet lag, and learn Guiao's system. At the end of that period, if Penny proved to be the stronger import, he would take over for Greer in the playoffs. If Greer turned out to be the better man, he could keep his job. The way Red Bull exploited its imports seemed cruel and cynical, but from the franchise's perspective, paying the Americans twice as much as the highest-paid locals gave management license to jerk them around for the greater good of winning. Also, within the frame of Philippine basketball, Red Bull had done nothing wrong. Holding mid-season tryouts between imports wasn't common in the PBA, but it was an accepted tactic. Red Bull was not the first team to do it and they would not be the last.

At practice, Greer and Penny seemed determined to restore some of the dignity that Red Bull had removed from the situation. They arrived together, since Red Bull had arranged to have the imports driven back and forth to practice in the same van, and although they had already met, they courteously shook hands at the beginning of the session. After that, they kept their distance, with Greer staying on one sideline and Penny the other during water breaks. Greer smirked when reserve center Omanzie Rodriguez dunked on Penny, who was still a step slow from the long flight and Manila's mid-morning swelter. As the practice wound down and Guiao called for a full-court scrimmage, everyone in the gym tensed up. This would be the first head-to-head confrontation between Greer and Penny. When the game began, the imports' contrasting styles were obvious. Greer showed flashes of brilliance: a dunk over Penny and two other players, then a crossover that left Penny flatfooted at the top of the key. But Penny's team was more cohesive. He passed to back door cutters for easy layups and set screens that gave his teammates open jumpers. Guiao, stoic on the sideline with his arms folded in front of his chest, nodded his freshly shaved head in approval. Penny wasn't going to score like Greer, but because he was better at creating scoring opportunities for his teammates, he wouldn't need to. Plus, the extra touches might boost the locals' confidence and spur them to hustle more on defense.

That night, I met Penny in his room. Red Bull had put him up in a hotel separated from Greer's Holiday Inn by a shopping mall. The view from Penny's window included a panorama of nearby skyscrapers in the Ortigas Center business district, as well as Greer's window a few hundred feet away. According to Penny, Red Bull wasn't entirely honest about their reasons for hiring him. They led him to believe that Greer had been injured, and Penny didn't find out until after his arrival that he'd be vying for a job against a healthy Greer. He was so suspicious of the team's machinations that when he saw me arrive at practice that morning, he thought I was there to compete for the import position. "You might be a shooter," Penny said.* He felt queasy about the whole situation: "I really have no idea what I'm doing here. Usually, when something like this happens, the team is struggling. You don't come in and try to replace somebody who's the leading scorer in the league with his team being in second or third place. The situation is kind of iffy to me, but it's a job, you know?"

With that, he summed up the reason why distinguished international players willingly subject themselves to the capricious whims of PBA teams. The salaries were competitive with other leagues around the world, and PBA franchises were known for paying their imports in full and on time. This was a major draw. Almost every import I met had a story about getting ripped off by a team somewhere, but they all said that PBA teams, despite their constant scheming over replacements, were honest and fair when it came to money.

As the tryout dragged on, Penny and Greer kept practicing together and the tension between them evaporated. During the van rides before and after practice, Penny even encouraged Greer to start acting like the vocal leader Guiao wanted. "You've been here working your butt off the whole time," he told Greer. "It's your job, man. Don't let anyone take your job from you. If they ask you to do something like be more of a leader, then why not do it?"

Red Bull's final regular season game, against Coca-Cola, was critical for the team as well as for Greer. If they won, Red Bull would tie for second place and force a one-game playoff for an automatic semifinal

---

* Coming from a pro with Penny's track record, that brief case of mistaken identity was the best compliment I'd received in years. Never mind that I couldn't hang with Penny and Greer on the court, the fact that I could pass for a player in their league—even if only in a moment of extreme paranoia—made me proud.

berth. Penny had been in the country less than a week and was still recovering from jet lag. Guiao decided it was too risky to play him and penciled in Greer as the starter. It seemed like Greer's last chance to prove he deserved to stay. The threat of replacement seemed to have an effect on Greer's performance. He looked like he ran the court harder than in previous games, and he avoided taking the low-percentage, pull-up three-pointers that drove Guiao mad. With twenty seconds left and the game tied, he stood at the three-point line with the ball in his hands. He blew by his defender, jump-stopped a few feet away from the basket, and drew a foul when three opposing players pounced on him. He made one of two free throws to clinch the game. The win was enough to earn Greer another chance to play, this time in the one-game playoff for second place against Barangay Ginebra. He scored 37 points and grabbed 13 rebounds, but he had zero assists and Red Bull lost.

Later that week Penny officially replaced Greer. In Red Bull's first playoff series, he led the team to a three-game sweep of Alaska (this was the same year they lost Victor Thomas to the six-foot-six height limit). "I am more convinced now that Penny is the right import for us," Guiao told the press after closing out Alaska. "He's some sort of savior." Six weeks later Penny led the team to a 4-2 win over the Purefoods Chunkee Giants in the championship series. Guiao and Red Bull's harsh treatment of Greer was vindicated.

Although it was easy to see Guiao as a villain, I developed an unexpected affinity for the loose-cannon coach. Guiao was the kind of character you were more likely to find in a movie than real life; he seemed to be applying the philosophy and even some of the moves of *The Karate Kid*'s wicked Cobra Kai dojo to professional basketball. It seemed ridiculous, yet somehow he was winning. Red Bull operated at a lower budget than rival teams and traded for lesser talents, and Guiao would whip them into a frenzy, send them onto the court, and turn overlooked players into emerging stars. He reminded me of some of the hot-blooded coaches I saw as a player in New York's Public School Athletic League, educators who looked like bag men and spent entire games spewing invectives at their players, opposing teams, referees, scorer's tables, crowds, even the dance teams. I never thought these characters made it to the elite ranks—the NBA was too buttoned-up to permit these shenanigans. Yet here was Guiao, consistently willing Red Bull into the semifinals and beyond. The ranting, the taunting, the occasional clothesline—Guiao had bottomless chutzpah, and I loved watching him blow his top.

Looking forward to Alaska's season, Roe had a few reasons to feel confident that he wouldn't suffer Greer's fate. The strongest factor working in Roe's favor was the difference in coaches. It wasn't a matter of Alaska coach Tim Cone having more integrity or feeling more sympathetic to imports than Guiao did. Every coach in the PBA had replaced imports several times before, and their attitudes toward sending players home tended to be callous, like changing parts on a car. The difference, however, was that Cone had turned the Aces into a very complicated vehicle by fine-tuning the team's triangle offense. It took imports weeks to grasp the basics of the triangle, and it required several seasons to master. With that lengthy learning curve, Cone did his best to avoid hiring new imports in the middle of the season, when a three-game losing streak could mean the difference between a bye in the playoffs and playing a succession of knockout games against teams at the bottom of the standings. Cone was also a cerebral coach who was at his best when trying to solve problems on the court. He relished the challenge of working around an import's faults to find ways for him to succeed; in fact, constraints like Roe's poor shooting stroke could inspire some of Cone's finest, most creative moments.

Guiao, on the other hand, helmed an offense that easily accommodated interchangeable parts. Red Bull ran the same four plays over and over, and each included options for the import to catch the ball in the low or high post, on the wing or facing the basket at the three-point line, with plenty of time and space to take his man. Guiao could plug in a replacement and watch him drop 40 points in his first game.

Guiao also seemed to enjoy tinkering with his imports and shaking up his roster to give the team a competitive edge. The shift from Greer to Penny in 2006 was a risky move (Penny was, after all, replacing the PBA's top scorer) that caught other coaches off-guard. The Red Bull that teams had seen during the regular season was a one-man show. If they could force Greer into an off night, they stood a good chance of winning. The Penny-led team Guiao fielded in the postseason played a totally different style, with more balanced scoring, heavy contributions from the local stars, and Penny orchestrating the offense from the high post.

That wasn't the first time Guiao took advantage of league rules that allowed franchises to replace imports at any point in the season. He might be the only coach in league history to hire a new import midway through a championship series. After game three of the 2002 finals, Guiao deemed import Antonio Lang too inconsistent and hired Sean Lampley to bring home the title. Once again his gamble paid off and Red Bull won; Lampley went down in the books as the championship team's import, and Lang, who'd survived the whole season, was written off as another lemon.

Other teams that have switched imports during the postseason have been less successful. While Red Bull was unveiling Penny for the 2006 quarterfinals, the Talk 'N Text Phone Pals, who already sported one of the league's deepest rosters of Filipino stars, stole headlines by signing former Detroit Piston Darvin Ham. Ham was a role player on the Pistons squad that trounced the Lakers in the 2004 finals, and local hoops scribes suggested that the simple fact that Ham owned an NBA championship ring guaranteed Talk 'N Text the title. It was not meant to be. Ham, playing just days after he arrived, struggled with jet lag and looked lost against sagging zone defenses that surrounded him with three opposing players every time he touched the ball. The referees seemed to take perverse delight in saddling the NBA veteran with dubious over-the-back and offensive foul calls, and after three games the heavily favored Phone Pals were eliminated and Ham was booked for a flight home.

I found Ham in a hotel bar a few hours before his departure, drinking fruity cocktails at a three-per-hour clip in a last ditch effort to spend his remaining pesos and ensure a sound sleep on the flight. Even though Ham's PBA stint was a tiny blip on a distinguished career, his week in Manila had frustrated him. Dealing with quadruple-teams, power-tripping referees, and management's absurd expectations, he said, was like "hooping in handcuffs." Ham had a point, but those were the exact conditions in which Roe had become accustomed to playing, and by the time he suited up for Alaska, he had nearly mastered the art of balling in bonds.

Roe started thinking about surviving the season before he signed with Alaska. He had seen in his previous PBA seasons that certain teams and coaches were more patient with imports, and he planned to put himself in the right situation. That meant if a team like Red Bull inquired about his availability for the upcoming season, the answer was no. Roe, in fact, vowed never to play for Guiao—"that little bald-head coach"—after the 2002 Antonio Lang incident. One of Roe's major gripes with the Philippine league was that even when coaches and local supporting casts underperformed, imports got the blame and the boot. Roe credited Chot Reyes, who coached the Swift Tigers in 2001 when Roe first played in the PBA, for standing by him after the team lost its first three games. An 0-3 start almost always spelled doom, especially for a rookie import, but Reyes blamed his local players for the losing streak. Roe's effort was there; theirs wasn't. The team came alive and made a deep playoff run with Roe as their import, a performance that earned him several invites to return to the PBA in subsequent seasons. If Reyes had followed the standard import playbook, Roe might never have gotten another chance in the league. When Cone spoke to Roe before the current season, he said all the right things about accountability to convince Roe to return to Manila.

Another aspect of Roe's PBA longevity plan was cultivating friendly and hopefully close relationships with his teammates. During his second week with the team, Roe remained in the gym after practice one day to challenge the Alaska mainstays in shooting contests. It didn't matter that the locals were more accurate shooters than he was or that he still hadn't found his offensive rhythm; he joined the games and tried to keep up with Alaska's deadeye guards. Roe had one long rally with Dale Singson, a backup point guard whose in-game specialties were three-pointers and improbable running scoop shots. Here, Singson and Roe were trading baskets from a spot on the right side of the court, about seventeen feet from the basket. First, Singson would catch a pass and flick a soft parabola through the dead center of the rim. The sounds—hands catching the ball like one soft beat on a bongo, then the frozen silence of flight, then a swish and a bounce in quick succession—were basketball poetry. Roe followed, opting to launch a line-drive bank shot off the backboard. It wasn't as mellifluous as Singson's shot but it was just as effective. They went back and forth for a dozen shots without either player missing the mark. A handful of Alaska players who hadn't yet hit the showers watched from the sideline. One of Singson's shots hit iron before falling through the net, and he grimaced and clucked his tongue over the missed swish. Roe threw one off the glass that rattled around the rim, popped out, and hung on the iron before rolling back through the net.

Neither player missed until somewhere around the twentieth shot, when Roe short-armed an attempt that glanced off the front rim. The penalty was *lusutan*, where the loser would have to crawl through the spread legs of his conqueror. It took a bit of jostling for Roe to squeeze his six-foot-five frame through the five-foot-eleven Singson's legs. Meanwhile, the other Alaska players hooted with delight. *Lusutan* was a form of friendly stakes that the Filipino pros had been playing for since they were children. When they were too young to bet actual money, they competed for the chance to lord it over the loser while he got down on hands and knees and slithered under their legs. It was a nostalgic ritual from pickup games—like shooting hit or miss to see who gets the first possession—that reminded these pros of the days when they played for nothing but bragging rights and love of the game. Short of speaking fluent Tagalog and downing the Filipino delicacy *balut*, a hard-boiled egg containing a partially developed duck embryo, there was no better way for Roe to say "I'm one of you guys" than to make *lusutan* with Singson.

Togetherness is one of the most rigid social norms in Philippine culture, and it played a major role in the chemistry of PBA teams. There's a powerful urge in Philippine society to be part of the group, whether it's a family, a bunch of classmates, or a basketball team. Being alone is a minor tragedy to many Filipinos. Often, when I'd show up at Alaska practice and greet the players, we'd make small talk and they'd ask what I did the previous night. My typical response included eating dinner and writing a bit. "You were alone?" they'd ask, and either raise their eyebrows in bewilderment or say that it must be sad to eat by myself. It wasn't that bad for me, but to them it sounded intolerable. Likewise, many of the players were surprised to learn that I didn't have any family in the Philippines. Even though they knew I had no Filipino relatives, they guessed that my father had remarried into a Filipino family or that I had distant Filipino in-laws to live with. To them, the real explanation—that I left my relatives behind to come learn about Philippine basketball—was the least plausible scenario. For many Filipinos, being separated from family was a trauma you only chose to inflict upon yourself when economic hardship forced you abroad to support your loved ones, as in the case of the country's roughly 10 million overseas migrant workers. It was not something you did for a journey of self-discovery in a nation of hoops junkies.

As part of the team and a temporary member of the Alaska family, it was important for Roe to join group customs like postpractice shootouts, pregame prayers, and slapping hands with every player, coach, and ball boy whenever he arrived at practice. He might have legitimate reasons to opt out. He could be too tired to shoot. Maybe he was an atheist. Perhaps he was just shy and needed time before he could give high-fives and crack jokes with his teammates. Any of these would be understandable excuses, but even so, if Roe were to set himself apart from the group and emphasize the difference between himself and his teammates, he could be labeled a snob. It sounds like a lame epithet, but in the Philippines an accusation of snootiness was a serious condemnation that had the power to turn Roe's supporting cast against him and end his season prematurely. On the other hand, if he continued to court his teammates with small, humble gestures, they would protect him from being replaced by playing harder, winning, and making the import look better.

Finally, Roe had an ace up his sleeve. He was already friends with several Alaska veterans, guys he had played with and against during previous seasons. Poch Juinio was the team's lanky and jovial third-string center. Now thirty-three years old, Poch had been one of the league's craftiest pivot men and toughest rebounders during his prime. This season his role was to teach the tricks of low post to Alaska's younger big men, although Poch also distinguished himself by being the most prolific farter on a roster full of fart-joke connoisseurs. Poch played for Swift in 2001 during Roe's first PBA season, and the two nearly came to blows during Roe's first practice. Typically, when an import joins a team there is some tension; the locals want to test him and see if the foreign star is good enough to lead them, while the import wants to establish his dominance. This is doubly true of rookie imports, so when Roe and Poch matched up in 2001, they went at each other. Hard.

Poch and Roe weighed about the same, but Poch was bulkier. At first Poch tried to overpower Roe on the block. He was bumping and banging with his hips, groping and hooking with his hands, and driving his shoulder into Roe to force him deeper into the paint. When Poch caught the ball, Roe didn't try to return the favor and muscle him out of position. Instead, he waited for Poch to face the basket. In a blur, Roe swiped the ball out of his hands. On the next possession, Poch caught the ball in the same position. This time, however, rather than pivot and face Roe, he tried to keep the ball far away from the import's quick hands by spinning into a hook shot. But before Poch could release the shot, the ball disappeared. Roe stripped him again, and this time he added a snort of disrespect for emphasis. Poch glared back at him. He caught a third pass and blasted Roe in the solar plexus with a lowered shoulder. Roe absorbed the blow, then threw a vicious chop that would have knocked some air out of the ball if it hadn't landed squarely across Poch's wrists. Poch wheeled around and pegged the ball into Roe's chest. Roe charged and Poch cocked his fist back, ready to swing, but the two were separated before the scuffle could escalate. Although they wanted to rip each other's heads off in that moment, Roe's response was actually just what Poch was looking for in an import: a player who couldn't be pushed around. When their tempers cooled, each had earned the other's respect. Roe was impressed that Poch had the balls to challenge him, and Poch felt secure that the team's new import had the *bayag* to lead the team.

Now, when Roe guarded Poch in Alaska's practices, the body language wasn't much different. Poch still scraped and shoved and did everything he could to manhandle Roe and get the upper hand, while Roe gritted his teeth and took the punishment, waiting for the right moment to snatch the ball. But their relationship had changed greatly since their 2001 scuffle. They had become good friends. Over the years, Roe became a regular at Poch's kids' birthday parties. Where their jostling had once been punctuated by pointed elbows and icy stare-downs, now it was filled with playful nudges and laughter. After practice, Gus Vargas, Alaska's trainer, went around the gym calculating each player's body fat percentage by testing how much flesh on the guys' stomachs and triceps could be pinched with a set of large plastic pincers. Roe and Poch were shooting trick shots when Vargas approached. Roe went first, and Vargas could hardly find any loose flesh over his ripped abdominals. His body fat was just 4 percent.

"You're bulimic, man!" Poch said, then lifted up his jersey and allowed his belly to tumble out. Poch called this single mass, which was completely devoid of muscle definition, his "ab."

"Poch, you crazy," Roe said, chuckling. "Put that thing away." Before Poch lowered his shirt, Vargas was able to grab a handful of tummy and announce the results: 32 percent.

Poch raised his hands like he'd won a contest and offered to take Roe to a Philippine fast food joint for fried chicken and spaghetti: "Come on, Roe. We'll eat at Jollibee, my treat!"

When Roe left the gym that afternoon, he sat down to ice his knees and chat with team captain Jeff Cariaso, who was sitting with his feet submerged in a rectangular basin filled with ice water and a pair of thermal footsies covering his toes to keep them warm. Jeff, thirty-four, was in his thirteenth PBA season, entering the twilight of a career that included multiple championships and all-star appearances. He was no longer among the league's scoring leaders, but Jeff remained Alaska's premier defensive guard and served as the bridge between Alaska's homegrown Filipino and Filipino-American players. Born and raised in San Francisco, he spoke the best Tagalog out of Alaska's Fil-Ams and was equally revered by players hailing from both sides of the Pacific Ocean. Jeff also played with Roe in past seasons, and the two had developed trust and confidence in each other. For Roe, having the support of Alaska's proven leaders, Jeff and Poch, meant that the team's younger players would embrace him.

Jeff pointed to a nearby Chinese food menu. "You ever eat soup number five?" he asked while a ball boy strapped ice packs to Roe's knees.

"Nah, what's that?" Roe asked.

"Bull nuts and vegetable soup. They gave it to me when I first came out here, then halfway through the bowl they told me what it was and I almost threw up right there."

Roe giggled. "Oh no, I never had that. I did buy this book about international aphrodisiacs, though, that's got tiger penis soup in it."

"What about *balut*?"

"I don't know why, man, but I can't eat it." Roe shrugged apologetically. "I eat eggs. I eat chicken. I just can't take that *balut*."

"You gotta eat it all in one bite. Sometimes I see a little bit of head or beak, but I just think of it as an egg."

"It just reminds me of this TV dinner I had once. I opened the box and just saw this nasty little wrinkled chicken lying there. I never ate a TV dinner since."

Jeff said he had just finished reading the personal finance book *Rich Dad Poor Dad*. Roe had read it months before in Australia. Both players were a few years away from retirement and thinking about life after professional basketball. As long as they didn't become desk jockeys, it sounded like Roe and Jeff could be satisfied. "I gotta own something," Roe said. "I don't want to get up every morning to go make money for somebody else."

"I don't know about stocks, but I think I could make it in real estate," Cariaso said.*

Roe shook his head. "I got halfway through my real estate licensing

* This was 2007, after all, before the housing bubble burst and the world economy dipped into recession. Even as far away as Manila, people heard of the fortune that could be made by flipping houses. Cariaso, who'd been living the PBA high life since Alaska drafted him in 1995, thought real estate might be his best bet after retiring and returning to California with his family.

course before having to leave for Australia last summer. There are some places outside Seattle where houses are real cheap. I could fix them up, sell them. Be a landlord or something. I'm not trying to get rich, but I wanna make my money work for me."

Jeff felt the same way. A couple years earlier, Alaska hired former Chicago Bull Dickey Simpkins as the team's import, and Simpkins's entrepreneurial spirit inspired Jeff. "He played eight, nine years in the league; played a lot overseas," Jeff said of Simpkins. "He's got real good money. So if he's still out trying to make more, how can I not do that? I've been making pesos for twelve years."

The two sat there, talking like old friends dreaming on a porch together in the late afternoon. Roe had hardly been in Manila a week, but his past relationships allowed him to find easy acceptance with the Aces. They were both looking ahead to life after hoops, but before long the ice dripping on their knees and ankles brought them back to the present and the season ahead.

6

The Birth of Paeng Bartolome and Other Initiations

hile Roe was busy ingratiating himself with Alaska's locals, I too was being initiated by the team. The Aces' relationship with Roe could mean the difference between another lost year and a championship, whereas their courtship with me was a matter of curiosity. The chances that I would somehow don a uniform and step onto the court as Alaska's import were practically nil. I did like to think, however, that if some freak occurrence knocked Roe out of commission—perhaps if, on the afternoon before a game, mutinous soldiers bent on overthrowing the government seized his apartment building*—Cone might consider tossing me into the lineup. Similar last minute swaps

---

* Such a coup attempt was not that far-fetched. Twice in the past decade apostate soldiers seized condominium buildings and hotels not far from Roe's apartment in Makati City. They held the buildings hostage and called for like-minded members of the armed forces and civilians to fill the streets in reenactments of the People Power revolutions of 1986 and 2001. The masses, however, stayed home, and the plotters eventually surrendered. A third ill-fated putsch might be just the ticket to get me in the PBA, where my goal would be to match the 11 points Cedric Ceballos scored in his one-game PBA career, then tell everyone I was as good as the 1992 NBA slam dunk champ.

had been made before, when imports suffered injuries or got sent home on short notice. Before the U.S. military bases north of Manila closed in the early nineties, teams responded to import crises by recruiting soldiers who had been decent basketball players in their civilian lives. Now, with the bases shut down and the talent pool of able-bodied foreign men severely depleted, the practice of hiring imports off the street had more or less ceased. It's probably safe to say that the PBA's loss was the country's gain, since too many of those American servicemen used their able bodies to patronize massive girlie-bar industries around the bases. Even so, the sad truth about the likelihood of me playing for Alaska was that even if Roe were struck by lightning en route to a game, Cone would almost certainly opt to field an all-Filipino lineup and hope for the best.

Still, the players were curious about me. Non–Peace Corps, nonretiree American expatriates are pretty uncommon in the Philippines, where the typical image of a Western man tends to be an overtanned lecher in his fifties or sixties married to or dating a Filipina half his age. I really, really wish this characterization were exaggerated or unfair. It's not. Several times a week, often in jeepneys, I would cross paths with inquisitive folks who wanted to know if I was a Mormon or a Marine. It was hard to explain that I was neither, because people just weren't used to seeing white American men in their twenties who weren't in the country to proselytize or fight terrorism. Even stranger, I was a foreigner interested in Philippine basketball, which had been in the country for almost a hundred years yet never attracted much interest from writers and scholars from any country, including the Philippines. Many Alaska players wondered how I ever heard of their league.

From the beginning the Aces seemed interested in me as a novelty. In the six weeks since Alaska lost in the first round of the all-Filipino playoffs, the team had done little but practice and wait for the import tournament to begin. Players found the preseason tedious—nothing but conditioning and endless drilling of the triangle offense. Cone, on the other hand, seemed to love this part of the season because he could focus on conducting the movement and flow of his offense. Cone's troops were less seduced by the abstract realm of hoops; they craved the packed arenas, referees' whistles, and hard fouls of actual competition. Alas, they could do nothing but wait, and during this lull, any diversion was welcome. I was one such diversion.

At one of these preseason practices, I sat on the bleachers and watched five-man squads race up and down the court in a simulated fast break drill. The team still didn't know me, but my plan to keep a low profile lasted all of two minutes, until reserve forward Eddie Laure left his lane in mid-drill and sprinted toward me. Eddie, with the triangular face of a pit viper, may have been the fiercest-looking player on a team full of tough customers. I froze as he strode toward me, as if a six-foot-three praying mantis was bearing down on me and my only hope was to stay still and hope it decided not to slice me into pieces. He stopped on a dime inches away from me. Still wondering what would happen, I gulped and stared at Eddie, who then broke into a toothy grin. He slapped me on the knee and said, "Good morning!" before hustling back into the drill in time to catch a swing pass and drill a nineteen-foot lefty jumper from the wing.

Next, I had to be baptized with a nickname. Partly because Filipinos tend to be named Spanish-style,* with three or four given names followed by a surname, and partly due to a cultural affinity for abbreviations and

---

* Hoops homages appear constantly in Philippine names. During my first month in Manila, I rode home from a pickup game in a taxi and learned that the driver had named his son Kobe Bryant Salem. My girlfriend, a Filipina-American from Los Angeles, had nephews named Clyde (as in Drexler) and Iverson (as in The Answer). In the PBA, Purefoods all-star forward Kerby Raymundo named one of his sons Kevin Garnett Raymundo. Basketball-inspired names were so common that people often mistakenly assumed that Tim Cone's son, whose first and middle names are Kevin and Charles, was named after the erstwhile Phoenix Suns duo of Kevin Johnson and Charles Barkley.

contractions, nearly all Filipinos have nicknames. Often, people are better known in public by their informal handles than their actual names. These sobriquets are often onomatopoeic, like Jinggoy or Ding, and a few have unfortunate double meanings in English—Dong and Bong being the classic examples. Bong, in fact, has nothing to do with pothead paraphernalia, but instead indicates the suffix "junior." Thus, Ferdinand Marcos's son, Ferdinand Emmanuel Romualdez Marcos Jr., the former governor of Ilocos Norte province, is commonly known as Bongbong. Foreigners, especially Western writers, have poked fun at these so-called "doorbell" names, but I'm going to resist the easy pickings. Truth be told, after a few months I stopped smirking whenever I met someone named Buboy, Biboy, or just plain Boy. Nicknames were so common they began to feel normal to me.

Nicknames were prevalent throughout the Alaska organization. Assistant coaches Rene "Bong" Hawkins and Isabelo "Jojo" Lastimosa* became household names as starters on Alaska's championship teams in the nineties. Among the current players, Poch Juinio's real name was Edward, while fellow center Joachim Thoss was always called "Sonny." Backup forward John Ferriols was nicknamed *Tisoy*, slang for mestizo, due to the Eurasian features that made him the team heartthrob. I'm not sure many people on the team knew the given names of Alaska's four ball boys. *Utol* and *Datu's* monikers meant "brother" and "chief," respectively, while Jun and Cabs shortened their full names.

After practice, Cone introduced me to the team. Almost immediately, team wits Poch and John began sounding out my name, inverting it, tossing it around with different prefixes and suffixes. They were searching for a suitably clever and crude nickname. In a matter of sec-

---

* Jojo actually had multiple layers of nicknames, such as "Jolas," a contraction of his already shortened first name and his surname. A powerful leaper with notably plump thighs, PBA yearbooks from the early nineties frequently singled out Jojo for his "sexy legs."

onds they pounced on the most obvious option: "Rafist." The letter F does not exist in Tagalog, nor does its sound occur naturally in most Philippine languages. So, in one of the more enduring ironies of Spanish colonialism, the archipelago was given a name—in honor of King Philip II—that its natives had to learn how to pronounce. The Tagalog spelling of Philippines is "Pilipinas," and a common verbal tick of Philippine English is the unconscious transposing of Fs and Ps. This was never a problem when a jeepney driver threw an arm over my shoulder and proclaimed, "My *priend!*" It was another story, however, when I visited friends' families and explained to their prim aunties and grandmothers that my name was Rafe, pronounced with a hard A and a silent E.

Their eyes would widen with alarm as the matriarchs sounded it out in their heads. Then they'd look at me with a sour face: "Ray—Ray—Rape? I don't like that name." Real fast I got used to going by Raphael, my given name, and its less incriminating forms like Raf. I even tolerated Raffi, a name I'd despised since kindergarten, when classmates would taunt me by caroling "Baby Beluga."

Decorum was less of a concern inside Alaska's locker room, however, and my vulgar name delighted Poch and John. "Stop! Rafist!" Poch yelled, while John chimed in with a falsetto "Rape me, Rafe!" Before long, however, they were back in brainstorming mode, challenging themselves to devise something fresher. The phonetic gag with Rafe was too easy. The players, given this crisp new canvas, wanted to create something special. They gave up on Rafe and started using Raphael.

"Paeng!" (pronounced pah-eng) Poch rejoiced, repeating a fairly common Philippine reworking of the name, which takes the last two syllables and adds the *ng* sound to the end. "Paeng Bartolome! You've been Filipinized, man!"

A puckish glint appeared in John's eyes. He was about to deliver the coup de grace. "Chu-Paeng! Chu-Paeng!" he announced, and when the rest of the team heard it, they burst into hysterics. This was a pun on the Tagalog verb *tsupain* (pronounced choo-pa-eehn), derived from the Spanish *chupa*, meaning "to suck something," where in most cases that something is a dong, and this time I don't mean the nickname. The "Chu-Paeng!" chorus continued for a few minutes, with different players and even ball boys joining in and laughing. The moniker stuck throughout the rest of the season; whenever I arrived in the locker room, I could expect a round of fist bumps and Chu-Paeng catcalls. Maybe I should have objected or lobbied for a downgrade to the tamer "Paeng," but I never did. Because the team had given me the alias, I didn't mind being named after a blow job. What mattered was that I had a nickname. I was in.

It wasn't just the players who wanted to break me in. Alaska's assistant coaches had a plan of their own. Two of them, Jojo Lastimosa and Dickie Bachmann, were devoted mountain bikers who rode through the hills and livestock trails of nearby provinces several times a week. One Saturday morning before practice they invited me to join them. Dickie and Jojo had played for Alaska when the team was still called the Milkmen. They were members of Alaska's 1996 Grand Slam team that swept the championships of all three conferences in a single season, a feat only accomplished three other times in league history. Dickie was a backup forward then and now served as the Aces' big man coach, and Jojo, who had been the team's shooting guard and most consistent scorer, was named one of the PBA's twenty-five greatest players during the celebration of the league's silver anniversary in 2000. These weren't the kind of guys who pedaled leisurely through the countryside to enjoy the fresh air. They were ex-athletes out to push themselves and whoever rode alongside them.

I had been mountain biking once before, when I took a visiting friend to Guimaras, a small Western Visayan island known for mango plantations. Our ride through the island's craggy hills had been gorgeous but grueling. My buddy had only been in the country a week, not enough time to acclimate to the tropical swelter, and he quickly became dehydrated. Every time we passed a roadside shack, I bought some kind of liquid for him—an imitation Mountain Dew drink called Sparkle, water-filled plastic baggies, even a pitcher filled with murky agua from a pump well. Before he fell into a woozy stupor and stopped talking, he joked that if I'd told him that morning he would be drinking water out of plastic bags, he would have called me insane. When we reached a real road, I hailed a tricycle, helped the driver strap the bike to the top of the sidecar, and sent my friend back to town while I rode back.

Before riding with Jojo and Dickie, I made it my goal to avoid getting strapped to a motorbike and carted off like a wounded animal. Jojo, who lived twenty minutes north of me, called at four-thirty that morning and told me to meet him at a nearby McDonald's. He picked me up and drove south for an hour to Santa Rosa, Laguna, where we met Dickie and the other bikers. Like recreational cycling in the States, mountain biking in the Philippines appeared to be a yuppie pastime for athletic types with an eye for spandex. Everyone, including Jojo and Dickie, was covered in specially engineered "performance" gear that clung to their bodies and supposedly kept them cool under the vicious sun. The coaches' bikes came equipped with cutting-edge accoutrements like long-stemmed, shock-absorbent seats and pedals that clipped into cycling shoes to make spinning the wheels more efficient. Meanwhile, Dickie walked me to the bike shop, where the owner set me up with his only rental—a creaky machine that looked like the Huffy I received for my eleventh birthday. Like that bike, it was perfectly sized for a five-foot-six rider. By the looks of things, I would have to ride standing most of the day. Jojo got a hearty laugh out of the sight of me giving the miniature bicycle a test-ride around the parking lot, and I got the feeling that only training wheels could have made the moment more perfect for him. The coaches filled their two-liter camel packs with mineral water and strapped them to their backs. I was given a sixteen-ounce bottle of orange Gatorade. In a moment of compassion, Jojo offered to loan me his spare set of biking gloves. That is, until he saw my hands, which are small for a six-foot-three guy.

"Hold up your hand," Jojo said. I raised my left hand and pressed it against his. He winced, unable to mask his disgust. "Damn, those are ladies' hands! I bet you have small feet too." He looked down at my size eleven feet and just shook his head before mounting his bike.* "Okay, let's go now," he said, and then took off at full tilt without looking back.

My middle school bike made an alarming clacking noise with each crank of the pedals, but it held together and the gears worked, which was all I needed to keep Dickie and Jojo in sight. We rode along country roads and water buffalo paths that zigzagged through parts of Laguna, Cavite, and Batangas provinces. The March sun had singed the grass brown in many of the fields, and whenever we passed houses, local kids ran out to slap hands and yell "Good morning!" as we passed. From the hilltops, we could see the highways, subdivisions, shantytowns, and malls of the southernmost parts of Metro Manila. It was a lovely way to see the country, if you could stand six hours of relentless sun. We passed one enchanting basketball court where four wood boards had been nailed haphazardly to a tree trunk and a netless rim dangled over the dirt playing surface. A pile of coconut husks lay parched and blackened at the base of the tree, with a ball waiting in the soil about ten feet from the hoop. My heart dropped and I stopped to daydream on the pastoral scene, one of thousands like it across the archipelago.

These homemade courts and balls worn so smooth that the rubber seams and cobblestone grips vanished were essential clues to unlocking the riddle of basketball's meaning in Philippine society. Jojo first played

---

* This moment made such a lasting impression on Jojo that months later, when I coached children at his Manila basketball clinic and all the coaches received a free pair of sneakers, he ordered size nines for me. When I told him they were too small, he frowned and said, "I thought you had tiny feet?"

on courts like these in his hometown in northern Mindanao, where he grew up without television and could only follow his basketball idols by reading sports magazines. For the millions of Filipinos who adored basketball, the game was participatory, something they played and watched in their own communities. The measure of the nation's passion wasn't the number of fans who bought tickets to Alaska games, but the fact that everywhere in the country, even in remote *barangays* with few television sets and hardly any Internet access, tiny burgs that felt disconnected from the rest of the world, people played hoops. It truly was a way of life. I understood this. For me, the love of playing basketball— missing a long bank shot, then dashing back to stop the others team's fast break, then rocketing back down the floor to finally score— trumped all.

When I snapped out of my pseudospiritual trance, Dickie and Jojo were gone, and I wore myself out chasing them. Until then I had nursed my Gatorade responsibly and managed to stave off the light-headed tingle that heralded dehydration. The twenty-minute sprint to catch the coaches changed that. When I found them leaning on their bikes at the top of a hill, I was seeing spots. I downed what remained of my drink and scanned the slope for a place to find more fluids. Jojo must have seen the panic in my eyes, because he wandered into the bushes and returned with a gourdlike fruit called *guyabano*, which resembled a dark green football covered with knobby spikes. With a flick of his wrists he split the *guyabano* in two and handed half to me. I plunged my face into the fruit and started vacuuming the juice, sugar, and flesh as fast as possible. Every bite sent waves of vitality back through my body, and by the time I tossed the leftover green rind into the grass I felt normal. I looked at Jojo like he had just saved my life, but he was already moving downhill.

We stopped at a small outdoor eatery where the trail met a paved street. Inside, a consortium of men in helmets and biker shorts sat at picnic tables, pounding Sprite and slurping bowls of *lugaw*, a hearty rice porridge seasoned with ginger and concealing hard-boiled eggs in its gooey depths. Once the cyclists recognized Jojo and Dickie, they formed a line to have their pictures taken with the ex-players. One father who had brought his son along was mimicking jump shots and dunks to explain why he was making the boy pose with the old-timers. After the autograph session ended, the three of us sat and ate. It was nearly noon, and we had a short ride back to the bike shop to return my rental and drive to Manila for practice. In the car, Lastimosa talked to me with a little more interest, like I'd earned some respect, not because I distinguished myself as a cyclist, but because I survived the ride without complaining.

A few days after the mountain biking trip, Alaska's season got off to an encouraging start. Although the team didn't even reach the quarterfinals of the previous all-Filipino conference, it had high hopes for the import conference, partly thanks to Roe, and also because the league had snubbed Alaska in selecting players for the Philippine national team that was preparing for the Asian Olympic qualifiers later that year. Many stars from rival teams had been picked to play for the flag and would be skipping this conference to train for the tournament that could earn the Philippines an invitation to the 2008 Beijing Games. The nationals plucked only one player from Alaska's roster, the versatile Filipino-American forward Tony dela Cruz, while other league powers lost as many as three starters. For the entire Alaska team, especially a former MVP still in his prime like Willie Miller, this was a slap in the face. In the eyes of the PBA higher-ups who controlled the Philippine team, all but one of Alaska's players weren't good enough. The Aces, with a mostly intact roster and a veteran import, looked to dominate the upcoming season and show the league its mistake.

From the beginning, Alaska seemed capable of fulfilling their quest for revenge, beating the Talk 'N Text Phone Pals and the Barangay

Ginebra Gin-Kings in their first two games. Although both teams sent players to the Philippine team, their rosters were so laden with talent that they could wave goodbye to their starting backcourts and still expect to manhandle a struggling team like Alaska. Before the opener against Talk 'N Text, Cone warned the Aces that having fewer stars on the Phone Pals' roster might improve their chemistry and allow its gifted young players to have breakout seasons.

Alaska, in fact, had few answers for the helter-skelter drives and one-handed floaters of Talk 'N Text's Macmac Cardona or the mismatches created by their six-foot-six half-American swingman, Jay Washington. The key to the Aces' win, however, was their team defense, which hounded the opposing import, J. J. Sullinger, into a nightmarish debut. There were few gaps in Sullinger's offensive game. A strong and explosive lefty with a shooting touch, he could barrel through the lane and dunk over a crowd of big men or bang three-pointers from twenty-five feet. But he was young. Just twenty-four years old and months removed from his senior year at Ohio State University, this was Sullinger's first PBA game, and he seemed overeager to prove his worth. It's likely that he heard about the league's cutthroat reputation and decided he needed to score 40 points. Cone, however, expected Sullinger to be aggressive and prepared Alaska's defense. When Sullinger drove, helpers cut off his path to the basket. When he spun away from his man, most of the time he whirled right into the chest of another defender. When he elevated to shoot, one of Alaska's import-stoppers, Nic Belasco or Reynel Hugnatan, always raised a hand to disrupt Sullinger's release. On some plays it looked like the entire Alaska team was guarding Sullinger.

The swarming defense confounded Sullinger. Back in the Big Ten, he probably would have responded to double and triple teams by passing, not by heaving ever more impossible shots. But perhaps the young player felt insecure in his first PBA game; he knew what was expected from imports, and he wasn't delivering. So instead of letting his teammates pick up the scoring slack, Sullinger played right into Alaska's hands and kept attempting acrobatic drives against four defenders and step-back three-pointers that even a legendary chucker like Kobe Bryant might consider bad shots. By the time Alaska eked out a 97-94 win, Sullinger had converted six of twenty-six shots.

A few days later Alaska beat Ginebra. The Aces were facing another dynamic left-handed import in Rod Nealy, but this time they couldn't contain his scoring. Nealy came close to netting 20 points in the first half while carrying Ginebra to a nine-point lead. Roe, who had been looking to create scoring opportunities for his teammates early in the game, became more offensive-minded in the second half. On several possessions he kept Alaska close by grabbing defensive rebounds and dribbling coast-to-coast to score on powerful layups. Roe pushed the ball upcourt like a runaway freight train, and no Ginebra player seemed willing or able to alter his path or take a charge. While he was having his way, however, the Ginebra shooter Sunday Salvacion* was draining three-pointers as if his shooting hand was possessed by the higher power that inspired his name. Entering the fourth quarter, Alaska still trailed by five points.

The Aces clawed ahead on the scoreboard with five minutes left, and from there the lead changed hands on nearly every possession until the clock ran out. The back-and-forth scoring created more suspense than the Alaska players' wives and daughters could handle, and during the last minute many of them covered their faces with Alaska Milk banners. With twenty seconds to play and the game tied, Nealy drove against Roe and drew a foul. He made a free throw to put Ginebra

---

* Salvacion's pious name was one of the coolest in the PBA, a league filled with great names. My other favorites included Aris Dimaunahan, whose last name loosely translates to "can't get in front of [me]" in Tagalog; Olsen Racela, whose parents named him after the holiday—All Saints' Day—on which he was born; and assorted less clever names that just sounded badass, like Nelbert Omolon, Homer Se, and Jimwell Torion.

ahead, but Alaska had time to run one last play to win the game. The ball went to guard Willie Miller, Alaska's top local scorer, who spun into the lane and collided with Ginebra's Ronald Tubid, who flopped backward, hoping to draw an offensive foul. The whistle never came, and Willie was left alone at the foul line. He flicked a jumper that skipped off the front of the rim to the backboard, then back to the front of the rim, and finally through the net. With three seconds left they were up one point. Alaska ended up winning 100-98, after Willie harassed Ginebra's inbounder into calling a timeout the Gin-Kings didn't have and Alaska was awarded a technical foul shot.

After the game the jubilant mood in the locker room was something the Aces hadn't felt for a long time. The players wouldn't settle down after the win. They kept jumping around, hugging each other, joking about the game and Willie's lucky bounce. Asia Agcaoili, an actress and television host who rose to fame as a magazine sex columnist, wandered through the locker room with a camera crew to conduct interviews for a PBA lifestyle show. She sat next to Roe and stroked his muscle-bound upper body, then did the same with Poch's sizable belly. It was the kind of attention that Ginebra, the league's most popular team and defenders of the recently concluded all-Filipino championship, usually received. It was the glory that Jeff Cariaso promised to restore three years earlier, when Alaska traded to get him back from the Coca-Cola Tigers.

The team's surprising start set up a showdown in the next game against Red Bull Barako, which had also won its first two contests. Around the PBA, Red Bull was already being hyped as this conference's team to beat. James Penny, the import who replaced Quemont Greer and led the team to a championship, had returned to defend his crown. The Barako supporting cast had also barely changed since last year's title run, and during the two intervening all-Filipino conferences the Red Bull locals completed successful runs to the finals and semifinals. If Alaska was a contender this season, the team would have to prove it against Red Bull, who likewise would be eager to show the league that they were still dominant.

Cone scheduled two consecutive days of pre-practice video sessions to scout Red Bull and develop a game plan for them. Typically, the team would only watch video on the day before a game, but Cone wanted to treat the Red Bull game with a sense of playoff urgency. That week, however, the team would have a particularly hard time focusing on the upcoming game because of the distraction caused by a criminal complaint filed against Alaska guard Willie Miller in his hometown of Olongapo City. Months before, Willie and three other men allegedly got into a road rage argument that escalated into Willie's group beating the other motorist and stealing a bag from his car that contained more than $10,000 in Philippine pesos. Willie claimed that on the night in question he wasn't even in Zambales, the province where the crime supposedly occurred. Instead, he said he was visiting neighboring Bataan. Nevertheless, he would be forced to miss two practices the week before Alaska played Red Bull to attend preliminary hearings at an Olongapo court.

Willie's absence at practice didn't seem too detrimental to the team. A former league MVP and Alaska's best overall player aside from Roe, Willie was an instinctual player whose raw talent and feel for the game would allow him to play like an all-star despite missing Cone's scouting reports. Instead, Willie's case hurt the team by distracting the players and coaches, whose sole concern should have been Red Bull's zone defense and three-point marksmen. It wasn't that they were sick with worry over their teammate's legal woes; on the contrary, the Willie Miller robbery scandal became Alaska's joke of the week, inspiring constant tomfoolery and howling laughter.

The first day of Red Bull video was also the day after Willie's first court appearance. He burst into the team lounge a few minutes late, arriving straight from Olongapo and waving a newspaper with the blaring headline EX-MVP IN ROB CASE alongside a grainy image of the normally jovial Willie with a scowl on his face. His willingness to laugh about the case set the tone for a scouting session that sounded more like a *Saturday Night Live* writers meeting than a team strategy summit. One player pointed out the resemblance between Willie and the character Fernando Sucre from the TV show *Prison Break*, thereby sparking a small riot of athletes hooting and rolling on the floor. Even assistant coach Joel Banal, known for his serene locker room presence, couldn't resist jumping into the fray. He asked Willie to bequeath him a few pairs of sneakers, since Willie wouldn't need them in prison. Finally, Cone shushed the team, dimmed the lights, and flipped on the Ginebra DVD to review Alaska's gaffes and successes. Willie, who had scored 26 points, was involved in many of the highlights, and before long his teammates were chanting "Prison Break" or "the robber" every time the video showed him driving to the basket. "You're so good, Willie," teased assistant coach Bong Hawkins. "It will really be a waste when you're behind bars."

I wasn't sure what to make of the team's antics. Were they in denial? I didn't believe the allegations against Willie, but the fact that they were being heard in court made the situation seem grave. The Aces were not an insensitive bunch, and they adored Willie. Initially, I chalked their reaction up to the Philippine penchant for gallows humor. From natural disasters like annual typhoons, landslides, and volcanic eruptions to man-made misery in the form of bombings in southern Mindanao and attempted military coups d'état, the nation was always recovering from some tragedy. Alaska's players had all lost property in a flood, hid from a violent storm, or lived through civil unrest. They understood that cruel fates were dealt daily in the Philippines, and that sometimes laughter was the only way to respond.

Later on Cone offered another explanation. He told me that the players could laugh at the charges against Willie because the allegations were so specious. The evidence supporting the supposed victim's claim consisted of his recollection of being beaten by a crowd of men that included someone who looked like Willie and not much else. The case was receiving more coverage in salacious tabloids with names like *Bulgar* (as in "vulgar") than in the country's respected broadsheets. Philippine courts, especially regional ones, existed in a sort of alternate reality, where a corrupt or crackpot judge could turn rumor and innuendo into legal reality. These frivolous lawsuits, known as "nuisance cases," were fairly common problems for wealthy public figures. Half trial and half shakedown, small-time judges would hear the cases to gain notoriety while plaintiffs would try to bluff celebrities into payoffs to drop the charges.

It also helped that Willie, the PBA's clown prince, never seemed to have met a situation that didn't inspire comedy. To his coaches and teammates, the idea that happy-go-lucky Willie attacked anyone was beyond comprehension. Rare, perhaps nonexistent, were the moments when Willie was not performing to amuse himself or his teammates. In just three weeks with the team I had already seen him make the impromptu decisions to use a giant yoga ball during shooting drills and, during another practice, to tuck a basketball under his jersey and scrimmage while pretending to be pregnant. These moments unexpectedly revealed the breadth of Willie's talent; he shot nearly as well with the yoga ball as many of his teammates did with basketballs, and even when he had a ball stuck in his shirt, no one could guard him. Before games, he liked to practice hesitation and crossover dribble moves in the mirror while winking, raising his eyebrows, sticking out his tongue, and practicing his entire catalog of facial contortions.

Just about any professional basketball player loves the game, but that affection was particularly evident and infectious in Willie. His Alaska teammates seemed to admire this quality even more than his formidable skill. After one of the first practices I visited, power forward Nic Belasco told me that he'd never met anyone who loved basketball as much as Willie, who was known to drive up and down the national highway in Zambales to search for pickup games during the off-season. A ten-year

PBA veteran, Nic normally had a gruff, seen-it-all manner, but there was a note of awe in his voice when he talked about Willie. Thanks to him, Nic and the rest of the team never lost touch with the joyous side of basketball. Willie's game—fearless, beautiful, and carefree—was an oasis of fun in the pro ball pressure cooker.

Yet Willie's playful demeanor had tormented coaches throughout his career. Every coach he played for since high school had tried to make him act more serious on the court. He confounded drill-sergeant coaches whose approach to the sport was the warrior code. A point guard is supposed to be a team's second coach, its floor general, but Willie, giggling and grinning with the ball in his palm, set a different tone from his combative coaches. Watching him botch a careless pass and then laugh it off made it look like he didn't take the game seriously. His flashes of brilliance—finishing blind floaters between three larger defenders; sinking bank shots at angles that Euclid would want to double-check—looked so effortless that even when Willie led teams to victory, coaches accused him of not trying. Coaches had such difficulty mastering Willie's psychology that despite his talent, two PBA teams had already traded him. He entered the PBA playing for Yeng Guiao at Red Bull, where he won the MVP award in 2002, but he was poorly matched with the pugnacious mentor. Banal, the Alaska assistant, was head coach of Talk 'N Text when Willie played there, and even though his coaching style was more relaxed and philosophical than Guiao's, he too tried to coax Willie into playing with grim-faced determination. It didn't work, and Willie was traded to Alaska. At first Cone tried to restrain his foolhardy on-court habits like pulling up for three-pointers on fast breaks and throwing ill-advised baseball passes. Eventually, however, the coach learned to give Willie space. More often than not, the team fared best when Willie was allowed to be himself. Cone tried to stay off the guard's back, although the extra wrinkles that had formed over the coach's brow since Willie joined Alaska attested to the psychic toll of admitting that some players shouldn't be controlled.

———

"They say the team we're playing today is the measuring stick. If we beat them, then we become the measuring stick." Tim Cone was standing in a cramped locker room at the Olivarez College Gymnasium in Parañaque City. As a nod to fans on the south side of Metro Manila, the PBA had scheduled the Alaska–Red Bull tiff away from the Araneta Coliseum. Olivarez could seat a few thousand spectators and held hot air like a greenhouse. Alaska's locker room came equipped with about twelve plastic chairs and low, irregular ceilings with buttresses cutting through the room at sharp angles. The players staked out territory on the tile floor and listened to Cone rehash the game plan: Keep Penny off the boards. He's long-limbed and jumps high. If he can't get easy put-backs he might get frustrated. When Red Bull runs the staggered double screen for Cyrus Baguio, go under the picks to deny his penetration. Red Bull's big men—Carlo Sharma and Mike Hrabak—are shooters. Guard them close.

Willie hadn't arrived yet. He was en route from a court appearance, but with a couple hours left before tip-off, there was little worry that he wouldn't make it in time. Despite the week's distractions, the players seemed locked in, nodding along to Cone's words with silent conviction. While the players stretched and had their ankles taped, the arena sound system blasted one grating eighties bar mitzvah jam after another: "Hey Mickey," "My Sharona," "Wake Me Up Before You Go-Go." Cone stewed over a recently released PBA stat sheet that compared the various imports' numbers. Somehow, Roe had been left off the list. To Cone, this confirmed once again that the league didn't give Alaska the respect it deserved. Roe, for his part, seemed unperturbed. He was wolfing down an unusual pregame snack for a man with almost no body fat—a Chicken McNuggets value meal. I was standing a few steps away, pondering what kind of chips I would eat for dinner at halftime. Would it be the barbecue-flavored tortilla chips that offered the highest caloric bang for the buck or the tastier salad-flavored multigrain snacks that never quite filled my stomach? At these small gyms there were no restaurant stalls selling rice meals or burgers, just hawkers roaming the crowd with wire baskets full of chips and cherry red, lukewarm hot dogs with gray innards.

Out of nowhere someone tapped me on the back. "Hello, Rafe!" The greeting was extremely cheerful. Too cheerful. I felt a tinge of alarm as I turned around to see who was responsible for all this effervescence. Who else but Willie, back from his court appearance and naked except for a bundled-up T-shirt held in front of his junk. He stood facing me, a mad grin on his face and his palm outstretched for an uncomfortably low high-five. I slapped his hand and Willie sauntered away, butt jiggling, for his pregame shower, while Alaska reserves Dale Singson, Eddie Laure, and Rensy Bajar collapsed in hysterics.

My encounter with Willie's birthday suit was another locker room rite of passage. There would be countless opportunities to glimpse Willie's unmentionables in months to come, but having this first brush with his ass meant I had passed another milestone. Willie had a fierce exhibitionist streak, and few things seemed to satisfy him more than surprising a teammate with his nakedness. Even on a basketball team, where men were constantly in various states of undress, Willie gleefully flouted the norms of privacy. That, of course, was the joke: that Willie was so sure of his masculinity that he made everyone around him a little unsure of theirs. It also allowed him to pull some epic stunts. Almost every player had seen a cell phone video of Willie running up and down the aisle of the team bus, with his shorts at his knees and his wang flopping while he screamed, "Snakes on a bus!"

Tony dela Cruz, the forward Alaska loaned to the national squad, may have possessed the team's best Willie story. Every weekend the PBA would schedule a provincial game and send two teams to some corner of the archipelago as a treat for fans outside of Metro Manila. On one of these trips during another season, Tony was taking a pregame nap in his hotel room. He knew it was time to get up because he could hear his roommate, Fil-Am point guard Mike Cortez,* dressing for the game. Tony hit his mental snooze button. He couldn't summon the energy to get out of bed yet, so he dozed flat on his stomach with his head buried underneath a pillow. A few dreamy minutes passed and he felt something soft touching the sole of his foot. It tickled a little. Tony couldn't tell if the sensation was real or part of a dream. He reflexively curled his toes and rubbed back. That's when he heard Mike and Jeff Cariaso, who had entered the room, snickering. He bolted upright and saw Willie, naked, standing over the corner of his bed. Upon realizing that he'd been playing footsie with Willie's penis, Tony ran screaming into the shower and started scrubbing his foot with soap. Willie followed him in and asked what was wrong. "You didn't like it? But you were rubbing back? Wasn't it soft?" The fact that Willie's teammates put up with these shenanigans, and even laughed about them afterward, may be the strongest proof of their deep affection for the unhinged star guard.

Between Cone's stone-faced spiel and Willie's loosey-goosey arrival, there was nothing left for the Aces to do but go out and beat Red Bull. By the time of the jump ball, the climate inside Olivarez gym felt like simmering molasses. It had been hot earlier, before fans filled all the seats and hundreds of spectators packed standing room only space in the aisles and behind the baskets. A handful of daredevil supporters even climbed to viewpoints in the rafters. With thousands of people jammed into the glorified high school gym, it felt like there was no air left to breathe. Two refrigerator-size air conditioners labored from opposite sides of the building, and two industrial electric fans rattled away next to the teams' benches, but on this night the machines were over-

---

* At this point in Alaska's season, Mike was still recovering from an ACL tear, but according to Cone, Mike was the Aces' best player prior to his knee injury.

matched. Somehow, despite these circumstances, Alaska and Red Bull ended up playing the most intense, fast-paced game of the young PBA season on a court that felt like Mother Nature's sweaty armpit.

Both teams scored on their opening possessions. Red Bull drew first blood when Penny hit a sixteen-footer off the tap. Alaska came back and found Willie on the left wing for a long jumper. Then Penny, sensing that Nic Belasco was playing off him to stop the drive, drained a three-point shot. Alaska big man Sonny Thoss hauled an offensive rebound on the following play, then strung together two dribbles and a shot fake to get his defender off-balance before rising for a textbook half hook. On plays like that it was easy to see why coaches hoped Sonny, only twenty-five years old with a ballet dancer's footwork, classic big man moves, and a soft shooting touch, might develop into a Filipino Tim Duncan.

The game's furious pace never let up in the first half. Penny, who made his mark as a pass-first import, switched gears and looked to score. He canned three-pointers, baseline floaters, and putbacks galore. Alaska tried three defenders on the Red Bull import—first Nic, then rat-tailed backup forward Rey Hugnatan, and finally, as a last resort, Roe. Even Roe, who was probably the league's finest one-on-one stopper, couldn't lock down Penny. Willie and Roe had to score on nearly every possession just to keep pace with the Red Bull import. Willie abused Red Bull's smaller guards in the post and sank pull-up jumpers that had fans smacking their foreheads in disbelief. Roe was steady as ever, dropping left-handed bank shots through the net almost every time he touched the ball within ten feet of the basket.

But the lucky bounces went to Red Bull. On one possession Penny swiped the ball away from Roe and appeared to be cruising for the game's first breakaway dunk. Roe somehow willed himself back into defensive position in time to poke the ball out of Penny's hands as he jumped for the slam. The ball bounced back toward half-court and both imports gave chase. Their feet became tangled, and Penny stumbled while Roe crashed to the floor. The ball rolled gently to Penny, who seized it, dribbled once, and delivered a feral two-handed jam. Roe, sprawled on the hardwood, could only watch. Extra possessions like this were enough to give Red Bull a 69-59 halftime lead.

In the locker room, Cone praised his players. They had weathered Red Bull's first half onslaught and only trailed by ten points. Eventually, the law of averages would take over and Red Bull's shooting would peter out. If Alaska played aggressive in the third quarter, the coach said, they'd be back in the game. That's more or less how it happened. Alaska scored six straight points to open the half. Behind the bench, the Alaska wives, who had been silenced by Red Bull's dazzling play earlier, became bolder. Bong Hawkins's wife Nancy screamed *"Bobo!"*— Tagalog slang for "stupid"—at Red Bull's Cyrus Baguio, who wore a six-inch-thick elastic headband[*] that covered his forehead and made his hair stand up like a pencil eraser. When Red Bull reserve Carlo Sharma entered the game a few minutes later, Nancy led the Alaska fans in rhythmic chants of "Shawarma! Shawarma!"[†] When she wasn't heckling the opposing team, Nancy plied me with chewing gum and chocolates from her purse.

On the court, Roe and Willie combined for beautiful give-and-go plays. Roe would flash to the free throw line, catch a pass from Willie, and either hand the ball off to him streaking for a layup or wait for him to fade into the corner, then whip the ball to him for a three-pointer. Every time Alaska cut the lead to two or three points, however, some Red Bull player, often some relative unknown on Guiao's roster, rattled in a three-ball to kill the Aces' momentum. First it was Larry Fonacier, a lanky second-year shooter. Then it was Leo Najorda, a defensive spe-

---

[*] Baguio's headband defies description. The best I can do is compare it to a tube top for your head, but even that doesn't do it justice.

[†] Nancy was able to devote extra energy to taunting Alaska's opponents during this game because it was played on a school night, and Neil, her kindergarten-age fireball of a son, had stayed home.

cialist who rarely scored but managed to make four three-pointers that game. And when the locals weren't scoring, Penny was. The import had hardly missed all night. Roe kept Alaska close during Red Bull's surges with an array of push shots in the paint, but the heat in the gym was starting to affect him. When players took free throws, Roe would trot to the bench to wipe off sweat and gulp down a couple swigs of Gatorade.

With less than eight minutes to play in the fourth quarter, Nic Belasco narrowed Red Bull's lead to two points on an up-and-under post move. As the ball was dropping through the net, Roe fell to the floor writhing in pain. The Alaska bench watched in horror as their import clutched his right thigh and rolled on the floor like he was on fire. "Cramps!" he yelped loud enough for the entire arena to hear. The bench players, relieved, sat back down. Roe would have to come out of the game, but the injury posed no long-term threat to Alaska's season. Cone called time-out to reorganize his players, who would have to complete the comeback without their import. Meanwhile, Alaska's trainers maniacally rubbed Roe's legs to loosen his knotted muscles. Cramps were one hazard of hiring an import with extremely low body fat. Playing in the country's saunalike heat, imports sweated more than usual, and in Roe's body there was no extra fat to burn. When he sweated out his water weight and his muscles became exhausted, they would simply clench up. It was one of the quirks of Philippine basketball that in a hot gym, an import in peak shape could be less reliable than a player who carried a few extra pounds. Nancy remembered Derrick Hamilton, a former Alaska import with a ripped physique like Roe's. Hamilton suffered the worst cases of cramps she had ever seen. Near the end of games he would remove his tank top on the sideline, and the spasms of his chest and abdominal muscles looked like a squirrel running laps under his skin.

Without Roe, the Aces' late surge started to fade. The team was down two with more than seven minutes to play and no import to lead them. But an unsung hero, Dale Singson, emerged. With Roe watching from the bench, the seldom-used backup guard connected on a three-pointer, then orchestrated a trip to the charity stripe for Rey Hugnatan, who trailed Dale on a drive and received a no-look drop pass a step away from the rim. Alaska finally took a lead, but gave it up when Penny was fouled on a drive. The teams traded leads until the game was tied at 108 with less than two minutes to play, when suddenly the frenetic shootout became a stalemate. Roe returned to the game, but the threat of cramps kept him in partial paralysis; he shuffled around the court with short, measured steps, as if any sudden movement might cause his muscles to seize up. Still, he managed to force a Red Bull turnover by harassing Penny into dribbling off his own foot. Alaska had a pair of chances to steal the game, but Sonny missed two foul shots after Sharma was called for pushing, and Willie got stripped on a drive.

Neither team scored in the last two minutes. The game went to overtime—a death sentence for Alaska. Roe made his last stand in the waning minutes of regulation. The cramps returned and Alaska was forced to start the extra period without him. This time no savior stepped up to carry the team while Roe sat. Fonacier returned for Red Bull and outscored the entire Alaska team in overtime. His nine-point outburst pushed Red Bull to a 124-113 win, with Penny tallying 44 points and Roe and Willie chipping in 27 and 24, respectively. Although the Aces lost, the postgame mood in the locker room was one of low-grade elation, like the players knew how well both teams had played, and they understood, as did everyone else in that tiny, sweltering gym, that they had been part of a special game. Also, the way Alaska and Red Bull withstood each other's surges and battled to an even score after forty-eight minutes of basketball suggested that both teams were destined for deep playoff runs, and that Roe and Alaska would have a chance to avenge the loss and rekindle this rivalry later in the season.

7

The Legend of the Black Superman

I couldn't get the Alaska–Red Bull game out of my head. A lot of PBA games, like regular season NBA games, were sloppy or just plain uninspiring. Between the all-Filipino and import conferences of a PBA season, most players suited up roughly sixty games per year. Imports like Roe and Penny played even more. Their seasons in the Philippines and other international leagues added up to something roughly equal to the NBA's eighty-two-game schedule, with the added burdens of carrying their teams and hardly ever resting during games. Over the course of these grueling seasons, athletes would sometimes cut corners. On defense, they might zone out and forget to help on the weak side. Or, on offense, they could settle for outside shots instead of scoring at the rim. Then again, some games were breathtaking.

There was no way to predict which contests would be epics and which would be footnotes. Before the loss at Olivarez, Alaska had plenty of excuses to take the night off. Willie's court case had distracted the team all week and forced him to miss practices. The podunk arena felt small-time. With only a couple thousand seats, most of the players had been performing on grander stages since they were teenagers. The air-conditioning was struggling. The tarpaulin banners strapped to the basket supports, adorned with the grinning visages of the Olivarez men (local politicians as well as founders of the school that hosted the game) brought to mind a neighborhood tournament sponsored by the beneficence of a crooked mayor. Yet, for some reason, both teams came out that night and played one of the best games I've ever seen in any league. The highlights reenacted a roll call of famous moments from sports movies and real life—Roe and Penny tripping simultaneously like Rocky Balboa and Apollo Creed; Roe pulling a mini–Willis Reed by returning to the game after his debilitating cramp attack; and unsung shooters like Dale Singson and Red Bull's Fonacier swinging the momentum with long-range bombs like the Hickory High boys from *Hoosiers*. If Filipino fans had been witnessing battles like this for the past fifty years, it was no wonder they worshiped the sport.

The game reminded me of another early season classic that occurred more than twenty years earlier, which I'd read about in old sports magazines and heard PBA old-timers describe as a night that jolted Philippine basketball into the modern era. It also established archetypes for PBA imports that have prevailed ever since. That game, in May 1983, was the first head-to-head match-up on Philippine soil of Billy Ray Bates and Norman Black,* who are still considered the best two imports in league history. It was the opening game of the import conference. Bates, then twenty-six years old, was hired to reinforce the Crispa Redmanizers, one of the PBA's storied franchises, which, along with the Toyota club, dominated competition throughout the league's first decade. Bates's four-year NBA career came to an end a month earlier when the Lakers cut him; this was his PBA debut. Black, already in this third PBA season, won the previous year's best import award and had signed

---

* Bates and Black had played against each other in the CBA and in Philadelphia's Baker League, and Black believes that this familiarity earned him Bates's respect.

to play for the up-and-coming Great Taste Coffeemakers. Along with Black, Great Taste had hired the PBA's first high-profile Filipino American, a former Pepperdine guard named Ricardo Brown, who had been drafted by the Houston Rockets but never made the team. They also signed a deadly shooter named Bogs Adornado, who was the league's first MVP. A knee injury had hobbled Adornado over the past few seasons, but he'd finally healed. If Adornado, Black, and Brown could lead Great Taste to victory over Crispa, it would herald the arrival of new PBA royalty.

No one knew what to expect from Bates, who was brilliant in his first season with the Portland Trail Blazers but eventually drank himself out of the NBA and into rehab. This wasn't the first time an NBA has-been washed up on Philippine shores, and judging by the skeptical coverage Bates received in sports magazines prior to his Crispa debut, the local basketball cognoscenti doubted that he could pull himself together. It didn't take long for Bates to turn them into believers. The first time he caught the ball, he blew by a helpless defender and threw down a vicious dunk over two others that shook not just the rim but the entire Araneta Coliseum, packed that day with more than 20,000 fans.

They had never seen anything like Bates, a six-foot-four, 215-pound guard with a chest like the trunk of a redwood tree and powerful, expansive thighs that gave him Jordanesque* hang time. That is no exaggera-

---

* I'm not sure if I will get another chance to mention this story, so here goes: Like all basketball devotees, Filipinos deify Michael Jordan. Once, a Manila advertising agency hired me to consult on a basketball-themed television commercial (Alaska put me up for the job). The storyline involved a girl basketball player scoring a game winner, and my job was to coach the child actresses in enough basic basketball skills to make them look somewhat believable on film. The director's vision was for the lead character to score on a last second crossover and jump shot identical to Jordan's iconic championship-clinching move against Bryon Russell in the 1998 NBA Finals. When I was showing the girl how to plant her foot and rise for the jump shot (I didn't teach her how to push the defender, like Jordan did), the director came over to emphasize the point. *"Jumujordan!"*

tion. He was a tank with wings. In terms of aerial grace, Bates was probably the closest most Filipinos ever came to seeing Michael Jordan or Julius Erving in person. With Portland, when he was focused and sober, Bates dunked with ease over legit NBA big men like Artis Gilmore and Darryl Dawkins. On top of that, he was a natural shooter. Off the dribble or catch-and-shoot, when Bates was hot he didn't miss. He had three-point range as well as the delicate touch required to make pull-up bank shots and floaters in the lane. There weren't a lot of men in the world who could average 25 points per game in an NBA playoff series. Bates was one of them. He did it in the first round of the 1980 playoffs against the Seattle Supersonics. Bates had all-star talent and all-world athleticism.

In that first Crispa game and throughout his career in the Philippines, Bates was an elemental force on the basketball court. Like the annual typhoons that blasted through the archipelago, he laid waste to anything that crossed his path. He was faster than the quickest local point guards, bulkier than the most brutish centers, and springier than the highest leapers. Against Great Taste, Bates scored 64 points while making five of six three-pointers, seventeen of twenty-five two-point shots, and fifteen of sixteen free throws. He dunked seven times and also managed to collect 12 rebounds, 5 assists, a steal, and a block. During one stretch in the fourth quarter he scored eleven straight points, nine of them on consecutive three-pointers, each a step farther from the basket than the last. The virtuoso display—a few commentators noted that Bates scored on every kind of shot imaginable—had fans' eyes rolling back in their heads. He brought the Jordan brand of high-flying, acrobatic basketball to the Philippines two years before Jordan perfected it in the NBA.

The fact that the Crispa–Great Taste game came down to the wire

---

He had turned "Jordan" into a Tagalog verb. Basketball was so much a part of Philippine culture that Jordan had not only entered the sport's pantheon, but also the country's lexicon.

and included two lead changes in the final ten seconds has been eclipsed by the story of Bates's performance. Great Taste, however, gave Crispa all they could handle, and the great Redmanizers needed every one of Bates's 64 points to win. Adornado torched his former team throughout the game to keep Great Taste close, and after Bates completed his eleven-point explosion in the fourth quarter, Norman Black responded by scoring nine straight points of his own. Black, in fact, nearly stole the thunder from Bates's "fantasmogorical" debut, as local writer Romy Kintanar called it, by scoring off a spin move in the post that gave Great Taste a one-point lead with seven seconds remaining. As it turned out, seven seconds was more than Bates needed to seal the win. With Black guarding him close to deny a game-winning jumper, Bates drove past the rival import and lured Black into committing a foul. He went to the free throw line, calmly sank both foul shots, and ran to the Crispa bench, where his teammates mobbed him and Bates lifted team manager Danny Floro in a massive bear hug that made the diminutive Crispa honcho look like a Cabbage Patch doll.

Any other night, Black's game would have been remembered as a masterpiece. He scored 56 points while making 74 percent of his shots and going a perfect six for six from the foul line, with 17 rebounds, 6 assists, 2 steals and a block. Next to the show Bates put on, however, Black's masterwork looked pedestrian. Black, a workmanlike forward, scored mostly on short bank shots, power moves in the lane, and put-backs of offensive rebounds. Almost every one of Bates's baskets, in contrast, came at the end of a highlight-reel move. Black was no slouch—he made it to the Detroit Pistons in 1980 on a pair of ten-day contracts. In fact, the PBA imports of the 1970s and 1980s were all impressive talents who were probably more accomplished than the league's modern-day reinforcements. Back then, the 1992 Dream Team that spread the gospel of hoops worldwide at the Barcelona Olympics was a distant dream. Big-time basketball had not yet caught on in Western Europe or East Asia. The PBA was the world's best-paying pro league after the NBA, and the Philippines' roundball-obsessed masses attracted several players with NBA experience. Yet even among this elite group, Billy Ray Bates was on another level.

Bates had been on my mind for years. In fact, if unlocking the mystery of basketball's place in the Filipino soul was the main focus of my quest, discovering what happened during Bates's PBA career was a close second. Bates, you see, had occupied a meaty portion of my hoops imagination since I read about him in David Halberstam's *The Breaks of the Game*. The Portland Trail Blazers signed Bates late in the 1979-80 season to fill in an injury-depleted backcourt, and over the book's final forty pages, Bates makes an indelible impression as one of the greatest doomed, tragic heroes in the history of the sport.

Bates was eleven years younger than my father, yet his Mississippi upbringing seemed straight out of the nineteenth century Reconstruction South. I read Halberstam's book when I was fifteen, and Bates's life bespoke a reality opposite everything I knew about civil rights and New York's relative racial harmony. He was the second youngest of nine children living in a sharecropper's shack on a white millionaire's farm in Goodman, a hamlet on the outskirts of a small town, Kosciusko, in rural Attala County—the godforsaken dot within the dot on the map. Their home had no plumbing and no electricity. Their alcoholic father died when Bates was seven years old, and Bates and his siblings worked the fields to support the family. He spent his youth picking cotton and soybeans, breaking clods of fertilizer behind tractors, and hooking logs for lumbermen; later, he credited his powerful physique to a childhood of manual labor. Bates went to school only to play basketball, and although he never learned to read full sentences in class, he was able to dunk by his sophomore year. By then, basketball had become his sole purpose in life.

In some ways it was fitting, because there was seemingly nothing he couldn't do on a basketball court. In high school and then at Kentucky State University, if Bates wanted to dunk, he'd dunk. If he wanted to shoot from twenty-five feet out, he did it. Any move he attempted, he pulled off. He may have been one of the most naturally gifted players to ever lace up a pair of high-tops. But because he had so few other opportunities in life, he became a basketball savant. Due to the hopelessness of being reared in a corner of the deep South that had hardly changed since slavery, Bates was never expected to do anything but pick cotton and drink himself to death. When his athletic gifts were discovered, they offered him a ticket out of Mississippi, but without any of the preparation he would need to survive in the world. He had little more than his instincts, which served him well on the hardwood but failed him away from the sport.

Initially, Bates's talent seemed to keep him out of the NBA. Because he'd been able to score since the moment he picked up a basketball, his high school and college coaches didn't bother teaching him to play a team game. He averaged more than 20 points over his last two seasons at Kentucky State, but NBA scouts worried that he couldn't be taught to play with discipline. Furthermore, they looked at his stunning athletic gifts and wondered how he ended up at a second-tier program like Kentucky State. In the scouts' minds, if a player could look as good as Bates and still get passed over by the major schools, there had to be some irreparable, unseen flaw in his game. Instead, Bates began his professional career with the Maine Lumberjacks—a PBA-worthy name—of the CBA, where he led the league in scoring for a season and a half until Portland gave him a chance.

With the Trail Blazers, Bates showed that he could put up points against the best players in the world. For Portland, he was instant offense, and his high-wire leaping ability and against-all-odds path to the NBA made him a fan favorite. It wasn't long before the national media got wind of his story. During halftime of one of Portland's playoff

games against Seattle, CBS ran a segment on Bates's upbringing, and
while watching him torch the Sonics for 25 points per game in the series, Brent Musberger dubbed him "the Legend."

Yet the fissures in Bates's dream-come-true were already widen-
ing. When he joined the Blazers, he reportedly had never heard of a
checking account. Although Bates was described as good-natured and
likable, some scenes from *Breaks of the Game* reveal how difficult it
was for Bates to relate to his teammates. Many of the other Blazers
also came from poor, predominately black neighborhoods, but Bates
endured a deeper level of poverty and stuck out as the locker room
rube. The book contains an account of a heartbreaking dinner Bates
shared with fellow rookie Calvin Natt and Portland scout Stu Inman.
Bates was excited to learn that Natt also hailed from the South and
asked Natt if he too had grown up eating squirrel and possum. Natt
burst out laughing while Inman was crestfallen. How do you save a man
like that? Soon, Bates attracted hangers-on, men and women who
leeched his fame and newfound cash flow. With them, he drank and
partied until it began to affect his game. The Trail Blazers gave up on
him after three seasons. He received second and third chances from the
Washington Bullets and then the Lakers, but squandered them. After a
few seasons on top of the world, Bates checked into a Phoenix rehab
facility.

Halberstam's book ends with Portland's season, and for years all I
knew about Billy Ray Bates came from those pages. Mixed in with every
heartbreaking detail, I saw a hint of inspiration in Bates's tale. Even
though I hadn't been born when Bates played for Portland, and had
never seen him dunk, I thought of him as a wonder to behold. Of course,
for all of his sheer, awesome ability, he seemed doomed to failure, and
his inevitable fall made him seem more legendary. Ever since I read
Breaks of the Game, a wedge of my mind belonged to Bates, and every
now and then I'd feel a mental itch to try and find out more about him.

Back in 1999 or 2000 my Internet-savvy cousin* told me to start using Google instead of WebCrawler or AltaVista. The first phrase I remember Googling was "Billy Ray Bates." These days, the Web is home to a wealth of Bates-related information. Back then, however, there were no Wikipedia or Basketball-Reference.com pages to research Bates's career. All I could find was a dinky fan page on GeoCities that said after his NBA career, Bates became one of the most celebrated players in Philippine history. At the time, I knew Manila was the capital of the Philippines, that the country had been an American colony, and hardly anything else. The idea of Bates becoming a roundball god in Southeast Asia was tantalizingly weird. I never thought that in five years I would get a chance to meet opponents who once tried vainly to guard Bates, and ex-teammates who tried—perhaps even more hopelessly—to keep up with him in drinking sessions. When I moved to Manila, I felt that Bates itch act up again. The more I discovered about him, the more I wanted to learn. Now I could begin to fill in the gaps.

I found local sports magazines that quoted an *Oregonian* story about Bates's rehab stay. Sports psychologist Bruce Ogilvie explained that Bates had nothing aside from hoops: "All he knows is basketball and he's in a situation where he knows his tools are not where they were before. He is a young man who lives for the recognition and the glory. He gets his recognition from what he does with a basketball. There is a terrible danger when someone is one-dimensional. If the basketball doesn't go well, how else can he define himself?" The man Ogilvie was describing sounded like an inside-out Shakespearean tragic hero. Bates

---

* He was also my business-savvy cousin, and he managed to sell our joint collection of "Magic: the Gathering" cards to an online buyer for several hundreds of dollars. The price impressed everyone except my father, who remembered how much I'd saved up to buy an Icy Manipulator the previous year. Now, we pretend none of this ever happened.

was all fatal flaws with one saving grace—hoops. But the sport was never enough to save Bates from the poverty and racism he'd come from; it was only enough to give him a taste of the good life and set up his next fall. In Bates's case, it was hard to tell if basketball was giving him opportunities he'd never had or giving him rope to hang himself.

There was no way Bates could maintain an NBA career while slipping into full-blown alcoholism. So what did he do? Get clean, pull himself together, and take another shot at the big leagues? Nope. By the looks of things, he found a place where he could keep playing without giving up the bottle. That place was the Philippines. In the PBA, Bates's talent was so overwhelming that he probably could have played in a drunken stupor and averaged 30 points per game. By most accounts, he almost always dried out before tip-off. His career average of 46 points per game is the highest of any PBA player to score at least 4,000 points, and Bates will probably always be remembered as the best import in league history. Throughout the eighties, he was a superstar in the Philippines, one of the nation's most famous and infamous ballers, whose legacy lives on today.

In the same breath, coming to Manila could be considered one of the worst things that ever happened to Bates. If, as Ogilvie suggested, Bates needed to find some foundation other than basketball for his sense-of-self, then he was in the wrong place. In the Philippines, all of Bates's self-destructive habits were enabled, if not encouraged. He could score at will, average almost 50 points a game, and be worshiped by a nation of devotees who treated his ability to put the ball in the hoop like it was proof of the divine. And here's the clincher: Bates never had to put down the bottle. Time would eventually catch up with him, but for a few wild years in the mid-1980s, he had found his proverbial free lunch. Catastrophe could wait.

I wondered if Bates ever recognized the similarities between his early years and the lives of many Filipinos. Even if he only glanced Manila's squalid shantytowns from the window of a passing car or looked down on farmers' bamboo homes and palm frond roofs from a descending airliner, did he ever think to himself that these people, who bathed in streams and hijacked electricity from nearby wires, knew more about the life he had come from than 95 percent of his fellow Americans? If Bates ever had this realization, it never led to much. He got along with fans, enjoyed their adulation, but never seemed to bond with the Philippine masses or demonstrate awareness that their struggles mirrored his own. Instead, he spent his time drinking, carousing, and playing ball.

Bates actually tried to stay clean when he first arrived in the country. In many of his preseason interviews with local sports columnists, the conversation touched on how alcoholism led to Bates losing his spot in the NBA and how he had become a changed man after rehab. By the end of these interviews, however, he was usually finishing off a bottle of beer. When a writer named Butch Maniego interviewed him for *Champ* magazine after a Crispa practice in May 1983, Bates had the team trainer bring him a couple of San Miguels. What better way to cool down than to double-fist some brews? Maniego, who'd been briefed on Bates's newfound sobriety, asked about the booze, and Bates told him: "I don't have those problems anymore, thanks to God. I'm a man's man, and a man is gonna have a beer. I'm all alone and I can't see why I can't have a beer. I'm in complete control of myself and I don't have no stacks of beer in my apartment. It's just a drink between friends." And with that, Bates fell off the wagon and into the Bacchanal.

Back then PBA players partied hard. In the eighties sports magazines I noticed almost as many pictures of teams drinking and smoking at postgame celebrations as images of them on the court. But even these seasoned drunkard-slash-athletes had never seen anyone drink like Bates. I met several of his former Crispa teammates—Atoy Co, Philip Cezar, Tito Varela—and inevitably the first word that came out of their mouths when I asked about Bates was "crazy." Cezar said Bates downed whiskey like the rest of them drank beer. Co told a story about the squeeze bottle Bates would bring to practice. The rest of the players filled their bottles with water. Bates usually filled his with orange juice, which seemed strange to Co, since OJ is heavy and acidic. One day, on a hunch, Co opened up Bates's bottle and took a whiff, then quickly jerked his head back and shook off a shiver. The Johnnie Walker fumes had stung his nostrils. Tommy Manotoc, Crispa's coach in 1983, remembered the first time he went out with Bates. After watching his new import drink enough liquor to knock out a horse, Manotoc left the bar with Bates, who was feeling restless. In the street, Manotoc said he saw Bates pick up the back end of a car by its bumper and do a set of curls with it. He's wild, the coach thought, but he's strong.

Then there was the womanizing. Bates wasn't just putting up Chamberlain-esque numbers on the court, but also in the bedroom. The intervening decades have no doubt led to some embellishment in the Bates mythology, but the guys who played with Bates recalled him hitting the town most nights with no fewer than four lady friends. A small-town boy who once said that the Mississippi town he grew up in only had two girls, Bates went hog-wild with Manila's groupies. To the women, Bates was a famous, physically stunning twenty-six-year-old American who tossed pesos around like they were Monopoly bills—why not enjoy his riches?

When Bates first joined the team, Crispa's managers tried to curtail his indulgent lifestyle. They hired drivers and bodyguards to make sure he always returned to his condo by midnight. No problem, Bates told them. And he always did ride back to the apartment before curfew. He just didn't stay there. Bates struck deals with local taxi drivers and the security guards in his building. For a good tip they would look the other way while Bates, after sending his handlers home, slipped downstairs, left the building through a rear entrance, and hopped into a cab. The whole charade was pointless, anyway, because the idea of any six-foot-four black American keeping a low profile in Manila was outlandish. Not to mention, Bates played for one of the league's most popular teams. A polar bear would have had a better chance of cruising the streets unnoticed. On a handful of occasions Manotoc and Crispa manager Danny Floro would arrive at the Araneta Coliseum on game day to hear that Bates was spotted leaving a bar at seven the previous morning. What could they do? Besides, more often than not, Bates could shake off a crushing hangover and still score fifty.

Manotoc and Floro didn't want to worry that Bates might be tipsy every time Crispa took the floor. Eventually, Manotoc feared, the hard living and late nights would cost the team an important game. So he cut his own deal with Bates. Manotoc told him that he would weigh him before every game and pay him a hundred-dollar bonus every time Bates came in under 210 pounds. That way, Manotoc figured, Bates would have to stop drinking a day or two before games to allow himself time to sweat out the bloat. For the most part, the plan worked. Back then, PBA teams played about every five days, so Bates could drink himself silly for the first three days, then fast on the fourth day and spend sixteen hours sleeping. On the fifth day he'd suit up, tip the scales at 210, hit the court and look unstoppable. In the PBA, Bates became known as "Black Superman" for the way he swooped to the rim, peaking higher and hanging longer in the air than anyone else on the court, but his ability to recuperate from drinking marathons was nearly as superhuman as his prowess on the hardwood.

Although Bates was hardly a role model to the Philippines' aspiring young athletes, he was beloved by teammates and fans. He was a drunk and a lothario, but he was a joyous one. When I spoke with his teammates and coaches, they all remembered their nights out with Billy Ray as the epic benders of their youth. Only once did Bates's drinking get him into serious trouble. After a game in Naga City, the biggest town in Camarines Sur province, Bates and another import, DeWayne Scales, went drinking. They ended up in some dubious nightspot, where, according to a report in *Atlas Sports Weekly*, the two imports ordered beers and started enjoying the "floor show," which is a polite term for a striptease. The story gets fuzzy here, but Bates somehow offended the other patrons. The article says his hooting and shouting at the go-go dancers bothered the locals. Who knows how Bates's behavior deviated from the accepted norms of strip club conduct, but one of the other customers threw a bottle that hit him in the head. At first Bates didn't respond. He was having too much fun cheering on the dancers. But when the song ended, he went on a rampage, storming around the club and demanding that the bottle-tosser face him. No one owned up to the attack, so he found the biggest table in the joint and flipped it over. Glass, beer, ashtrays, and bar snacks crashed to the floor, and then the real melee broke out. Bates and Scales hid behind the table while the local customers threw everything within reach against the makeshift shield.

When the hail of projectiles ended, the bar owner kicked everyone out and walked Bates and Scales back to their hotel, where he met a Crispa assistant coach and demanded several hundred dollars for his trouble. Was the near-riot actually just a shakedown? A choreographed fracas to give the bar owner a reason to insist on payback? There's no way to tell. One thing is for sure: the *Atlas* article ended on a disturbing note. "Maybe, the next time Bates wants to unwind after a game," it said, "his Crispa handlers ought to give him what he wants in the solitude of his hotel room." The suggested solution—to ply Bates with willing love slaves in a private place where he couldn't cause trouble—speaks to a common and unfortunate Philippine attitude toward black athletes. Players like Bates were idolized for the way they could dunk a basketball, but off the court they were often viewed as borderline savages devoted to sating their appetites for food, alcohol, and women. Part of the reason teams hired drivers for imports was to keep an eye on them. A driver was supposed to prevent a player's inner Mandingo from emerging at an inopportune moment that might tarnish the team's image or lead to the import getting hurt and wasting the team's investment in him. As long as the booze-fueled escapades were kept behind closed doors, however, no one seemed to mind.

This paternalistic, dehumanizing attitude toward black players was widespread, not only among teams but also with fans, who seemed willing to accept and sometimes even encourage sleazy behavior from their imports as long as they put on a show at gametime. A transcendent player like Bates could get away with almost anything. To the fans, all that mattered was his game. To his coach and teammates, all that mattered was winning. And Bates never failed them. His performances were electrifying. The three-point shot and the dunk were arguably the two innovations in basketball's modern era that lifted the sport to its global status. Bates excelled in both. His hot streaks from beyond the arc could have been lifted straight out of the video game *NBA Jam*; he could score 15 points in a matter of minutes, shooting a series of deeper and deeper three-pointers that seemed drawn through the hoop by a force greater than gravity. His drives were even more astounding. If a defender pressed Bates to deny his jump shot, that player would be left behind and Bates would already be soaring through the lane with the ball cradled beside his hip, about to be windmilled in another patsy's face.

Bates's character only amplified his game. He never simply let his play speak for itself, but added flourishes of showmanship to excite crowds even more. When he heard that TV announcers were calling him Black Superman, Bates came to games with a cape flapping behind his back and dunked during warm-ups while wearing the hokey outfit. When Bates arrived at Crispa, he brought not just a jaw-dropping skill set, but also a flamboyant personal style from the twilight of the disco era that was new to many Filipinos. He was one of the first players to wear a headband—a white rag wrapped around his forehead and knotted Rambo-style in the back. The tendrils of a lush, shimmering jheri curl tumbled over the top of the headband. Bates's hair and its accessories became the subject of a barrage of sports features, in which journalists asked Billy Ray to explain the look: with all the activator he was putting in those curls, he told them he needed something to keep the greasy mix of sweat and moisturizer out of his eyes. He was the first and only import in PBA history to have a line of signature sneakers made for him. The Black Supermans, made by local shoemaker Grosby, looked like a rip-off of Nike's Air Force Ones sans the Swoosh. He further accentuated his look with wristbands, striped knee socks, and loads of swagger. Shortly after Bates joined Crispa, one of his boasts became the quote that summed up his PBA career: "The only way I can be stopped is to handcuff my right arm to my leg."

Bates had a natural star quality that allowed him to glide across the razor's edge between two opposing values in Philippine culture. In many cases, being called *mayabang*—arrogant—is a condemnation. There's no doubt that Bates was that, but he also projected another quality, *diskarte*—a celebration of skill and flashiness with a dash of machismo. People loved to watch a great player who knew how good he was. Somehow, Bates always managed to stay on the right side of these contradictory concepts. The fans never turned on him and called him a conceited jerk. They embraced Bates's bravado on and off the court. Perhaps his instincts told him how far he could push his antics, or maybe Filipinos simply appreciated his otherworldly basketball brilliance enough to forgive his excesses. It was helpful that Bates was willing to share the fun with everyone around him. After games, he'd walk out of the Crispa locker room with a boom box on his shoulder and boogie with the fans waiting outside.

Most importantly, however, Bates was a winner. This defused any arguments that his marvelous one-on-one game and garish antics prevented his teams from thriving. Crispa won its first nine games with Bates and cruised to the finals of his first PBA conference. The best-of-five series was a rematch of their epic season opener, and Great Taste actually jumped out to a 2-1 series lead thanks to the hot shooting of Bogs Adornado and the defensive efforts of Alaska assistant coach Joel

Banal, who was Great Taste's import-stopper. Banal frustrated Bates with tight defense and a few well-timed flops. The import got his points, but Banal made it hard for him and earned a standing ovation for his efforts in Great Taste's game one victory.* Banal couldn't keep up with Bates for five games, however, and the import took over in games four and five. This time it wasn't his scoring that won the games, although he did notch his customary 50 points. Instead, Manotoc credited the championship to Bates's decision to guard Norman Black for the rest of the series. Bates didn't completely shut down the Great Taste import, but he managed to outplay Black, and Bates's willingness to step up on defense inspired his Crispa teammates to match his effort. They ran the Coffeemakers out of the gym, winning both games by an average of 24 points and clinching the conference title.

Bates stayed with Crispa for the third and final conference of the 1983 season—this time, teams were allowed two imports—and led the team to another championship. For Crispa, the win made a clean sweep of the year's three conferences (Crispa won the all-Filipino crown before Bates arrived). Only four teams in PBA history have achieved that level of dominance, known as a Grand Slam. By the time Bates returned to the league in 1986, the Crispa franchise had dissolved, so he teamed up with another high-scoring import named Michael Hackett and the league's biggest Filipino star, player-coach Robert Jaworski, to win a title with Ginebra. No PBA import aside from Bates has won three championships in his first three seasons. In 1987, Bates returned to Ginebra and averaged a career-high 55 points per game while nearly dragging the undermanned club to the finals. It was his only full season in the league that didn't end with his team cutting down the nets.

---

* At practice more than twenty years later, Banal told me that holding Bates to 28 points in a game earlier that season was the proudest moment of his playing career.

Over the months I spent tracking down Bates's teammates and pulling clips about him from newspaper and magazine archives, I always sensed his lurking denouement. Each passing season seemed to hurtle Bates closer to disaster. Honestly, it was excruciating. I was reading about the exploits of a great basketball player whose rare talents not only won games but left crowds feeling inspired and awestruck. I was listening to Bates's teammates reminisce on the highlights of their careers, many of which might not have occurred without him. But Bates's fall from grace was always around some corner. There wasn't a question of if, but of when he would lose basketball, the game that fueled his entire being. When it happened, it would be ugly.

The death knell of Bates's PBA career rang in 1988. He returned for another season with the Ginebra franchise, which changed its name to Añejo to promote a new brand of rum.* Bates was thirty-two, and in the six years since he first played in the Philippines, he must have put fifteen years' worth of mileage on his body. Jaworski made him promise not to stay out drinking and partying, but the import couldn't resist the temptations of Manila nightlife. At Añejo, Bates still managed to average a respectable 31 points, but the team lost its first four games, and Bates, playing passive, hesitant basketball, looked like a shell of his former self. When fans saw him struggling to defend rookie guards and getting his shots blocked by local forwards, they saw the Black Superman cut down to size. Bates was spared the biggest embarrassment of his career the night of his final PBA game. He scored a career-low 17 points and

---

* Changing names to boost sales of a new or struggling product is a cherished PBA tradition. The increased television and print media exposure a brand receives through PBA coverage is generally associated with enhanced business. Since it entered the league in 1988, the Purefoods franchise has played as the Tender Juicy Hot Dogs, Coney Island Ice Cream Stars, Corned Beef Cowboys, Chunkee Giants, and Tender Juicy Giants.

looked helpless against younger, healthier competition, but few people witnessed the game because a violent storm caused a blackout in Manila. It was as if fate had intervened to prevent television audiences from seeing Bates at his humiliating nadir.

And so, because he had already broken his sobriety pact and was no longer Superman, the best import in PBA history suffered the fate of every other lemon. Bates was sent packing after four games. On one of his last nights in Manila, in a final delusional moment, Bates called the manager of Purefoods and asked for a chance to replace their import. It was 2:00 a.m., and he was calling from a place called Faces disco. The team manager, who had been asleep, simply hung up. Columnist Ronnie Nathanielsz penned a eulogy to Bates's career in *Champ* that week. "Basketball has become an integral part of our everyday lives," he wrote, "and Bates was its most brilliant character."

After the Philippines, Bates's deteriorating skills drove him deeper and deeper into the backwaters of international basketball—first Switzerland, then Mexico, and eventually Uruguay. In 1998, back in the States, the inevitable finally occurred. Bates, soused on vodka, robbed a New Jersey Texaco station at knifepoint and slashed an attendant's ear. When he was arrested, police found that he had netted seven dollars in the heist, which earned him five years in prison. This had to be one of the world's all-time telegraphed passes; it was the rock bottom Bates had been approaching for fifteen years. His life in ruins, he fulfilled his tragic destiny.

Yet even at this disgraced juncture in Bates's life, fans felt connected to him. From people who actually saw him play to those like myself, who were merely captivated by his legend, if you had a drop of compassion in your heart and you loved basketball, then part of you hurt for Billy Ray Bates. The online comment page of a 2004 *Willamette Week* article about him reveals a multilingual mash of nostalgia, adoration, and sorrow that reflects the complicated life of one of the sport's great antiheroes. On one hand, there are comments like this:

> i am an avid fan of billy during his crispa and ginebra
> days here in the Philippines . . . i saw how wild he is when
> he was young, i saw him hanging around with some of
> his friends having beers, i saw him when he took a mas-
> sive piss on the streets . . . those were wonderful mo-
> ments of my childhood seeing an NBA great hanging
> around the place like an ordinary kid.

Yet there are also comments from young women in Switzerland and the United States, claiming to be Bates's daughters and requesting help in contacting him. Reading these, the consequences of all those amusing tales about Bates's drunken red-light follies became evident. There's no doubt that life dealt Bates a miserable hand, and the fact that he managed to rise from such depths, however briefly, is inspiring. Yet for all the heartbreak he endured, he caused just as much.

Even though it had been more than twenty years since Bates played his last PBA game, and many Filipinos were aware of his criminal past, people in Manila still considered him a hero. Internet message boards devoted to the PBA were clogged with glowing remembrances of Bates, and newspaper columnists gushed over his possible return to the archipelago as late as March 2009, when a Filipino blogger found Bates online and learned that he was living in a drug-and-alcohol-treatment center in New Jersey. Before long Grosby shoes, which had been planning a comeback, offered to bring Bates back to Manila, perhaps to promote a throwback version of his signature high-tops. So far the trip hasn't occurred, but if it ever does, Bates's homecoming may rival that of General Douglas MacArthur, whose return to the islands in World War II was credited with liberating the Philippines from Japan. In a country with such a deeply felt, sometimes irrational passion for basketball, Bates's hardcourt wizardry mattered almost as much as driving out the hated Japanese. He revolutionized the Philippine game by showing fans and players moves they'd never imagined, and for that he will always be the Black Superman.

Although Bates was the man who brought the spark of change to the Philippine game, it was his rival Norman Black who remained in Manila to help implement the transformation of local basketball that Bates inspired. While Filipinos revered Bates as the best individual player in PBA history, Black, and maybe Bobby Ray Parks, who won seven best import awards, were acknowledged to have had the greatest careers.* But no other import held his own against Bates as well as Black did. In their head-to-head match-ups, Black always kept his teams close, and through the first three games of the 1983 Finals, it looked like Black might even lead Great Taste to an upset.

Black, known as Mr. 100 Percent throughout his ten-year playing career, earned fans' respect for the passion and effort he brought to every game. He was not a flashy player. At six-foot-six he was a prototypical undersized power forward, with an unreliable shooting touch and so-so ballhandling skills, but Black was a tireless rebounder and defender who could score anytime he caught the ball within ten feet of the hoop. Humble, self-effacing, relying on hard work as much as talent, he was the perfect foil for the boisterous and sensational Bates. And after Bates flared out and Ginebra cut him, Black remained in the PBA. Thanks to his consistent effort and winning ways, teams just kept hiring Black. Eventually, in the late 1980s, San Miguel made him the team's player-coach. Black would suit up during import conferences and direct the team from the sidelines during all-Filipino tournaments. In 1989,

---

* To anyone who notices the similarity between the names of Billy Ray Bates and Bobby Ray Parks, the PBA indeed seemed to have a knack for hiring black ballplayers with hillbilly names. Toss in Donnie Ray Koonce, a contemporary of Bates and Black, for good measure.

Black's Beermen became the third team in league history to win a Grand Slam, matching Bates's 1983 accomplishment with Crispa.

In 1991, Black retired from playing, but he stayed in the Philippines. Little by little the nation had become his home. He continued to coach the San Miguel Beermen, then moved on to coach other PBA franchises, and at each of his stops he brought his teams to the playoffs and usually won championships. Over the years, Black coached some of the Philippines' most brilliant individual talents like San Miguel's Samboy "the Skywalker" Lim, who could jump, hang twist, fake, and hang some more before releasing his shots. These players were clearly inspired by Bates, but it was Black who helped them combine their breathtaking moves with the discipline it took to win championships.

Black is still in the Philippines and has no plans of moving back to the United States. He now coaches college ball for hoops powerhouse Ateneo de Manila University. From 2008 through 2010, Black led Ateneo to three consecutive collegiate championships. He was the first American player named to the PBA Hall of Fame in 2007. Just as Bates and Black took disparate roads to success as players, their lives after basketball followed starkly different paths. In the Philippines, however, the two are forever linked by their classic 1980s battles. Moreover, they have become the basis for the prevalent archetypes of foreign stars. When I first met Tim Cone, he told me there were two kinds of imports. The first was a guy with NBA talent who was so crazy that he played himself out of the league. The second was a player who wasn't as gifted but would work tirelessly to win every game. Sound familiar? He was explaining that he preferred workhorse imports like Roe, but Cone might as well have been talking about Norman Black and Billy Ray Bates.

8

A Rim in Every *Baryo*

Just wait till we go out of town." I heard this mantra dozens of times, from the Alaska ball boys on up to general manager Joaqui Trillo and owner Fred Uytengsu. When you see the team travel to the provinces, and see how fans away from Manila's basketball-spoiled masses treat the visiting athletes, then you'll truly understand how enthusiastically Filipinos worship basketball. A month into the season, it happened. The Aces piled into a bus headed for the former U.S. Navy base at Subic Bay, where the team was set to clash with the Purefoods Tender Juicy Giants. I was psyched for some overenthusiastic, foaming-at-the-mouth, downright scary hoops idolatry.

A couple weeks had passed since Alaska's loss to Red Bull, and the team recovered with two straight wins. The first was an expected blowout against the Welcoat Dragons, a first-year expansion team owned by a paint company. The second game was a ragged encounter against the Coca-Cola Tigers.* At the time, Coke was bunched with Alaska near the top of the standings. Two of the Tigers' local stars, Filipino-Americans

---

* Somehow, the Coke management beat back the urge to name the team the Soda Poppers or Carbonation Classics, and for that I applaud them.

John Arigo and Ali Peek, had been Alaska's team leaders until 2004, when the team traded them to begin the rebuilding effort that Cone hoped would culminate in a championship. With Coke, Peek and Arigo had been talented but inconsistent, yet they reliably saved their best efforts for revenge games against Alaska. On top of that, Coke's import, Anthony Johnson, was a deadly scorer who had so far carried the team to a promising start. In the game, many of Cone's worries came true. Coke got inspired low-post play from Peek, a six-foot-two center whose bodybuilder physique made him look more like the Philippine entrant in a World's Strongest Man competition than a basketball player. Johnson, the import, was unstoppable in stretches. Yet Alaska held Coke off with balanced scoring from Roe, Willie Miller, Jeff Cariaso, Sonny Thoss, and backup guard Rensy Bajar, all of whom hit double figures. A win in Subic would return Alaska to a first-place tie with Red Bull.

Early in the morning on the day before the game, the team met in the parking lot outside their practice facility. Shuffling around the pavement in their flip-flops or sitting on their Alaska duffel bags, the players looked into the cloudy distance with droopy eyelids and expressionless faces. While everyone waited for the bus, the ball boys handed out plastic McDonald's boxes. The containers held the fast food chain's take on Filipino breakfast, a meal that typically includes a mound of rice, a fried egg, and some kind of meat. In a restaurant, the options would include *longganisa*, sweet pork sausages; *tapa*, strips of beef marinated in sugar and vinegar; *tocino*, sweet cured pork; and *daing na bangus*, milkfish marinated in vinegar and garlic, then fried hard. At McDo, as it's called in the Philippines, there's only one traditional choice—*longganisa*. Other than that, they serve standard McMuffin fare. *Longganisa* are little red sausages. Some are fat and short, others are like lumpy, irregular hot dogs, but almost all variants come in the form of a tube encased in skin. Except at McDonald's, that is. When I popped open my container, I saw two pale brown meat slugs bracketing a cup of rice and a fried egg. I looked at the players. They were mashing pieces of egg and composite meat into their rice and scarfing it down. I tried it, and found that like other McDonald's meat products—the immortal McRib and its bone-shaped mold come to mind—the *longganisa* looked foul but tasted pretty normal. Just when a trash bag had been passed around and the empty receptacles stuffed inside, our ride pulled into the lot.

The bus offered surprisingly few frills. It was a rented version of the passenger liners that plied the Manila-Subic route every day, and came equipped with air-conditioning, cushioned seats, and a DVD player. This was one of the high-end buses; thrifty commuters had the option of riding forty-year-old diesel belchers with passengers stuffed five per side into wooden benches and gritty air rushing through the vehicle's open windows as the only cooling system. My most unforgettable ride occurred in Catanduanes, an island province off the southeastern coast of Luzon, where I sat next to the driver of a ramshackle, partly homemade bus headed to a small beach on the Pacific Ocean. Before I boarded, porters loaded the bus with a boatload of cement sacks that just arrived from the mainland. I squeezed into a sliver of open space and stared at a three-foot stick shift sprouting from a gaping crevice in the thin metal floor. To keep the engine from overheating, the driver rigged a system of rubber hoses leading from the top of the bus through a window and down into the engine pit. Whenever we passed a rainwater-filled ditch, the driver would pull over and bark instructions at a pair of teenage helpers perched on the roof, one of whom would leap to the ground and fill buckets of water for the cooling system. When one of the tires blew out, the teens climbed down the side of the vehicle with shovels and sledgehammers to dig a hole under the wheel that would provide space to change the flat (believe it or not, this was easier than unloading all the cement and using a jack). Not bad for a two-dollar ride.

Alaska's tidy, efficient bus couldn't match those thrills, although that was surely how the team wanted it. Aside from the fact that the

Aces had the bus to themselves, the vehicle wasn't different from a standard "luxury" model. The privacy was key, however, because it allowed the players to spread out and avoid being jammed into tiny seats built for average-height Filipinos. The first hour of the ride was sleepy. Most of the players nodded out against their windows. The lone exceptions were Willie Miller and rookie forward Christian Luanzon, who split the ear buds on an iPod to sing along to "I Believe I Can Fly."

The driver dug into his collection of pirated DVDs. First he played *Turistas*, a cautionary slasher film about fratty American bozos lured into an organ-smuggling ring while vacationing in Brazil. Next came the first season of *Heroes*, which Poch Juinio requested. To me, these choices were a bit of a letdown, as previous trips had taught me to look forward to the bus drivers' gonzo cinematic sensibilities. During one twelve-hour drive I watched the first three installments of Chuck Norris's *Delta Force* series,* followed by *The Chronicles of Narnia*. On another half-day slog to northern Luzon's Mountain Province, I managed to fall asleep despite the high-decibel pyrotechnics of *Rambo: First Blood Part II*, but was roused a few hours later by the excruciating techno theme music of *Mortal Kombat*. Perhaps I should have been more worried that the man steering our bus through hairpin turns and mountain passes had the same taste in movies as my old college suite mates after they'd been drinking forties of malt liquor, but finding a nation that loved schlock cinema as I did helped tamp down my visions of bus-plunge doom.

With no Norris to captivate me on Alaska's bus, my attention drifted instead to the view from my window. Outside of Manila, the landscape abruptly turned rural. Solitary farmers were bent over in rice paddies the size of football fields, some brown and muddy and others green and lush. Massive water buffaloes plodded along, their slate muscles shining

---

* By the time *Operation Delta Force 3: Clear Target* was made, the franchise had sunk so low that Chuck Norris was no longer starring in it.

with muck. I caught glimpses of three-on-three games being played beneath the elevated highway. In the shade of the underpass where a local road crossed the northbound expressway, shirtless players juked and shimmied their way to rims hung from the tunnel walls. In Pampanga province, we passed a sign urging voters to reelect Vice Governor Yeng Guiao, the Red Bull coach who dabbled in dynastic politics. Guiao's father Bren had been governor of the province for nearly a decade starting in 1986, and its flagship public gym and convention center still bore the elder Guiao's name. The cheerful campaign image of Guiao the politician was a far cry from the scowling coach whose Red Bull team handed Alaska its first loss.

After a couple hours the bus pulled into the Double Happiness rest stop in Lubao, Pampanga. Almost every bus headed north from Manila made a stop at this snack and restroom depot. There were no other buses in the parking lot when we arrived; business was slow, and the employees—hamburger vendors roaming a phalanx of empty picnic tables, women ladling noodle soup and rice porridge into take-out bowls, bathroom attendants—seemed half asleep. That is, until they realized that a PBA team had arrived. Cue shrieking. "Willie!" "Hi Poch!" "Idol! Jeffrey! Da Jet! Idol!" The workers abandoned their posts and followed the players to the men's room door, where many of them peeked around the corner at the queue of famous athletes peeing into an aluminum trough. They lined up to slap five with the players as they emerged from the bathroom, a gauntlet that resembled the line Alaska's players formed when the starters were announced before games, only with more urine exchanging hands. Willie found himself on the receiving end of a few kamikaze hugs as he walked back to the bus, while other players signed autographs and made small talk with the employees.

I wondered if twenty years ago, before Twitter became the closest way to interact with NBA players, casual fans in the United States were able to rub elbows with professional athletes like this. Before every team had a private jet and a public relations staff that tried to orchestrate the players' every move, might I have bumped into A. C. Green or Vinnie "the Microwave" Johnson at a TCBY along the highway? Players may have been more accessible then, but the situation still seemed far-fetched. In the Philippines, however, it was reality. This was partly due to the economic realities and infrastructure deficits of a developing nation. The cost of a private jet would probably eclipse the Aces' entire payroll, and the bus stopped at Double Happiness because it was the biggest rest stop on the only major road headed north. But familiar relations between fans and players were longstanding in Philippine basketball. Athletes had chance encounters with the public in malls, at church, at the movies, and just about any other gathering place you could imagine. As the price of gasoline skyrocketed in 2007, I even spotted a few PBA bench players riding commuter trains to save money. Fans didn't merely gawk at the players they encountered; they asked questions, sought autographs, talked hoops, demanded warm embraces, and requested cell phone numbers to become players' "textmates." It was hard to imagine a Miami Heat fan getting close enough to Dwyane Wade to surprise him with a bear hug, and perhaps Dwyane prefers it that way, but there was something touching about the way Double Happiness employees lined up to wrap their arms around Nic Belasco's shoulder—or his waist, for those who couldn't reach beyond the six-foot-six forward's chest.

The word "fans" also seemed inadequate to describe the Double Happiness throng. Not just a few fans among the workers rushed to greet the players. Everyone—from burger boys to bathroom attendants to soup ladies—reacted with the same utter joy. We tend to think of fans as people with an above-average interest in a team or sport, but here at the rest stop and indeed throughout the Philippines, there was nothing exceptional about following and loving basketball. This was a hoops nation and these were just a few of its millions of patriots.

Of all the people who stepped off the Alaska bus, I may have been the only one the PBA disciples didn't recognize. That doesn't mean, however, that people didn't notice me. In fact, my role on the team inspired much confusion and disbelief. I was tall enough to be a basketball player, and I was traveling with the team. But I wasn't actually a baller? This story, although true, did not pass muster with the Double Happiness crowd. They cornered me with beaming faces and held out napkins to sign. "Idol! Idol!" I posed for cell phone pictures with a hawker and his tray of burgers, who then turned to one of the ball boys and asked if I was John Arigo, the former Alaska guard whose height and build were similar to mine. Suddenly, the rumor spread that I *was* Arigo, and more napkins were thrust at me, now forcefully, as if to say I wouldn't be able to leave if they didn't get their John Arigo signatures. By now the actual players had finished their courtesy calls and returned to the bus, where Jeff, Nic, Poch, and John Ferriols watched my humiliation with delight. I wasn't trying to impersonate a real professional athlete. Really. It just happened. I gave the people what they wanted. After a dozen or so Arigo autographs, I was on my way back to the bus. When I climbed the stairs, I faced a crowd of hysterical, chanting players and ball boys: "A-ri-go! A-ri-go!"

As the bus got closer to Subic, the pastoral farm scenes and homemade hoops began to vanish. First, we passed through Olongapo, a city of 220,000 residents that grew alongside the U.S. Naval Base at Subic Bay. Billboards and campaign posters for members of the Gordon clan—Senator Dick, Mayor Bong, and Zambales vice governor Anne, whose family had run Olongapo since the U.S. Navy relinquished the town to Philippine rule in 1959—were plastered everywhere. In many ways, Olongapo resembled other provincial hubs. The main drag, Rizal Avenue, formed a backbone for the entire city. The road was choked with jeepneys and tricycles that carried locals down side streets and away from the banks, restaurants, and department stores along the central axis. The big difference in Olongapo, and the cause of its ignominy, is the sex industry that grew in tandem with the base, which by the time of its closure in 1992 had become the U.S. military's largest overseas installation. In fact, Olongapo and prostitution had been linked since the turn of the twentieth century, when America first occupied the Philippines. In 1904 an ex-Marine named John Jacob Gordon settled in Olongapo and opened Gordon's Farm, a watering hole for off-duty servicemen that Americans called "Gordon's Chicken Farm" because of the loose women who hung out there. More than a hundred years later one of Gordon's grandsons was a senator and the other was Olongapo's mayor.

Driving through Olongapo on the way to Alaska's hotel in Subic, the bus passed clusters of girlie bars with names like Geisha Club, Gentleman's Paradise, Girlfriend Bar, and Girlfriend II. Elsewhere in the country, red light districts contained clubs with names like Classmates and Dimples—seamy, no doubt, but with a kitschy side that left room for a speck of dark humor. There was no such levity in Olongapo, just one pitifully named, dilapidated shack after another—neon-clad houses of desperation. The austere lifestyle and pure love of hoops I'd been promised on this provincial jaunt was nowhere to be found.

This was Willie's hometown. He's the product of a relationship between an African-American military man and a local woman, although his parents met under innocent circumstances and his father kept in touch with the family after he returned to the States. Aside from that skeletal outline, Willie demurred whenever I asked about his family and experiences growing up near the base. He insisted that there was nothing exceptional about it, just kids shooting hoops like they did everywhere else. Willie's restraint was a drastic departure from his playful norm. This was, after all, a guy who routinely flashed his teammates for laughs. He had an uncanny ability to sense people's eyes on him, and he always rewarded their attention with a maniacal grin or goofball raised eyebrow. The never-ending act could have been Willie's way of deflecting outsiders' focus to his clowning, and if so, his teammates respected his privacy by keeping mum about the star guard's serious side.

Alaska's hotel and the gym where the game would be played the next day were inside the confines of the old naval base, which had been renamed the Subic Bay Freeport Zone. In an attempt to replace some of the jobs lost when the base closed, the Philippine government created tax incentives for foreign businesses to operate in the area, and some companies had moved in, although the post-base Subic Bay was known mostly for Sea World–type attractions and duty-free shops that sold five-pound hunks of Toblerone. The wide, empty boulevards looked nothing like the Philippines I knew—no traffic, no crowds, no vendors hawking fried quail eggs on the sidewalk. Nor was there anything provincial about the area. It might as well have been an underdeveloped Florida suburb.

After checking into the hotel, Cone was eager to practice. It took longer than expected to extract the players from the comfort of their rooms and load them onto the bus, and by the time the Aces arrived at the gym, Cone was tapping an exasperated beat with his foot. He let out a hoarse sigh. "We're here?"

"Yes sir!"

"I can't believe this. Let's practice. Just get out and go."

Sensing Cone's frustration, the players and assistant coaches hustled to a set of double glass doors that served as the gym's main entrance. Assistant coach Bong Hawkins was the first to the door. He pulled on the handle and it didn't budge. He tightened his grip, bent his knees, and yanked with his whole body. Nothing. Cone found a young woman sitting in the box office and rattled off a list of questions and demands. Who runs this arena? Why aren't they here? Why are the doors locked? Did you know we were coming? It's the middle of the afternoon! It's damn hot out here. Do you understand that we need to prepare for a game tomorrow? We have a job to do, and you're keeping us from it. When will you let us in?

The flummoxed girl probably had nothing to do with the lockout, but when Cone confronted her, she absorbed all of the shame for the mistake. She reacted by going catatonic behind the window and staring wordlessly at her desk. Her lack of a response further incensed Cone, who looked like he was about to ram his head through the glass, when a janitor unlocked the doors and scampered down a dark hallway before the coach could scold him. For a moment, it looked like Cone might follow the custodian, but he thought better of it and led the team into the gym.

With the players stretching at center court, Mang Tom, Alaska's elderly practice referee and stat keeper, struck up a conversation with head trainer Gus Vargas on the sideline. While Tom wasn't looking, Sonny Thoss crept behind him and pinched the old man's butt cheek. Tom leaped and spun and cursed Gus, who had purposely distracted Tom while Sonny approached. When Gus and Sonny apologized to Tom, Willie circled behind and goosed him again. Tom yelped and hopped and grabbed his ass. Minutes later, when Tom relaxed, Jeff Cariaso jumped up and tweaked his nipple. With one arm covering his chest and the other guarding his rump, Tom backed away from the players, vowing to make them all pay.

No one knew for sure when the team started poking Tom—usually in the ass—but it had become one of the Aces' favorite pastimes. Whenever someone was bored or needed to blow off steam, he snuck behind Tom and took a fistful of sixty-seven-year-old butt. Violating Tom had become as much a part of Alaska's routine as taping ankles and drinking Gatorade. Some teams smacked a poster with an inspirational message like THE TEAM ITSELF LEADS THE TEAM on their way out of the locker room; this team smacked a senior citizen's booty. Tom thought they did it because his reactions were so spasmodic. They loved to see the old man squirm.

After Tom's retreat, the players turned their attention to me. I was shooting on a side basket, and each time I made a shot, one of the Acess would yell, "John Arigo!" Mang Tom sensed a connection and sat down to impart some wisdom. On this team everybody makes fun of everyone else. Some days it was Willie the robberman. Other times it was *Lolo* Poch, when his teammates called the creaky center "Grandpa" in Tagalog. Today, with the Arigo wisecracks on me and the coordinated ambush on Tom's ass, was our turn. Tom grabbed my elbow and shot me a broad smile—it's a good thing he was wearing his dentures. He explained his country's love for look-alikes* and practical jokes.

"I hope you don't mind us calling you that name. It is a very Filipino thing. Once you have a name of someone you look like, you are stuck with it. It's the same with them always touching my butt. I don't know why it started, but now I am stuck with everyone doing it. Even my children are touching my butt to laugh at me."

It didn't look like I'd be able to learn much about basketball's role in the rural Philippines during the team trip to Subic. There was more to gain in hanging around Mang Tom, who hailed from Bicol, a region of southeastern Luzon where the coastline lurches in and out like it was drawn by a blindfolded drunk in the back of a rickety jeepney. Tomas

---

* Spotting *kamukha* (look-alikes) was a tier-two national pastime just behind basketball, cockfighting, and karaoke. That weekend in the hotel, I spent hours sitting in front of a TV with five players, all of us watching and pointing out look-alikes for each other and anyone else we happened to know. Fil-Am guard Alvin Castro's resemblance to Makati City Mayor Jejomar Binay (whose name is a contraction of Jesus, Joseph, and Mary) was the hit of the night until the albino Filipino comedian Redford White came on screen, and then my white ass was toast. But no matter how realistic—or, as was more often the case, unrealistic—the resemblance between two look-alikes, the response was the same: uproarious laughter.

Urbano was born in Daet, the provincial capital of Camarines Norte. The region sits dead center in the Philippines' hurricane alley and catches the business end of about a dozen typhoons every year. The destructive storms, combined with the unfriendliness of Bicol's volcanic, mountainous terrain, have made it one of the most poverty-stricken parts of the country. It seemed like every year a batch of farmers lost their homes and land to natural disasters and were forced to start from scratch or migrate to Manila and chance it in the slums. A few months before Alaska's season began, Typhoon Durian lashed Bicol with 155 mile-per-hour winds and dumped more than eighteen inches of rain on the region, which sent layers of mud and boulders cascading down Mount Mayon, the area's iconic volcano, whose name means beauty in Bicolano. More than seven hundred people died in landslides, and hundreds more were entombed in the mud. They're still missing, their deaths confirmed by the passage of time.

I began hearing the story of Mang Tom's journey from Daet to the PBA one evening on my way home from practice. While walking home from the train station, I heard someone yell from across the street. There was nothing inherently strange about this. The neighborhood had adopted me as their foreign mascot, and anytime I left my house, I expected to pay respects to everyone from street urchins to bank security guards. Everyone had a different name for me. Some called me Raphael, others used the generic "Joe," and the tricycle drivers reveled in naming me Wowowee, after a local variety show where I once got pulled from the audience to answer trivia questions on national television. But there was something different on this occasion.

"Shit, man! Is that Raf Bartholomew?"

Who here knew my last name? The voice was coming from the back room of a streetside eatery. I crossed the street, ducked through an opening in the yellow gate and peered inside. Mang Tom was sitting with his back to the wall and a mountain of rice in front of him. It turned out that Tom was my neighbor. Aside from being one of the Aces' longest-serving employees, Tom operated this *turo-turo*ˢ restaurant and lived in the adjoining back room with his wife, married children, and a herd of toddler grandkids. I had actually eaten there, before I started following Alaska and met Tom. The price—about a dollar for your choice of main course, plus a cup of rice and a small mug of beef stock—was tough to beat, and Tom's *ginisang monggo*—stewed mung beans with pork—was charged with a smoky aftertaste that made it the best in the *barangay*. Tom, it turned out, did most of the cooking himself. He didn't trust his employees with anything other than the simplest dishes like fried fish and pork adobo. After that night, I ate dinner with Tom a couple times each month, and over all those meals he spun the story of a life in basketball that spanned generations and brought him into contact with just about every important figure in the game's post-WWII history, like the Leonard Zelig of Philippine basketball.

Growing up in Daet, the harsh realities of life in Bicol were the least of Tom's problems. By the time he turned eight he was an orphan. Both his parents died of illness within two years of each other, leaving him to be raised by an older sister. In the late forties the country was still recovering from the ravages of World War II. Medical care was hard to come by, and contracting a serious illness in the provinces was often a death sentence. When Tom finished sixth grade, his sister sent him to Manila to live with their brother, who could afford to put him through high school. But when he arrived in the capital, the eleven-year-old Tom didn't cotton to the idea of being a charity case. "I had relatives here but I was too ashamed to stay with them," he told me between spoonfuls of rice drizzled with a pungent yellow broth. "I don't want to be a burden to them. So instead of staying, I ran away, you know?"

---

* A Tagalog term meaning "point-point," which described how people selected meals from the array of pots and steam trays of stewed meats and vegetables at these eateries.

Tom waved over one of his daughters, who carried a pot bubbling with more of the jaundiced-looking brew. It was *papaitan*, an infamous soup that I had been dreading ever since I heard about its ingredients—a chopped medley of lung, intestine, and assorted innards, cooked in water, garlic, ginger, and goat bile. Now, I'm no skittish eater. Pig face and ears, chicken and pork intestines, *balut*—I breezed through these. Assistant coach Bong Hawkins had even showed me how to bite the head off a roasted pigeon at a Chinese wedding. But *papaitan* seemed uncomfortably close to sipping vomit. At the same time, when Tom offered me a taste, my fear of bile made me more eager to conquer it. In the gross-out food kingdom, this was big-game hunting.

"Come on, Raf! You try this *papaitan*." Mang Tom plucked a winged ant out of the bowl and ladled the soup over my rice. Once inside my mouth, the sour and bitter tastes mingled with the acrid smell, and soon I was gagging. My cheeks blew up with air and bile (at this point, I wasn't sure if it was the goat's or my own), but I took a breath and swallowed it, then smiled and told Tom how great it tasted.

"I was one of the best wash-your-car boys in Manila," Tom said, jabbing the air to emphasize how skillfully he performed as a 1950s precursor to the squeegee man. To hear him tell it, Tom was a Pinoy Odysseus, skilled in all ways of contending, from scrubbing windshields and cleaning pork intestines for *papaitan* to handling the rock and refereeing basketball games. After he left his brother's home and took to the streets, polishing cars earned him enough money for rice porridge and *siopao*, a Filipinized version of Chinese steamed buns. Tom's childhood sounded terrifying—an adolescent eking out a subsistence living without knowing where he'd sleep each night. Fairly often, his bed was a patch of concrete. But he sounded almost exhilarated while describing the same kind of youth that had doomed millions of Filipino kids to lives of poverty. For Tom, who would eventually let basketball carry him to a comfortable life that would be out-of-reach for many of his countrymen, a childhood on the brink was an adventurous interlude.

Tom only lasted a couple months on the street before he was picked up by a government paddy wagon and taken to a state reform school for wayward boys. Once again his recollection of what sounded like a nightmare scenario was rosy. At the group home, he could count on three meals a day. The school had a basketball court, and when Tom wasn't doing schoolwork or chores, he spent every moment shooting hoops and playing against the other boys. After a year he was released to his brother's custody in a Manila suburb. When Tom started high school, he found that his games of three-on-three with other street kids gave him an edge against his new classmates—he was faster to loose balls and a little more ruthless on defense.* With coaching, he began to show talent. Tom wasn't much of a shooter, but he had an elastic body with long arms and sharp elbows. He learned to use shot fakes and jab steps to get his defender off balance and then slash to the rim. "I was flexi," he bragged. It was a word that only Mang Tom used, with no firm definition in English or Tagalog. "Flexi" had little to do with flexibility and more with being quick and shifty, a high scorer with pretty moves. Often, when Willie made a breathtaking drive during Alaska workouts, Tom could be heard clucking his tongue in appreciation and saying "flexi" to himself.

"I could move, evade the guard doing some acrobatic shots," he said. "When I noticed your footing is the wrong way, it's done. You're finished. Oh shit, maybe you think I'm bragging. You don't believe me because of my size."†

---

* Wealthy former players like Franz Pumaren sometimes took their kids to play in Sunday morning games at *barangay* courts to toughen them up against poorer opponents. Of course, as a Quezon City councilor, Pumaren also used the games to mingle with constituents.

† Tom was only five-foot-seven, but most centers in his era topped out around six-foot-two, so his scaled down height seems about right for a wing player.

Tom took me by the wrist and headed to the back room, where the cinder-block walls were covered with framed blow-ups of his photographs. Alaska's championship teams adorned one side of the room. In one image of a victorious pile-up, only Tom's strained, elated face and right hand, forming a number one sign, were visible under the heap. Hanging on the opposite wall were his celebrity photos—a shot of him and the PBA Hall of Famers who played in a legends game to celebrate the league's twenty-fifth anniversary. Another of Tom next to Manny Pacquiao, the Filipino boxer who would soon become known as the world's pound-for-pound best fighter. Tom walked to a dresser in the corner of the room and pulled open a drawer to retrieve a stack of moldering scrapbooks, their pages pasted with box scores and news accounts from his playing days.

After high school Tom returned to Camarines Norte and began starring in Daet's neighborhood and commercial tournaments. He was selected for a provincial all-star team that entered a national tournament in Manila, and there his play caught the eye of college scouts. He accepted a scholarship to play at the Mapua Institute of Technology, Manila's premier engineering school. In three varsity seasons at Mapua, Tom started at small forward for the Cardinals and was one of the team's top scorers. He left school before graduating to play semipro ball in the MICAA and Interbank commercial leagues that predated the PBA. Tom's Mapua scrapbooks were destroyed years ago in a flood, but his commercial league artifacts had survived more or less intact. He poked the doughy, waterlogged pages, pointing to headlines and box scores clipped from sixties newspapers with Tom's name alongside the likes of Olympians Caloy Loyzaga, Loreto Carbonell, and Lauro Mumar. On the score sheets, next to "Urbano," I saw his point totals: 16, 24, 30. "See that?" He squeezed my shoulder. "Top-notcher in everything! To see is to believe, Raf!"

I also saw, rendered in blurry, forty-year-old newsprint, pictures of Tom driving to the hole. There were fewer wrinkles and his mouth was less puckered back then, but Tom was instantly recognizable thanks to his narrow, rectangular face, stubby crew cut, and giant ears. The two pancakes jutting from the sides of Tom's head became his trademark, the signature feature that everyone who crossed his path seemed to remember. Decades later, when Tom was reunited with greats like Loyzaga and Carbonell at PBA events, they saw his ears and knew it was him. In the seventies, when Tom was rising in the referee ranks, he called a game of the Manila International School when the teenage Tim Cone was playing for the team. When Cone was hired as Alaska's head coach in 1989 and Tom was already with the team, Cone recognized the old ref. I asked Cone about it and he said, "How could anyone forget those ears?"

So by 1979, when Tom became a PBA referee, there was no question how angry players and fans would target him for verbal abuse. Every questionable call was met with a maelstrom of Tagalog curses, followed by "*tenga*," the word for "ears" and Tom's de facto name among PBA stars of the eighties. It was also the last word he heard from a section of rabid fans before they pelted him with peso coins. Tom's Dumbo ears played a headlining role in the most memorable moment of his career. He was reffing a game of the Toyota franchise, then led by Robert "The Big J" Jaworski, an excitable guard who became the PBA's most beloved player. Jaworski took the sport-as-combat analogy literally. His physical, bullying style, along with his outsize popularity, probably made him the toughest player to referee in league history. He was constantly hacking other players, and whenever refs called these violations, they could expect an earful from the foul-mouthed Big J. His tirades had a way of whipping the crowd into a frenzy, and in those days Filipino fans were not shy about expressing their discontent with a barrage of stinging projectiles. It's easy to imagine the chilling effect Jaworski's presence had on referees, who might understandably wish to avoid being threatened by 20,000 raging spectators.

Tom was one of the few referees who refused to back down. During a now infamous game, he called Jaworski for a simple nonshooting foul. The Big J was defending his man on the perimeter, got a little too close while trying to body him, and committed a pushing foul. Tom blew his whistle, pointed to Jaworski, then headed to the scorer's table to repeat the call. Turning his back to the Big J's theatrics, Tom signaled a pushing foul and flashed seven fingers—Jaworski's number—to the scorekeeper. All the while, Jaworski had been flailing his arms in disbelief, pointing to the crowd and ranting about the terrible call. Then he tiptoed about six inches behind Tom. Jaworski cupped his hands to his ears, simulating Tom's expansive lobes, and wagged his tongue at the referee. Suddenly, the arena burst into laughter. Tom, sensing something was wrong, wheeled around and saw Jaworski mocking him. He ejected Jaworski on the spot for unsportsmanlike behavior, a decision that might seem obvious to fans of modern-day NBA basketball but was practically unthinkable at the height of Jaworski's popularity.

"I showed them that my balls are here," Tom told me, pointing to his crotch, "not here," then to his throat. Days later the commissioner summoned Tom and Jaworski to review the confrontation, and Jaworski dropped his tough-guy act. "You're my favorite of the referees," he said to Tom. "You're the only one with courage. You're the only one with guts."* The incident has entered PBA lore as one of the funniest on-court encounters in league history, one of the moments ex-players and lifelong fans mention when they talk about Jaworski. The Alaska coaching staff certainly remembered it; they speculated half jokingly that Tom's ejection of Jaworski led the PBA to retire him as a referee in 1986,

---

* Or so goes Tom's recollection of the event. Tom has been known to apply a grandiose glaze to stories, but the quote sounds an awful lot like many of the John Wayne–worthy quotes attributed to Jaworski over the years. Perhaps the best known is *"Kung ayaw ninyong masaktan sa basketball, mag-chess na lang kayo."* If you don't want to get hurt playing basketball, play chess instead.

when league officials suggested him to the fledgling Alaska franchise as a practice ref and in-house scorekeeper. Since then he'd become an elder statesman—not just for Alaska but for the entire PBA, and by extension, all of Philippine basketball. Watching him on the sidelines, you might mistake Tom for a top league official, a visiting politician, or some kind of mafia don. There, Tom would greet a steady stream of players from various teams and generations; the commissioner and other representatives of the PBA top brass; journalists and agents; and casual fans who remembered him as a referee. They all stopped by to pay their respects. When I rode to practice with Tom, I usually spotted subway and jeepney passengers eyeballing him, then nudging one another and whispering, "That's the guy from Alaska!"

I asked Mang Tom what basketball had meant to him, and he pointed back to the room where he kept his scrapbooks. It was part living room and part hoops shrine. This time, however, he wasn't referring to his basketball relics but the framed photographs of his children dressed in cap and gown for their graduation portraits. "Basketball is the bread and butter for me," he said. "I got four kids. All of them studied from nursery, intermediate, high school, college because of basketball. All of them now are professionals. I can retire if I want and they're already on their own, because of basketball. That's life for me."

Now, Tom's children work as bank tellers and call center agents. Even in those white collar professions, the wages were low and the hours long. But it was enough for them to live fairly comfortably and raise their own families, and for Filipinos who aren't born into wealth, it doesn't get much better than that. Tom didn't obtain stardom and riches via basketball, but the sport brought him from his bleak beginnings to a decent life. For the ball boys and support staff of teams not only in the PBA but in semipro and regional leagues around the country, basketball was a way to inch forward in the Philippines' hopelessly stratified class structure. Tom's life may be a modest hoop dream, but it is one of the most inspiring stories Philippine basketball has to tell.

———

Away from the team, I got to witness the central role hoops played in provincial towns. As a matter of fact, a basketball court was literally at the center of every Philippine municipality I can remember visiting. There must have been a handful of burgs dispersed across the nation that weren't situated around a pair of rims and backboards, but I never found them. Basketball courts were so uniformly located in central plazas, alongside the other touchstones of Philippine society—city halls, public markets, and Catholic churches—that people widely (and mistakenly) believed that local governments were required by law to build public courts. Now, there was a constitutional amendment I could support! Such a regulation, however, would probably be unnecessary, since the sport had no trouble penetrating the most remote *barangays*. In fact, considering the feats of engineering and ingenuity that were required to build courts on the slopes of mountains, it was surprising that they hadn't been constructed by decree. How else could a place like Adams, Ilocos Norte, end up with what looked like a regulation-size court?

I visited Adams on a lark while staying with a Peace Corps volunteer in Laoag City, the capital of Ilocos Norte, a northern province facing the South China Sea. Through the ages, the Ilocos region has built a reputation as a harsh place to live—a not particularly fertile sliver of scorched earth sandwiched between the ocean and the rugged Cordillera mountains. The Ilocanos, who toiled over their inhospitable territory to cke out a subsistence living, had a reputation for being hardworking, hard-headed, and cheap as all hell. Their unwelcoming land and willingness to work made Ilocanos some of the Philippines' earliest migrants. They spread through neighboring provinces like Cagayan, Abra, and La Union, until Ilocano became the primary language of northern Luzon. Nor did their diaspora end there: Ilocano farmers settled as far south as Mindanao, and they made up the bulk of the first Filipino immigrants to the United States in the early 1900s, when they toiled in pre-statehood Hawaii's sugarcane plantations, California's lettuce patches, and Washington's canneries.* In the past half century, however, the province became associated with its most prominent native son, Ferdinand Marcos, who, despite his regime's record of plunder and human rights abuses, remains beloved in Ilocos Norte, where he reinvested sizable portions of his embezzled fortune.

When I hopped off the bus near the provincial capitol building in Laoag City, a row of tarpaulin banners celebrating then-Governor Bongbong Marcos served notice to the family's enduring dominance in the region. It was early December, and the park across from the capitol featured Christmas-themed sculptures made from recycled goods, including a pile of empty mayonnaise jars shaped like the baby Jesus. That first day, I hit the tourist staples before linking up with Tom, my Peace Corps host, who was working at a local high school. In Batac, about fifteen minutes from Laoag, I saw the strongman himself, or at least what was left of him, since Marcos died in 1989. There, next to the dictator's boyhood home, lay his preserved remains under a backlit glass case in an otherwise pitch-dark, chilly room where the only sound was an air conditioner's hum. Throughout his reign, Marcos's opponents called him a puppet of the United States for favoring American military and business interests over the needs of Filipinos, and the state of mild decay in which I encountered him seemed like poetic justice. He resembled a shriveled marionette: a preserved head, a limpid face with the sheen of a glazed doughnut, and nothing but a bag of bones beneath it.

The following day, Tom and I headed for Adams. We had a vague notion of how to get there—take a bus up the coast for several hours, then jump off when you see a dirt road crawling up into the mountains.

---

* A 1955 agreement between the Philippines and British North Borneo requested the migration of Filipino laborers, "preferably Ilocanos," to Borneo for work in the logging industry and on rubber and coconut plantations.

From there, find a motorcyclist willing to take you to the top. We had no clue what we might find—jungle, waterfalls, blood-thirsty gorillas like those from the movie *Congo*. Even in Laoag, few people seemed to know much about their upland neighbors. The city folk wondered why anyone would want to visit a place so far out of the way. Their voices turned grave to warn us that communist rebels lived in the mountains. This belief was widespread among urban Filipinos, and it wasn't wholly false. The country's communist rebel army had long been associated with the unforgiving terrain of upland jungles where the government had little authority. Still, the communist threat seemed wildly exaggerated. It got to the point where every time I passed a deserted, grassy hill, I expected someone to lean close and whisper, "Communists."

When we got to the Adams turnoff, the young Red waiting to take us up the slope didn't look too radical—a fourteen-year-old in a denim jacket and a faded Orlando Magic hat, leaning against a mud-splattered Yamaha. He grinned when we jumped down from the bus and gestured up toward the green unknown. Tom, who spoke Ilocano, negotiated a ride to the Adams town hall. We squeezed ourselves onto the back of his dirt bike and began to crawl up the mountain. The teenager weaved around pools of sludge and dodged rocks as big as coconuts throughout the vertiginous climb. All the while, the gulf on our left kept growing. We hardly saw anyone else along the road—just a father and son plodding down the path with the curved, eighteen-inch blades of their bolo knives dangling from their belts. Later on, while crossing a drooping bridge of wooden planks, we passed over a naked, middle-age man bathing in a creek. When he looked up and saw two Americans above him, he giggled deliriously. When the road became too steep for the Yamaha's engine to haul us up, me and Tom would hop off and walk until we reached more level ground. Close to Adams, small cinder-block houses mushroomed up along the road; after a sharp turn we found ourselves in the center of Adams, where a few modern buildings rose mirage-like out of the jungle. The town's tallest structures were the municipal hall and a regulation-size, open-air basketball court with a concrete floor, surrounded by a ring of cement bleachers and topped with a high pitched roof.

Tom and I walked to the municipal hall and found the town tourism director brimming with enthusiasm at an opportunity to do his job. He confirmed several obvious facts about Adams—that it was Ilocos Norte's most remote town, that most of its population lived off the land, and that most people lived in houses made of cinder blocks and corrugated iron or bamboo and palm leaves. "Actually, I am proud to say that you two are not the first foreign visitors we have had here in Adams," he told us. He took a marble composition book from his desk, shook the dust off and opened it to the first page, where we saw the beginnings of a ledger. Two Israeli travelers had already signed. "Will you please sign?" he asked.

I asked him about the basketball court, which was on par with some of the nicer ones in Manila. It was still in decent condition with just one bent rim, but other than that and a couple weak spots in the roof where water leaked during heavy rains, it was good as new. Long fiber mats were laid out on the court, with rice spread out to dry on them. A small group of women sat in the bleachers and guarded the harvest. For the people of Adams, the court wasn't just a place to practice reverse layups, it was the center of social life, the place where the town held singing contests, beauty pageants, and community meetings. During Christmas and New Year's celebrations and the town's annual fiesta week, festivities started at the basketball court and radiated out through the forest paths to people's homes.

The basketball court's all-purpose role in rural living was not particular to Adams. Throughout the Philippines, in coastal fishing villages, pastoral rice-farming burgs, and isolated mountain hamlets, basketball courts were used in every conceivable way. At midday, when it was so hot that trying to play five-on-five would have people keeling over from heat stroke, farmers dried rice on the courts. This arrangement benefited drivers on provincial roads, who otherwise would have to dodge patches of grain scattered in the street. Parties for holidays, graduations, weddings, and debuts for girls on their eighteenth birthdays were all held on basketball courts. I even saw wakes where families mourned loved ones under the backboards. But provincial Filipinos who lived miles away from funeral homes weren't alone in attending courtside wakes; shortly after former President Corazon Aquino died in August 2009, one of her public viewings was held at the same high school gym where I played Thursday-night pickup games.

With so many different uses for basketball courts, folks in the provinces often jerry-built their own playing surfaces so they wouldn't have to compete with farmers, mourners, and revelers every time they felt like shooting around. In places like Adams and beyond, people often lived miles away from their towns' central courts. So, like their urban countrymen, rural Filipinos improvised. They lashed the rusted hoods of broken-down cars to coconut trees to use as backboards. They dribbled, sprinted, slid, and leaped through clouds of dust on earthen courts surrounded by hulking tamarind trees. I saw entire hoops built from felled trees, from the backboard all the way to the supports. In some of the most isolated and impoverished areas, where a trip to Foot Locker might as well be a mission to Mars and a family's income might struggle to cover the cost of food and medicine, some rims sported handwoven nets made out of abaca fiber, a local banana plant. I saw many of these courts (played on them too), and although the ball didn't bounce as high off the dirt as I would have liked, and the gaps between the backboard's hacked-together planks pretty much killed my bank shot, visiting them felt more spiritual than anything I ever experienced in a church. The devotion it must have taken to build an entire court from scratch touched me. It was one of the most sincere expressions of love I'd ever laid eyes on.

Aside from marveling at the beauty of rural basketball courts, I also played in provincial tournaments. Friends from pickup games recommended me as an "import" for small-town leagues. Although the term "import" was borrowed from the PBA, it had a different meaning in these competitions. Here, imports were rarely foreigners—I was an exception—but instead, ringers from major cities like Manila, Cebu, and Davao who beefed up crews of neighborhood ballers. The team sponsors, often local big shots who operated somewhere in the gray area between politics, business, and organized crime, hired imports to boost their teams' chances of taking home some championship brass, earning some heavy duty bragging rights, and also making money. Thousands of dollars were often wagered over the outcome of these tournaments, and an owner whose squad won the title would cover the cost of his imports with plenty of cash to spare.

I should probably explain that the tournament I joined didn't take place in a typical small town. I played in Boracay. The tiny, kidney-bean-shaped island may have been a speck on the Philippine map, but its profile among the country's tourism destinations was unmatched. Boracay generated hundreds of millions of dollars in tourism revenue each year, a remarkable sum for an island not quite six miles long and less than a mile wide. Much of this was due to White Beach, a mile-long lawn of sand the color and texture of talcum powder. A diverse range of visitors found their way to Boracay; there were fairly normal travelers eager to see if the island could live up to the hype, but also a gallery of oddities and grotesques endemic to Southeast Asia—impenetrable cabals of Korean scuba divers, Filipino elites enjoying the spoils of their little corruptions, Western "sex-patriates" with comb-overs and fish-bowl bellies rolling in the sand with local women half their weight and one-third their age.

Boracay was no typical seaside community. With its multitude of resorts, chain restaurants, and an outdoor mall replete with a sex-toy shop, Boracay was unlike any other place in the Philippines. Many foreign tourists there left without encountering a Filipino who wasn't serving a rum-spiked fruit shake, guiding a sailboat, or tidying a room. But in the hills behind White Beach there was a local population whose lives weren't too different from those of Filipinos elsewhere in the nation, and the tournament I came to play in belonged to them.

The man responsible for bringing me to Boracay was Leopold "Bong" Tirol, scion of one of the island's leading landowning clans. Boracay's earliest resorts were founded in the seventies in an ad-hoc, homesteading style. People arrived, claimed plots, and started building. The Tirol family was an exception among resort owners; they were titled landowners who not only owned and operated hotels and golf courses, but also leased land for other entrepreneurs to develop. Yet although Bong could call much of Boracay his family bailiwick, he hadn't been able to extend his dominion over the local hoops scene, where a Canadian bar owner named John Munro had built a small dynasty with teams named after his Javas Jerseys' basketball uniform company.* The fact that Bong had also once been involved with real big-time basketball, as manager of a team in the now-defunct Metropolitan Basketball Association, possibly fueled his annoyance over losing to Munro.

Bong's plan to take back Boracay hoops relied on me and three other Manila-based ringers. Bong had entered two teams in the tournament, and we would be split up, two imports per squad, with the objective of stopping Javas from winning another title. My teammate was Jonathan "Jonats" de Guzman, a bulky five-foot-eleven guard with a boxy crew cut and veined stovepipes for arms; he had played for Bong's MBA team, the Pasig City Pirates, and was taking a week's break from his normal

---

* Boracay, although gorgeous, is a small place; so small that bored resort owners with island fever might develop heated rivalries over who could assemble the most powerful team of balling beach bums.

job as a practice player for Talk 'N Text to aid Bong's quest. Our counterparts on Bong's other squad were Ravi Chulani, one of my closest friends in the country and a three-point specialist, and Francis Sanz, another ex-pro from the MBA. Jonats and Sanz, who had meaningful credentials, received a daily allowance from Bong throughout the week; me and Ravi, just a couple of pickup ballers, were happy to be receiving room and board and spiffy new uniforms.

Fresh off the plane from Manila, I caught a glimpse of the Tirol family's clout when we arrived at their golf club in Caticlan. We were waiting to board a pumpboat headed to Boracay, more or less blending in with the other tourists there; it was one of the few places in the Philippines where a six-three white guy and a couple Filipino six-footers could remain fairly inconspicuous. But when Ravi told the receptionist we were Bong Tirol's hired guns, the telephone receiver slipped from the stunned employee's neck.

"You're the guests of Sir Bong?" he asked, voice quivering. "Why didn't you say? I'm sorry to keep you waiting."

The mercenaries had officially arrived to restore basketball glory to Tirol's fiefdom. His name worked like a secret password; we spoke it and servants sprung into action. The receptionist clawed frantically at the air to summon a crew of porters, who scrambled in from a back room to gather our bags. The porters led us to the beach, hoisted the luggage onto their backs, and climbed over the bamboo pontoons of a private motorboat to load the bags. Had we allowed them, they might have also tried to carry us onto the boat.

When we arrived on the shore in front of Bong's resort, the White House, he was entertaining guests next to the pool and watching the creamsicle sunset. Dressed in khaki shorts and a polo shirt, Bong was holding what looked like a glass of Johnnie Walker on the rocks; he was five-foot-seven, maybe, with sun-pinked cheeks and a carefree manner that made him seem more like a ruddy nineteen-year-old on spring break than a thirty-something resort magnate. He asked if we had a comfortable trip, then told us to put our sneakers on. He wanted to see us play ball. The sun was all but gone, but Bong had installed overhead lights on the island's cracked blacktop court. As we warmed up, I felt worried. Did Bong have the motor running on his pumpboat, ready to banish whoever failed to impress him? I remembered Quemont Greer's bitter sendoff from Red Bull, and all the other PBA imports who complained that their teams canned them unfairly. Was I headed down that road?

Not this time. Over about a dozen short games of three-on-three, all of the imports looked good. I was quick and long enough to guard anyone on the court, plus my outside shots were falling and I scored on some tough contested drives. Ravi's shooting was blistering. Sanz was a lazy defender but solidly built and the best low-post player on the court. Jonats was flying to the island early the next day, but Bong already knew his game from their days together with the Pirates. Jonats was a legit pro on the cusp of playing in the PBA; in fact, he might have been able to start for a lesser team, but according to the league's strange economics, he had greater job security as a reserve for a rich team like Talk 'N Text than as a vital cog on a shaky team that churned through players.

When we returned to the White House, two members of the Sacapaño clan were waiting for me. They owned Charlh's Bar (pronounced "Charles"), one of the island's oldest beachfront pubs and a choice spot for listening to Eagles cover bands, nibbling pig organs, and spotting Western Lotharios. They were also my teammates; Bong was sponsoring the Sacapaño squad in the tournament. I wouldn't be playing under the Charlh's Bar flag, however, because the Sacapaños wanted to promote their new cockfighting arena.

They brought me the weirdest basketball uniform on the planet. The jersey was a navy blue V-neck with my number, thirteen, over the left shoulder. An image of two gamecocks in mid-flight, their beaks poised to strike and their talons bearing down on each other, covered the chest. The words BORACAY COCKPIT ARENA, appeared above the roosters, and just below was an orange bubble proclaiming NEW! in white print. On the back of the jersey, my last name, Bartholomew, had received the Ellis Island treatment, and now read BARTOLEME. This was my moment. I had made it. What twelve-year-old, shooting baskets in the playground and dreaming of his future career, doesn't look into the clouds and imagine himself as Bartoleme, import of the Boracay Cockers?

That night, we went to Cocomangas, the bar owned by Javas headman John Munro. It was one of the oldest and best-known watering holes in Boracay, but over the years the vibe in Cocomangas had turned increasingly seedy. Ten years ago, I was told, Cocomangas had been *the* nightclub in Boracay, a place where Filipino scenesters and moneyed travelers partied hard enough to keep them in bed until the following afternoon. Over time, however, the upper class crowd migrated to newer bars that opened closer to the beach. What remained was a meat market. When we arrived at Cocomangas, a group of women in halter tops and shorts were smoking outside. The moment they spotted me, they started shouting prices: "One thousand!" "Seven hundred!" "Free!" Sanz and Ravi found this hilarious, but I was already feeling queasy. Inside Cocomangas the gallery of horrors included balding men in fanny packs grinding against teenage Filipinas to a Black Eyed Peas song; a grab bag of lady boys and unfortunate-looking women, all half-naked, waiting for customers to approach them; older Australian men with leathery sunburnt skin pounding mason jars of mixed drinks while sizing up their prospective dates; and teenagers from Manila's elite high schools tying on their first benders. The music was loud and overbearing; the air was thick with cigarette smoke and mosquitoes. If Munro was in charge of this joint, then I was eager to give him some basketball comeuppance.

Before we played Javas, however, we had to dispatch a few weaker squads made up of busboys and cooks from local hotels and dive shops, as well as a gruff crew of public servants from the Boracay precinct of the Philippine National Police. The style of play was straight run-and-gun, with full-court passes leading to contorted, crowd-pleasing layups and hardly any defense. In Tagalog, they called this style of play *bato*, a word that meant "rock" but could also mean to hurl something as far as possible. After I pulled down rebounds, it was usually the first word I heard—*"Bato!"*—from a teammate dashing down court. Basketball players all over the world like to avoid playing defense, but few seemed to disdain it as much as Filipinos. Of course, PBA and college teams ran intricate defenses and fielded hard-nosed stoppers in their lineups, but in more disorganized competitions, the sport was about showing off your moves. There was even a sense of collusion between players on opposite teams: "I'll give you the lane to try a spinning layup if you let me scoop a finger roll from the foul line."

I grew up under a different basketball ethic. I felt embarrassed when someone scored on me, and I got back at him not with a gaudy drive of my own, but by trying to shut him down for the rest of the game. I couldn't rewire myself to give up on defense, which made me even more of a novelty to the Boracay spectators, many of whom seemed to enjoy me as a cross-cultural hoops study: *White Americans are monstrously tall, have hairy arms, and play intense defense!* I even earned the approval of Bong, who pulled me aside after a game and said, "The crowd is talking about you. They say you never stop going after the blocks and rebounds, like you're crazy. They never see players like that."

We won each of our first three games by more than thirty points, and people started to recognize us around the island. During the day, when we walked along the beach, waiters at seaside bars would give us the thumbs-up, and people would run in from the street to yell, *"Ang galing ninyo!"* which was like saying, "Damn, you guys are good!" At night, every fifty feet, a group of guys huddled around a bottle of rum would stop us by shouting "Idol!" as we passed. "One shot!" they'd plead, holding out a plastic cup containing a snort of rust-colored liquor. They'd slap us five, reenact moves we made on the court, pass the communal cup and invite us home to meet their wives, sons, daughters, nephews.

Yes, the thought of myself as anyone's idol was absurd. I should mention that these people didn't mean "idol" in a religious sense; instead, they were using the word as a greeting, kind of like saying, "Dude! I'm a fan." True, the thought of me having fans was only slightly less ridiculous than the one of me inspiring worshipers, but whenever somebody called us "Idol!" we couldn't help but play along. The next morning they'd tell their buddies about sharing a slimy cup of cheap rum with the Cockers imports, and that was an honor for us players. But with the first game against Javas looming, I also got the feeling from the Boracay regulars that they expected our winning streak to end. After anointing me and Jonats as their idols, they would usually mention that it was too bad we had to play Javas next. *"Sayang!"* they'd say. What a waste.

It felt like Boracay's entire adult population showed up to watch the Cockers challenge Javas. When I arrived at the court on the back of a teammate's motorcycle, the lawn surrounding the pavement was so dense with onlookers that I had to tiptoe through the tangle of splayed limbs to reach our bench. The standing crowd backed up all the way across the plaza to the church steps overlooking the court. Kids sat on top of a fence that separated the blacktop from the road; tricycle drivers lined their rigs up bumper-to-bumper along the curb and climbed on top of the sidecars to watch from homemade upper decks. Across the street, a guy wearing a faded jersey from a past tournament waved at me. "Bartoleme! *Kayang-kaya mo!* You can do it!"

Both teams were undefeated, and while the stakes weren't particularly high for that game—we were on target to meet again two days later in a win-or-go-home semifinal match—both sides seemed eager to prove themselves. We jumped on Javas from the opening tip-off. Jonats came out firing. He sent looping three-pointers splashing through the net from spots all around the arc, like someone playing around-the-world in an empty gym. I rebounded Javas misses and rifled passes to Jonats at midcourt, where he blew by defenders for layups and trips to the foul line. He passed to me on the right baseline; I turned and saw nothing but empty space between myself and the basket. As I approached the hoop, Munro rushed in and chest-bumped me. I absorbed the blow, jumped straight up and banked a one-hander off the backboard. On Jonats's rare misses, I rebounded and scored. Our success energized our local teammates, who made shots, came up with steals, and slipped under the basket for layups when defenders double- and triple-teamed me or Jonats.

Midway through the first half the Cockers had built a seventeen-point lead. Javas, stunned, called time out. Then things changed. Jonats was whistled for three phantom fouls in rapid succession and had to leave the game for the remainder of the half. Every out-of-bounds call went in favor of Javas. The referees were whistling Cocker locals for traveling violations before they'd taken a step. The crowd, which had been reveling in the apparent demise of Javas, was hushed. Then the whispers began.

"*Luto, pare. Luto talaga.*" The game is cooked. They're being cooked. *Luto* is the Tagalog root for all words related to cooking. If a contest or contract is fixed, they call it cooked. In provincial tournaments, games were always slightly fixed, especially when you ran up a double-digit lead against the tournament organizer's team. Munro was responsible for hiring referees, announcers, and scorekeepers, and he had even sold discount uniforms to the teams, all so the people of Boracay could enjoy playing in and watching the tournament. For all his generosity, it just seemed natural that the calls might favor Munro's team. Even in these small-time tournaments, basketball seemed to reflect larger themes of Philippine society. In this case, it was patronage, political or otherwise, which persisted throughout the country and was especially strong in the countryside. Munro was treating Boracay to a lovely basketball exhibition; didn't he deserve a reward for his hard work? Didn't he deserve to win?

As the game went on, the depth of the Javas roster also began to show itself. Munro could play. He stood a shade under six feet tall, with a built upper body and elbows like daggers. He was a consistent shooter, but what made him dangerous—as a player and as someone likely to injure you—was his frenzied approach to the game. On offense, he didn't drive around his defender as much as barrel through him like a threatened rhinoceros. He was similarly berserk on defense, where he liked to crowd his man chest-to-chest and swipe at the ball in a blunt, chopping motion. And, of course, the referees rarely penalized him for his kamikaze style. Javas also fielded the tournament's most decorated import, Rommel Daep, a former guard for Purefoods. Their other import was six-three with a lights-out jumper from the free throw line, and their big man, a good-natured, heavyset six-four local, learned to throw his weight around in the Philippines' top semipro league. Even their less decorated players could all make open threes and handle the ball.

On the other hand, the supporting cast playing with me and Jonats could have been the Pinoy Bad News Bears. After us imports, the best player was Trinidad, who was a legitimate threat from the three-point line, but his slight frame allowed Javas' grown men to overpower him. Besides Trinidad, our other teammates were more memorable as oddities—a guy with a giant potbelly, one with an Elvis Presley pompadour, another with a cleft palate—than as basketball players. If we were going to beat Javas, me and Jonats would have to carry the team, and after the referees sidelined Jonats, that weight shifted onto me.

My Cockers got rattled during the Javas comeback. Now, when I rebounded the ball and threw long outlet passes, instead of driving to the hoop, my teammates would freeze and wait helplessly while Munro, practically foaming at the mouth, closed in to snatch the ball from them. Daep, the heady professional, settled down the Javas offense. He directed the shooting big man to the high post and sent the six-four heavyweight under the basket. Playing in the middle of a zone, I could only guard one of them, and Daep was clever enough to always pass the ball to the player I wasn't defending. By halftime the Cockers lead had shrunk to four points.

Early in the second half Jonats attempted to protect his dribble by blocking one of Munro's chops with his forearm. The ref whistled Jonats for a fourth foul. He was one call away from fouling out, or "graduating" as many Filipinos call it, so he returned to the bench to save himself for the last eight minutes. I went back to playing almost one-on-five, with my local teammates drained of poise and ready to succumb to Javas and their referee henchmen. Before long I reached an elevated state of pissed-off exasperation. I didn't care who paid for what; I wanted a fair game.* When the referees allowed a Javas big man to camp in the lane for about ten seconds past the three-second limit, then shove me out of the way to secure an offensive rebound and score, I hawked a loud, exaggerated loogie and spat at the ground near an official's feet. I was engaging the refs in icy stare-downs during dead balls and celebrating made baskets by cursing loudly in English. This behavior was definitely not what the State Department envisioned when they granted my Fulbright scholarship (the program's implied goal is to improve the country's image by sending clean-cut young Americans abroad), but my violent remonstrations seemed to endear me to the Filipino crowd more than anything else I did on the court. Spectators started hooting with delight at my approaching meltdown. After one call, a referee answered my death glare with an apologetic shrug and raised his eyebrows as if to say, "It's nothing personal."

---

* This was, in retrospect, a pretty arrogant and very American attitude, to which a local would probably reply, *"Ganyan ang buhay"*—That's life.

My outbursts might have helped the Cockers stay close. I found a new ferocity in my inside game, bumping and jostling my way to offensive rebounds, tip-ins, and trips to the foul line. The cleft palate guy got hot, and I penetrated into the lane and kicked out passes to him for three-pointers that kept the Javas lead to five or six points. We still had a chance when Jonats returned, but by then he'd sat for so long that his shooting touch went cold. The long jumpers he'd made early in the game stopped falling. Meanwhile, Daep took control of Javas' offense and immediately returned to the high-low game. When the high post big man made a jumper to extend Javas lead to seven points with ninety seconds to play, I knew we would lose. The Javas empire was shaken, but in the end it prevailed.

On the morning of our rematch I woke at seven to squeeze in some shooting practice. My legs felt rubbery from playing five games in four days, but my touch felt good. I worked around the court from baseline to baseline, making ten jumpers in each spot. Catch-and-shoot five times, then off-the-dribble five times. I kept it up until I'd made a few hundred. I wanted to step on the court that night feeling like I could singlehandedly beat Javas. If the game turned out like the last one, I might have to. After one mid-range jumper, somebody hissed at me. A tricycle driver, resting in the shade of his sidecar, was watching from the street. "Bartoleme! *Pssss!* Don't do that! Don't make that shot. You lose tonight. I bet one thousand on Javas." A thousand pesos was only slightly more than twenty dollars, but it was probably several days' worth of earnings for the driver.

Our semifinal game against Javas followed the same script. We built an early lead off hot shooting and Jonats's superior talent. The refs turned on us and fueled a Javas comeback. The rest of the way it was nip-and-tuck basketball, with the lead changing practically every time either team scored. This time, however, the refs were saddling me with dubious fouls. A few minutes before halftime they whistled me on three straight possessions. First, I set a pick for Jonats just above the foul line. Munro didn't see it and slammed into me. We were both shaken by the collision, but the foul was called on me. The next play, I was guarding a Javas big man in the post and was whistled for pushing him with my knee. Less than a minute later, I picked up another knee-in-the-back violation. I hadn't committed any fouls, but suddenly I was in foul trouble.

Midway through the third quarter Munro stripped one of our locals and came charging through the lane. I stood with my hands straight up as he barged through and swung an elbow that split open the bottom of my chin. With my blood spilling onto the blacktop, the referee blew his whistle, pointed at me, and puffed his chest out to make the sign for a blocking foul.

"What'd I do? Foul his elbow with my face?" I wiped the blood off my chin and shoved a red palm in the ref's face. "How did this happen?"

Not only was I one call away from fouling out, but I had to run across the street to have my wound treated at the medical clinic. The dim, yellow-lit room was empty except for an examination table and a scale. The doctor was snoozing on a cot in the back room. When I woke her she told me I needed stitches. I asked her to just bandage my chin so I could return to the game. I'd come back later to be sewn up. She pressed gauze under my jaw and wrapped three strips of medical tape lengthwise around my head. I had a full-skull chinstrap.

I crossed the street and subbed myself in for the beginning of the fourth quarter. The small lead we were holding when I left had swung in favor of Javas. My first time downcourt, Jonats missed a jumper, I snagged the rebound and scored while being fouled. It was a momentum-turning play, and we followed it with a defensive stop and another basket to tie the game. Someone—a referee perhaps?—had to swing the game back in Javas' favor. With three minutes left, just after we reclaimed the lead, I was called for another kneeing foul, my fifth. I graduated. I still don't understand what I did wrong, but I was so incensed that I tore off my blood-stained chinstrap, threw it to the ground and stomped on it, then pulled my shorts down and waddled away in my boxers while the crowd hooted its approval and chanted "Bartoleme."

Filipino basketball crowds love a good tantrum. In my histrionic moment, I had channeled Jaworski and other celebrated hotheads of PBA past and present. There was something about watching a man crumble in the face of flagrant crookedness that drove people wild. Not only was it great spectacle, but people could relate to it. For many Filipinos, it was the story of their lives. If the odds were stacked against you, you might as well fail with some chutzpah and let everyone know that—to paraphrase Mang Tom—your balls are down where they belong. Of course, the Cockers lost. But our two battles with Javas wore them down, and they hardly put up a fight against Bong's other team in the finals.*

The postchampionship revelry over Javas' downfall was a whole-island affair. Bong bought two spit-roasted pigs to celebrate and served one at a private team party and another at center court for the crowd. At the party, a disco cover band serenaded the imports with Bee Gees tunes and we stood for an ovation from Tirol's family and friends. Even though the Cockers lost, I was cheered all over the island by fans who enjoyed my pantless antics. Everyone I talked to asked me to reenact the moment where I pulled my shorts down and stormed off the court.

We were up all night, eating and drinking, swimming in the moonlight and soaking up adoration we probably didn't deserve. The next morning, we flew back to Manila. In the capital, no one would confuse me with an import. But in Boracay, the Bartoleme legend endured. When Ravi returned to the island six months later, he was greeted by

---

* I also heard the rumor that Bong threatened to turn off the court lights, which he had paid to install, if he felt the referees were jobbing his team in the championship game. If true, that may have helped level the playing field.

familiar calls of "Idol!" and people asking about his friend Bartoleme, the fiery, half-naked import.

The Boracay tournament had raucous crowds, small-time malfeasance, and overblown local rivalries—all ingredients in the beloved, combustible jambalaya of Philippine grassroots basketball—but something was still missing. When people told me about these tournaments, they usually spoke with reverie for the raw emotion that games inspired in entire communities. I hadn't felt that in Boracay; instead, the freewheeling, high-scoring games and somewhat nonsensical cajoling from amateur coaches reminded me of New York youth tournaments I played in as a teenager. More than a year later, when I watched the finals of a similar league in my own neighborhood in Quezon City, I realized there hadn't been anything missing in Boracay, but that there was no way to fully appreciate these tournaments without being a true local.

In Loyola Heights, where I had been living for three years, I was as close to "local" as any gargantuan foreigner could hope to be, and I could recognize the links between the games and the teeming mass of families, local politicians, and drifters in the crowd. The league had been ongoing for months, but I hadn't paid much attention aside from occasionally watching a quarter when I passed the court on my way to dinner. Then, on a blustery Sunday afternoon, while I was lugging a sack of sweaty clothes to the laundromat, I heard the hi-hat patter of rubber flip-flops slapping the concrete behind me, followed by the familiar call of "*Kuya* Raphael! *Kuya* Raphael!" As the street children closed in on me, I fumbled in my pocket for enough change to treat them to *hopia* pastries and RC Cola. For once, however, snacks weren't on their mind.

"*Kuya*! Are you watching the game tonight?" one kid asked in Tagalog, and I replied that I hadn't heard about it.

"Championship *na*! Lots of people are going." It was settled. I would come to the court around eight.

Later on, when I set out to walk to the game, the streets were deserted. Rain poured down in buckets and turned entire streets into shallow puddles; everyone, including the tricycle drivers and the telltale buzz-saw din of their motorcycle engines, seemed to have stayed home. The wind shredded my umbrella and I was tempted to turn back and skip the game, but I soldiered on, half wondering if I'd arrive at an empty court. When I arrived, however, I saw that the weather wasn't the only reason the streets were empty. There, under the court's overhead lamps, I saw the whole neighborhood on the court and packed into its concrete bleachers. It felt like walking into a demented version of *This Is Your Life*, with three years' worth of faces and memories hugging the sidelines. There were dozens of kids—Jeff Boy, Angelica, Ronnie, Jennylynn—who scaled me like a human jungle gym, stroked my exotic forearm hair, and asked questions ranging from "How many siblings do you have?" and "Where does your family live?" to "How did you learn to speak Tagalog?" and "Why are you so white?" These were some of the same children who watched me practice on this very court when I first arrived in the Philippines, and now I saw them gathered with their entire families. I bumped into Jay-Arr (because J.R. was so passé), the neighborhood MJ, an older teenager who had played me in some epic one-on-one duels. I man-hugged the tricycle drivers who turned me from a Tagalog student into a Tagalog speaker during dozens of drinking sessions, where they passed around a cup of Red Horse beer, fed me fried fish balls, goat, and dog meat,* and tried to teach me to curse like a local. One of them had made me an honorary godfather to his grand-

---

* Perhaps. They were always coy about where our snacks came from. If it was indeed dog, as a few tricycle drivers claimed after the fact, then it tasted fine to me. Rather, it seemed normal after six shots of Ginebra, which is sometimes called *gin bulag*, meaning it's so strong you'll go blind (or eat dog).

daughter. I saw the elderly twins who roamed the neighborhood selling "dirty" ice cream, cold scoops served out of a pushcart and stuffed inside *pandesal* bread rolls. I smiled and yelled "Red Horse!" when I saw the night watchman from a nearby construction site, because that's what we did—for no apparent reason—every time we saw each other. I had never seen these disparate characters gathered together in one setting, yet here they all were at a basketball game.

Throughout the tourney, each squatter community in Loyola Heights fielded a team. The private subdivisions where the area's wealthier residents lived, including the one where I stayed, hosted their own leagues and didn't participate in the public one. The local congressman, Mat Defensor, had sponsored the tournament, and the navy blue and gold reversible uniforms had LOYOLA HEIGHTS printed on the front and a University of Michigan-style M over one knee that actually stood for "Mat." The teams from Ronas Garden and Daan Tubo had reached the championship, and I knew most of the Ronas players, since my town house was on the opposite side of Diliman Creek from their improvised village of plywood and corrugated metal. The game itself was a sloppy mess. Most of the players were quick and agile, and a couple could really shoot, but aside from a few pretty drives, they spent an awful lot of time losing the ball, then scrambling to pick it up, then losing it again. This kind of bewitched game, where everyone handled the ball like they were wearing butter-soaked oven mitts, was common enough to have a Tagalog name—*larong buko*—which compares such slapstick basketball to hoops played with a coconut.

It didn't matter, however, that the game itself wasn't impressive. The energy radiating from the court made me feel starry-eyed. This was what all those people had been talking about when they raved about *barangay* hoops. Although I wasn't in the province, the atmosphere was still parochial. Even though my neighbors lived a ten-minute jeepney ride away from malls that housed multiplexes and sold all sorts of pricey staples of first-world living, they spent most of their lives selling cigarettes, driving tricycles, and collecting five-peso donations to assist parking along Katipunan Avenue. Their whole lives took place in that neighborhood, and on this night the whole neighborhood was at the court. If the players bobbled the ball so much because they felt nervous, it was no wonder; their entire extended families as well as almost everyone else they knew were in the stands, pressed against thin yellow ropes tied along the sidelines to keep the crowd from spilling onto the court. If a player scored 30 and sealed the championship with two clutch free throws, or if he threw a boneheaded pass that cost his team the game, he would hear about it until next year. I remember thinking that playing in front of that crowd would intimidate me, and I was only a temporary, fringe member of the community. For the born-and-bred Loyola Heights crowd, this game meant everything. When I played for the Cockers, the Boracay lifers must have felt the same way.

Back in Subic, before Alaska played Purefoods, there was one similarly meaningful moment. Just before the teams finished warm-ups, the big-city PBA took on the outsize passions of small-town basketball. With the game clock ticking down its final minute before tip-off, Willie Miller sauntered away from Alaska's layup lines and stood at the sideline near half-court. He worked his gaze over the crowd baseline-to-baseline, making eye contact with all the people he recognized from his hometown. Meanwhile, practically everyone in the stands seemed to be standing to yell something at Willie, or if they didn't know him, snap a picture with their cell phones, because they might not get another chance to see him and the other PBA ballers playing in their hometown.

The game played out like a typical PBA affair, only in a slightly smaller, hotter arena. Alaska beat Purefoods 94-80 and improved their record to five wins against one loss, which put them in a first-place tie with Red Bull. The Subic win came as a minor surprise because Roe had been suffering from back spasms that week. Cone wanted him to rest, even if it meant risking a loss against the Tender Juicy Giants and their high-scoring import, Marquin Chandler. But Roe refused to sit and further won the adoration of his teammates by playing despite his injury. In limited minutes he handcuffed Chandler, and even soared for a breakaway dunk that left the Alaska coaching staff wincing. If Roe aggravated his back and had to miss upcoming games, Alaska's emerging confidence might have vanished and the season could have been spoiled. Luckily, Roe dunked comfortably and then ran back smirking at the coaches, their faces ashen with worry. With the game in hand, Roe rested for much of the fourth quarter and let Willie lead the team with 23 points in front of a hometown crowd.

After the win, hundreds of well-wishers stormed the court and surrounded Willie. While the rest of the team showered and Cone congratulated Roe on a gutsy performance, fans outside the arena found the locker room windows—a pair of smudged portholes eight feet off the ground—and took turns boosting one another to press their faces against the glass. It was their last glimpse of basketball royalty, as well as the final glimmer of provincial zeal during Alaska's out-of-town trip. Just as Cone finished explaining the Aces' upcoming schedule and led the team in its customary "One-two-three . . . together!" chant, he realized that Willie never made it back to the dugout. He was still on the court, kissing babies and posing for photographs.

"Shit, he's been gone the whole time?" Cone asked as the team headed back to the bus, back to Manila, back to their normal lives. "I didn't even notice. No wonder it was so quiet."

9

Fil-Am or Fil-Sham?

"**P**re-cise-ly! Ab-so-lute-ly! How do you do?" Inside the Alaska players lounge, Willie Miller was showing off his command of genteel English. He was speaking in a put-on British accent with lilting, effeminate flourishes because that afternoon he decided to sit in the "English section" for a change. Leather couches ran along two walls of the lounge, and most days the homegrown Filipino players sat on one side while the Filipino-American Aces and Roe sat on the other. When Willie's King's English failed to garner much reaction, he turned to Roe and started slapping the import's hand in a way vaguely reminiscent of a fist bump and hugging Roe with one arm.

"What up, son? Yeah, son, I be chillin', son." Unable to keep a straight face through any of his jokes, Willie greeted Roe in mock American slang, but couldn't stop a giggle from intruding whenever he said "son." Now, at least, Willie wasn't the only one laughing. His imitation Ebonics had Roe and the team's four* Fil-Ams howling. His clown-

---

* Including Tony dela Cruz, who was on loan to the national team but occasionally stopped by Alaska practices, the team had five players who grew up in the States, all in California.

ing created a tableau of the Philippines' unique and muddled cultural blend, a legacy of hundreds of years of Spanish and then American colonial rule, followed by a contemporary society in which poverty drove a tenth of the population to work abroad as sailors, nurses, nannies, maids, and at countless other jobs. The nation's web of cross-cultural influences sometimes seemed most snarled in Philippine basketball. Here was Willie, a half African-American, Zambales-reared Filipino, regaling the team's black import from Seattle and their full-blooded Filipino—yet still American—teammates with goofy renditions of American hip-hop culture.

Willie, with his shaved head and dark complexion, looked a lot more like the stereotypical image of someone who might say, "Do your thing, son." To an untrained eye, he might not even look Filipino. But it was Alaska's Fil-Ams like Jeff Cariaso, Nic Belasco, Mike Cortez, and Alvin Castro—none of whom would blend in on the set of a Jay-Z video—who spoke fluent American slang. All were part of the mash-up of ethnicities and cultural backgrounds that came together in the discussion of Filipino identity, which, curiously, was often viewed through the prism of basketball.

When Willie sensed he'd milked the English section for all its laughs, he reverted back to his natural state, blurting out rapid-fire Tagalog laced with his high-pitched English catch phrase, "Oh yeah!" and skipping across the lounge to re-join Alaska's local players.* The seating arrangements on each side of the room could not be any different. On the Fil-Am side, every player occupied a well-defined sliver of personal space. Of course, with four large guys packing themselves into a standard size couch, some contact was unavoidable. Nic had no choice but to be pressed between Jeff and Mike, who were themselves smushed against Alvin and the end of the couch, respectively. Still, it was clear

---

* Those born and raised in the Philippines, along with Fil-German Sonny Thoss, who grew up in Papua New Guinea.

that each player did his best not to touch his neighbors. They turned slightly to face each other while talking, but personal space was sacred. This code of conduct seemed normal to me. I had obeyed it hundreds of times on subway cars and in cramped vans headed to basketball games.

On the other set of couches, something very different was going on. The homegrown Filipino players were seated in one tangled, conjoined mass. Willie was in the middle of it all, with one leg splayed in front of him and the other resting on Poch Juinio's pale, fleshy thigh. On his other side, Willie was reaching behind Eddie Laure with one arm to sprinkle scraps of blue fuzz on an unwitting Dale Singson's head, and doing so meant Willie had to bury his face in the crook of Eddie's neck. Poch was leaning into Willie to create enough separation between the couch and his butt to pass gas on John Ferriols, who had already stuffed his head inside Rey Hugnatan's shirt to escape the smell. Laure, with his endless arms, was giving one-handed shoulder rubs to the players on each side of him, and Rensy Bajar had decided to rest his head in Sonny Thoss's lap.

The contrast between Philippine and American norms of male camaraderie, acted out on opposite sides of the lounge, couldn't have been more stark. To Roe and Alaska's contingent of Californians, their teammates' snuggling was excessive and borderline disturbing. Of course, they understood it was a simple cultural difference, but that couldn't change the fact that seeing their teammates draped on top of each other evoked all sorts of homoerotic discomfort. The locals, no doubt, considered themselves just as manly as their Fil-Am teammates, but their notion of machismo didn't preclude clutching a teammate's inner thigh. And so, due to cultural preferences like this, most PBA teams split into cliques depending on where their players were raised. This de facto segregation seemed divisive, but it was just natural. I always enjoyed trying to figure out which legs belonged to each player when Willie and company formed a human knot; the players also exchanged some genuinely tender moments when they weren't farting on each other, such as when Poch would massage Willie's scalp. Still, I was never eager to sit with those guys, and I wouldn't have felt comfortable when someone started caressing my shoulder. I sensed that I belonged on the anglophone side of the room.

Yet even though the Philippine- and American-raised factions separated amicably, relations between the PBA and its Fil-Ams had not always been simpatico. Over the past decade, an influx of players raised in other countries forced the league to consider what makes someone Filipino and how Filipino a player needs to be to join the Philippine Basketball Association. Competition for jobs created tension between homegrown players and their foreign-born counterparts. Largely thanks to Jeff Cariaso, Alaska dealt with that tension as well as any other team, which made the Aces' team chemistry a key advantage in their drive for a championship.

The Philippine Basketball Association possesses the unenviable duty of deciding who qualifies as Filipino and therefore is allowed to play. This sounds like a simple classification task, but history and geography have contrived to make determining Filipino identity utterly baffling. Even before the Spanish arrived and drew the Philippine archipelago's national—some might say arbitrary—borders, the country was a melting pot. Although much of the population shared some Malay heritage, rough seas, imposing mountains, and impenetrable jungles ensured that groups who settled in different areas developed distinct languages and cultures. Arab merchants arrived in the South and spread Islam. Chinese traders lived alongside the local population in major ports like Cebu and Manila. Three-hundred-plus years of Spanish colonialism were followed by American control, which gave way to a short, violent period of Japanese occupation before the Philippines finally became independent. Each foreign power left behind not just a colonial legacy, but also a sizable gene pool. By the time the PBA played its first games in 1975, the Filipino "race" was a mix of Malay, Chinese, American, Spanish, and Japanese backgrounds, among others; the country was not just a melting pot, but a blender.

Ethnic tensions had always strained relationships between different groups, especially between the darker-skinned masses of Malay background and the Caucasian and Chinese mestizo elites who controlled a disproportionate amount of the nation's wealth. In the early days of the PBA, however, ethnic rivalries were not an overriding concern. Two of the league's greatest shooters, Fortunato "Atoy" Co and Lim Eng Beng, were Chinese citizens who became naturalized Filipinos and were welcomed by the PBA. Divergent ethnic backgrounds mixed harmoniously in the seventies and eighties because players and fans alike shared a Filipino cultural heritage. Co and Lim may have looked more Chinese than their teammates, but they were both raised in the Philippines, spoke Tagalog, ate rice at almost every meal, and loved basketball for as long as they could remember.

Not counting imports, the first player raised outside of the Philippines to play as a local in the PBA was Ricardo Brown, a half-Filipino guard who starred at Pepperdine and came to the Philippines in 1983. Before Brown ever played a quarter, observers of the Philippine game worried that he could set a dangerous precedent. In *Champ* magazine, Butch Maniego warned that Brown could be "some sort of test case before a whole horde of players with similar lineage come in and take over roster spots which would have gone to our homegrown cagers." Brown's heritage was confirmed, he was naturalized, and he joined the Great Taste Coffee franchise and led the team to two Finals appearances in the 1983 season, where they lost twice to Billy Ray Bates and the Crispa Redmanizers. Brown was scrutinized and picked apart by sports writers in his first season; they expected more from the heralded American, who was chosen by the Houston Rockets in the third round of the 1979 NBA draft. Over time, however, he won them over with his low-key manner and by letting his remarkably steady play speak for itself. A squat, five-foot-nine point guard with a fullback's massive thighs and a deadly pull-up jumper, Brown won the league MVP award in 1985 and was named to five All-PBA first teams. Although a heart ailment forced him into early retirement in 1990, his career scoring average of 23.1 points per game is still the highest of any Filipino player in league history.

Over the course of Brown's seven-year career, the dreaded "horde" of Fil-Am conquerors never materialized to usurp local players' jobs. Something else, however, was developing within the Philippine national team. In 1980, Ferdinand Marcos appointed his crony Eduardo "Danding" Cojuangco to restore Philippine basketball to its perch atop the Asian hoops hierarchy.* Cojuangco formed a training pool of the country's top collegiate talents and recruited Americans Jeff Moore, Dennis Still, and Chip Engelland to practice with them, as well as an American coach, Ron Jacobs, to train the team. He planned to put the Americans on a path to Philippine citizenship in time for the 1988 Olympic Games. While Moore, Still, and Engelland waited to become naturalized, they would compete with their local teammates and share the skills they had learned at top U.S. college programs. (Engelland was a member of Mike Krzyzewski's first teams at Duke University and now works as the San Antonio Spurs' shooting coach.)

Cojuangco's experiment never got a chance to play out. As public

---

* At the time, many of the continent's finest players were Filipino, and a team of PBA stars could have challenged China's supremacy in regional tournaments. But professionals were barred from international competition back then, so the Philippines had to send college-age amateurs to play against more seasoned opposition from countries that hadn't yet formed professional leagues. The Philippines actually suffered for being ahead of its time, and it probably cost the country a few regional medals and maybe even a trip to the Olympics. Not so coincidentally, the Philippines last qualified for the Olympic basketball tournament in 1972, three years before the PBA was formed.

sentiment turned overwhelmingly against the Marcos regime and civil unrest grew throughout 1985 and 1986, the team disbanded and the program was scrapped. Although its run was brief, Cojuangco's national team left its imprint on Philippine basketball. For starters, they were the only Filipino squad to defeat an elite U.S. national team. In 1985 the team beat the United States in the championship of the William Jones Cup, an invitational tournament in Taiwan. Team USA included six-foot-eleven Joe Wolf, who became a multiyear NBA veteran mostly remembered for his mullet; Tommy Amaker, Jay Bilas, Kenny Gattison, and other NCAA standouts filled out the roster. The American team was coached by Purdue University's Gene Keady, who, with his trademark greasy comb-over and forehead blanketed by a galaxy of liver spots, seems like the perfect curmudgeon to fall victim to such an upset. The Philippines won 108-100 in overtime in a game that many middle-age Filipinos remembered as one of the happiest moments of their lives. I met a resort manager in Palawan who professed to own a poster of Samboy Lim scoring over an American defender in that game. He said the poster still hung on the wall at his mother's home in Manila. It was the dazzling, acrobatic Lim, along with sharpshooter Allan Caidic, who outplayed the American guards that night and inspired Keady to name them "Heckle and Jekyll."

In January 1986, a month before Filipinos flooded the streets in the name of People Power and drove Marcos into exile, the national team defeated China and South Korea to win the Asian Basketball Championships and qualify for the World Championship tournament. It was the team's last hurrah; to the new Philippine government, Cojuangco's squad was tainted, and Cojuangco himself fled the country for several years to avoid prosecution for his role in Marcos's regime. Lim, Caidic, and the others joined the PBA as a new generation of stars, and Philippine basketball insiders learned that recruiting foreign talent could pay large dividends, a lesson they wouldn't forget.

Heading into the 1990s, a new generation of Filipino-American basketball players were coming of age in the States, mostly in Filipino hubs like Hawaii, California, and New Jersey, but also in less typical immigrant destinations like Michigan and South Carolina. They were the children of Filipinos who arrived after the United States lifted national-origin quotas in 1965 and made it easier for Filipinos and other non-European immigrants to move to the States. These American-born Filipinos learned basketball on high school and traveling teams with bigger, stronger, more diverse competition than existed in the Philippines. A six-foot-two teenager in Manila would probably be taught to play like a forward, or in some cases a center; a Fil-Am of the same height learned guard skills and competed against big men who might be six or eight inches taller than him and just as agile. In the early nineties, the PBA and semi-pro leagues in the Philippines invited Fil-Am all-star teams of high school- and college-age players to tour the motherland and compete against local teams. The best Fil-Ams stayed behind to try their luck in the PBA.

Jeff Cariaso was one of these Fil-Am pioneers. Alaska drafted him in 1995, and, along with other U.S.-reared talents Vince Hizon, the brothers Dwight and Elmer Lago, and a handful of others, they changed the face of the league. At first the novelty of Fil-Ams made them the toast of the PBA. Cariaso was the league's rookie of the year in 1995, while Hizon, playing for fan-favorite Ginebra, parlayed his mestizo looks and three-point touch into heartthrob status. Fil-Ams brought a new style to Philippine basketball—they attacked the basket with more fury than local slashers, whose artful finger rolls and scoop shots seemed dainty by comparison. The American-raised players had a swagger that was more hip-hop and more NBA than the way Philippine-bred athletes carried themselves. Some homegrown Filipinos even tried to mimic the puckish, American attitude, like two-time MVP Danny Ildefonso, who made the "raise the roof" gesture every time he dunked.* Unfortunately, Ildefonso's celebration looked goofy and forced, like Mark Madsen's dancing during the Lakers' 2001 championship parade. For Fil-Ams, wearing headbands or pounding their chests Iverson-style didn't seem foolish; it was natural.

When word trickled back across the ocean that players like Jeff Cariaso were becoming PBA stars, other Fil-Ams planned to make the leap, although until the turn of the century there weren't much more than a dozen foreign-bred Filipinos in the PBA. That began to change in 1998, thanks to a start-up pro league that hoped to challenge the PBA's twenty-three year reign over Philippine basketball. The Metropolitan Basketball Association boasted promotional and financial backing from prominent politicians and ABS-CBN, one of the nation's two largest television networks. With ABS as the prime mover behind the league, the MBA had a built-in media apparatus that offered teams and their owners some of the country's most valuable television exposure. With the network's deep pockets and nightly audience of more than 20 million viewers, the new league was well-positioned to give the PBA a run for its money.

Still, it wouldn't matter how much clout the MBA received from its network if the league could not attract talent to rival that of the PBA. Since PBA teams had already signed the best local players, the new league courted Filipino Americans aggressively. They loosened regulations so teams could hire players whose Filipino bloodlines were hard to prove and in rare cases nonexistent. In its first season, the MBA's strange brew of Filipino journeymen and over-the-hill stars, hungry Fil-Ams out to prove themselves, and pseudo-Pinoy anomalies was a

---

* To this day Ildefonso has not stopped raising the roof, although age and injuries have conspired to make his dunks, and therefore his celebrations, less common than they were during his MVP years in 2001 and 2002.

hit. The local game was preserved but infused with American influences like fluid, ankle-breaking ballhandlers, big men with three-point range, and slashers who finished their drives by dunking over defenders.

The MBA's great innovation was to form a truly national league with teams based in different provinces. Because all the PBA's corporate-sponsored teams were based in Manila, the league never developed regional fan bases and rivalries. Sure, PBA teams would visit provincial towns from time to time, but the MBA gave real home teams to areas outside of Manila—like Cebu and Negros in the Visayas, and Davao City and Cagayan de Oro in Mindanao.* Often, MBA teams signed top players from their home province's college and commercial leagues to boost local appeal. It worked. MBA games almost always played to sell-out crowds, while the scene at the Araneta Coliseum for subpar PBA match-ups on Wednesday afternoons could resemble a ghost town.

The MBA, with its trans-Pacific talent pool and simmering local rivalries, seemed like the PBA's riveting, renegade kid brother. The young league was rough around the edges, and overall the PBA still had better players, but no one seemed to have more fun at basketball games than the fans, players, coaches, and even announcers of the MBA. Take, for example, Bill Velasco, a sports broadcaster and journalist who has covered the sport for almost three decades. Every month or so I would meet Bill at a coffee shop and pump him for hoops gossip. Bill's observations on Philippine basketball tended to come laced with the wry cynicism of a media veteran, but when we talked about his days on the MBA circuit, he launched into exuberant, hour-long soliloquies about the great league that was.

---

* This allowed teams to finally break free from the shackles of corporate sponsored names, a contribution that should not be overlooked. Filipinos had endured decades of teams like the pesticide-inspired Shell Azodrin Bugbusters, the Manhattan Shirtmakers, and the N-Rich Coffee Creamers. For once they could cheer for teams without embarrassing names, like the Laguna Lakers and Davao Eagles.

Basketball fervor was reputedly most intense in Cebu City, the country's second-largest metropolitan area and the nerve center of the Visayas region. So when the MBA gave Cebu its own team, the Gems, that passion boiled over. Bedlam ruled the Cebu Coliseum during any Gems game, but Cebuano fans were most frenzied when the Manila Metrostars or Negros Slashers came to town. For these games, the organizers knew to hire a platoon of truncheon-wielding peacekeepers to contain the riotous crowd. Facing the Metrostars, the Cebuano masses looked to exact revenge for decades of slights that stemmed from being the Philippines' second city; against Negros, they aimed to flaunt their supremacy over a less prominent Visayan island. Both rivals, however, faced the same abuse—bombardment by peso coins, water bottles, and AA batteries—and survived by hiding under massive beach umbrellas. Whenever Bill described these scenes he appeared invigorated by reliving those harrowing moments, which he survived more or less unscathed. Bill's colleague, on the other hand, a winsome courtside reporter who once found herself—her head, to be precise—on the receiving end of a flying Mono-block chair, might not view the MBA through the same rose-tinted glasses.

Traveling with the MBA also unearthed loony interprovincial superstitions and prejudices. Occasionally, the Iloilo MegaVoltz would schedule a game in Antique, a neighboring province just a few hours' drive up Panay Island's idyllic west coast. During these games, the broadcasting crew's foremost concern was to finish the game and get out of town before the *manananggal* came out. Somehow, the mountains looming over Antique's sleepy farming and fishing communities became known as the ancestral home of *manananggal*, a breed of female vampires that sprouted wings and detached from their legs to become flying torsos. The beasts would fly through the night, looking for open windows or roofs that weren't properly sealed. When a *manananggal* found a good spot, it would unfurl its long, proboscis-like tongue and lower it into a sleeping victim's bed. The tongue would pierce the skin and suck blood (organs too, sometimes) from its prey. Supposedly, the *manananggal*'s favorite meal was a fetus still inside its mother's womb. Yes, these myths sound outlandish, but many Filipinos take them seriously, not as absolute truth but as the kind of fate you didn't want to test. Even urbane Manileños like Velasco, who attended the country's top schools and enjoyed the same modern lifestyle as most Americans, reserved a corner of their belief system for these superstitions.*

These regional quirks, the violent crowds, the bitter rivalries, and the mix of local talent and Filipino-American players, gave the MBA a vitality that the PBA—playing every week in the same Manila arenas, with many of the same teams and even some of the same players from 1975—lacked. The MBA even managed to poach some of the PBA's stars, such as Vince Hizon, who signed with the Iloilo MegaVoltz in 1999 for a salary that was reportedly double that of the highest-paid PBA players. In overall status and audience, the PBA was still the dominant league, but the mere fact that the upstart association had established a fan base and stolen headlines from the older league spooked the PBA. A basketball arms race followed, with both leagues luring the other's players away with overpriced salaries and a Fil-Am hiring spree that sent scouts to stateside Filipino communities from San Francisco to Staten Island. From 1998 to 2001 the PBA drafted or hired more than twenty-five Fil-foreign players, who suddenly made up about 20 percent of the league. Butch Maniego's horde had finally arrived.

At the same time, the Asian financial crisis hit the Philippines. The peso lost half its value compared to the dollar from 1997 to 2001, and team owners in both leagues began to cut costs. In the MBA, travel

---

* Velasco's ABS crew is not alone. In 2007 the *Wall Street Journal* profiled a Metro Manila judge who was removed from the bench after he claimed to consult three mischievous elves known as *duwende* while he tried to decide cases. Their names were Armand, Angel, and Luis.

expenses sent franchises' balance sheets deeper and deeper into the red. The home-and-away schedule that made the league so popular would eventually lead to its undoing. MBA owners could no longer afford their teams, and some of them stopped paying the players' salaries.* For PBA franchises, playing to a half-full Araneta Coliseum was better for business than playing to packed houses in the provinces. Meanwhile, MBA teams were dropping like flies. Several franchises collapsed by the end of 2000, and the whole league folded in 2002. The PBA had survived the MBA's challenge. Now the league would have to learn to live with its Fil-Ams.

A few minutes before the opening whistle of an 8:00 a.m. practice, Alaska's assistant coaches stood in a circle near half-court. "There goes one more Filipino job right there," Joel Banal said to Dickie Bachmann, Jojo Lastimosa, and Bong Hawkins. According to the latest PBA gossip, Alex Compton, the American player I met my first week in Manila, who had toiled in the semipro Philippine Basketball League after the MBA folded, then retired and became an assistant coach in the PBA, was finally going to be allowed to play in the big league.

For most Philippine basketball fans, this was a feel-good story. When Compton came to the country in 1998, the MBA permitted him to play, even though he wasn't Filipino, because he was born in Manila. He charmed fans with his clutch shooting—Alex led the Manila Metrostars to a championship and won the league's MVP award in 1999—and embraced Philippine culture in a way that was almost unprecedented for a foreigner. Compton's assimilation touched Filipinos, who had tolerated years of American imports who knew little more about the country than where to find a Big Mac. Compton, on the other hand, could

---

* Vince Hizon, who bolted the PBA for MBA riches, reportedly still hasn't received all the money the Iloilo MegaVoltz promised him.

pass for a native Tagalog speaker.* During his MBA days he would drive team managers crazy by disappearing into crowded markets to mingle with working-class Filipinos as they shopped for rice and squid. Fans knew that Compton, like many Americans before him, could have gotten by without learning Tagalog; his studying the language was a gesture of respect that warmed their hearts. When the MBA collapsed, many of its players jumped to the PBA, but Compton's lack of Filipino lineage meant he couldn't play unless a team hired him as an import, and that would never happen because he was only five-foot-eleven. Yet he chose to remain in the Philippines because he considered it home. He was grandfathered into the rugged, mostly ignored PBL, and he took part-time TV gigs as a college hoops analyst and host of a men's health program. All the while, Compton sent letters to the PBA, requesting that he be permitted to compete as a local. His plea became a minor cause célèbre, with Manila sports columnists arguing that his commitment to the Philippines and mastery of the national language made him Filipino enough to play. But the PBA wouldn't budge.

By 2006, Compton had his fill of the PBL and retired, even though he probably could have played three or four more years. A few times when I was out with him, shopping for groceries or eating gyros in a mall before church, strangers approached Compton to say he deserved to play in the PBA. In the 2007 import conference, it finally happened. Because Welcoat's roster was full of PBA bric-a-brac—rookies and expendable role players bequeathed to the team in an expansion draft—the league allowed Compton, who was already the team's assistant coach, to suit up as a second import. In one stroke the league made Welcoat more competitive, granted Compton's wish, and pleased his

---

* Becoming absorbed in Asian cultures probably came naturally to Compton. His father is a development scholar specializing in the Asia Pacific region, and his mother, a linguist, translates Lao poetry. He was born in Manila in 1974 because his parents were passing through on a research trip.

thousands of fans, all while avoiding a precedent that could lead to other Philippine-born foreigners claiming a right to play in the PBA. When I heard the news, I called Alex to tell him how excited I was to finally see him play in the PBA. He called it a dream-come-true. But to Alaska's assistant coaches, it was a travesty.

"How did that even happen?" Bachmann asked, providing his own sarcastic response. "Speak Tagalog in public whenever you can."

"Pray all the time," Joel added, "say hello to the commissioner every time you see him, come out on TV." The coaches' bitter laughter made one point clear: to them, it didn't matter that Compton was a model citizen, that he could address them in their native language, that he was a leader in his church, or that the commissioner and even most Filipino fans felt he deserved this chance; to them, all that mattered was that Compton's roster spot could have gone to a real Filipino, but instead it was going to a popular and well-connected American.

This protectionist impulse was at the root of many Filipino players' objections to the influx of Fil-Am players in the early 2000s. Even though in most cases the American-born Filipinos were no more than a generation removed from the islands, many native Filipino players and fans felt that Fil-Ams didn't share their culture and didn't deserve the fame and riches they received in the PBA. Always first on their list of complaints were the Fil-foreign players' language skills. Many of the league's Fil-Ams could understand Tagalog and hold an adult conversation in the language. But it often seemed that they only spoke Tagalog when absolutely necessary, like when telling their drivers where to pull over or asking their kids' nannies when the children left for school. Even more importantly, the homegrown Pinoys felt that Fil-Ams didn't share and couldn't comprehend the local devotion to basketball. Sure, they also grew up playing the game. But did Fil-Ams build their own baskets out of twisted clothes hangers and rummaged two-by-fours? Did they play in bare feet or flip-flops until they were thirteen? Did they worship Atoy Co, Ramon Fernandez, and Alvin Patrimonio as kids, or

The author dribbles a ball while kids watch at the Cagsawa Ruins in Albay Province.

A basketball-inspired multicab (a cousin of the jeepney) in Surigao City, Mindanao.

Roe drives past Talk 'N Text import James "J.J." Sullinger.

Photo courtesy of Joaqui Trillo, Alaska Aces

Photo copyright 2007 Patrick Michels

Photo courtesy of Rafe Bartholomew

Coach Tim Cone discussing strategy with his staff.

PBA officials measure an import's height in the mid-Nineties.

Center Sonny Thoss
takes a break.

A trio of smitten fans watch the Aces work out.

Guards Jeffrey Cariaso and Mike Cortez on the sidelines.

Willie Miller, laughing as always.

"Mang" Tomas Urbano, a PBA lifer and Alaska's longtime stat-keeper and in-house referee.

A homemade hoop in Puerto Princesa, Palawan.

A dirt court in Guimaras.

A rim and a jeepney, two staples of Philippine life, in the mountain town of Santol, La Union.

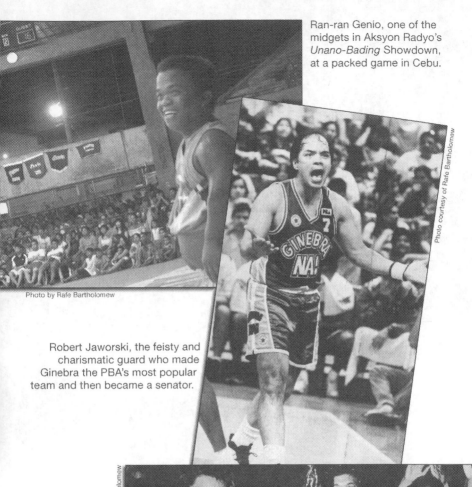

Ran-ran Genio, one of the midgets in Aksyon Radyo's *Unano-Bading* Showdown, at a packed game in Cebu.

Photo by Rafe Bartholomew

Photo courtesy of Rafe Bartholomew

Robert Jaworski, the feisty and charismatic guard who made Ginebra the PBA's most popular team and then became a senator.

Photo courtesy of Rafe Bartholomew

The Crispa Red-manizers gathered around one of the many champion-ship trophies the team collected in the PBA's first decade.

A glimpse of the PBA's high-scoring, low-tech beginnings in the 1970s.

Mike Cortez looks for the pass on a fast break.

Tim Cone argues a call in the Finals.

Willie Miller gets a step ahead of Macmac Cardona.

Tim Cone gets hoisted by Roe,
Nic Belasco, and Rensy Bajar
after Alaska wins game seven of
the PBA Finals.

Willie and Roe hold the championship trophy.

were their idols Hakeem Olajuwon, Scottie Pippen, and Karl Malone? With no more than 150 active PBA players and a nation of 90 million people who revered the sport, Philippine hoops nationalists believed the roster spots should belong to players who had devoted their entire lives to the dream of playing in the PBA, not to guys from California who never considered playing in Manila until an agent convinced them they could make a lot of money overseas.

Chris Guidotti, a former team manager in the MBA who supported Compton's drive to join the PBA, summed up this attitude for me: "Some Fil-Ams are not even interested to learn the language. They just want to take Filipinos' money and bring it to the States. Alex doesn't have any Filipino blood, but he's more Filipino than all these Fil-Ams in the PBA." Guidotti's take was harsh, but it accurately reflected the animosity many people felt toward Fil-Ams. Like many other prejudices, this bias was based in some fact and a lot of misunderstanding. When Filipino Americans entered the PBA en masse during the MBA years, the basketball community began to notice the differences between players who were raised in the Philippines and those who grew up in other countries.

Fil-Ams lacked the common touch that local players had cultivated for decades. Every PBA team had a corps of die-hard fans who attended every one of their teams' games, waving glittery, personalized banners embroidered with the players' names and screaming maniacally in support of their chosen franchise. These groups of fans were like off-the-books cheerleaders; they received blocks of free tickets from team management and players, and many enthusiasts even received cash per diems to cover travel expenses and meals. These fans tended to be the misfits of Philippine society—raggedy teenagers badly in need of dental work; crutch-wielding midgets; and poor souls bearing limps and gimp limbs as reminders that the Philippines wasn't polio-free until 2000. The leaders of these motley crews tended to be flamboyant gay cross-dressers. The drag queens were called *bakla* in Tagalog, and they made up a meaty cross section of the PBA's most avid devotees. In a crowded mall or some other nexus of the Philippine mainstream, the *bakla* might be pariahs, but they somehow carved out a niche in the world of professional basketball. At PBA games they led the entire crowd in chants for their teams, and the drag queen fans had a knack for stealing the show during timeouts with racy stripteases. Most of all, the players accepted these fans and even developed genuine friendships with them.

On days when Alaska played the later game of a PBA double bill, the players and coaches would arrive early, usually in time to watch the beginning of the first match before heading to the locker rooms to stretch and change. During this downtime, the locals worked the crowd with the calm assuredness and affable demeanor of natural politicians. Poch Juinio would sit with his arm around Hector, a gay fan whose rendition of the "Go Alaska! Fight! Fight! Fight!" chant was a raspy, effeminate warble capable of cutting through thousands of roaring fans. Bong Hawkins would join two elderly, partially toothless women and gab about everything from his mid-nineties glory days to the pre-renovation Araneta Coliseum and the stench of its old locker rooms, which the PBA shared with cockfight breeders. Willie Miller would stand in the aisle, uncorking various combinations of smiling, cross-eyed, tongue-wagging facial expressions for a self-replenishing line of kids and female fans waiting for a hug and a photograph.

For Poch, Willie, and Bong, these fans were as much a part of Philippine basketball as bounce passes and the pick-and-roll. Many of the fans had been following the homegrown players since their college careers. They had been sharing pre- and postgame chats with each other for years. Likewise, Filipino fans had come to expect this level of intimacy in their relationships with pro athletes. Two of the PBA's greatest and most beloved players, Robert Jaworski and Alvin Patrimonio, were legendary not just for their hardwood heroics, but also for their endurance when it came to pleasing their fans. Stories abound of the two players mingling for hours after practice and games, refusing to go home until they had honored every request.

Alaska's Filipino-Americans, on the other hand, didn't have years of interactions to develop bonds with the fans, nor did they grow up in a culture where rubbing elbows with transgender cheer squads was the norm. They honed their hoops instincts in the United States, where common spectators enjoyed no access whatsoever to NBA stars, and where professional athletes rarely connected with the American underclass except in stage-managed publicity events. Even then, NBA players were more likely to be donating their time to underprivileged or sick children, not to the plethora of misfits who dominated the PBA die-hard ranks. Indeed, many of these marginal characters, with their ill-fitting sequined tube tops and haggard, wan faces, looked like they came to games straight from a casting call for third world indigence. When most Fil-Ams signed their PBA contracts, they were newcomers to Philippine basketball; they didn't possess the lifetime of experiences and ingrained attitudes that allowed local players to mesh naturally with common fans, so they struggled to live up to the image of a PBA star.

The American-raised players were never rude or cruel to the Alaska supporters; they were courteous but not warm. When Mike Cortez or Nic Belasco walked through the stands on the way to or from the locker room, they might slap some outstretched hands, but they rarely lingered with fans. Jeff Cariaso made an effort to give his devotees the attention they craved by smiling and making small talk, but even a twelve-year PBA veteran like Jeff didn't feel comfortable around the den mother drag queens. It was hard to blame a guy who was raised in the States for being wary when packs of emaciated cross-dressers with blush bull's-eyes painted on their cheeks beckoned with calls of, "Daddy, come here! Come talk to us!" Or for acting annoyed when semibelligerent fans grabbed their shoulders and squeezed like they wanted to take a piece home with them. But even though Fil-foreigners might have had legitimate reasons to feel reluctant about getting up close and personal with local hoops addicts, their public image suffered for it. As fans observed similar standoffish behavior in Fil-Ams around the league, the public reached their own conclusion: Filipino Americans were snobbish. They were *mayabang*.

There's that word again. *Mayabang*. The same label of arrogance that could prematurely end an import's season had dogged Fil-Ams since they entered the league. Velasco, the broadcaster, explained the chasm between Fil-Am players and PBA followers: "The Fil-Ams didn't behave like Filipinos, and that alienated the fans. The general attitude when the Fil-Ams came over was that, 'This is a job, I'm getting paid well for it and anything beyond what I do on the basketball court is none of your business.'" No one told them that there was another part of the job, a social contract of touchy-feely bonhomie between fans and players.

I wasn't sure how to feel about the antipathy toward Fil-Am players. For obvious reasons, I found it easy to relate to Alaska's Fil-Ams. I really liked those guys—we could riff for hours on everything from hoops and rap music to *The Fresh Prince of Bel-Air* and goofy Steven Seagal movies. Even though I was becoming conversant in Tagalog, I couldn't hold as rich a conversation with Willie in his native language as I could with Jeff in his. Often, I felt Fil-Ams were blamed unfairly for cultural differences that were beyond their control. I too felt nervous when I sat behind the basket surrounded by giggling drag queens who wouldn't stop asking me to take them home with me. I just had to ignore the alarm bells ringing in my head and remind myself that they only meant to share a harmless laugh.*

---

* These *bakla* fans also managed to score a prominent role in one of Roe's favorite PBA memories. A few years back, when Roe was playing for the Coca-Cola Tigers, he kept hearing someone call his name during warm-ups. "Ell-ees! Ell-ees!" He remembered, "Just by the way he was saying my name, I knew something was funny. I knew better than to look, but I'm laying the ball up and he's right under the basket. So as I come down, I just happen to look. Gay dude, just had breast implants, whipped them out and showed me. I knew right then, I done seen it all."

At the same time, however, I couldn't help but observe something wonderful in the warmth and closeness between Filipino fans and homegrown players, and that spark was absent in their wooden interactions with Fil-Am players. The opportunity for hoops junkies to interact with pro ballers who were genuinely happy to pal around with them was rare and perhaps unique to Philippine culture. In the States, fans could only admire NBA stars in the abstract, through highlight reels and Twitter feeds and occasionally humorous television commercials. Through no fault of their own, it seemed like Fil-Am players had undermined one of the PBA's most elemental characteristics—the athlete-fan relationship—and I hoped that eventually more American-raised players would make the extra effort to preserve that bond.

PBA fans had good reason to suspect that Fil-Am players who didn't walk or talk like Filipinos might actually be impostors. At the peak of the PBA-MBA rivalry, a few opportunistic scouts and franchises saw how eager the PBA was to hoard Fil-Am talent and recruited American players with no Filipino blood, fabricated their local family trees, and helped them forge documents that confirmed their right to play as Philippine citizens. Thus, Fil-shams were born.

The first Fil-sham was Sonny Alvarado, the number one pick in the 1999 PBA draft who became a dominant six-foot-seven forward for the Tanduay Rhum franchise until the league discovered his false papers had been shepherded through the verification process by a PBA office worker. Alvarado, it turned out, was Puerto Rican. How could someone with no Filipino or even Asian heritage fly to Manila and masquerade as an authentic Pinoy? Fairly easily. Friends sometimes joked with me that Filipinos could pass for any race on the planet. Just look at the Alaska organization: rookie forward Christian Luanzon was Chinese; Willie Miller, half black; assistant coach Dickie Bachmann was part German; even team owner Fred Uytengsu had mixed Chinese and

American blood and the boyish good looks of a pre-Parkinson's Michael J. Fox. All of them were Philippine citizens. With this much diversity in just one PBA franchise and many thousands more mixed-heritage Filipinos throughout the country, it wasn't hard to see how Alvarado could impersonate a Filipino, especially with prominent backers ready to grease the palms of any officials who sniffed a hoax.

In 2000, midway through his second season, Alvarado was deported and the PBA tried to play his case off as an isolated incident. Meanwhile, however, two other rumored Fil-shams hailing from parts obscured—Purefoods' Al Segova and the Santa Lucia Realtors' Rob Parker—left the country and were never heard from again. The departures of Alvarado, Segova, and Parker marked the beginning of the Fil-sham debacle. Obtaining counterfeit documents in Manila was as easy as riding a jeepney to Claro M. Recto Avenue. This sprawling east-west thoroughfare was home to the country's largest facsimile flea market, where dozens of open-air stalls sold fake diplomas, marriage and birth certificates, and even medical licenses that were nearly indistinguishable from genuine documents. For PBA fans, it was easy to imagine how teams and agents could have phony documents made to prove Fil-shams' Filipino heritage, then secure their official clearance from government agencies with well-placed bribes.

For Fil-foreigners to play in the PBA, they had to meet the criteria for Philippine citizenship. They had to be at least half Filipino by blood, and one of their Filipino parents had to have been a Philippine citizen at the time of their birth. This meant that Fil-Ams born in the United States to parents who had already become naturalized American citizens were technically not eligible to play in the PBA. Before Fil-Am prospects could be drafted or hired as free agents, they had to gain clearance from the Bureau of Immigration, then have that endorsement reviewed and affirmed by the Department of Justice. Both agencies were supposed to base their decisions on a dossier of evidence that documented the players' Filipino background and their parents' citizenship—passports, birth and marriage certificates, immigration and naturalization records, sworn affidavits from parents and extended family members. The MBA, on the other hand, didn't impose such strict rules on its franchises. As challenger to the PBA's throne, the upstart league allowed exceptions—Alex Compton* among them—for novel and marketable players with more tenuous connections to the motherland. The MBA received an initial ratings boost from these players, but hiring them ended up being like inviting vampires into the house of Philippine basketball; once they were in, there was no way to get them out. By the time the MBA folded, the league's Fil-foreign stars were already rooted in Philippine society, and several found their way onto PBA rosters where their dubious Filipino pedigrees were set to collide with the league's eligibility rules.

The suspicion that many Filipino-American players who entered the league between 1998 and 2002 couldn't prove their heritage, along with the cultural differences that divided locker rooms, led Alaska's Jojo Lastimosa and Purefoods' four-time MVP Alvin Patrimonio to draft a "manifesto" on behalf of Philippine-born players in 2002. The statement protested the special treatment Fil-Ams received from teams and called for an investigation of their claims to Philippine provenance. In those years, many Fil-foreign players who were hired directly from

---

* Even Compton once found himself on the verge of becoming a Fil-sham. The first team to recruit him out of Cornell was a PBA franchise, and negotiations went so far that Compton was twice told to pack his bags and head to the airport, where tickets to Manila would be waiting for him. Both times, the tickets weren't there. When Compton, upset and confused, called his then-agent for an explanation, the agent explained that the paperwork had hit a snag: He couldn't play in the PBA because he had no Filipino blood. No worries, he told Compton. It would just take a few extra weeks to prepare documents that made it look like his biological mother was a Filipina who died when he was young, and that his actual mother was his stepmother. Compton refused to go along with the hoax and thought his dream of playing overseas was dead, until the MBA offered the born-in-Manila exception.

other countries received the kind of perk-laden contracts usually reserved for imports, including high-rise condominium units and chauffeured cars paid for by the teams. To Jojo and other provincial stars who came to Manila to play professional ball, this seemed unfair; teams never offered that level of assistance to athletes from Cebu or Davao, even though, just like Fil-Ams, players from other regions might find Manila overwhelming. Jojo and company drove themselves to practice. Why couldn't the American newcomers do the same? The possibility—no, likelihood—that there were more Fil-shams among recent signees rallied support from local players, who were incensed by the notion of impostors robbing Filipinos of their livelihood. Almost a hundred players, about two-thirds of the PBA, signed the petition, which Jojo and Patrimonio forwarded to the Philippine Senate.

For legislators seated on the Committee on Games, Amusement, and Sports, the Fil-sham issue was political paydirt. Basketball had been an essential element of Philippine identity for decades, and now a foreign blight had infiltrated the beloved pastime. Between November 2002 and May 2003 the committee held seven hearings to investigate the controversy. It gave politicians a chance to wear their nationalist hats, wave the Philippine flag, and save the PBA from Fil-Ams, Fil-shams, Uncle Sam, and any other foreign entities who might be stealing not just food from the mouths of Filipino players' families, but highjacking the hoop dreams of every Filipino boy practicing spin moves in his flip-flops and praying to make it to the PBA. Oh, and by the way, the Fil-sham scandal also guaranteed top-notch TV exposure for the participating senators, whose hearings would be broadcast live and re-capped on nightly news broadcasts. Let the posturing begin.

The Senate investigated citizenship claims of several Fil-foreign players, but throughout the hearings it was clear that the prize buck, the player they wanted to snare most, was Asi Taulava, a six-foot-nine

Fil-Tongan (or possibly just Tongan) and the league's preeminent big man. Taulava had already been deported in 2000 for failing to prove his Philippine citizenship, but just months after his exile immigration officials allowed him to reenter the country on a temporary visa so he could be reunited with his Filipina fiancée and children. Once he was back, Taulava's lawyers, with support from his team, Talk 'N Text, filed additional documents and affidavits to support his claim of Philippine heritage. Through these machinations, immigration officials were made to see the light; they certified Taulava's citizenship and he returned to the PBA. Now, Senator Robert Barbers and his committee seemed determined to reverse the ruling and expose Taulava once and for all.

Chairman Barbers, who died three years after the hearings, sent Senate staffers to Northern Samar, the province where Taulava traced his roots. Samar island, somewhat remote, very poor, and reputed to have the Philippines' most decrepit roads,* was precisely the kind of place where someone trying to fake his Filipino background would base his imagined ancestry, because who would bother going there to check the facts? Senator John Henry Osmeña, sounding a little flustered, expressed that exact sentiment in the first hearing: "Some of these players are claiming to have their mothers coming from faraway places like Samar and Kabankalan and God knows where." But the staffers managed to find these places—in Taulava's case, San Jose, Northern Samar, where his Filipina mother Pauline Hernandez Mateaki was supposedly born. The investigators couldn't find a soul in San Jose who recalled Hernandez Mateaki or any member of Taulava's extended family, which was very strange for a small community like San Jose where everyone knew each other. The most damning evidence against Taulava, however, was a con-

---

* If true, this would be quite an honor. I never made it to Samar—the closest I got was neighboring Leyte—but judging by some of the rough roads I traveled on, the country's worst roads might be able to shred the tires of a truck after a quarter mile and turn entire vehicles into slow-rolling fireballs somewhere around the first mile marker.

fession from San Jose's civil registrar, who testified that he added Taula-va's mother to the municipal register in 1998, after the town mayor set up a meeting between the registrar and Don Raymundo "Boy" Daza, the local congressman's brother. Daza asked the registrar to add Hernandez Mateaki's birth to the record as a personal favor, and it was done. During the registrar's testimony, Senator Barbers asked if he knew his actions were illegal, and why he would help falsify the records. The registrar's response, in Tagalog, was "Who could possibly refuse that man?"

Senate investigators crisscrossed the archipelago to visit the ancestral homes of suspected Fil-shams and in several cases found similar discrepancies between the players' claims and the facts on the ground. There was never a reliable record that the players' relatives had been born or actually lived there. Still, I found it hard to accept the committee's findings as definitive proof. This was, after all, a country where records were regularly lost to floods and natural disasters, where even the card catalogs in some of the nation's top university libraries were incomplete. Was it really unthinkable that the baptismal records from a *barangay* in Northern Samar or La Union might be missing a few names? Nevertheless, the committee's final report called for the deportation of Taulava and four other players and recommended continued scrutiny of three more suspected Fil-shams.

The transcripts of the hearings possess a vaudevillian absurdity, thanks to a rotating cast of PBA representatives and government paper-pushers whose testimony resembled a rendition of Who's on First. When managers of individual PBA franchises faced the senate panel, each of them denied knowledge of the process by which Fil-Ams gained clearance to play in the league. Despite the fact that team representatives scouted and recruited overseas talent, the managers claimed their organizations had hardly any involvement with Fil-Am players before the Bureau of Immigration cleared the athletes and they entered the PBA draft. It was as if the senators asked, "Which way did they go?" and the teams answered, "Thataway" while pointing in all directions to an alphabet soup of government agencies—the Bureau of Immigration (BI), the Department of Foreign Affairs (DFA), the Department of Justice (DoJ), the Commission on Immigration and Deportation (CID). Employees of these offices appeared before the panel, and the senators repeatedly asked why Fil-shams' papers had been approved when a thorough review of the facts would have revealed falsehoods. Time and again the witnesses would point the finger at another government body. That office would then send another bureaucrat to testify that yet another agency was responsible for investigating Fil-Ams' citizenship applications, and the same pointless charade would begin with new characters. No one from any of the government offices that examined the paperwork seemed to understand their role in the process aside from collecting processing fees, gathering documents, and rubber-stamping them.

The senators seemed equally dimwitted at times. Robert Jaworski, who left his PBA coaching job in 1998 when he was elected to the Senate, delivered a smirk-filled reminder that this issue was important to him because he never officially retired as a player. Never mind that he was in his mid-fifties. Senator Osmeña, while questioning Coca-Cola human resources director Jesse Macias, seemed unable to grasp the concept that a Filipino American could mean someone born in the United States to Filipino immigrant parents.

MACIAS: We have four Fil-foreign players. William Antonio, Jeffrey Cariaso, Rudy Hatfield, and Rafi Reavis.

OSMEÑA: Why do you call Jeffrey a Fil-Am? Jeffrey, I think—both parents are Filipinos. In fact, they're from South San Francisco. So, why are you leveling him as a Fil-Am?

One of the richest ironies embedded in these hearings to protect the mythical indigenous Filipino basketball player was that Barbers, Osmeña, and Jaworski all had Caucasian parents or grandparents. But it was Barbers, grandson of an Italian-American soldier who settled in the Philippines, who treated the hearings like a Fil-Am witch hunt. He was their most bellicose interrogator and a champion of so-called pure Filipino talent. Still, it was hard not to detect a whiff of posturing in his aggressive manner, because of his mixed blood and also because Barbers had owned an MBA franchise, the Surigao Miners. The Miners were known for hiring only local players, but could Barbers really be unaware of his league's role in opening the door to Fil-Ams? Whether Barbers was shameless or just oblivious, he lambasted the Fil-Ams, in this case, Andy Seigle, a six-foot-ten forward from Scranton, Pennsylvania.

BARBERS: Of course, your mother has told you her origins as to what part of Eastern Samar she comes from. Could you not recall where in Eastern Samar?

SEIGLE: I can recall, sir. I know I've been there before because my grandfather was really sick and I brought him here to Manila. I'm just unaware of the name where they are from.

BARBERS: How many times have you been in Eastern Samar?

SEIGLE: I've been there once.

BARBERS: And you know your relatives there, of course.

SEIGLE: Most of them are in Santa Ana. There's two more in Mariveles, Bataan.

BARBERS: Can you tell us the names and addresses of these relatives of your mother?

SEIGLE: I can tell you their names. I can tell you what city they are in, but I don't know the exact addresses. There's my aunt Preciosa and Terry; they are both there in Santa Ana.

BARBERS: Slowly, so we can take note of the first name and the family name and the address.

SEIGLE: Just my aunt Preciosa. I don't know the last name.

BARBERS: It's beyond comprehension for a Fil-Am to not even know his own relatives, especially if your mother is a native of this country. So you must, at least, know these people if you do not know your relatives in Eastern Samar. You forgot about the name of the place where your mother comes from. At least your own relatives in Manila, as you mentioned, you should know their address and their names.

SEIGLE: Well, my uncle's name is Ricardo Yadao and he lives in Mariveles, Bataan.

BARBERS: Where? In Mariveles, Bataan?

SEIGLE: Yes.

BARBERS: No particular address, no specific address?

SEIGLE: On a mountain.

BARBERS: On a mountain?

SEIGLE: That's where he lives.

BARBERS: So we have to use a chopper in going there?

Of course, the players didn't do themselves any favors by being unprepared to answer the senators' questions. In a country where close family ties were very much the norm, Seigle couldn't have looked more alien than when he testified he didn't know his relatives' last names and admitted he had only visited them once or twice after living in the country for years. Yet Seigle and other Fil-Ams were anything but alone in their gaffe-prone ways. When Jojo Lastimosa testified, one senator asked about his petition on behalf of native-born Filipino players, and Jojo answered, "I just want to clarify, your honor, because we did not really read the whole manifesto."

The shortcomings of the PBA's citizenship model of integrating Fil-Ams were revealed throughout the hearings. None of the senators, lawyers, players, agents, or bureaucrats involved seemed to understand the legal process for certifying Fil-foreign athletes. In many cases the players' backgrounds didn't fall neatly inside or outside of the league's definition of a Fil-Am, but somewhere in between. The hearings showed how muddled the question of Philippine identity could be. "It becomes interesting now," was all Barbers could say when he questioned Fil-Am Rob Wainwright and learned that his mother's family migrated to Hawaii before it became the fiftieth state. This meant she became an American citizen when Hawaii gained statehood in 1959, but she never renounced her Philippine citizenship. Had she been grandfathered into dual citizenship? If so, then Wainwright was a Fil-Am. If not, he was a

Fil-sham. And Wainwright's case seemed simple compared to Andy Seigle's. Back in 1998, a year after Seigle joined the PBA, he was selected to play for the national team in the Asian Games, but he wasn't eligible because he never obtained a Philippine passport. Time was short, so the PBA pulled some strings and set up a meeting with President Joseph "Erap" Estrada, the former action movie star who in 2001 was chased out of office for various acts of plunder and corruption. By presidential order, Seigle was given a passport, but at the Fil-sham hearings, officers from the Department of Foreign Affairs, which issued the document, weren't certain that Estrada's decree had been legal. In another farcical twist to Seigle's case, his younger brother, Danny, was widely accepted as a legit Fil-Am. Andy, however, was born in 1972, a year before the Philippine constitution was rewritten to include the modern definition of Fil-foreign citizenship. Instead, Andy was born under the 1935 constitution that required children born to Filipino parents outside of the country to elect citizenship by their eighteenth birthday. Andy had waited until he was twenty-six, which, in the committee's opinion, made him a Fil-sham.

If all this sounds hopelessly convoluted, it is. The questions surrounding Rob Wainwright and Andy Seigle's right to play in the PBA were the stuff of Supreme Court cases, not legislative publicity stunts. In fact, I got the feeling that the Philippine bureaucracy was purposely mind-numbing. That way, it would drive most people who encountered its Babel-like labyrinth of paperwork to pay fixers to grease the wheels of government. That's what I did. The first time I extended my visa at Manila's Bureau of Immigration,* I wandered up a side staircase and saw the room where foreign passports got processed, a cavernous hall filled with rows of desks and electric typewriters. Workers in blue uni-

---

* Actually, the second time. The first time I was turned away for trying to enter a government building while wearing shorts, or "shortpants," as the blockhead guard who sent me home called them.

form shirts were slumped over, sleeping with their faces mashed in their keyboards, while others draped washcloths over their faces and snoozed on benches lining the walls. The sight didn't leave me brimming with confidence when I headed downstairs to submit my visa application. A wall-size flow chart that resembled the blueprint for a nuclear power plant hung in the entrance; it showed the path my documents would take—a small-scale Bataan Death March through a jungle of government offices—once I paid my fees. That's when I felt a tap on the back. One of the blueshirts, Bobby, was standing behind me. He explained that he could guide my papers through the thicket in an hour. It would only cost me an extra twenty dollars. Was I interested? Hell yes! But Bobby didn't just take care of my visa that one occasion; he became my *suki*, the Tagalog word for a regular vendor. Bobby, it turned out, passed my neighborhood every day on his way to work, so every two months when I needed to extend my visa, I called him. I was filled with low-grade dread the first time I met Bobby in the back of a local McDonald's and slipped him an envelope stuffed with my passport and a wad of cash—but it sure beat dealing with the chaotic and nonresponsive government.

This was probably the same attitude PBA teams adopted when they sought government clearance for Fil-Ams they wanted to hire. Paying a fixer wasn't the underhanded way to get things done; it was the reasonable and efficient way. The citizenship papers of genuine Fil-foreign players might contain the same irregularities as Fil-shams like Alvarado, but that wouldn't mean they were also bogus Filipinos. The more the Senate committee pulled the threads of the Fil-sham scandal, the more it unraveled and revealed that the core disgrace didn't belong to a few con-artist players but to a system that encouraged bending the rules. In the end, the Senate hearings resolved very little. Two players were deported, while Taulava and the others fought their deportation orders in court and won, partly because their bosses owned some of the Philippines' most powerful corporations, but also because the cases against them were weak. They went on to lengthy, productive, and lucrative PBA careers, and three players once labeled Fil-shams by the Senate played for the Philippine National Team in 2007.

After an Alaska practice one morning, I got a closer look at the lifestyles of some of the local players. An upcoming game would be played at the Ynares Center, an arena that looked down on Manila from the hills of Antipolo in neighboring Rizal province. Cone scheduled a few workouts there so the players could develop a feel for the gym's dimensions. Antipolo, about an hour's drive from Quezon City, was home to a familiar Philippine blend of vacation homes for wealthy Manileños and absolute squalor. The Ynares Center, named for the province's ruling clan,* was Antipolo's Taj Mahal—a glittering white temple of basketball that dwarfed its humble surroundings. I figured out the jeepney routes between my neighborhood and Antipolo and used them to zip back and forth from practice without much hassle. When I left practice that day, I walked a few blocks from the arena and waited on the curb for the next jeepney. The sky was gray and threatening rain, but it would be a few hours before thunderheads formed, and until then the overcast breeze was a welcome respite from Manila's pounding heat.

Not more than a minute after I sat down, a white pickup truck stopped in front of me. The window rolled down and Aaron Aban, Alaska's rookie shooting guard, peered out at me with a perturbed squint. "Paeng! Why are you in the street? Who will fetch you? Do you need a ride?" The back door swung open and there was Dale Singson, Alaska's backup point guard, laughing uncontrollably at the thought of me riding home in a jeepney.

"Where do you stay?" Dale asked. I told him Katipunan. "You take

---

* Since 1992 there have been three governors of Rizal: Casimiro Martin Ynares Jr.; then his wife, Rebecca; then Casimiro again; and now their son, Jun Ynares.

the jeepney and train everywhere?" He too was incredulous. Aaron and Dale had some distant notion that Americans, with their untold riches, all rode around in chauffeured SUVs, which wasn't far from the truth for embassy types and corporate consultants flown in to work for local businesses. I, on the other hand, was trying to stretch a stipend meant to cover one year of living expenses into three. "Not even taxi?" Dale said. I could have afforded Philippine taxis, which can drive for hours and cost less than twenty dollars, but my New York upbringing had hard-wired in me a love for public transportation and a principled objection to wasting money on cabs. "Expensive!" I explained. Dale and Aaron nodded.

Dale was a journeyman. He'd played a season or two for a handful of teams but never caught on as a full-time starter. Alaska signed him when starting point guard Mike Cortez went out with a knee injury during t he previous conference. In practice, it was easy to see why Dale's career had sputtered, but also why teams kept giving him chances. He was all guile on the court. Dale reminded me of a junk-ball pitcher in baseball. He had an array of bizarre, unteachable moves—running hook shots, finger rolls released from the free throw line, some kind of shovel shot that he'd set up with head fakes and then release from his hip while the defender was frozen. But he was erratic. When Dale's bag of tricks worked, he was enchanting. But other days, when the shovel shot was ricocheting off the backboard and the running hooks were sailing clear over the rim, he was useless.

Aaron was a different kind of player. He was a genetic wonder, a six-foot-one bundle of fast-twitch muscle fibers that made him faster, stronger, and more explosive than practically everyone on the team except Roe. I wondered, however, if Aaron's athletic gifts stunted his growth as a basketball player. In the amateurs he probably just overpowered defenders, but against pro caliber players who could keep up with him, Aaron seemed lost. He hadn't yet learned how to use his natural advantages to set up scoring opportunities. Instead, he would use them to shoot hopeless fadeaway three-pointers. Aaron wowed teammates in practice with powerful dunks and soaring rebounds in traffic. *"Hayop!"* they'd say. "Animal!" But it was beginning to look like he might never impress them in a real game.

Maybe it was because Dale and Aaron recognized they were opposite halves of a near perfect player; maybe it was because they shared Cebuano as a mother tongue; or maybe it was because they warmed adjacent spots on Alaska's bench—whatever the reason, the two grew close. The day they scooped me off the corner in Antipolo, they were carpooling to save gas money. For the second- and third-stringers, this level of thrift was necessary, because unlike Willie, Jeff, and Sonny Thoss, they couldn't count on staying in the league for years and earning piles of pesos every month. Inside the pickup, the overriding concern was not playing time or the upcoming game against the Air 21 Express, but where to eat lunch. It didn't seem to matter that all three of us were tearing apart KFC meals the ball boys handed out after practice; the lead-battered chicken thighs with gravy and a lump of rice were just *meryenda*, a mid-morning snack. Dale and Aaron spoke for a few minutes in Cebuano; I had been in the country more than a year by now, and was at the point where I could follow Tagalog conversations. I knew enough to tell the difference between the language I was studying and Dale and Aaron's utterly confounding (to me) polysyllabic prattle.

After a few minutes I felt Dale tapping my shoulder. He'd tilted his head forward and was looking at me with a lecherous, open-mouthed smile. "Paeng, you eat *fek-fek*?" Dale, in his early thirties, was the only Alaska player who still had braces. The guffaw lurking beneath his glinting, metal-mouthed smirk made him seem like a mischievous teenager, so I paused for a beat to decode his question. A moment later it clicked. I snapped back in my seat, and Dale, seeing the recognition in my face, was giggling and hooting before I could speak. If he had said *pek-pek* from the beginning I wouldn't have needed any extra time to think about it. *Pek-pek* means "pussy" in Tagalog. The same linguistic quirk that led so many Filipinos to wonder what kind of parents had been twisted enough to name me "Rape" had possessed Dale. He was mixing F's and P's.

We had already turned onto Ortigas Avenue, the wide thoroughfare that would take us back to the heart of Metro Manila, and we were feeling hungry. "Uy! *Lugaw!*" Aaron jerked his head in the direction of a tent across the street with a tarpaulin banner promising LUGAW—GOTO—MAMI. Once we pulled over and got out of the pickup, Dale scanned the avenue for a crosswalk. There was none, so we waded into the street, three human froggers looking at four westbound lanes, a concrete divider, and four more lanes heading back to Antipolo. Dodging traffic was a fact of pedestrian life in Manila. I had already maneuvered through dozens of these thoroughfares, but it always felt dangerous.

Crossing Ortigas along with two PBA players, even bench players like Dale and Aaron, was like having a force field. Normally, approaching jeepneys would accelerate to scare any pedestrians who might be considering a dash to the other side. But when the drivers saw Dale and Aaron, they stopped. Arms shot out the window slats of jeepneys, and Dale and Aaron walked through the column of vehicles to slap hands with the passengers. "Dale! *Saan kayo pupunta?*" Where are you guys going? One woman jumped out of a van to hug Dale, then had her husband snap a quick picture of her with the players. Even though the cars made it easy for us to pass, I still almost killed myself when I reached the divider. Dale and Aaron had already vaulted over it and sprinted to safety. I stepped up on the four-foot concrete barrier and realized that if I jumped down to the other side I would land on the hood of an approaching Honda Civic. I would have to wait for a better moment to cross. I stepped back down, close enough to a passing jeepney that I could feel the cackling driver's breath on my neck as he swerved to avoid me. At the next chance I jumped the divider and jogged to the far side, where Dale and Aaron shook their heads at me and headed into the restaurant.

The premises were just some plastic tables and stools under a corrugated iron roof. Sitting on each table were bottles of soy sauce and vinegar, calamansi limes, and skinny two-inch chili peppers. Two matronly cooks wearing grayish smocks stirred black cauldrons of bubbling porridge. Each bowl would cost between a dime and fifty cents, depending on add-ons like hard-boiled eggs, chicken thighs, and beef tripe. The tables were filled with construction workers and garbage pickers whom the Metro Manila Development Authority had hired to sweep trash from the street. For some of them this might be their only full meal of the day, and the heavy *lugaw* seemed engineered to stave off hunger for the longest possible period of time.

Dale and Aaron ordered *lugaw* with egg, extra bowls of *mami*, a beef broth noodle soup cribbed from the Chinese, and the ultimate luxury, *sisig*, a tossed salad of chopped pork jowls and ears, onions, and chilis that was served in a sizzling lake of margarine. Dale and Aaron tore into the crunchy and gelatinous *sisig.* They came to eat and didn't spend a lot of time preening for the laborers, many of whom happened to be PBA fans. They signed a couple of autographs, smiled for a few snapshots with porridge-glazed lips. But the pace of the other diners' meals slowed down noticeably once we sat down. They watched the players, men who probably hailed from the same provinces as some of them, consume a quintessentially Philippine feast. It was the kind of moment that Fil-Ams might never share with lower class Filipinos, because many American-born players wouldn't be caught dead risking typhoid and hepatitis and God knows what else by eating *lugaw* and *sisig* off the street. Instead, they ate at places like Chili's, where the only interactions they'd have with common fans would be slipping five-peso coins to the scruffy teenagers who prowled the parking lot.

In the PBA, fans couldn't base their loyalty on regional pride, so feeling a personal connection with the players became crucial. Not too many people could identify with a Purefoods hot dog or a can of Alaska condensed milk. They could, however, feel close to players like Dale and Aaron, who weren't just wealthy athletes, but guys who ate at the same curbside *karinderias* as construction workers; hell, they even ate from the same bowls, with the same spoons, and by doing so sent a powerful message of unity to the league's fans. The populist bent of Philippine basketball was so different from my knowledge and experience in American sports that I wasn't sure how to react to it. If I were eating at Subway around the corner from my apartment in New York, I would never expect to see one of the Knicks walk in, and if one did, I wouldn't expect him to talk to me, aside from—at best—an obligatory "What's up?" It would be foolish to expect more. Besides, as a New Yorker, I was raised to act unimpressed around celebrities; the only one I ever approached was Bill Walton. Philippine culture was clearly different. It wasn't the fan's duty to remain aloof in the presence of stars; it was the player's responsibility to show gratitude to the average Filipino.

The perception of Fil-Am players as a uniform gang of churlish Americans who considered themselves above the lowly masses was anything but true. Just on Alaska, each Fil-foreign player came to the PBA with his own set of attitudes and experiences. Sonny Thoss, the team's six-foot-seven center, was born in Papua New Guinea to a Filipina mother and a German father. He lived there until college and learned to play basketball on summer trips to Cebu. In the eyes of the league Sonny was a Fil-foreigner, but inside the Alaska lounge he caucused with the locals. Reserve guard Alvin Castro, on the other hand, was born in the Philippines and moved to Los Angeles as a child. His Tagalog was pure and the PBA considered him a homegrown player, but he identified more closely with Fil-Ams. Alvin sat in the "English section" with Jeff Cariaso, Nic Belasco, and Mike Cortez; he preferred his homemade beef chili to *kare-kare*, the Philippines' signature oxtail stew; and he hoped to hold his PBA job for another two seasons, long enough for his wife to finish a nursing degree. After that they planned to move back to California with their daughters.

Nic was part of the second mini-wave of Fil-Ams to join the league in 1997, two years after Alaska drafted Jeff. But Nic's family history differed from most other Filipino Americans' experiences. His grandfather was one of roughly 30,000 Filipino migrant laborers who settled in California by 1930. Nic grew up in the northern California* town of Stockton, home to one of the country's oldest Filipino communities. His parents, both full-blooded Filipinos, were born in the United States and English was their first language. "Man, my father hardly speaks Tagalog," he once told me, to explain why he had learned to understand the language over his ten-year career but still rarely spoke it. And, thinking of how many third-generation Italian- or Polish-Americans were fluent in their grandparents' mother tongues, I couldn't blame Nic for not speaking much Tagalog or Ilocano. If I did, then I also deserved a stern rebuke for never learning my grandfather's native Slovak.

Lost amid the criticism of Fil-Am players' foreign mannerisms were the ways in which they improved Philippine basketball. Take Mike Cortez, Alaska's injured point guard, who grew up in the Filipino-American enclave of Carson, California. He was still a couple weeks away from returning to the Aces' roster from a torn knee ligament, but when healthy, Mike wasn't just one of Alaska's best players, he was one of the best in the league. His surly—some might say American—on-court attitude was an important aspect of his game. When he made a move off the dribble, he didn't just try to beat his man to the rim, he wanted to demoralize the defender. If a player scored on him, Mike wanted to come back and score twice. If the player scored again, Mike would

---

* Back in 2007, Nic's bio on the Alaska Web site claimed he hailed from North Carolina, which, as far as the team was concerned, was more or less the same as California.

spend the rest of the game making him stumble over his own feet. He was the PBA's most fluid ballhandler. He could make an opposing guard look like a cat chasing a string; he dangled the ball in front of defenders, tempted them to lunge for the ball, then whipped it behind his back and vanished in the opposite direction. If the PBA kept a stat for the number of times a player left his man standing in the open court, looking over his shoulder and wondering, "What just happened?" Mike Cortez might be the career leader. Yes, he carried himself with an imperious air—stared down opponents, didn't make eye contact with people he deemed unimportant—but he wouldn't have been the same player without that pugnacious attitude.

Before Mike arrived in Manila, the country had never seen a player who handled the ball with such composure and slickness. He combined crossovers, hesitations, and spins into an elusive ballet that confounded local opponents when he entered the league. Over the years, however, local Filipino guards added similar sleight-of-hand touches to their ballhandling repertoires. Nic was one of several Fil-Am big men who finally proved that Filipinos taller than six-foot-four could run the floor without tripping over their own feet, and do it faster than some guards. He was known as one of the only local players, big or small, who could defend imports straight-up, without help from double-teams or sagging zone defenses. Jeff brought technique and intensity to perimeter defense that hardly existed in the PBA before him. For much of the league's history, a stopper was someone who could put the other team's best scorer in traction. Jeff could slide his feet to stay in front of a slasher just as easily as he could bump an opponent out of the lane. Owners and coaches, whose primary goal was always to win more games, noticed the impact Fil-Ams had on the league. They brought new skills, greater size, and hard-nosed defensive mentalities to the Philippine game, and by doing so forced local players to improve and raised the PBA's level of play.

Yet it seemed unlikely that Fil-Ams would receive much recognition for this contribution or be able to escape the perception that they were standoffish and arrogant. Jeff, who had fought against the label throughout his career, agonized over this reality. Even his wife told him that before they met, she saw him give a halftime interview on television and thought, "Who's this Fil-Am guy? So *mayabang*; speaking English." Over the years, however, Jeff became comfortable with the language and the Philippine way of honoring fans. Now, with Alaska, he was the key to team chemistry, the bridge between the Philippine-bred players, who felt at ease with Jeff's fluent Tagalog, and the Fil-Ams, who considered Jeff one of their own.

One afternoon before practice I followed Jeff on his monthly rounds to collect two hundred pesos from each of his teammates to be divvied up as tips for the ball boys, trainers, and Mang Tom. Inside the players lounge, he found Alvin on the couch with his head lolling back on a cushion and an ice pack strapped to his groin. *"Kulang? O sobra?"* Jeff asked while pumping his fist. *Not enough? Or too much?* "For the boys, Vin," Jeff said, and Alvin groaned, reached into a duffel bag and pulled out two crinkled hundred-peso bills. Outside of the lounge, Jeff found Poch, Sonny, and John Ferriols sunk into a wooden bench, their arms around each other's shoulders and a Kanye West song blaring from a miniature boom box John carried everywhere. "Guys, for da boys," Jeff said. They decided that Sonny would pay for all three and the others would treat him to dinner. Just then, Willie was walking in from the parking lot. "Roommate!" Jeff shouted. "For da boys *na!*" Willie pretended to run away, then turned around and gave Jeff the money. In fifteen minutes Jeff had kidded and prodded his way to more than 3,000 pesos, which he handed over to Mang Tom to split with the others. When Tom turned around to sort the money into equal shares, Jeff tweaked his ass for good measure, and, as always, Tom's sixty-seven-year-old legs propelled him a foot into the air. He wheeled around and shook a fist at Jeff: "Shit, man!"

The players would kick in for the ball boys no matter who collected the tips, but no player but Jeff could have made the rounds so comfortably. Willie got along with his teammates as well as Jeff did, but no one—not even Willie himself—took Willie seriously. Jeff was able to interact so naturally with all his teammates because he worked at it. When Jeff finished with Tom, I asked him what he thought about the negative attitudes toward foreign-born PBA players. "As Fil-Ams, we have to be the ones to adjust," he said. "I don't blame people looking at Fil-Ams that way because it's the way they carry themselves. Fil-Ams act and dress the way they do because it's their culture. It's the way we were raised. But we're the new guys here, and we can't expect the whole country to adjust to us."

Jeff's enlightened approach to Fil-Ams' role in the country, as well as his ability to blend seamlessly with his local and American-born teammates should have made him a beacon of Fil-Am success, an example of how Fil-foreigners should conduct themselves in the PBA. Instead, he was so adored by local players and fans that public opinion rechristened him as an honorary native. Jojo Lastimosa had been one of the most vocal critics of the PBA's Fil-Am policies during the 2002 Senate hearings. I asked Jojo if his complaints also applied to Jeff, his former teammate, and Jojo answered, "Well, I don't really think of Jeff as a Fil-Am. He's really local." But Jeff was unequivocally Filipino-American. He was born and raised in San Francisco, but because he assimilated successfully into Philippine society and didn't fit the unflattering Fil-Am stereotype, people reclassified him. They didn't question the attitude that Fil-Ams were bad guys, they just removed Jeff from the negative category. On a personal level, Jeff could feel honored that local players and fans considered him no different from themselves. But as a Californian, it tormented him: If every "good" Fil-Am was no longer thought to be American, then the remaining Fil-Ams would always be maligned.

10

Courts of Public Opinion

One stuffy May afternoon, I met Roe Ellis and his brother Tim at a branch of the fast food chain Jollibee across the street from his apartment building. For a month Tim had been staying with Roe—sleeping on the couch, tuning his jump shot alongside Roe after practice, and even trying out for a few PBA teams that were looking to swap imports. Like Roe, Tim racked up accolades at Rainier Beach High School and went on to play D-1 ball, but unlike his brother, Tim had yet to establish himself as a reliable import. Roe intended this visit to be an exposure tour for Tim, something to give the younger Ellis a taste of life on the road.* Tim's workouts with other teams had been pretty success-

---

* One lesson Tim surely took home with him concerned hair care. Veteran imports knew to bring a girlfriend or cut their hair short before going overseas. In the Philippines, as in other countries where expertise with black hairstyles was scant, finding a barber or stylist could be close to impossible. Tim arrived with his hair in cornrows and never managed to meet someone capable of undoing and rebraiding it. This forced him to endure a month of tropical heat without a chance to adequately wash his hair. As the sweat slowly pickled his scalp, he tried covering the unruly, pungent mess with an ever-present do-rag, which helped but couldn't totally prevent wisps of stray hair or traces of stink from escaping the wave cap's seal.

ful. He was a step quicker than Roe, with smooth moves to the hoop and a graceful, hanging jump shot that was far prettier than Roe's. San Miguel supposedly came close to signing him, but eventually decided against it. Tim stood just six-foot-three with a slight frame and the team doubted he could match up with other clubs' larger, rugged imports.

Enough food to feed a Filipino family of six sat on the table between the brothers—a pair of fried chicken meals with tubs of gravy and plum-sized clumps of rice; a gloomy chicken sandwich composed of a breaded patty, shredded lettuce, one slice of unidentifiable cheese and mayonnaise; a Champ burger, Jollibee's obligatory Whopper clone; two smaller hamburgers, called Yums, dressed with a pink approximation of Thousand Island sauce; and french fries scattered everywhere over their two trays. The feast should have been a grand start to the brothers' last day together, but Roe was in a foul mood and unable to focus on anything but Alaska's loss the previous night to the Coca-Cola Tigers.

A win would have given Alaska a 10-4 record and sole possession of first place with only four games to play before the playoffs; instead, the defeat left the Aces mired in a four-team race for second place. What's worse, Roe sensed that Coke would have rolled over for Alaska. The Tigers were near the end of a tumultuous year, with a poor postseason outlook. Weary and ready to collapse, Coke was ripe for a knockout blow, but the Aces couldn't deliver. A mid-season trade had replaced half of Coke's starting lineup, and their once spectacular import Anthony Johnson had been dismissed. Rumors around the league blamed the Manila nightlife for sapping his vitality. Jeff Varem, a brawny and energetic forward fresh from the NBA developmental league, took Johnson's place, but he was a younger, less effective version of Roe.

Throughout most of the game, Coke tried their darnedest to mail it in. They allowed Alaska guards to blow by them, then chanced a few futile pokes from behind while watching the Aces cruise to the rim. Coke lobbed errant passes to Roe and Jeff Cariaso and stood nonchalantly as Alaska steamed downcourt for dunks and layups. Alaska held double digit leads at the end of each of the first three quarters, yet none of the players aside from Roe seemed to realize that the scoreboard concealed how poor Alaska was playing. The Aces were winning because Coke had given up, not because Alaska had done anything right. In fact, the Aces seemed equally lackadaisical that night; they flubbed layups, hoisted three-pointers before Roe or Sonny Thoss got to touch the ball, and mimicked Coke's lax defense. Roe attempted to whip the team into shape, first by example—he tried to swat every shot within reach, dove for loose balls, and dribbled coast-to-coast through the Coke defense to score on multiple occasions. When that failed, he stalked into the huddle with a killer's scowl and snarled, "Quit bullshitting! Let's play!" Then he kicked a guardrail behind the bench so hard that I could see it vibrating from the stands. Even this made little impact on the Aces—they glanced at the JumboTron, saw Alaska up twelve, and looked at each other, eyebrows knit in confusion: "What's Roe's problem today?"

When the fourth quarter began and Alaska managed only three points over the first six minutes, they finally understood, but it was too late. The Aces' thirteen-point cushion evaporated, and Coke took the lead on a pair of foul shots with two and a half minutes to play. The teams traded baskets down the stretch, and Coke came out on top, 94-90. In the locker room, the players covered their heads with towels and stared at the floor. No one spoke; no one relaxed. The tension, equal parts shame and disbelief, was thick as pâté. Cone delivered his postgame talk in the kind of low, monotone mumble men use to break up with their girlfriends. He rested a palm on his forehead and cast a blank look at the wall: "A lot of things going through my head right now, fellas. We really didn't take care of business there. We let them get momentum. We kind of screwed around at the end of the third quarter and we paid for it. We'll put it away and we'll go forward, but damn it, we need to learn something from this." By the time he finished, Roe was dressed and halfway to the door. He said nothing to his teammates on the way out and slammed it behind him.

Sitting across from his brother and their deep-fried smorgasbord the following afternoon, Roe was still livid. The game revealed flaws that had been nagging him throughout the first two months of the season, and he couldn't bear them silently any longer. "Those guys need to stop fucking around," he said, gouging the air with a half-eaten drumstick. "They ain't used to winning. All of a sudden they win a couple games and they think they can coast." He couldn't believe some of the boneheaded plays his teammates made. Foremost in his mind was a two-on-one fast break in the third quarter. Rey Hugnatan and John Ferriols had the ball with a single Coke defender between them and the basket. Instead of going strong to the hoop and passing off after the defense committed to one man, they tried to be cute. John and Rey tapped the ball back and forth between each other as they approached the goal. When John caught the ball with an open lane in front of him, he didn't take it. He shot-faked and passed again to Rey, who jumped like he was going to lay it in, then dropped a behind-the-back pass to John, who pumped at least five more fakes before attempting a shot, which was now contested by three defenders who arrived during John's fit of fakes. The shot rolled around and out of the rim, Coke regained possession and John and Rey ran back on defense with Alfred E. Neuman grins. Alaska had a double-digit lead. What, me worry?

John, especially, was developing a habit of fast-break swashbuckling that led to missed opportunities. Earlier that week, in a win over Ginebra, the burly power forward tried an inside-out, stutter step dribble that bounced out of his hands, over his head, and into the clutches of a trailing defender. The PBA crowd howled with delight at this play. It reminded them of the free form, silly brand of hoops played in Philippine playgrounds, where everyone attempted his most rococo move and the turnover-addled hijinks fueled the fun. But winning, not whimsy, inspired Roe, and he was sick of John's shenanigans. "Fuck all that playing to the crowd with seventeen pump fakes," he said, using an unwrapped Yum burger to reenact John's spasms with the ball. "You can pump your ass right on over to the bench." By now Tim was pounding the table in laughter, and even Roe had to take a break from his diatribe to chuckle at his impromptu roast of the Alaska roster.

But underneath Roe's frustration was real concern about the team's chances, and his chagrin over the Coke loss led to the cruelest assessment I heard from him all season: "Let's be honest, a lot of the guys on this team are the scraps of the PBA." The roster, he explained, included role players like Rey, John, Eddie Laure, and Rensy Bajar, ex-MBA stars who struggled to find their niche in the PBA; aging studs like Jeff Cariaso and Nic Belasco, who were traded to Alaska after the teams they played for during their primes lost faith in them; and Willie Miller, a former number one pick in the PBA draft and league MVP who, despite his breathtaking talent, had been traded twice by franchises that thought his comedic approach to the game didn't breed success in the results-oriented world of professional basketball.

It turned out that Willie was the root cause of Roe's frustration. After the riff on pump fakes, Roe's diatribe seemed to be losing steam, but then he mentioned Willie and the look in his eyes hardened. "Willie thinks he's a star, but if he's so great why has he been traded two times?" he said. "After a while people get tired of the funny man, all that joking and playing around. Sometimes they want a businessman."

Alaska's two best players, Roe and Willie, couldn't have had more divergent basketball styles. Roe had the classic workhorse mentality. He succeeded by taking every element of the game seriously, by treating every loose ball and rebound like it could lead to a game-winning possession. Before games, he psyched himself up to a level of feverish intensity that didn't subside until the final buzzer. Willie, on the other hand, goofed around as if his life depended on it; as if every fifteen minutes his biological clock told him to laugh. He played with a joyous, improvisational flair that made him impossible to guard but also prone to errors—quick shots, risky passes, careless ballhandling, daydreaming on defense. Willie was guilty of every hoops sin, but when he committed them, he never seemed penitent. He smirked at his own foolishness, maybe gave his bald head a light smack and shrugged it off. *Bahala na.* It was the Tagalog expression for "leave it to God" or "it's out of my hands," and it was Willie's standard response to a bungled play.

If Roe and Willie were Alaska's yin and yang, there was hardly any harmony between them. After the Coke loss, Roe began to see Willie's nonchalance as a scourge that could spread through the team and derail the Aces' championship run. Early in the season, before Alaska had established itself as a top team, the players mimicked Roe's tenacity. A forward like John wouldn't have tried to lead a one-man fast break; he would have concentrated on rebounding, post defense, and knocking down baseline jumpers. Before the team's first game, I told friends I would be following Alaska, and they asked why I didn't choose a better team. Back then John and the rest of the overlooked Aces had a chip on their shoulder. They wanted to prove themselves, and behind their workhorse import they exuded toughness and scrappy play. Now that Alaska had become a top team, the players lost their edge. They relaxed and started taking cues from Willie. But Willie was a singular talent. His carefree style was an effective way for him to play, but when less gifted players tried it, disaster, à la John's head-fake fiasco, was never far behind. Willie's game was a thing of beauty, but it needed a disclaimer: DO NOT TRY THIS AT HOME.

At this late point in the conference, with a winning record and the post-season looming, Roe no longer had to worry about Alaska replacing him. But being assured of a paycheck until season's end wasn't enough for Roe, who was feeling the weight of the sacrifices he made this season. Foremost among them was rest, something most thirty-two-year-old athletes need in much greater quantities than Roe received. Including the Australian league, he had been playing for nine months straight, and Alaska's playoff run would probably last another two months. Not long after this PBA stint was up, he was expected to report to Townsville, Australia, for another season. With Alaska, Roe was holding back his scoring for the sake of Cone's triangle offense and to anchor the defense. He was averaging about 20 points a game when he could easily norm 30. Money alone wasn't enough to make the grueling schedule and his selfless output worthwhile. He already had a house, a BMW, motorcycles, and tailored suits at home in Seattle; his goal was something less tangible and more meaningful—a championship in an international league, something he'd never won before.

Other annoyances of life in Manila were also wearing on Roe. During practice, his friend and former teammate Jojo Lastimosa had made it his mission to correct Roe's shooting form. Jojo, one of the best guards in PBA history, had the ruthless self-confidence of an all-time great. In his mind, no task, no matter how formidable, was beyond him. Roe was ten years into his pro career, and he'd succeeded at every level except the NBA. Yes, there were chinks in his game, but changing them now was pointless. Still, Roe played along with Jojo's coaching, tucking his elbow in and shooting free throws under the coach's guidance after practice. He didn't intend to use Jojo's suggestions in a real game, but he put up with them out of respect.

Roe's relationship with his driver Neil had become strained. This was Neil's first job chauffeuring a PBA import, and he was having a little too much fun. Neil happened to resemble PBA journeyman Joey Mente, so when he traveled with the team Neil pretended to be Mente and signed autographs as him.* He enjoyed shooting around before practice, a perfectly acceptable pastime until he began wearing Roe's discarded headbands and challenging reserve guard Rensy Bajar to em-

---

* Yes, I am also guilty of signing autographs, sometimes as Coke guard John Arigo and sometimes as other names that popped into my head—Tiger Woods and R. Kelly became my regulars—but I never lost sight of the fact that I was actually nobody, while Neil seemed to embrace faux-fame wholeheartedly.

barrassing games of one-on-one. Neil's transformation from humble employee to wannabe baller coincided with more serious transgressions. He acted as Roe's de facto translator when they shopped in Metro Manila's sprawling flea markets, talking vendors down from their asking prices. Sometimes, Roe noticed Neil telling shopkeepers to add extra DVDs to his tab. Later, in the car, Neil would slip the additional movies into his own bookbag. When Roe went to the mall for dinner or coffee and Neil noticed women eyeing the import, he would take it upon himself to ask if they wished to visit Roe's apartment.

There was no way to know the nature of Neil's scam. Roe guessed that Neil offered to set the women up with Roe for a finder's fee. It didn't matter that Roe never requested Neil's matchmaking services and even ordered Neil to stop; Neil would still show up at the apartment with unknown females, and Roe would turn them away. Yet Roe didn't have the heart to report Neil's deceits to Alaska management. If they found out, Neil would be fired in a heartbeat, and although Roe was fed up with his driver's stunts, he didn't want to be responsible for Neil losing his job.

Finally, Roe had long since tired of the constant, sometimes unwelcome and often bizarre attention he received as a six-foot-five black celebrity in Manila. When he walked through a mall food court with his brother, people stared like a pair of pterodactyls just flew past. Their eyes would widen and their jaws would gape, sometimes with rice tumbling out of their mouths. Most Manileños had seen black tourists before, but African-Americans were still novel enough to inspire some pretty ugly behavior. For Roe, the staring was bearable. So was the pointing. The whispering of *"Negro!"* was bad; but worst were the people who treated him like an attraction in a petting zoo. They'd hold their forearm next to his and compare the difference in skin tone, or sneak behind him while he was shopping to measure how tall they were against his back. If he leaned down to shuffle through a stack of pirated DVDs, the dealer might reach out to touch his hair, just to see how it felt.

Roe could handle it: The racial insensitivity, Neil's swindling, Jojo's tinkering with his shot, the grind of an endless season, giving up his scoring to favor his teammates, even Willie's infectious clowning. Roe knew he could take it. But to feel like the decisions and compromises he made weren't mistakes, he had to win a title.

The Ellis brothers were able to hold their afternoon summit because it was Election Day in the Philippines and Cone canceled practice. The coach wanted to drag all his players into the gym and run them ragged after losing to Coke. He even announced that practice would push through, but then the Aces began murmuring and looking to Jeff Cariaso to speak up for them. Jeff squinted at assistant coach Dickie Bachmann. "Dick," he pleaded. "Tomorrow? Come on." Dickie followed Cone out of the locker room, then returned a couple minutes later. "Tuesday *tayo*." A sigh of relief swept the room. John Ferriols rapped on Poch Juinio's back in approval. "Vote tomorrow," Dickie said. "Be safe."

Civic duty had nothing to do with the coaches' decision to cancel practice. Half of the Senate and all the seats in the House of Representatives were up for grabs in the national election, as well as governor, vice governor, and local government positions throughout the country. Cone determined that the safest plan would be for the players to stay home when they weren't voting. The Philippines had a long history of political killings, and anyone who had lived through a few national elections took the threat very seriously. In the months leading up to the 2007 election, more than a hundred people were killed in poll-related violence, and more murders were expected as candidates vied for control over the vote-counting process.[*]

---

[*] The long fuse leading to the May 2010 elections started with a horrifying bang last November, when fifty-seven people en route to file the candidacy papers of

Philippine elections were literally power struggles. The candidates, often from political clans whose bloody rivalries went back generations, competed for access to government riches. The winner gained control of a slice of the pie for the next three or six years. Many, perhaps most, Filipino candidates entered politics not because of their devotion to public service, but because it was seen as the most effective way to get rich. Philippine political parties hardly bothered creating ideological platforms; instead, they formed convoluted alliances designed to control the vote in enough disparate regions to capture victory at the national level. The zero-sum nature of Philippine politics made it fairly easy to predict the targets of election violence—candidates, their operatives, and the journalists who covered them. Average voters with little stake in the outcome were generally safe, and PBA players fell into this category. Still, there was always the chance of being in the wrong place at the wrong time—sitting in traffic when the armed henchmen of rival candidates started spraying shots—and because of this Cone and the Alaska coaching staff gave the team a day off and encouraged the players to stay home.

Aside from the scant chance of being peppered with buckshot, the campaign period was a festive time in Metro Manila. Candidates for positions from *kagawad*, the neighborhood council, to senator sent van convoys through neighborhoods to drum up grassroots support. The two principal means of impressing voters in these processions were campaign jingles and handouts. The vans were plastered with beach-ball-size images of candidates' smiling faces and giant hands giving thumbs-up signs. They crawled through nearly every street of every *barangay*, blasting political theme songs from loudspeakers strapped to the vehicles' roofs. Each jingle tried to repeat its candidate's name as

---

a gubernatorial candidate in southern Maguindanao province were waylaid and massacred by a private army believed to be working on behalf of a rival office-seeker.

many times as possible in thirty seconds or a minute. No definition of torture would be complete without these tunes.

One incumbent senator, Joker Arroyo, had a ditty that was nothing but his name repeated over a synthesized clamor of game show sound effects. He was reelected. Miguel Zubiri, another Senate hopeful, melded his name to the melody of *"Boom Tarat Tarat,"* a ubiquitous tune that was normally accompanied by rhythmic pelvic thrusting. He also won a seat. For office-seekers, it didn't much matter if listening to these looped monstrosities inspired hatred for the men behind the music. What mattered was that people remembered their names. Because Philippine voters were required to write the names of their preferred candidates, name recognition was a key to electoral success.* Once voters were alone with their ballots, it was better to be Zubiri, the Senate bet with the irksome song, than what's his name, the other contender who seemed nice on television.

During the cacophonous motorcades, staffers would stroll alongside the vans and hand out branded tchotchkes to sear the aspirants' names even deeper into voters' minds. Before the election, I watched people in my neighborhood eagerly glom umbrellas, backpacks, calendars, shoulder bags, hats, T-shirts, and even sponges. The goal, apparently, was to accumulate so much poll-related swag that you wouldn't have to buy new clothes until the next election rolled around and the politicians returned with their goodie bags. The cherry red shirts distributed sometime during Mel Mathay's stint as Quezon City mayor,

---

* In 2010 the country planned to switch to an SAT-style ballot, where voters would choose government officials by filling in bubbles, and optical scanners would tally the votes. Less than a year before the election, however, the government was still unsure if it would be able to implement the scheme. If they pulled it off, it would be a major step toward ending the tyranny of the jingle. Then again, the government's voter education campaign about automated elections was disseminated via a jingle sung by the Sexbomb Girls, so perhaps it's naïve to think that jingles won't survive the electoral change.

which ended in 2001, were still worn daily by local tricycle drivers. Basketball seemed to occupy its own category of promotional merchandise. Politicians handed out numbered jerseys, multicolored miniballs, and plastic backboard-and-rim sets small enough for bedroom walls, all emblazoned with the candidates' names. I sensed something sinister in this basketball-for-votes quid pro quo. The roundball love that awed me every time I spotted a homemade basket also had a dark side.

For decades, Philippine politicians have manipulated the nation's hoops passion for electoral gains. Take, for example, the legions of ex-players who parlayed their celebrity status into elected office. The practice went as far back as Ambrosio Padilla, captain of the 1936 Olympic team. Padilla won a Senate seat in 1957 and held it for fifteen years until Ferdinand Marcos declared martial law and dissolved the legislative body. After the 1986 People Power revolution ousted Marcos, President Corazon Aquino reinstated the Senate and, within five years, the chamber welcomed Freddie Webb, another ex-baller. Webb played for the 1972 Olympic team and became one of the PBA's quickest, highest scoring guards while playing for the Tanduay Rhum Makers in the seventies. Webb worked his way up the political ladder, serving as a councilor in southern Metro Manila's Pasay City during his playing career, then winning a seat in the House of Representatives in the late eighties. Robert Jaworski jumped from the hardwood to the Senate in 1998 without any government experience. Fifty-two years old at the time and still manning the sidelines for Ginebra, Jaworski was only able to win the election by promising fans he would not retire.[*]

---

[*] This is why, during the 2002-2003 Fil-sham hearings, Senator Jaworski reminded PBA players that he was still one of them, even though he was in his mid-fifties. Such reminders were knowing winks to the masses of Filipinos who worshiped Jaworski and delighted in the senator's refusal to announce his retirement. This running joke between fans and the great old-timer continues today.

Because senators in the Philippines are elected in nationwide polls, not province-by-province or state-by-state as they are in the United States, celebrities like basketball players had a natural advantage in name recognition. Many conventional candidates (often called *trapo*, a double entendre that is short for "traditional politician" and a Tagalog word meaning "dirty rag") came from dynasties that controlled certain regions but weren't known outside their spheres of influence. Webb and Jaworski were household names before their Senate runs. And, even though they came to the legislature with fewer credentials than many *trapos*, who had studied at top U.S. universities and served in high positions of the Philippine military and academic establishment, the hoop-it-up senators were hardly the most preposterous members of the group. That honor belonged to the actors, action movie icons like Ramon Revilla Sr., who served from 1992 to 2004 and was known for having sired somewhere between forty-five and eighty illegitimate children; or Joseph Estrada, another cinematic tough guy who reinvented himself as a populist politician and served a term in the Senate before being elected vice president and eventually president.

Even more former PBA stars found their way into local politics. The ranks of city councilors, mayors, vice mayors, and governors were thick with basketball players. Franz Pumaren, coach of college powerhouse De La Salle University and a former guard for the San Miguel Beermen, represented my neighborhood as the District Three councilor in Quezon City. When I walked to the corner store and passed freshly paved sidewalks that had been outfitted with new underground drainage cylinders, I had Pumaren to thank. Months later, when segments of the new road caved in and became murky cesspools, I had Pumaren to blame. Who could forget Yeng Guiao, the Red Bull coach who pulled double duty as vice governor of Pampanga province? Elsewhere in Metro Manila, former PBA guards Yoyong Martirez and Luis Varela were vice mayors in Pasig and Caloocan cities, respectively. In the recent past, Crispa greats Atoy Co and Philip Cezar completed terms as

Pasig City councilor and vice mayor of San Juan; Jaworski helped his son Dodot win a seat in the House of Representatives, and onetime Great Taste guard Joey Marquez had been mayor of Parañaque City. The NBA has also had its share of players turned politicians, like Bill Bradley in the Senate and Dave Bing as mayor of Detroit. But the pro-basketball-to-elected-office career track is still a novelty in American politics. In the Philippines, government service had become a logical, even expected, career move for retired PBA stars.

Politicians didn't need to be able to sink a reverse layup to exploit basketball. Government officials who never played organized hoops were just as likely as ex-Olympians to use the sport for electoral gain. Every candidate's political bag of tricks included stunts like attending PBA and college games to receive face time on television, or sponsoring local tournaments where players received uniforms branded with the donor's name. When Senator Robert Barbers investigated Fil-shams, critics assailed the hearings as a ploy to gain media attention. Stirring the pot of basketball and Philippine nationalism allowed Barbers and his fellow senators to portray themselves as crusaders fighting to restore honor to Philippine hoops. But the hearings, supposedly "in aid of legislation," produced no new laws and failed to banish several alleged Fil-shams from the league.

More than publicity stunts and sponsoring teams, the go-to tactic in politicians' hoops playbook—the pick-and-roll, so to speak—was constructing basketball courts. Like the neighborhood court where I took my first jump shot in Manila, and the concrete roundball fortress I discovered in Adams, Ilocos Norte, most of the nation's full courts—tens of thousands of them—were built by politicians. The public officials who built them argued that courts were worthy investments. They insisted that basketball gave communities an enormous boost in esteem, kept teenagers away from drugs, and instilled disciplined, healthy lifestyles in children. In addition, courts were used for more than just basketball games. They became community centers—surfaces where farmers dried rice and stages where towns hosted singing competitions and coronations during annual fiestas. For politicians, courts were cheap, easy to build, and easy to claim credit for with painted murals: *A gift to the people from Mayor Santos!*

Critics of basketball's role in politics pointed to opportunity costs. Too often the most modern structure in a town whose health clinic badly needed improvements would be a state-of-the-art outdoor court. Occasionally, a newly elected mayor wanted to impress his constituents, but the municipal plaza already had a functional court. So he made his mark with nonessential add-ons like spring-loaded rims and fiberglass backboards; sometimes, defying all logic, politicians built new courts right next to perfectly good ones, as if they couldn't think of any other use for public funds. At the University of the Philippines, Diliman, Aries Arugay, a lecturer in political science, told me that basketball courts offered good bang for the politicians' bucks: they were cheaper to build and more popular with constituents than projects like roads and hospitals. Aries, in his late twenties, was only a few years older than me, but he had already seen enough craven hoops-related politicking to have the outlook of a cynical campaign veteran. "The politician merely wants it so he can put his name on it and collect brownie points," Aries said. "With a government that fails to provide for their basic needs, Filipinos are easy to please. If they feel any government presence, they appreciate it." I felt queasy listening to him. It sounded like the sport I adored had been used to bamboozle people and deny them the better lives their elected leaders should have worked to provide.

The same week in 1983 that Benigno "Ninoy" Aquino was assassinated upon his return to the Philippines, the Crispa Redmanizers and Great Taste Coffee Makers met in a storied PBA finals. For the first time, Billy Ray Bates and Norman Black went head-to-head in a series, and judging by write-ups of the games, the avid fans who poured into the Araneta Coliseum that week were more captivated by the clash between two great imports than the event that would change the course of Philippine history. Juaniyo Arcellana wrote in *Atlas Sports Weekly*: "Ninoy Aquino's assassination notwithstanding, the world remains the same inside the coliseum during the heat of a PBA championship game . . . Basketball as escapism, who would have dreamed?"

Marcos, maybe? Few Philippine leaders have been as adept at manipulating basketball to serve their political ends. The PBA, after all, was founded during the heyday of martial law, when the Marcos government exercised near total control of media and clamped down on individual freedoms through curfews and the persecution of dissidents. Basketball was promoted as clean, wholesome entertainment, and the PBA rose to heights of popularity that the league probably never would have reached in an open society. Hoops, however, served as more than just a diversion during martial law; the fierce competition and occasionally downright violent action on the court provided a government-sanctioned release valve for the frustration simmering within the masses, who rarely had such opportunities to blow off steam in Marcos's police state.

The two dominant teams of the era, the Crispa Redmanizers and Toyota Tamaraws, spent the PBA's first decade locked in one of the most heated rivalries in Philippine sports history. Whenever they clashed, crowds upward of 20,000 fans jammed every seat, catwalk, and staircase in the Araneta Coliseum. At the very least, fans knew they'd be treated to a seesaw battle played by the country's finest ballers; and, if the spectators were lucky, they might witness a brawl.

Rough play was a hallmark of the early PBA, which Bill Velasco liked to call a "street fight in shorts." Forearm shivers, Muay Thai elbows, and running clotheslines were essential skills, just like bounce passes and bank shots. When blows started flying during Crispa-Toyota games, the crowd felt a vicarious jolt of adrenaline. Fans booed and cursed the thuggish fouls committed by the opposite side and celebrated when their heroes mauled the opponents. The fans shrieked themselves hoarse with the filthiest obscenities Tagalog, English, Cebuano, and other Philippine tongues had to offer. If the referees missed a particularly dirty foul, bedlam followed, as fans pelted the court with as much debris as could be dredged from their pockets, handbags, and backpacks. The peso coin was the projectile-of-choice, but bottles, beer cans, and batteries were also lobbed at the hardwood. Unruly behavior that would have gotten spectators arrested in public was tolerated inside the arena, and even fans who only watched on television felt cathartic thrills.

Marcos also used the Crispa-Toyota rumbles to demonstrate his control over Philippine society. In 1977, after the Redmanizers defeated Toyota 122-121 on opening day, Crispa guard Atoy Co saw Toyota center Ramon Fernandez bump Crispa coach Baby Dalupan as the teams walked off the court. Co rushed to defend Dalupan and tagged Fernandez with a punch to the chin, sparking a free-for-all between both teams. The donnybrook began in the tunnel leading to the locker rooms and then surged back onto the court, where frenzied supporters threw chairs and whatever else they could lift off the ground at the grappling horde. The small-scale riot lasted until the police arrived to restore order. A few days later, both teams were invited to Camp Crame, headquarters of the Philippine National Police, who were then called the Philippine Constabulary. There, General Prospero Olivas chastised the players for setting a bad example. As athletes, the general said, they had to be role models for the masses and exhibit the discipline that was central to President Marcos's governing philosophy. The jingoistic speech inspired snickers in at least one player, and that was enough to convince Olivas to send both teams to Fort Bonifacio, the military base where political prisoners—including Ninoy Aquino—were detained. The players spent the night in a holding cell and were released the next day, but the legend—the country's biggest sports superstars, the Kobe

Bryants and Dwight Howards of their day, jailed for fighting—endures to this day. The message was clear: no one received special treatment in Marcos's New Society.[*]

I asked around, and the PBA never produced a Muhammad Ali–type athlete who used his platform to decry political injustice. This was likely due to the fact that under martial law, dissidents weren't merely harassed, discriminated against, or, as in Ali's case, arrested and banned from boxing. Filipinos who spoke out against the Marcos regime risked being tortured, detained indefinitely, or murdered. Also, basketball players in that era felt little political consciousness or moral imperative to speak out. For starters, their bosses were all devoted Marcos toadies; at the time, there was no way to own a major corporation and a PBA franchise without supporting the regime. Second, Philippine society's still-operational patronage system, where personal debts could take precedence over broader ethical concerns, was particularly strong in the Marcos years. Many players lived in team dorms during the season and remained loyal to the businessmen who cut their checks and gave them free meals, vacations, and sometimes even cars. Today, many of those players, although aware of Marcos's excesses, couldn't help but look back on this dark period in Philippine history as the best time of their lives. Their families were secure, they earned money hand over fist, and every time they donned a uniform the nation's adoring eyes

---

[*] Of course, this was hokum. Marcos's family and cronies, the police and the military, and American corporations, all operated above the law in the dictator's authoritarian kleptocracy, but public displays of force like jailing Crispa and Toyota reminded the public that disrupting the social order would not be tolerated. Basketball players were not the only celebrities who were made into examples of state power. A similar urban legend concerns Ariel Ureta, a comedian and television host who publicly ridiculed the martial law slogan, "*Sa ika-uunlad ng bayan, disiplina ang kailangan.*" It means: For progress of the nation, discipline is needed. Ureta repeated the catchphrase, then substituted *bisikleta* for *disiplina*. It was a harmless phonetic gag, but soon afterward, Ureta was invited to Camp Crame and forced to spend an entire day biking around its perimeter.

focused on them. With a setup so sweet, athletes didn't ponder social justice, they just went with the flow.

The linked personal debts created a chain of command from Marcos to team owners to players, so when the president called on the PBA for political favors, the teams obliged. In the months leading up to the 1978 parliamentary election—a stage-managed sham to demonstrate Marcos's respect for democratic rule—Crispa and Tanduay wore special uniforms bearing the initials of Marcos's party—KBL, for *Kilusang Bagong Lipunan* or New Society Movement—and played outdoor exhibition games around Metro Manila to promote the establishment cause. Naturally, these free spectacles drew enthusiastic crowds numbering in the hundreds and sometimes thousands, depending on the venue. The fans probably could have cared less about the election, which the KBL was certain to sweep, but they scaled trees and stood on top of trucks to catch a glimpse of the PBA stars competing on their neighborhood blacktops. After the games, each player gave a short spiel praising Marcos and encouraging fans to support the KBL slate. For Redmanizers like Atoy Co, Tito Varela, and Philip Cezar, all of whom held office after their PBA careers, the rallies may have introduced them to the sport's political value.*

Marcos also used PBA teams to reward regions for their loyalty. In February 1983 he sent Crispa and the San Miguel Beermen to Paoay, Ilocos Norte, a ten minute ride from the strongman's boyhood home, as a Valentine's gift for his fellow Ilocanos. That year Crispa's connection to Marcos became even stronger, when the team hired Tommy Manotoc as head coach. Manotoc, a champion golfer, had recently married Marcos's eldest daughter, Imee. Crispa, a textile manufacturer, outfitted its coach-

---

* I returned to the Ateneo de Manila library to dig up old articles in *Champ* and *Atlas Sports Weekly* about Marcos's connections to basketball. Aside from the newsprint images of spectators' legs dangling from tree branches, I stumbled across a misguided attempt at political correctness in a feature devoted to the Special Olympics with a subtitle that joyously proclaimed, "Retardates are Beautiful!"

ing staff in custom T-shirts for the occasion. That night, playing in an outdoor game with Marcos himself in attendance, Manotoc and his assistants wore shirts that professed a common emotion in a region that often found itself the beneficiary of the dictator's largesse: I ♥ MARCOS.

Not long after the elections, as Alaska's season was beginning to wind down, hype was building for the country's preeminent collision of hoops, politics, and business. Ever since the students returned to my neighborhood at the end of May (the academic year began in June), I noticed a change in the way female students at Ateneo de Manila University looked at me. When I passed groups of coeds, they would hide behind their textbooks and follow me with their eyes. After I passed, I would hear a chorus of giggles. What was going on? Weeks later I stopped at a local bakery to buy some chocolate cookies, and the guy working the counter wouldn't let me pay for them. "No, sir, we cannot accept that," he said, arms folded across his chest and shaking his head at the crumpled twenty-peso bills in my hand. "We are very big fans of the Blue Eagles." I took the sweets but left confused. What did I have to do with Ateneo sports?

A few days later the answer was revealed when a student riding sidesaddle on a motorcycle wiggled her fingers at me and yelled, "Hi Kirk!" They thought I was Kirk Long, the Ateneo basketball team's prize recruit. Like me, Long was white and above six feet tall. He came to Ateneo from a high school for foreign missionaries' children on the outskirts of Metro Manila. Never mind that I was more than five years older than Long and a couple inches taller; being a pale beanpole and wearing a pair of long nylon shorts was enough to convince Ateneo boosters that I was the Blue Eagles' new white knight. For one glorious, ethically dicey month, I high-fived autograph seekers, gorged on free confections, and returned the ladies' smiles. Maybe I should have tried harder to correct them, but the way I saw it, I had earned the right to enjoy a case of mistaken identity. The previous year, I could hardly step outside without hearing some horrified matron shriek "Daniel Smith!" Apparently, I also resembled Smith, a U.S. Marine who had been convicted of raping a Filipina at the former Subic Bay naval base. It was unlikely that anyone actually mistook me for Smith, since at the time he was locked inside the U.S. Embassy, but my whiteness alone made the comparison fair game. Needless to say, no one ever fed me sweets because I reminded them of a sex criminal.

Throughout the seventies, eighties, and most of the nineties, college basketball trailed the PBA in popularity. Fans preferred the more glamorous professional league because it employed the biggest and most talented players. Over the past decade, however, the popularity of college ball had skyrocketed, and by the time I found myself posing as an Ateneo heartbreaker, the country's two major leagues, the NCAA and University Athletics Association of the Philippines (UAAP), were on almost equal footing with the PBA. Some sports commentators believed this occurred in response to the PBA's influx of Filipino-American players. When the PBA lost its local flavor, fans migrated to the college game. Others suggested the amateurs played with more passion than the avaricious pros. Both arguments had the familiar ring of stateside NCAA platitudes, and they were similarly hollow. College teams in the Philippines recruited Fil-foreigners and even players without any Filipino blood, like Long and a host of other import-slash-students from Australia, Eastern Europe, and various African nations. Most of the players couldn't even be called amateurs in the United States, since they already received payment in cash and goods as paid endorsers of Nike, Adidas and other products.

New technology and niche markets contributed to a more plausible explanation for college basketball's recent prominence. Throughout most of the PBA's existence, Filipinos had scant access to other professional basketball leagues. As late as the mid-1990s, local television stations only broadcast a doubleheader of tape delayed NBA games on weekends, and fans who wanted more had to visit flea markets where predigital VHS pirates sold videotaped NBA games shipped from abroad. In recent years the introduction of satellite cable granted widespread access to the NBA, especially among upper class Filipinos. Not long after I arrived in the country, a new channel, Basketball TV, began showing live NBA games every morning, with nightly replays.*

The PBA was no longer the only game in town, and the TV audience for basketball became fragmented. Many wealthy Filipinos who could now watch Lebron James and Kobe Bryant stopped paying attention to Willie Miller and Jeff Cariaso, and the PBA lost a chunk of its elite audience. Moneyed Filipinos did, however, remain engaged in college ball, with many prominent alumni becoming vociferous supporters of their alma maters. The advertisements during PBA and college broadcasts illustrated the leagues' changing fortunes. PBA commercial breaks tended to be filled with spots directed at working-class Filipinos like pig farmers, construction workers, and cockfighting breeders. Some memorable ads included cockers singing about their roosters' fortitude and farmers injecting vitamin formula into the necks of squealing hogs. Ads during college games, on the other hand, reflected their viewers' high disposable incomes: imported sportswear, digital cameras, sport utility vehicles.

The main events of the college season, and arguably the grandest occasions in all of Philippine sports, were the two bouts between Ateneo de Manila and De La Salle universities. These were the nation's

---

* That's not all. When BTV first went on the air, the channel was a hoops geek's wet dream. Put aside the fact that I saw more televised NBA games in Manila than I ever saw on basic cable at home. The midday filler was a scatterbrained grab bag that included classic NBA games like Reggie Miller's 25-point fourth quarter against the Knicks and the 1995 Finals game where Orlando's Nick Anderson choked four straight foul shots; episodes of NBA Inside Stuff from the early nineties that were heavy on Dana Barros and Craig Ehlo highlights; Australian and European leagues; and the occasional championship game between Manila elementary schools.

most elite private institutions.* Their combined roster of distinguished alumni read like a list of Metro Manila's major roads: Rizal, Epifanio de los Santos, Recto, Osmeña, Chino Roces. When the schools' basketball teams met at the Araneta Coliseum, an arena owned by La Salle loyalists, the metropolis shut down. The schools' rancor was born of similarities—the affluent, educated Jesuits of Ateneo versus the wealthy, sophisticated La Salle Brothers. With so much in common, basketball became the tiebreaker that students, professors, and luminaries from each school used to distinguish themselves from the other. The victors earned the right to call themselves—always a tad too pompously— richer, smarter, and holier. They were the true cream of Philippine society.

Months before I got to witness the rivalry, I heard about the legendary milieu drawn to Ateneo–La Salle matches: equal parts joint session of Congress, PBA all-star game, diplomatic summit, the Luna Awards (the Philippine equivalent to the Oscars), and a Miss Philippines pageant, with a sprinkling of Forbes' forty richest Filipinos in attendance. Call it an alignment of stars, an eclectic brew of dignitaries, or a bloodthirsty madhouse. It was a uniquely Filipino throng that only basketball could bring together. I couldn't think of an event in the States that could summon such an all-encompassing cross section of the American power structure. Even the Harvard-Yale game wouldn't come close; not to mention that such a contest would never have national championship implications. Yet La Salle and Ateneo had won five titles in the previous ten years. Before the teams' first encounter of the season, I bumped into La Salle coach Franz Pumaren shortly after he'd been reelected to the Quezon City council. Even Pumaren, who had led

---

* Students and alumni of the equally venerable, public University of the Philippines, Diliman, are quick to point out that their school is actually more selective and academically rigorous than Ateneo or La Salle, but since U.P.'s basketball program is famously inept, the Maroons don't make a dent in the hoops scene.

the Green Archers to several titles, sounded starstruck when he described the crowd: "The janitors in Araneta always say if there's an Ateneo–La Salle game, once everybody's out of the coliseum, it still smells good because of all the socialites watching."

On the day of the big game, I wasn't even sure I'd be able to get in. The staff at Araneta knew me from the PBA, but this event required a higher level of security clearance. Two armed guards stood outside the coliseum service entrance, checking names off a list of credentialed media guests. I wasn't on the list, but I carried a handful of expired IDs and media lanyards from the PBA, the Malacañang Palace press corps, even my local ATM card. These were basically useless, but I planned to use them as subterfuge, something to flash at inquisitive officials while I smiled and disappeared into the crowd. I passed the first checkpoint by telling both guards that my name was on the other one's list. On the other side of the green metal gate three women sat behind a desk checking names on yet more lists. These gatekeepers worked all the PBA games; when I saw them I figured I was in the clear. Not so fast. The dowager of the lists, after scouring her spreadsheets, looked at me and shook her head. "This is UAAP," she said. "Not PBA."

I had to see this game. In my mind, I had built it up as the pinnacle of Philippine enthusiasm for basketball, and a positive counterpoint to the manipulative hoops politics I'd discussed with Aries Arugay. Yes, business moguls and government officials attended Ateneo–La Salle matches for reasons—school spirit, networking opportunities, to flaunt their status—that had little to do with the sport, but the fact that only hoops could unite these people buoyed my spirit. I wasn't going to miss it. I kept pleading my case with the gatekeeper while she checked credentials. I tried to charm my way in with Tagalog. Her icy response: "You speak well." I tried various American accents—Brooklyn, southern, midwestern—at different speeds and volumes, hoping that a Yankee imbecile act might exasperate her to the point that she'd wave me through just to get rid of me. She was unflappable: "I'm sorry, sir."

I got desperate. When the name-checkers were all occupied, I snatched the red access stamp from the table and pressed it against my wrist. I tossed the stamp back on the desk and strolled through the final turnstile. The beefy security guard there knew me from PBA games. "My friend!" he said, and slapped me on the back. "You made it!"

About forty-five minutes before tip-off, the arena began to fill. The students, infantry on this hoops battleground, arrived first. Ateneans sporting blue and La Salle fans donning emerald swarmed through the upper deck, then gradually segregated themselves into opposing semicircles. This was the "ocean of green and blue" that local writers romanticized, with each half of the venue wholly colonized by a color. Long before the players took the court, the students started working themselves into a lather with opposing chants punctuated by the school bands' thundering kettle drums.

"An-i-mo La Salle! An-i-mo La Salle!"

"One! Big! Fight!"

Next, the well-heeled alumni trickled in to take their courtside seats. They arrived fresh from corporate boardrooms and government ministries, still crisp in their blue or green button-down shirts and matching ties. Their patrician air, however, was a charade. Even the most highfalutin fans had to pull every available string to get those seats; some bribed media pals for press passes, some flew in from Jakarta and New York, and some paid scalpers more than a hundred bucks for tickets with a five-dollar face value. For Pumaren, this was one of the occasions when life as a coach-cum-politician wasn't so sweet. He only received four comp tickets but had to pay steep premiums on scalped passes for campaign donors and business partners. Due to the travails of obtaining tickets, fans defended their seats like hyenas guarding a juicy carcass, and the handful of interlopers who arrived early with hopes of squatting on front-row real estate were swiftly removed. Still, amid all the glamour and pomp, I was pleased to see a couple of the same gaunt drag queens who attended every PBA game wandering the stands. It lent a hint of oddball social justice to the proceedings, a reminder that Araneta was usually the capital of cockfighting, the habitat of Ginebra, and the home court of the hoi polloi.

Soon the entire arena was packed except for one row behind the Ateneo bench. There, alone, sat Ateneo alumnus Manuel V. Pangilinan, chairman of the Philippines' largest phone and Internet conglomerate, which also owned the Talk 'N Text franchise. It was hard to figure out what mattered most to Pangilinan, who was known throughout Manila as M.V.P: being a telecommunications mogul or the godfather of Philippine basketball. The basketball programs at Ateneo and another school he attended, San Beda College, would have been in the poorhouse if not for Pangilinan's beneficence.* He also served as president of the Philippine national basketball federation, and his mobile phone company, Smart, sponsored the developmental team that hoped to qualify for the 2012 Olympics.

Pangilinan was the ringleader of a group of donors who restored Ateneo's basketball program from a UAAP laughingstock to a national championship contender. Their money sent the team on overseas training jaunts to the same gyms NBA players used during the off-season, and it allowed Ateneo to hire the gold standard in Philippine coaching, PBA Hall of Famer Norman Black. Blue Eagle benefactors even paid a six-figure fee to have the floor used at the 2000 NBA All-Star Game installed at Ateneo's university gym, a purchase that was supposedly made to provide athletes with a first-class playing surface but was probably also inspired by the alums' desire to play pickup games on

---

* When Typhoon Ondoy hit Manila in September 2009 and floods submerged entire neighborhoods, Pangilinan dispatched a helicopter to deliver food and supplies to Ateneo guard Jai Reyes and his family, who were stranded in the top floor of their home.

hardwood that once absorbed sweat droplets from Karl Malone and Kevin Garnett.

At the game, Pangilinan occupied his solitary row, surveying the court through small oval glasses with his arms folded across his chest—the empty seats around him like a gesture of deference. When the teams emerged from the tunnel and both sides of the crowd erupted, Pangilinan peered a little more intently at the layup lines; the Blue Eagles, after all, were his investment, and beating La Salle was the payoff. Before long a conga line of unctuous hustlers approached Pangilinan. Some chose to beam their widest smile and chance a quick embrace, while others opted for a steely, professional demeanor. They wished each other good luck, paid their respects, and disappeared to their seats. Commentators liked to say that business flatlined on afternoons when Ateneo and La Salle played, but instead the deal-making just migrated to Araneta's lower deck. Pangilinan's procession of suitors continued for ten minutes, until the coaches put the finishing touches on their pregame rhetoric and the referees' whistles heralded the start of the game. Finally, Pangilinan was joined by an Atenean of equal stature, Senator Jinggoy Estrada, and soon there were no more empty seats.

Across the court, La Salle's alumni sugar daddies—men like shipping mogul Enrique Razon Jr., who donated about $1 million to refurbish La Salle's sports center and finance athletic scholarships—blended into the green expanse. Fronting the La Salle side was U.S. Ambassador Kristie Kenney, guest of La Salle devotees José T. Pardo, a former finance secretary, and the Araneta clan. At first glance it didn't look very diplomatic, but when I took time to decode Madame Ambassador's symbolic attire, I could see that although Kenney sat with the La Salle crowd, she wore a modest blue blouse and held a pair of Ateneo balloons. Kenney may have been serving the Bush administration, but the way she played both sides smacked of Clintonian triangulation. With her cropped blond hair, perky composure, and clever neutrality, she brought to mind the woman who would become America's Secretary of

State, Hillary Clinton. Naturally, the ambassador's aides professed that attending Ateneo–La Salle games had nothing to do with her diplomatic agenda. Kenney, they said, had been a basketball fan since her college days at Clemson University. Perhaps that was the case, but I suspect the ambassador also didn't want to miss the country's most politicized and commercialized sporting event.

The game began, and when Ateneo secured the jump ball, the blue side whooped in joy as if big man Ford Arao had just hit a game-winning hook shot. The crowd's feral enthusiasm was cranked up to soccer hooligan levels, even though the sloppy first-half play didn't give either side much reason to cheer. La Salle's backcourt, a pair of smurf-sized guards, T. Y. Tang and J. V. Casio (whose name sometimes appears as Jayvee and the abominable Jvee), were as abbreviated in height as they were in name. Time and again they drove into the heart of Ateneo's defense only to miss off-balance runners or kick the ball out to three-point gunners whose shots rarely fell. Ateneo wasn't much better. They pounded the ball into Arao and Rabeh al-Hussaini, effective but clunky big men who managed a few buckets despite shooting with a shotputter's touch. However dull the action, the fans preserved their fever pitch. They screamed for defensive rebounds, loose balls, and out-of-bounds calls that favored their teams. When La Salle's slinky six-foot-five Rico Maierhofer slipped free for a baseline dunk, the green mob burst into chaos.

Despite the ragged play I was able to discern the teams' opposing styles. Ateneo was nauseatingly clean-cut, like they weren't just Blue Eagles but Eagle Scouts. Kirk Long, my American look-alike, was literally holier-than-thou. His parents were missionaries and Ateneo recruited him out of a high school called Faith Academy. Fellow guard Eric Salamat's last name meant "Thank you" in Tagalog, although with Salamat's quick hands and penchant for stealing the ball, a more ironic, sneering interpretation of his name seemed appropriate. Then there was team captain Chris Tiu, a Filipino Ken doll and scion of a wealthy

Chinese family. Tiu, pronounced "choo" and greeted by unfortunate "Tiu-perman" signs throughout the arena, was revered as the consummate student-athlete, a top player who left the team in 2005 to study abroad in France and returned to eventually become "King Eagle." At the time, Tiu said he was unsure if he wanted to pursue a career in professional basketball, business, or politics.* Ateneo played textbook basketball, with classic man-to-man defense and an inside-out offense that relied on post-up moves and outside shooting. The squeaky clean image, the royal blue uniforms—I felt like I was watching a Filipino cover band perform as the Duke University Blue Devils.

La Salle walked the court with a more menacing swagger, with more of the accessories—baggy shorts, headbands, tattoos, elaborate beards—that signified basketball toughness. Maierhofer was a gifted leaper whose chin-strap facial hair and Teutonic name added extra malice to his shot-blocking and dunking prowess. Guards like Casio were more streaky than steady. They didn't always make the smart play; they forced the ball into hopeless situations and relied on skill and gumption to finish with two points. The Green Archers played aggressive, intimidating basketball anchored by Pumaren's vaunted full-court press. Alaska assistant coach Joel Banal, who coached Ateneo to a championship in 2002, admitted that La Salle's press gave him nightmares. He knew the Green Archer defenders would converge on his ballhandlers and that after being hounded by Pumaren's charges, they'd cough up the ball. If Ateneo was Duke, La Salle had to be the Blue Devils' early nineties nemesis, the UNLV Runnin' Rebels, whose brash, dominant athletes humiliated Duke in the 1990 NCAA title game but were upset by the Blue Devils the following year.

---

* Before graduating from Ateneo, Tiu had already been elected to his neighborhood council. When I taught a sports writing class at the college, I included John McPhee's profile of Bill Bradley at Princeton on the reading list, and my students all agreed that Bradley reminded them of Tiu.

Basketball connoisseurs may not have found much to enjoy on the court during the Ateneo–La Salle game, but the real spectacle was in the crowd. In the lower deck, posers tried to blend in with tycoons by bog-arting courtside seats with their bodyguards. It made an impression— "I'm important!"—but when I asked other society types about the guy in the brown shirt with his private army in tow, no one could identify him. If the U.S. ambassador could leave her SWAT team at home, so could these guys. The Quezon City government and Philippine National Police had already pledged enough manpower to reconquer parts of Mindanao from Muslim separatists, and the peacekeepers were in plain sight, huddled together in camouflaged cabals beside each entrance to the arena.

Three contestants in the *Binibining Pilipinas*⃰ national beauty pageant also stood near a corner entrance, looking like they got lost on the way to the prom. Or perhaps they had found an environment that suited them perfectly: Ateneo–La Salle provided ample pomp for the beauty queens, who seemed more interested in pouting for photographers than following the game. Their heavy makeup reminded me of that popular American style of histrionic fandom—face-painting—only these hoops fashionistas lacked beer bellies and used glitter. With their hair teased up into shimmering black meringues and held together by enough hair spray to cause a minor explosion should a cigarette fall from the rafters, these stunners probably posed the greatest fire hazard in the building, but the paramilitary trio leering at them looked unconcerned.

As the game progressed—neither team had broken out of its slump, so it was close—the tension in the arena transformed people. Led by some of the most mannered and educated members of Philippine society, the fans reached a state of frothy lunacy that until that point I had never seen outside of zombie films. Sophistication, etiquette, and self-

---

⃰ *Binibini,* aside from being a phonetic fiesta, is the literal translation of the titular "Miss," as in "Miss Philippines."

control were discarded as assorted bigwigs cried like babies, hurled invectives like street-corner drunks, and chanted together like cult followers. Senator Richard Gordon, a member of Ateneo's Blue Babble Battalion cheerleading squad during the sixties, was jumping up and down in the aisle, stomping his feet and waving a blue T-shirt in circles. This was Gordon lite; the senator was renowned for leaping onto the scorer's table in fits of passion and sneaking behind La Salle colleagues to whisper "La Salle *bulok!*" La Salle is rotten trash! At this game, Gordon faced the Ateneo congregation and raised his palms toward the ceiling to rile them up. It worked. The crowd hardly sat during the fourth quarter, and when Maierhofer stole a rebound by pushing an Ateneo big man, Gordon led his side in a synchronized gesture. Hundreds of shame-filled index fingers pointed at the La Salle forward like they were preparing to burn him at the stake. Those who felt that the index finger lacked emotional charge flashed middle fingers. The rivalry actually had a long history of violence dating back to the 1960s, when the universities were still all male and games ended with parking lot brawls. Even in recent years, high emotions had boiled over into ugly incidents. In 2005 the "Dream Game," a friendly exhibition between PBA players who came from La Salle and Ateneo, was marred by an on-court melee that inspired fans to launch trash and a full can of San Miguel beer onto the court.

As the fourth quarter wound down, the teams also transformed to live up to the heightened atmosphere. In crunch time, players who hadn't found their touch all game became world-beaters. Maierhofer was hitting turnarounds at the high post and beating his man to the basket for acrobatic layups. Chris Tiu rose to the occasion after missing most of his shots in the first half. In the last two minutes, with his team trailing by six points, Tiu sliced La Salle's lead in half with a three-pointer over a trio of bum-rushing La Salle defenders, then scored a double-clutch, go-ahead layup a few possessions later. Ateneo won 65-64.

The rivalry had a way of staying with players and coaches throughout their careers. When Banal's Ateneo team won the 2002 title, squelching La Salle's run at a fifth straight championship, it was the coach's "most fulfilling accomplishment." Ateneo published commemorative books about that season, and Banal was immortalized, at least among the Blue Eagle flock, as the miracle coach. "After that championship," Banal told me, "it was like the whole Filipino nation knew me. Like if you go to a restaurant and you're paying your bill, somebody from Ateneo got it already." But the sword cut both ways. Alaska point guard Mike Cortez had been dominant throughout his three-year La Salle career. He was so good, in fact, that when his last game in green turned out to be a dud—he missed eleven of thirteen shots in 2002's deciding loss to Ateneo—he was branded a game-fixer. The accusation was based on nothing but bitterness and innuendo, but it followed Mike into the PBA, where even though he helped Alaska win titles and made all-star teams, many fans whispered, *"Benta,"* Tagalog for "Sold," anytime he missed an important shot.

Ateneo–La Salle enmity even loosened the bond of friendship between the teams' coaches. Norman Black and Pumaren won several professional titles together with the San Miguel Beermen. But those eighties glory days meant little now. "If you're part of the rivalry, you just don't like each other," Black, plain-spoken and deadly serious about all things basketball, told me. "Franz played for me and he was my assistant coach, but that has little bearing on what's happening right now. He's the coach of La Salle; I'm the coach of Ateneo. Let the chips fall where they may."

11

My Big Break

Basketball sat at the junction between politics and entertainment in Philippine pop culture, with all three sharing common borders that allowed ballers, actors, and elected officials to cross into each other's realms. As far back as the early days of the PBA, television and film producers sought to turn players' popularity into ratings, with mixed success. Politicians supported basketball and occasionally owned professional teams, largely because their involvement with the sport provided an electoral boost. Athletes not only converted their fame into acting and government jobs, but also married into elite political and entertainment families.*

---

* Purefoods guard James Yap, the reigning MVP during the season I followed Alaska, may have been the PBA's most popular player, not because of his three-point accuracy but because he had recently married Kris Aquino, the country's biggest television star and Ninoy and Corazon Aquino's youngest daughter. Kris had a well-known, star-crossed infatuation with basketball players that included very public failed relationships with two already married PBA titans, Alvin Patrimonio and Joey Marquez, the latter of whom, Kris admitted on national TV, gave her chlamydia. Aquino's marriage to Yap was also plagued by rumors of Yap's infidelity, and the couple's 2010 separation rivaled the election of Aquino's brother Noynoy as President of the Philippines as one of the country's biggest media events."

Freddie Webb, the fleet-footed guard who played on the last Philippine Olympic team in 1972, probably pulled off the politics-entertainment-hoops hat trick most successfully. Webb was the face of the Tanduay Rhum Makers for most of the seventies. He never managed to win a championship with Tanduay, but he did ride his celebrity into a post in local government, a starring role in a prime time sitcom, and an eventual Senate seat. Webb, a natural showman with good comic instincts, still appeared in romantic comedies as his stock character—a buffoonish, over-the-hill beefcake.

Robert Jaworski also made television forays before becoming a senator, although his theatrical talents were less inspirational than his behind-the-back passes. Jaworski headlined an early eighties police procedural, *Manila Files*, which a handful of people told me was the worst show ever broadcast on Philippine television. That would make it the Mona Lisa of schlock entertainment. This was, after all, the land where no fewer than five adaptations of the telenovela *Betty La Fea* (all from different countries) had been aired and where one of the current top-rated programs was a sitcom called *Show me da Manny,* starring the world champion boxer Manny Pacquiao.[*]

Atlas Sports Weekly called *Manila Files* a Filipino answer to *Starsky & Hutch*, with Jaworski and Francis Arnaiz, the real-life starting guards for the PBA's Toyota team, playing members of a Manila police "Special Operations Squad" bent on showing the world that "crime does not pay." The show was filled with production values so poor that they would make the effects in low-budget Blaxploitation flicks look like *Avatar*. Episodes would end with so-bad-it's-good action sequences, usually shot in abandoned warehouses, where Jaworski and Arnaiz threw stage punches at gangs of petty crooks who crumbled instantly and permanently; then the backcourt duo would mow down a second

---

[*] Benjie Paras, a two-time PBA Most Valuable Player, also appeared in *Show me da Manny* as one of Pacquiao's rivals.

wave of bad guys with dozens of shots from revolvers that never needed reloading. When the smoke cleared, another criminal mastermind was thrown in the slammer, while Jaworski and Arnaiz exchanged satisfied looks through aviator sunglasses. Basketball could get you on TV, but it couldn't make you an actor.

It was fitting, then, that my entrée to the proud Philippine tradition of hokey television also came through hoops. Not long after I arrived in Manila, I started playing pickup games with a group of ex-pros, guys in their early thirties who had played some college and MBA ball and managed to last a couple years in the PBA. They spent enough years on the fringes of Manila's celebrity scene to know some prominent actors and directors. After a game one night, I got a call from Chris Tan, one of my pickup buddies. Chris had played for Santa Lucia and was re-membered for hitting a deep three-pointer that clinched a champion-ship for the Realtors in 2001. His wife was a talk-show host for the GMA network, one of the country's two ruling TV conglomerates.

"Chris? What's up? Did I take your rubbing alcohol?"*

"Hi Rafe, do you want to come out in a *novela* on GMA?"

"Sure." I accepted even though I hardly knew what he was talking about. I understood that GMA meant channel seven, and that *novelas* were *telenovelas*, prime-time soap operas filled with overheated ro-mance, backstabbing connivance, and inconsolable weeping.

"Great! The director needs some American guys," Chris said. "Come to the restobar on Scout Borromeo, corner Mother Ignacia, tomorrow night at seven. You're going to be in *Bakekang*. You get to have a bed scene with Sunshine Dizon."

And then he hung up. Back home, if an acquaintance gave me a time and place and said to be there because he wanted me to act in a "bed scene," my next move would be to change my telephone number. In

---

* In Metro Manila there was no better way to freshen up than a quick dousing with rubbing alcohol. It's a shower in a bottle.

Manila, however, it seemed to fit with life's unpredictable rhythm, the same way my landlady's septuagenarian dad sometimes came to my door unannounced at six-thirty in the morning to collect rent checks. Besides, I was more concerned with Googling Sunshine Dizon to see how my costar stacked up in the realm of gorgeous TV starlets.

Sunshine seemed like an enchanting young woman, also in her early twenties. She started as a child actress in the late eighties and played supporting roles in dozens of popular movies and TV shows. With her baby face, round eyes, and button nose, Dizon conveyed a tenderness that most of her sex symbol colleagues lacked. Her character Bakekang, however, looked nothing like the actress who portrayed her. I read online that the show, based on a 1970s comic book and film, told the story of a mythically ugly woman—think Medusa without snakes—struggling to get by in a cruel world. To transform into Bakekang, Dizon wore a swollen, lightbulb-shaped prosthetic nose covered with pockmarks and inserted crooked brown dentures that looked like the novelty redneck teeth sold in supermarket gumball machines. "Bakekang," I was told, conveyed something similar to "ugly duckling" in English, but without the happy ending of becoming a swan. If you were *Bakekang* ugly, you stayed that way for life.

The next day, as I rode a jeepney west across Kamias Road, my head kept banging against the exposed metal spot where the interior's Naugahyde cushion had worn away. My one good shirt—a blue button-down—and my jeans were hanging from a handrail that ran lengthwise down the center of the jeep, and the garments whipped into irritated passengers' faces as the driver careened through traffic. It didn't matter. Nothing could puncture my high spirits. I was living the dream! I would never get a chance to act on national television in the States. Not that I ever dreamed of starring on *General Hospital,* but who could say no to the opportunity? Plus, this gig had fallen into my lap by the grace of hoops.

I thought of Alex Compton, who once told me how a network cast him in a Tagalog sitcom before he could speak the language, and Jaworski and Arnaiz and the other ballers who stumbled into showbiz careers. I wasn't in their league, but somehow basketball led me to *Bakekang* the same way it led them to movies, billboards, and, in some cases, politics. I couldn't wait to upload the scenes on YouTube and hear my friends' bewildered reactions: "*Why are you on TV, and moreover, why are you in bed with a woman wearing a duster and Billy Bob teeth?*"

I hopped off the back of the jeepney and walked a few blocks to the shoot. "Are you Raphael?" a voice called out from a tent. One of the producers, Miss Mona, introduced herself and insisted I sit down and eat from a pink tray of rice, squid, and vegetables. After dinner she would tell me about my role. While I chewed squid, I saw another basketball friend, Twan Clinton, loping toward me. Twan was a six-foot-eight Jamaican-American from Miami with shoulder-length dreadlocks and long arms as skinny as the string beans I was pushing around my tray. No one seemed to know precisely why Twan was in the Philippines, and everyone had heard a different rumor: he managed a call center, he was on the lam, he was CIA.

One undisputed fact about Twan was that he was a man about town, and standing a foot and a half taller than everyone around him meant that people noticed him. Twan could definitely hoop, but he had never played professionally, whether in Florida, Manila, or anyplace else. Still, he seemed to make the most of the common misconception in malls and nightclubs that he was a visiting NBA player. That is, he rarely went out of his way to correct anyone who mistakenly identified him as a onetime member of the Miami Heat. To many Filipinos, he was tall enough, black enough, and he could dunk like a pro. Twan earned pocket money as a ringer in corporate leagues and neighborhood tournaments around Manila. I went to watch him play in a mayor's cup playoff game in nearby Rizal province once, and as our van rattled into the town plaza, people shook the chain-link fence surrounding the court and chanted, "Cleen-tone! Cleen-tone!" The clamor grew as Twan walked toward his grimy cement stage. When he reached half-court, a young boy ran out and presented him with a ball. Twan took it, galloped toward the basket with two big dribbles, then sprang high into the air off two legs and jammed the ball through the rim with two hands, while people screamed and hugged like they had won the lottery.

In the tent, Twan explained that Chris Tan had also called him the previous night. We were to be costars in *Bakekang*. Miss Mona came over to explain the show: Bakekang was an ugly girl from a poor family. She lived in a slum where everyone made vicious jokes about her dark complexion, her bulbous nose, and her hideous teeth. Without money or beauty, her situation seemed hopeless. Television was her escape. Her rare happy moments came while watching *novelas*, and she dreamed of falling in love with a hunky actor named Kristof. One day Bakekang vows to take control of her destiny and make something of her life, to show the people who hurt her that she was indeed someone special.

And there was only one way to make her dreams come true: find a white foreigner and have *mestizo* babies. That's where me and Twan came in. I looked at Twan with a raised eyebrow, and he lowered his face into his hands and chuckled. We were finding out that the main character wasn't the only ugly thing about *Bakekang*. The show was built on racial attitudes that stretched my conscience to its breaking point. Every day, makeup artists transformed Sunshine into Bakekang by flattening her nose and darkening her skin. Bakckang believed her best shot at a better life was to find a Caucasian man—more of a sperm donor than a husband—and have whiter, more European-looking children who could support the family by starring in commercials. These mores were nothing new; I encountered them every time I went shopping and struggled to find a bar of soap that *didn't* tout its whitening abilities. In *Bakekang*, however, I wasn't merely observing an unpleasant fixation with skin color. I was perpetuating it by helping a fictional Filipina, a character created to relate to average viewers, achieve her dream of raising a *mestizo* love child. I was the whitening ingredient.

Bakekang's racial themes reflected long-standing color prejudices— an ugly and indisputable colonial legacy—that kept wealthy, often mixed-race elites separate from darker skinned *indios* who toiled in rice fields or peddled cigarettes in urban slums. This rigid class structure was as responsible as any government policy for making social mobility no more than a fantasy for most Filipinos. Some of the "offensive" themes in *Bakekang* could also be attributed to cultural differences in the way Americans and Filipinos talked about people's appearance. In Manila, if someone gained weight, their friends might giggle and say, "Wow, you got fat!" A guy with dark skin might hear something along the lines of "You're really black, dude!" I tried to tamp down the indignant—or was it uptight?—American raging in my mind: *Why is it your business if I gained weight? So what if someone has dark skin?* Also, I reminded myself that the Philippines had a different kind of historical baggage than the United States when it came to institutionalized racism. The country had its own set of racial hang-ups.

After that responsible discussion of Philippine attitudes toward race, I should also admit to being a sellout. *Bakekang*'s subject matter made me uncomfortable, but I never really considered taking a principled stand and refusing to act in the show. While Miss Mona ran through the sordid details, I looked at Twan again, and he shrugged as if to say, "What can you do?" If he could live with it, so could I. Besides, this was our chance to appear in prime time!

Now that we'd sold our souls, it was time to do some soap opera acting. My character, Brad, was an American businessman living in Manila. In my first scene, Bakekang notices me in the street and introduces herself. Before the first take, two flirtatious gay makeup artists patted foundation on my cheeks, then opened up several sachets of jet black conditioner and rubbed it into my scalp to make my hair darker. According to the show's inscrutable racial calculus, *Bakekang*'s audience liked their white men tall, dark, and handsome, not tall, fair and blondish. Sunshine Dizon introduced herself and thanked me and Twan for agreeing to work on short notice, then she settled into the massage chair where she waited between takes. I asked Miss Mona if I could see a script. She cocked her head and squinted at me like I had asked for a still-beating goat heart. Eventually, she nodded and left to find my lines. Because *Bakekang* aired five nights a week, the crew worked at a blinding pace. So fast, it seemed, that the acting was based on broad narrative arcs more than scripted lines. A script did exist somewhere, but the stars didn't bother memorizing lines. Instead, they improvised within well-worn genre tropes.

It took Miss Mona fifteen minutes, but she managed to scrounge together three pages of dialogue for the scene I was about to shoot. I hadn't acted since high school, when I played a raccoon-eating mountain man in a five-minute comedy skit, and I had no clue how to carry myself in front of a TV camera. Peering at my lines through brown *adobo* sauce stains on the crinkled sheets at least made me feel more prepared, although I'd hardly whispered my way through the pages when director Gil Tejada touched the small of my back and asked, "Ready?"

I didn't know the lines. Nobody cared. I knew the gist of them and it was time to shoot. Once the camera was rolling, it was like I was transformed, except instead of stepping into my character, I became a walking parody of bad acting. When Bakekang chased me down on the street, calling "Mr. Foreigner!" and offering to serve as my tour guide, I turned her down in a voice I'd never heard before. Higher-pitched than my normal timbre and with a foppish inflection, it was like I was trying to do an accentless Hugh Grant impression. Even worse was the vacant look in my eyes. There was no anger, no confusion, no human quality whatsoever.

We kept shooting deep into the night. As the story progresses, Bakekang follows me to a restaurant, where I bump into Carl, my black

American friend played by Twan. My character finds Bakekang repulsive and wants to get her thrown out of the restaurant, but Twan fancies her and invites her to stay. Twan convinces me to play wingman and let Bakekang hang out with us so he can seduce her, while Bakekang plots to use him to get closer to me. Before long we're pounding San Miguel beers and belting out karaoke standards at a local watering hole. At the end of the night I'm plastered, so Bakekang stuffs me into a cab and gives Twan the slip. He jumps into the next taxi and follows.

And so the stage was set for the climactic bed scene. It was past midnight, and the crew was pressed to finish before 1:00 a.m., when the overtime clause in Dizon's contract kicked in. There was no time to bother reading lines, so instead Tejada just ordered me and Twan to take our shirts off and get under the sheets with Bakekang. He explained how the scene would unfold: The shot opens on Bakekang. She yawns and looks to her left, where she sees me nuzzling peacefully at her side. Success! Then she glances to the right, sees Twan's black foot and wails in horror when she realizes we engaged in a booze-fueled threesome. "Brad, then you wake up," Tejada told me, "and you say, 'We had sex with this monkey?'" Until then my character had been mean and dismissive, but none of the lines I butchered earlier in the evening had been this reprehensible.

I asked if I had to call her a monkey.

"Of course you have to call her monkey," Tejada said, while the crew nodded in agreement. "That's what makes it funny!" After delivering the primate punch line, I was supposed to drag Bakekang out of bed, down the stairs and out the door, then throw her on the ground while calling her "ugly bitch." I was outnumbered. I caved. I did it. So now not only do I have a clip I can use to seek more soap opera work, but also proof for future generations of Bartholomews that grandpa was a racist monster.

We filmed the scene in a small bedroom, baking under television lights that felt like heat lamps. The temperature climbed past a hundred degrees before the director ordered all three of us under the covers. It took six or seven attempts to find the right angle for the shot, and between takes me and Twan jumped out of bed so the giggling makeup artists could pat our sweaty chests with Kleenex. Once we were rolling and Bakekang started screeching, Tejada ordered us to "react." It was pretty common in Philippine *telenovelas* to cut between close-ups of characters making assorted forlorn, lusty, outraged, or dumbfounded faces. These reaction montages could stretch for minutes without dialogue, just actors beaming emotion into the camera. For a talentless amateur like me, this was terrifying. The passing seconds felt like eons, and Tejada kept urging me to "React!" My well of expressions ran dry almost immediately; after that I racked my brain for any configuration of features that might make an impression, but I mostly came up empty. Whatever my "reactions" looked like, Tejada wisely edited them out of the episode.

If you watch the show (it's available on YouTube),* you may notice a plot inconsistency in my bed scene. Bakekang and her beaus get drunk enough to have a *ménage à trois* and black out, but when we wake up the next day, me and Twan are both wearing pants. This suggests that after the threesome, we had the presence of mind to put our pants on before passing out. Our inexplicable moment of clarity was made necessary by Philippine TV's decency laws, which say that men cannot appear on screen in their underwear. Violence against women? Check. Frothy hate speech? No problem. Man in boxer shorts? Forbidden. Makes sense, right?

That was pretty much the end of my role in *Bakekang*. I continued

---

* The YouTube comment pages on my scenes contain an astonishing variety of reactions delivered in English, Tagalog, and the hybrid Taglish. For example: "Bakekang's a slut!" "Wow! Good for you Bakekang! You got two *amerikanos*, coffee and milk!" "LOL! SHE DID BOTH OF THEM!! THEM GUYS TALK HELLA FUNNY!" "Wow! That Brad is phenomenally BAD! (I'm referring to his acting.)"

following the show over the next few months to see what happened. Thanks to a little showbiz magic, Bakekang gave birth to fraternal twins fathered separately by me and Twan. This, I learned, was called a heteropaternal superfecundation, an extremely rare but possible occurrence. Throughout the show, Bakekang committed various acts of shameful neglect against Charming, the half-black and therefore ugly baby. First, she placed the infant in a chute marked IF YOU'RE EMBARRASSED at a nunnery. Then she tried to sell the child to a blind woman. None of it made me particularly proud, although I briefly became a minor celebrity. People recognized me in malls and on jeepneys wherever I went. Horrifyingly, children really seemed to enjoy my character; I hoped it was the overwhelming goofiness of my performance. It became hard for me to walk down the street without hearing some seven-year-old voice chime, *"Bakekang!"* The kids, often too young to understand the difference between fiction and reality, wanted to know why I was so mean to Bakekang and asked if we still lived together. On a few occasions, parents asked me to pose for cell phone pictures while holding their babies, which felt every bit as creepy as it sounds.

In fairness, *Bakekang* tried to have a moral ending. As Charming and my fictional daughter, Kristal, grew up, it became apparent that the ugly sister was kinder and more responsible than her fair-skinned twin. Kristal did become a showbiz baby, but she was selfish and mistreated her mother. Charming, on the other hand, loved Bakekang unconditionally and repeatedly bailed the family out of trouble. At the end of the series, Kristal sacrifices herself for Bakekang, who was going to be shot by a rival stage mom (this is a *telenovela*, after all). Kristal took the bullet for her mother, and Charming's loving example was credited for inspiring the selfless act. By then, however, the series had been contaminated by so many vile prejudices that this message of hope seemed like too little, too late.

The series eventually ended and I was forgotten. I was pleased, however, to have continued the proud Philippine tradition of following basketball into entertainment, and I liked to think my wooden performance was worthy of my hoops forebears like Jaworski and Arnaiz. At the end of *Bakekang*'s run, I drifted back into the basketball world, ready to follow the bouncing ball to other strange corners of Philippine society.

The Alaska clubhouse was quiet for a change when I arrived before one late season practice. For once, Willie Miller wasn't pouring all his guile and gumption into some prank like jolting unsuspecting teammates with a low-voltage prod the trainers used to stimulate strained muscles. Dale Singson and John Ferriols weren't snickering over some Cebuano video meme downloaded to their cell phones. Roe and Mike Cortez weren't cocooned in their noise-canceling headphones. The players were leaning forward to get a better look at a television—they squinted, nodded in response to what they saw, whispered observations into each others' ears. They were engaged.

Rightly so, I thought as I took in this studious tableau on my way through the narrow hallway that opened up into the lounge's main room. I figured they were watching game tape of the Barangay Ginebra Gin-Kings, the team the Aces were preparing to face in a one-game playoff for second place and an automatic berth in the semifinals. Alaska and Ginebra finished the regular season with 12-6 records, tied behind 13-5 Red Bull. In the PBA, the top two teams skipped the first two rounds of the postseason while the rest of the league battled to reach them in the final four. That made the sudden death Ginebra game the biggest of Alaska's season. Winning would give the Aces two weeks to relax—time for lingering injuries to heal and for the coaching staff to plan a championship surge. In recent weeks a strained hamstring had forced Roe to miss a rematch with Red Bull and James Penny, the only import who'd bested him all season. Cone's all-Filipino lineup gave Penny and Coach Yeng Guiao a scare; Alaska even took an eight-point lead in the third quarter, but the undermanned Aces eventually lost.

Roe returned and looked healthy in a season-ending victory over the Santa Lucia Realtors, but the extra weeks of rest would improve his chances of surviving the playoffs without reaggravating the muscle. Mike's comeback from torn knee ligaments was only a month old, and while he had shown flashes of his preinjury brilliance, he still hadn't found a consistent rhythm on the court. A bye to the semifinals would mean more time for his game to return.

Most of all, Cone wanted to avoid the early playoff rounds, a battle royale that began with a single-elimination tournament of the bottom four teams, one of whom would prevail with a spot in the best-of-three quarterfinals. The loser of the Alaska-Ginebra game would drop to the quarters, where Cone suspected they'd play the San Miguel Beermen. Aside from being the PBA's hottest team—the Beermen won eight of ten games after losing their first six—San Miguel was a frightful match-up for Alaska. With a stingy defense, playoff veterans and an experienced import,* they mirrored the Aces' strengths. A month earlier the Beermen dealt Alaska one of their worst losses of the season, and Cone was determined to avoid facing them in a best-of-three joust where one bad game could put the Aces on the brink of elimination.

It came as a slight surprise, then, to emerge from the hallway and see that the players weren't absorbed in Ginebra tape but were instead enraptured by a local variety show called *Wowowee*. This shouldn't have been such a shock. The most important game of the season would get its share of the players' attention, but not at the expense of *Wowowee*, a two-hour program that commanded a massive TV audience every afternoon. Pop culture experts had even cited *Wowowee*'s frenetic pace to explain why Filipinos loved basketball. *Wowowee* first aired in 2005,

---

* Galen Young, the San Miguel import, had actually been Cone's first choice for Alaska that season, but on opening day Young was still in Washington, playing for the Yakama Sun Kings of the CBA. After winning the CBA title, Young was ready to come to Manila, but Alaska already had Roe. Instead, Young landed with the Beermen and helmed their mid-season turnaround.

but its format, the "noontime show," had been a broadcast staple for decades. The myriad entertainments offered in a given *Wowowee* episode included gigs by popular musicians; lengthy booty-shaking sessions performed by a platoon of half-naked lasses; karaoke belted out by sundry members of the Philippine underclass; humiliating and heartrending testimonials of poverty; and a delirious crowd ready to erupt at every punch line dropped by Willie Revillame, the effervescent, everyman host whose very soul seemed to be carbonated.

The *Wowowee* segment that so enthralled Alaska's players that afternoon was a performance by an R&B strumpet once linked to John Ferriols, the team's resident hunk. Roe was impressed: "This show got some thick Filipinas." Then Pokwang, a comedienne cohost with the bony physique of a sixties pole vaulter, a severe, angular face, and an affinity for colored wigs, made her grand entrance. With her machine gun patter, delivered with the same aggressive intonation as the barkers who herded commuters into the backs of jeepneys, Pokwang struck a jarring contrast with the dulcet femininity of John's chanteuse. Nearly everyone in the room was laughing, except Roe, who reconsidered his earlier assessment: "That shit is nasty." The joke was on him and anyone else naive enough to take *Wowowee* seriously.

The binding agent in *Wowowee*'s unsavory brew was money, or the lack thereof. The show was structured around a series of games, with preselected contestants competing against each other and against participants pulled from the crowd, often based on their willingness to humiliate themselves. Throughout the program, Revillame rewarded each correct answer with cash from a bottomless stack of 1,000 peso bills, each worth about twenty dollars. In one regular segment, Revillame interviewed guests from a chosen, often neglected niche of Philippine society: orphans, construction workers, jeepney drivers, women who work as "guest relations officers" in girlie bars. Baring their souls for millions of viewers while the in-house keyboardist set the mood with somber, reflective chords, *Wowowee* contestants often had tears rolling down their cheeks by the time Revillame finished with them. Then, with hardly any transition, he would ask: "What's your talent?" and the contestants would choose to sing or dance. This formula enabled *Wowowee* to televise surreal moments like dishwashers' children serenading the crowd with tone-deaf Air Supply covers and macho security guards' deluded attempts at dirty dancing.* After performing, contestants received a few bills from Revillame's pile. But the prizes weren't limited to these minor disbursements. The show also gave away million-peso rewards worth between $20,000 and $40,000, and occasionally participants won jeepneys or even new homes.

Another of Revillame's favorite ploys was to recruit the most disoriented members of the studio audience—drooling senior citizens, clueless Americans, or overenthusiastic naifs who would gladly debase themselves for two minutes of fame and a fistful of cash. These were cheap laughs, but they were damn funny. Try suppressing a laugh when Revillame convinces an elderly woman in a duster to dance sexy for him, or when he talks Tagalog circles around a portly Westerner in a trucker hat. The show reached its exploitative zenith when children appeared as guests. *Wowowee* often selected kids from poor families as contestants, and Revillame milked their hard-luck stories for a nation of captive viewers. The children, too young to be self-aware, would reveal tear-jerking details of their lives, such as when Revillame asked one girl what she wanted to tell her father, who was watching at home. She looked into the camera, eyes welling with tears, and said in Tagalog, "Daddy, please don't get drunk tonight." The revelation made my stomach turn; then I inched closer to the screen to see what she'd say next. I thought I'd never see that kind of twisted intimacy on live television again. Then I started watching more *Wowowee* and realized the show averages two or three such breakdowns per month.

---

* Once in a while the show produced a jaw-dropping moment, wherein a paunchy, middle-age tricycle driver unveiled his silky falsetto and belted out a Stylistics tune superior to anything sung by local cover bands.

Wowowee cast a spell on its audience. The daily carnival of nubile bodies, inane humor, and voyeuristic thrills pulsated from segment to segment with snowballing momentum. The longer you watched, the deeper your trance. By the time you emerged the credits were rolling and two hours had vanished. This time-warp quality seemed like an important part of the show's appeal. Millions of Filipinos, in the city and the provinces, employed or jobless, spent multihour chunks of their day just waiting. Waiting for a customer to buy a can of corned beef. Waiting in line at the Philippine Overseas Employment Administration. Waiting on a twelve-hour bus ride to Manila from the Mountain Province. Nothing killed time like *Wowowee*.

I didn't understand the full magnitude of *Wowowee*'s stranglehold on Philippine TV audiences until I actually appeared on the show. When a friend of mine from Queens visited me in Manila, I wanted to make sure he'd have a funny story to share back on Bell Boulevard, so I took him to a live taping of *Wowowee*. The producers looked at us and saw comedy gold. We were seated in the front row. Like everyone else in the audience, we sang along with the theme song and tried to keep up with the dance steps. At some point during this orgy of forced happiness and orchestrated pelvic thrusting, a female cohost thrust a microphone in my face and asked for shout-outs. The next thing I knew, confetti was raining down on me as Revillame pointed and shouted, *"Ikaw ang Bigatin!"* You're a big-timer! Along with nine other handpicked patsies, I was led backstage and told how to play *Bigat 10*, one of the show's trivia games.

My *Wowowee* debut felt pretty insignificant. I stood on stage, recited the *Bigat 10* catchphrase, spoke to Revillame in kindergarten Tagalog, and buzzed in too late to answer my trivia question. A dancer handed me a cardboard box full of miniature juice boxes and sent me back to my seat. But what seemed like an anticlimax to me had actually made quite an impression on the TV audience. After the taping, while riding Manila's light rail train, other commuters recognized me. They slapped me five, hugged me, asked to take pictures with me. Inside a mall, a

KFC diner who saw me through a window dropped his drumstick and made *Wowowee*'s signature gesture, a right-to-left diagonal swipe under his chin. Later that week I took my friend biking in Guimaras, a sleepy Visayan island covered with mango plantations. Somewhere in the middle of a deeply rutted livestock trail, we stopped for drinks at a thatch hut next to a dirt basketball court with a hoop nailed to a coconut tree. The store sold tiny packets of peanuts and crackers, bars of detergent for hand-washing laundry, and sachets of shampoo draped over the window bars in long, perforated chains. They had no mineral water for sale, only warm bottles of Pepsi. I paid for the soda with a twenty peso bill, and the teenage girl who took my money studied my face. "Are you the foreigners from *Wowowee*?" Once our identities were established, the girl ran into a cinder-block house behind the hut and returned with her mother and a gaggle of younger siblings. "We've never met a celebrity!" she said.

The recognition continued for months. In my neighborhood it became permanent. Whenever I walked from my house to the train station, tricycle drivers buzzed by and yelped, *"Wowowee!"* This might sound strange, but the show was often compared to basketball because of its devoted following and fast-paced action.* When I asked sports journalists and basketball old hands why Filipinos adored hoops, many of them mentioned *Wowowee*. According to their theory, people loved the game show for the same reasons they loved the game: There wasn't a dull moment. There was drama in every Revillame trivia question and every hardwood lead change; there were laughs behind each geriatric undulation and each contorted layup. Both noontime shows and hoops appealed to Filipinos' short attention spans.

One major difference, however, was that basketball hadn't attracted as many detractors as *Wowowee*. Sure, there was plenty to bemoan about the excessive side of Filipinos' basketball jones. But to many

---

* Willie Revillame, by many accounts, is himself an avid pickup baller.

opinion makers, *Wowowee* was the bête noire of Philippine society. The show's cynical trade-off with its mostly impoverished guests—cash prizes for dignity—has been likened to dangling meat in front of wolves. In February 2006 that desperation turned fatal when the show's producers offered free tickets for *Wowowee*'s anniversary show to a crowd of 40,000 people waiting outside an arena in Pasig City. Much of the mob had been sleeping on the street outside the entrance for days, and when word spread that a limited number of tickets were being given away, a stampede broke out. More than seventy people, mostly elderly women, were trampled to death.

Less than a week later, investigative journalist Sheila Coronel took a stand against *Wowowee* in a speech to Philippine advertisers:

> Shows like these offer a way out of poverty through the magic, the razzmatazz of television. Never mind hard work or social reforms. The key lies in the luck in the draw, the promise of salvation provided by a celebrity entertainer. Is it any wonder that the following of TV programs like *Wowowee* resembles that of a messianic cult? And isn't Willie Revillame some sort of messiah of the idiot box?

Coronel's criticism was measured compared to the bloodthirsty rhetoric of politicians and columnists who called for Revillame's head, but *Wowowee* weathered that public relations storm and others that followed. Yet despite the program's rollicking debasement of the most vulnerable Filipinos, watching *Wowowee* remained a hypnotic, almost unavoidable experience, and the show continued to lure rubberneckers from the tricycle driver hangouts along Katipunan to the Alaska players lounge. The show was eventually taken off the air in 2010 and replaced by a nearly identical, perhaps less risqué program called *Pilipinas Win na Win*.

"**Let's go, fellas. Time to** work." Tim Cone breezed out of his office, cast a disdainful eye at *Wowowee*, and shut off the TV. The coach's legs were a little wobbly as he wheeled a dry-erase board in front of the television. His hair seemed unwashed and matted down, and his cheeks sagged a little lower than usual. The kidney-shaped bags under Cone's eyes were puffier and more purple. If Alaska lost its tiebreak to Ginebra, it wouldn't be due to Cone's lack of effort. Yet the trickiest part of the coach's strategy—instilling his game plan so the players could execute it in tomorrow's game—was just beginning. "We've got to stop Nealy," Cone was referring to Rod Nealy, Ginebra's prolific southpaw import. "No one's gonna stop him one-on-one. The only guy in the league who could even do it on a fifty-fifty basis would be Rosell."

Roe rolled his eyes at the backhanded compliment but kept listening to Cone. The coach seemed propelled through his exhaustion by a final adrenaline rush, a coach's high. In Nealy and Ginebra coach Jong Uichico, Cone had found worthy adversaries, and he'd spent much of the previous forty-eight hours devising a scheme to shut down the Gin-King import. For Cone, who relished the cerebral side of hoops, this was an opportunity to turn the basketball court into a chessboard. Nealy was Ginebra's queen. He was their primary ballhandler, scorer, playmaker, and rebounder. Nealy did it all, and Cone was ready to spring a trap on him. "When you have a dominant, dominant import like they do," he told the team, "you've got to have a disciplined game plan. You can't approach him lightly."

Ginebra was a throwback to the import-dominated teams of the early and mid-nineties, when Cone was crafting his coaching style and leading Alaska to its first championships. Back then he had to think up ways to contain players like Bobby Parks, a seven-time PBA best import who routinely put up 50- and 60-point games, and Tony Harris, who scored 105 points in a game. "Every night we had to go against a Michael Jordan," Cone reminded the team about the old days. "Every game there was a Michael out there that we had to stop." Over the years, imports receded into more subdued roles—if scoring just 30 points per game could ever be considered "subdued"—as coaches learned to slow the game down and attack foreign gunners with double teams and match-up zones. Modern PBA teams favored more balanced scoring, with roughly equal contributions from their imports and locals.

A mix of circumstance and patriotism forced Ginebra to revert to the one-man-team model. The Gin-Kings owned the league's most talent-laden roster that year, starting with Jayjay Helterbrand and Mark Caguioa, two American-bred guards who had been unstoppable while leading Ginebra to the most recent all-Filipino championship. Like Alaska forward Tony dela Cruz, Helterbrand and Caguioa had been called to duty for the Philippine national team and weren't playing in this conference. Ginebra began the current season with Rudy Hatfield, a chiseled six-foot-three Fil-Am who was the league's preeminent garbage man, a human perpetual motion machine who could average 15 to 20 points on offensive rebounds and broken plays alone. But the same relentless energy that made Hatfield a terror on the court made him impulsive away from the game. He had already gone AWOL once in the aftermath of the Fil-sham scandal. After the Senate hearings, the Department of Justice ordered Hatfield and a handful of other players deported. In Hatfield's case, the order was reversed, but by the time he was cleared to play, Hatfield wanted nothing to do with Philippine basketball. He returned to Michigan, where he pursued various flights of fancy, first exploring a professional wrestling career, then training to become a firefighter because, as he later told *Philippine Star* columnist Quinito Henson, "chicks dig guys in suspenders." At the end of 2006, Ginebra was able to lure Hatfield back to the PBA, and he helped the Gin-Kings win the all-Filipino title while also enchanting fans with his brand of Rodmanian lunacy.* Hatfield played for Ginebra when Roe and Alaska beat them in the second game of the season, but a few weeks later he drifted away again, this time to provide moral support for his Stateside fiancée, who was embroiled in a child-custody suit.

Without Hatfield and their all-star backcourt, Ginebra's roster read like a basketball contingency plan, all journeymen and backups. Uichico's decision to use Nealy as an old-fashioned "me against the world" import was the coach's way of making the most of his options. The outdated strategy proved effective, and Ginebra finished with one of the league's best records because Nealy was, in Cone's estimation, one of the best imports the league had seen in years, a player capable of scoring 30 or 40 points per game and creating shots for teammates who couldn't get free on their own. Also, opposing coaches got so used to preparing team-oriented game plans that they seemed to have forgotten the decades-old tricks for handcuffing Godzilla imports like Nealy. But Cone remembered Tony Harris and Bobby Parks, and he unveiled his plot with a hint of nostalgic glee.

"We're gonna scheme him, fellas," Cone announced while drawing a full-court rectangle on the whiteboard. "Nic, Rey, it's gonna be one of you two guarding Nealy." Cone looked at his import-stoppers, Belasco and Hugnatan. "You have to play him baseline to baseline: ninety feet of defense." Ginebra liked to have Nealy handle the ball as a point-forward so other teams couldn't deny passes to him on the wing. Cone

---

* Throughout the 2006-2007 All-Filipino conference, Hatfield created a wrestling persona, "H-Bomb," and delivered halftime and postgame interviews in character as if he were auditioning for the WWE. His pièce de résistance was a ninety-second diatribe after Ginebra clinched the title, in which he referred to Coach Uichico as "Jong U-Cheeks" and team executive Henry Cojuangco, a member of the powerful Cojuangco clan, as "Big Bank Hank." After thanking teammates and the Ginebra organization, Hatfield most of all thanked himself for being the only one who believed in himself two years ago, when he was at home in Michigan "with a bag of Milk Duds and some Doritos."

wanted the ball out of Nealy's hands, so he planned to sic his defenders on him full-court. "Then Willie, Mike, Dale—you guys are gonna play the backcourt chasers," Cone said. To make sure Nealy passed before he crossed half-court, Alaska would send one of its guards—the quickest on-ball defenders—to pester him into getting rid of the ball. "If he doesn't pick up that ball, then *tuloy, tuloy, tuloy* until he picks it up and passes," Cone said, injecting a little Tagalog to emphasize that the guards should pursue Nealy until he gave up the ball. "Rule number one is he never crosses half court with a dribble."

As soon as Nealy passed, the chaser would scramble back to cover his man, and Nealy's defender would jump into a full denial defensive stance, staying between Nealy and the ball at all times and hopefully preventing him from receiving it again. "When they see you're denying him, they're probably gonna send him down to the right block and look to post him up," Cone instructed Nic and Rey. "If he gets it, Roe is going to leave his man and double. When he passes out of the double, Roe is going to stay on Nealy, and Nic or Rey, you guys are going to rotate back to Roe's man." By then, Cone reasoned, the twenty-four-second shot clock would be winding down, so if Ginebra "reposted"—passed back to Nealy after the double team—he would have at most eight seconds to score against the league's best one-on-one defender. "We want to cut his touches from sixty or sixty-five to thirty," Cone said. "We want him to either score under 20 because he has to give the ball up or score 30 and shoot 30 percent because he has to force shots."

Before dismissing the players, Cone took a deep breath and looked at his team. "Remember, fellas," his voice became grave. "We got a Ginebra crowd waiting for us tomorrow."

12

Hee-neh-bra!

For more than twenty years the Ginebra crowd has been the PBA's most intimidating force. Before facing Ginebra in a recent playoff series, Air 21 Express' Coach Bo Perasol described the match-up as his team "versus the Philippines." The Gin-Kings seemed to have more fans than the league's other nine teams combined, and opponents knew that playing Ginebra meant confronting an overflow crowd of tens of thousands of fans, 90 percent of whom would be Gin-King fanatics. Wherever Ginebra played, they claimed the home-court advantage. The team's full name, *Barangay* Ginebra, alluded to a neighborhood; a nationwide community of working-class fans who supported the Gin-Kings as if their lives depended on it. The mob's constant din was impressive, but even that clamor paled in comparison to the impact of its signature chant, pronounced with a Spanish G: "Hee-neh-bra! Hee-neh-bra!"

That one voice, many thousands strong, could swing the momentum of games in Ginebra's favor. Referees couldn't help but be influ-

---

* In 2009 the team was rechristened the Burger King Whoppers, but they have since reverted to Air 21.

enced by the crowd's energy, so borderline calls favored the Kings. Some opposing players, determined to silence the horde, submitted their best efforts against Ginebra. Others turned into cowering pill bugs. For the Ginebra players, the crowd was like a drug. Chito Loyzaga, a Ginebra mainstay of the eighties and nineties, once told me about the chant's ability to lift the players' performance: "When you hear them, you're in Heaven. You're not standing on solid ground." Altogether, coaches guessed that Ginebra's crowd advantage was worth about seven extra points per game.

The crowd's passion had a menacing side. During Alaska's 1990s glory days, the road to the title often went through Ginebra. Cone remembered heated playoff games when the referees waited in the arena until three or four in the morning after Ginebra losses, time enough for the team's vengeful militia to disperse. Only then could the officials go home safely. The benchwarmers' habit of wearing hand towels on their heads had its origins in the rugged Ginebra crowd of old. The cloth, players found, took the sting out of falling coins.* During those years, Alaska made the mistake of printing promotional bumper stickers, which the players and coaches pasted on their cars. The bumper sticker era ended promptly after the team played Ginebra, when Cone and the Aces walked to the parking lot and found their vehicles keyed.

Ginebra consciously cultivated its flock. While the tradition of fans mingling closely with players after practices and games reached back years before the PBA existed, Ginebra was among the first pro teams to make community outreach a staple of its public image. In the eighties and nineties, Ginebra scheduled practices in the late afternoon so supporters could visit on the way home from work. Gin-King players

---

* According to Cone, the ball boys were the one faction within the Alaska organization who actually looked forward to the crowd throwing coins. Once the spectators emptied their pockets and it became safe to step onto the hardwood, the ball boys would scurry across the floor collecting as many pesos as they could carry.

brought pastries and the noodle dish *pancit* to practices to throw surprise birthday parties for longtime fans. Between conferences and during lulls in the season, Ginebra sent players to town fiestas across the
archipelago to give far-flung devotees a chance to meet the athletes they
adored. Ginebra wasn't the only team that catered to its fans. After all,
such generosity was a standard facet of Filipinos' renowned hospitality;
but Ginebra made the custom team policy. Beyond that, Ginebra had
been one of the Philippines' leading gin brands for decades. Throughout its existence the liquor has been among the cheapest routes to sloppy
drunkenness the country has to offer. During my time in Manila a third
of a liter cost less than a dollar, and one-ounce shots in plastic packets
sold for less than a quarter. In rural areas it wasn't uncommon for men
to finish work in the fields and then slowly drink themselves to sleep by
passing around a bottle of Ginebra.* The problem of chronic alcohol
abuse aside, the gin and the team reinforced each other's popularity and
generated profits for their owner, the San Miguel Corporation.

Imagine if NBA or NFL franchises planned practices around their
fans' schedules? Or if the Lakers baked cupcakes and cooked spaghetti
for their season ticket holders? If basketball were so vital to our daily
routines that we stopped by our favorite teams' practices after work?
Life in the States felt too cluttered to make a beloved hobby such a large
part of my daily routine. In the Philippines, I encountered basketball
everywhere, even when I wasn't looking for it. The game was woven into
nearly all aspects of everyday life. Such an existence probably wouldn't
work for everyone, but for me it was ideal. Ginebra fanaticism was a

---

* The societal ills of this behavior are self-evident, especially in places like Ba-
tanes, an isolated island province halfway between the northern tip of the Philippine mainland and Taiwan. During typhoon season, the islands are continually
battered by some of the region's most violent storms, and people wait out the
tempests by tippling a bottle or three in the safety of stone-walled houses. Local
health officials have estimated that the province of about 16,000 people consumes 2,600 bottles of liquor—mostly gin, most likely Ginebra—per month.

prime example of how deeply basketball was embedded in Filipinos' lives. But open practices and birthday cake weren't enough to explain the irrational passion of Gin-King fans. For the Ginebra mystique, there was another answer. His name is Robert Jaworski.

Over the course of Jaworski's thirty-some years at the highest levels of Philippine basketball, the fiery point guard inspired a cult of personality that remains the heart of Ginebra mania more than a decade after he left the team in 1998. He was the most charismatic athlete in the nation's history. On the court, Jaworski was beyond intense; he was driven by a violent need to win. The moment the final buzzer sounded, however, he became gentle, amicable, and willing to grant practically any request a fan might ask of him. His dual personality was perfectly suited to woo Filipino hoops lovers. Even Tim Cone, whose technical philosophy of basketball could not have been more different from Jaworski's battle-of-wills approach, remembered worshiping Jaworski. "He was my absolute hero," Cone told me in the days before the Ginebra game. "I was a die-hard fan. He doesn't remember this, but I used to go to their practices when I was eleven or twelve years old."

A barrel-chested six-foot-one point guard, Jaworski wasn't particularly graceful, but he possessed uncanny basketball instincts. He could survey the court and see the future. He sensed where teammates would be and how defenses would react a couple seconds before they moved. Jaworski's Polish-American father didn't play much of a role in his son's life, but by the looks of things, the younger Jaworski inherited a brawny physique not uncommon in certain pirogi-loving precincts in Chicago. Jaworski's compact frame may not have been the prototypical basketball body, but he used it to great effect against the skeletal players of the seventies and eighties. His bullish drives to the hoop were famous for leaving trails of aching defenders scattered in his wake. Still, even in his prime, Jaworski wasn't his generation's premier talent. He wasn't even the best on the Toyota team; that player was Ramon "El Presidente" Fernandez, a four-time MVP who owns the PBA all-time scoring record.

Being one step below the truly peerless players may have spurred Jaworski to play every possession like a true believer in a holy war. There was nothing he wouldn't do to win games. Pushing, holding, tackling, tripping, stomach-punching, hip-checking, forearm-shivering—to Jaworski, every tactic was on the table if it meant winning. His presence intimidated opponents, who knew competing against him would test their fortitude as much as their skill. He might have been even more imposing to teammates, who could incur his wrath by showing any trepidation on the court. When Jaworski told a player on his side to hack someone on the other team, the order was obeyed. His teammates had no choice but to be fearless. Philip Cezar would know. Near the end of his career, Cezar played with Jaworski at Ginebra, then retired and served as one of the team's assistant coaches. "Even if you're a *bakla*," Cezar told me, referring to that distinctively Filipino genus of hypereffeminate transvestite, "you will become tough. He will see to it."

In 1971, four years before the PBA came into existence, Jaworski's hot-blooded nature led to the low point of his career. He was playing for Meralco in the MICAA league and his team was trailing in a game that had been marred by one-sided officiating. Jaworski had already been ejected for arguing bogus calls, so when he watched a frustrated teammate peg the ball at a referee over another bad whistle, he sprung from the bench and flattened ref Jose Obias with a right cross. After the punch, Obias needed five stitches over his left eye, and Jaworski earned a lifetime ban from basketball. Yet even at that early point in his career, the public sensed he would be vital to the sport. The next year, Ferdinand Marcos reinstated Jaworski by presidential decree and returned Philippine basketball's emerging icon to his adoring masses.

Jaworski seemed driven to personally express his gratitude to as many fans as possible. The man was a natural baby-kisser with unlimited stamina for signing autographs, mugging for cameras, and making small talk. After games, the walk from the Araneta Coliseum to his car could take hours, as Jaworski hugged and thanked every fan who stopped to say "Good game" or "Better luck next time." In three years of listening to Jaworski stories, I never heard anyone—his contemporaries, his admirers, or even his critics—say that he denied a fan's request. He was a one-man Make-A-Wish Foundation, dropping by schools to deliver inspirational pep talks, visiting ailing cancer patients, and stumping beside a longtime Toyota and Ginebra ball boy who in 1989 ran for *barangay* captain of his hometown in Pampanga.

Jaworski's appeal grew stronger as he aged and his presence in games became more and more improbable. By his late forties he didn't just have a natural rapport with fans, he actually resembled them. With a receding hairline and doughy loose flesh hanging from his triceps, Jaworski looked too lumpy for pro ball in his GINEBRA NA! jersey. Yet there he was, waving a towel from the sidelines and haranguing the referees. When he would finally check himself in, usually during the fourth quarter, the crowd would explode. Jaworski's three-point shots and behind-the-back passes, once hallmarks of his venerable talent, had become something of an inside joke with his followers. The idea that he had the balls to step onto the court and pull his old tricks against guys twenty-five years younger than him, and the fact that many of those tricks still worked inspired the crowd to its wildest, giddiest frenzy, which in turn boosted Ginebra's momentum. The people loved him, and in their eyes he could do no wrong.

Jaworski entered the basketball mainstream in the late sixties, when he led the University of the East to a pair of national championships. He remained in the spotlight long enough for successive generations of fans to watch him progress from a fiery upstart with a flashy floor game to a crotchety fifty-two-year-old man jockeying for position with men young enough to be his children. In fact, toward the end of his career he actually drafted his son Robert Jr., or "Dodot," as he was widely known. The two were teammates for the last three years of Jaworski Sr.'s career.* To put Jaworski's Methuselah act into perspective, consider this: among his many nicknames—Sonny, Jawo, the Living Legend— one particularly famous moniker was the Big J, a name coined by commentators who compared Jaworski to one of his NBA contemporaries, Oscar "the Big O" Robertson, who retired in 1974.

As the years dragged on, Jaworski became a flesh and blood memento of Filipinos' erstwhile pride in the hoops. He was old enough to have played on some of the last national teams to win the Asian Basketball Championships and qualify for the Olympics. The coach of those teams was Caloy Loyzaga, the all-time great who brought glory to Philippine hoops when he captained the bronze medal team at the 1954 World Championships. The Philippines hasn't been back to the Olympics since 1972, three years before the PBA was launched. As the Philippine legacy of basketball achievement receded into the past, Jaworski stuck around as a living and breathing, passing and dribbling monument to the country's former grandeur. As the PBA grew over an almost twenty-five-year period, Jaworski was there as a constant counterpoint to changing times, a symbol of the sport's better days.

The golden age in Philippine hoops peaked with the 1970s and 1980s PBA rivalry between the Crispa Redmanizers and the Toyota franchise,

---

* Dodot, widely considered one of the worst players in PBA history, surely deserves a spot in the Pantheon of Philippine nepotism. His father supposedly drafted him to raise Dodot's public profile in preparation for a career in politics. It worked; Dodot won Pasig City's seat in Congress in 2004. Unbeknownst to Dodot, he also played a complementary role in Nic Belasco's journey from Division Two college ball to the PBA. A Filipina exchange student convinced Nic he should join the PBA. "Dodot Jaworski is this fat, short guy," she said, "and he's a big-time superstar over there. He wouldn't even be able to play in open gym with you!" Nic's confidante failed to inform him of one essential detail—Jaworski's pedigree—and her encouragement set Nic on a path to becoming one of the league's pioneering Fil-Am big men.

which played under various car model names like the Tamaraws, Comets, Silver Coronas, and Super Corollas. Crispa and Toyota were the nascent PBA's premier teams. The league had yet to instate a salary cap or rookie draft, so Crispa and Toyota built their roundball arsenals by paying the highest salaries, outbidding other franchises until practically all of the nation's best players were either Redmanizers or Tamaraws. Crispa and Toyota played each other in the league's first six championship series.* It took nine years before a team other than Crispa or Toyota claimed an All-Filipino title, the most coveted of the conference championships. It was no surprise, then, that most fans cheered for these powerhouse squads.

Head-to-head meetings between the rivals were society events nonpareil, with the Araneta Coliseum even more saturated with tycoons and celebrities than in the present day Ateneo–La Salle match-ups. Imee and Bongbong Marcos (whose wife's family owned the coliseum) became true-blue Crispanatics and Big Dome regulars after Imee married Tommy Manotoc, the coach who took over the Redmanizers in 1983. The back pages of sports magazines were filled with gushing fan correspondence like tribute acrostics based on the players' names and letters asking for "colored pics of the fantastic players that comprise the mighty Crispa Redmanizers . . . including their imports and even their water boy." The most devoted supporters even became minor celebrities. Felicisima Bais, a nondescript middle-age woman, was widely known as Mommy Crispa, the enthusiastic conductor of the Crispanatic masses who constantly waved her homemade CRISPA MABUHAY! banner. When she died at the beginning of the 1978 season—she fell down a flight of stairs and suffered a fatal head injury—the press eulogized Mommy Crispa in mournful, glowing obituaries, fondly recalling her frantic exhortations: "Eyes to the ball! Eyes to the ball!"

---

* Remember, the PBA played three conferences per year back then, so those six championship series occurred over just two full seasons.

The Crispa-Toyota feud, divisive among fans, also managed to unite people from vastly different and even antagonistic segments of Philippine society. Manileños and *probinsyanos*, prodemocracy activists and government shock troops, Manila Polo Club patrons and squatters— they all chose a side. Crispanatics and their Toyota foils could even be found within the ranks of Muslim separatists fighting against the government in southern Mindanao. You could not get farther away from the Philippine mainstream than these rebels, who lived in remote jungle fiefdoms. Yet in the eighties, after Crispa and Toyota disbanded, the anthropologist daughter of Crispa Coach Virgilio "Baby" Dalupan traveled through territory controlled by the Moro National Liberation Front and found that Crispanaticism was alive and well. She was leading a relief mission to Basilan, an island not far from Borneo. Her team planned to deliver food and clothing to the Yakan, an indigenous group living on the island, but before they could enter Yakan communities they needed permission from the guerilla commander. When the rebel posse arrived, the devout Muslims refused to acknowledge Dalupan's daughter because she was a woman. For two days the commander avoided so much as looking at Dalupan's daughter. Then, after lunch on the second day, he broke his silence. "How are you related to Baby Dalupan?" asked the commander. "You know when I was a student in Mapua [an engineering school in Manila] I was really a fan of Crispa!"

The rivalry's real heat derived from the fact that none of the other PBA teams posed much of a threat to Crispa or Toyota. Most years, they met in the finals of at least one of the season's conferences, and a succession of playoff battles engendered bad blood between the teams. Crispa, a textile firm that sold men's undershirts and briefs, fostered a populist image for the Redmanizers, whose confounding name came from Crispa's signature technique. Crispa's "Redmanized" garments didn't shrink in the wash. The company probably used a popular preshrinking technique called Sanforizing, which was developed in the

United States in the 1930s, and renamed it to avoid infringing on the Sanforized trademark. Almost anyone could afford Crispa, and the company's basketball players dressed and acted like jeans and T-shirt kinds of guys. Toyota, playing under the banner of a foreign automaker, was the glamour team. Guards Jaworski and Francis Arnaiz and center Ramon Fernandez, the faces of the team, were nearly as famous for their light-skinned, *mestizo* looks as they were for anchoring Toyota's inside-out attack. They arrived at games dressed like the Bee Gees, with sunglasses and silk shirts buttoned only halfway up to reveal chest hair and gold necklaces. Toyota attracted its share of the masses, but the average Filipino's bond with the team was primarily aspirational.

The likelihood of fisticuffs was one element of the Toyota-Crispa allure for Marcos-era basketball fans, but people were equally drawn by a unique Philippine style of play that the early PBA stars perfected and disseminated. These players hadn't learned the game at basketball camps or through the endless drilling of coaches. They learned by watching their fathers and uncles play in *barangay* leagues, then mimicked the moves and hurled shots at the hoop until they discovered the right touch. Seventies and eighties basketball had a beautiful, idiosyncratic flair. Each player possessed an oblong hoops genius all to himself, developed according to the particular irregularities of the dirt or cement courts where he practiced. This helped create an array of offensive moves and defensive tricks that hardly existed outside of Philippine basketball, and probably wouldn't have evolved away from courts where coconut trees set picks at center court or where backboards were wooden planks nailed together, with each board requiring a different combination of force and spin to sink a bank shot.

Crowds adored not just the creativity apparent in these self-taught shots but also the familiarity of that kind of hoops. The run-and-gun, improvisational style was no different from the sandlot *barangay* games that fans played, only with elevated levels of skill and artistry. The basketball layman could attempt a magical shot; the pro could make it eight times out of ten. Toyota's Arnaiz was known for his "loop" shot, a running underhand layup with range out to the free throw line. On a dead sprint, he would scoop the ball from his hip, almost like a no-look pass destined for the hoop. Despite its low release point the shot was nearly unblockable because Arnaiz did nothing to telegraph it. One moment Arnaiz would be dribbling, and the next, the ball would be airborne. By the time defenders could react, the ball was already curling over their heads toward the rim. His teammate Fernandez, a bony six-foot-five stickman, patented a running one-hander in the lane that he set up by juking his defender left and right. It became known as the "elegant shot"; halfway between Kareem's sky hook and Olajuwon's dream shake, it defined big man grace for the Philippine game. Atoy Co, a lanky six-foot-two shooting guard, was Crispa's most flamboyant player and almost certainly the deadliest gunner in PBA history to sport a Beatles-style bowl cut. Co perfected the standard jump shot, then added flourishes like the turnaround, fadeaway, and a leg kick that caused him to land with his legs split. Spinning and fading on jumpers are standard evasive maneuvers, but Co used them as garnishes, occasionally executing a turnaround from sixteen feet when he was alone on the fast break. The spread-eagle landing, which seemed like the least practical piece of Co's mechanics, was actually made necessary by Jaworski's tendency to slide his foot underneath opponents' landing spots.

Dirty play during those years was as integral to the game as boxing out. Teams hired designated enforcers, burly hitmen like Crispa's Johnny Revilla and Toyota's Alberto "Big Boy" Reynoso, whose *raison d'être* on the court was to clobber opposing teams' scorers. Arnaiz's looper, Fernandez's elegant shot, and Co's gaudy jumpers all developed from a mixture of *diskarte*—flash, the desire to show off their talent—and survival. All that gorgeous finesse helped players avoid a knee to the thigh or elbow to the solar plexus. There were other ways to score without getting body-slammed. Freddie Webb and Yoyong Martirez, two of the league's fastest guards, got most of their points by sprinting ahead of the lumbering hatchet men. Jaworski was the rare perimeter player who consistently challenged enforcers. He used his blocky physique to blast through defenses. When he got close to the basket, he would jump with one foot extended like a battering ram to clear space for his layup. Yet even Jaworski, the PBA's foremost practitioner of smashmouth basketball, had a go-to finesse move that sports writers called his "don't care" shot. Sometimes, when he was close to the hoop with a defender smothering him, he'd just flip the ball up underhanded and bank it in. The shot drove opponents mad.

The Crispa-Toyota throng undoubtedly dug the fireworks incited by the enforcers' thuggish takedowns, but fans and players reserved a higher level of appreciation for trickery. Some players studiously cultivated a technique of cracking open the side of the mouth to shoot a thin stream of saliva at an opponent on the free throw line. Once a spitter established his reputation, the mere threat of his disgusting ability could wreak havoc. Just clearing his throat would plant fear in shooters' minds. From the perspective of American basketball—and the hundreds of imports who were tormented by cunning Filipino opponents—these plays seemed just as dirty as a kick in the shin, and maybe worse because at least the kick was a direct attack. But in Philippine basketball ethics, taking advantage of less experienced players was a skill as esteemed as boxing out or denying the ball. The word for this craftiness, *gulang*, is also the root of the Tagalog word for "parents." The double meaning implied that for young players, being fooled by their hardwood elders was part of the game—a fact of life.

To learn about *gulang*, I visited Crispa defensive stopper Philip Cezar at his home on a quiet side street in San Juan, the Metro Manila city where he was once vice mayor. Cezar was known as, among other nicknames, "the Scholar." The wiry six-foot-three forward was renowned as the premier thinking man's player of his generation. He revealed his best trick: "I love to hold the hand." His guttural, chain-smoker's rasp and deliberate cadences oozed wisdom, like Yoda mixed with Morgan Freeman speaking in a Filipino lilt. Under the boards, against the pick-and-roll, even while defending the low post, all Cezar needed for an advantage was a grip on his opponent's palm. Once he had the hand, he had his opponent on a leash. A player would try to cut across the lane only to find himself tethered by Cezar's gentle grasp. Against massive imports, Cezar would give up five or six inches in height and fifty pounds in weight but still outduel them for rebounds by grounding their momentum with a tug on the hand. "When I hold his hand," Cezar grumbled and gave a self-satisfied nod, "that's it. He cannot jump."

Ed Cordero, a six-foot-four shooter who joined Toyota in the early eighties, filled me in on the cherished art of tormenting imports. Many foreign players were *pikon*—easy to piss off—and local ballers quickly learned to take advantage of opponents with short tempers. Holding the hand à la Cezar was a good way to get under their skin, but if you really wanted to mess with an import's head, you had to get homoerotic: "When I was playing, we noticed that imports would be very icky when you touched their butts. Here in the Philippines, you can be with some gay guy, but it doesn't mean you're gay. My impression is, in the States, people think if you're friends with some gay guy then you must be gay too. So the fact that you hold the import's butt, they would think you're gay. And you don't just touch them, you touch the center part." Cordero broke into a joyous cackle while outlining the contours of an imaginary ass with his hands, then stroking the middle with two fingers. Once Cordero had violated an import in this manner, the freaked foreigner would usually settle for outside shots rather than drive to the rim and face Cordero's wandering hands.

Diskarte and *gulang* were alive and well in the PBA when I followed Alaska. Poch Juinio and John Ferriols possessed the full arsenal of tactics—handholding, shorts-grabbing, elbow-throwing, and who knows, maybe even spitting—passed down through generations of big men. Now, their role was to instruct Sonny Thoss in the dark art of below-the-backboards skulduggery. During the second half of a late-season win over Air 21, John noticed that import Shawn Daniels's shoe fell off after a battle for an offensive rebound. A foul was called on the play, and while the players lined up around the free throw line, John kicked the sneaker away from the roly-poly import known as "the Incredible Bulk." He nudged it softly enough to avoid attracting the referees' attention but with sufficient force to drive the high-top into the first row of seats behind the basket. Daniels gave John a quizzical look—why would you do such a thing?—and let out an exasperated sigh before trudging into the crowd to retrieve his footwear. John nodded at Sonny. *Gulang.*

Willie Miller had enough *diskarte* for two teams. He was Philippine basketball incarnate, a compendium of every herky-jerky stutter step and improbable scoop shot practiced daily on almost every *barangay* court in the country. His spoken English may have been merely proficient, but when it came to English, the art of placing spin on the ball to bank it through the hoop, Willie was Charles Dickens. He was a maestro of *pektos*, PBA lingo for "spin," and a flick of his wrist was enough to send the ball ricocheting off the glass and into the net at seemingly impossible angles.* Willie also mastered the sidestep, a one-on-one move that served as the capstone to many of his drives. American players are usually taught to finish strong at the hoop with a burst of speed and a leap toward the rim. For most Filipino players, no matter how hard they drive to the hole, they aren't going to finish above the rim.

---

* *Pektos* is such a part of Philippine basketball's standard operating procedure that when Nic Belasco arrived from California in 1997 to play for the Pop Cola Bottlers, he baffled his coaches and teammates by shooting plain layups with no spin. Even though the shots went in, Nic's teammates took time after practice to enlighten him on the proper way to rotate his wrist: "Do it like you're unscrewing a lightbulb!"

The sidestep presented an alternative. To execute the move, the player jumps sideways before shooting instead of jumping forward to the basket. His defender is left stranded, while the ballhandler frees himself for a short scoop or bank shot. Willie's sidestep was especially deadly because of his girth. His upper body was as thick as the meaty torsos of Alaska's big men, which made his quickness all the more otherworldly. He had the shape and heft of a bowling ball, but changed directions as sharply as a balloon with the air running out of it.

"Some of the shots he will make, guys in the States would go, 'Where'd that come from?'" Cone told me, describing the distinct flavor of Willie's game. "He makes them all the time. Those are shots that he learned. It's not different from the style you learn growing up on the playgrounds of New York. Willie learned it growing up on the *barangay* courts of Olongapo." Cone was right. I had been so mesmerized by the Philippine game's *pektos* and *diskarte*, so absorbed in cataloging every move and tracing it back in time from Willie to Jaworski and beyond, that I never really stepped back and looked at the bigger picture. The New York game I grew up playing and fell in love with had a lot in common with Philippine hoops. New York is a basketball town, and even though the sport may not reach every New Yorker the way it penetrates Philippine society, it seemed like everyone I knew when I was young played ball. Not just my teammates and kids my age, but also out-of-shape old guys who wore goggles and knee socks. Everyone knew how to play. They didn't necessarily have polished basketball skills, but they all had some self-taught go-to move—a two-handed bank shot, a back-you-down hook—that never missed. It was their version of *diskarte*, although a lot of the time it wasn't so pretty. I rarely saw these peculiar moves make it to the NBA, perhaps because of the pros' technical superiority. But the best Filipino players had somehow smuggled oddball, personalized skills into the PBA, and I wasn't just fascinated by how Jaworski's or Willie's style was different or exotic, but by how it felt familiar.

There were a few staples of the Philippine game that Willie lacked.

His stocky frame was not built to fly. The PBA's brilliant acrobats, guys like Samboy "Skywalker" Lim, Vergel "the Aerial Voyager" Meneses, and Paul "Mr. Excitement" Alvarez,* perfected the yo-yo shot, a downright miraculous floating layup named for the way its practitioners brought the ball up and down in midair before flipping it through the net. These shots, along with Willie's full array of jaw-dropping moves, were Philippine basketball's answer to the NBA's highlight reel. Compared to Lebron James rising into the stratosphere before a dunk, the Filipino moves lacked raw power, but I found it just as exhilarating to watch these smaller players create shots I had never even imagined. Willie's shooting touch, at times, was magical; after he scored, stupefied crowds couldn't help but wonder, "How'd he do that?"

Another shot missing from Alaska's inventory was the *kilikili*, or "armpit" shot, which was something of a dying art among PBA big men. It was a Philippine take on the up-and-under move, except that instead of stepping past a defender to find open space to shoot, a player executing the *kilikili* shot tried to reach under the defender's raised arms and fling the ball upward while drawing contact. The shot emerged from the defender's armpit and, when successful, was a guaranteed "And one." Over the years, referees grew wise to the *kilikili* shot's artifice and stopped rewarding its practitioners with foul calls. Since it was a low percentage move on its own, the gambit had been largely abandoned. The lone exception was six-foot-nine Marlou Aquino of the Santa Lucia Realtors, for years the league's tallest full-blooded Filipino. I couldn't think of a more frivolous move for a player nicknamed "the Skyscraper," but Aquino never gave up reaching under the arms of shorter players to release his *kilikili* shot.

---

* "Mr. Excitement" indeed. Alaska drafted Alvarez in 1989 and had high hopes of pairing him with Jojo Lastimosa to form the league's deadliest swingman tandem. But Alvarez was a one-on-one *artiste* who struggled to fit in with Cone's triangle offense. Alaska eased him out of the lineup in the early nineties, shortly after Alvarez was shot in the butt outside of a massage parlor.

The twin essences of *gulang* and *diskarte* had antecedents tracing back at least to the fifties, but they weren't enshrined as the stylistic soul of Philippine hoops until Crispa and Toyota electrified nationwide audiences in the seventies. After a decade, the teams disbanded and the PBA instituted a draft and salary cap. Parity soon followed. With more evenly matched teams, coaches could no longer succeed simply by hoarding talent. They needed strategy. The overall quality of PBA games improved. Turnovers became rarer as teams learned to execute specific game plans. But Philippine basketball lost a smidgen of its vitality as coaches took greater control. There would always be irrepressible talents like Vergel Meneses and Willie Miller, whose hearts pumped pure *diskarte*, but only Ginebra fully preserved the Crispa-Toyota ethic. When Toyota disbanded after the 1983 season, Jaworski and Arnaiz joined the Gilbey's Gins. By 1985 the team name changed to Ginebra. Jaworski, already pushing forty, was named player/coach, and he stacked his roster with former Toyota and Crispa mainstays like Philip Cezar, Arnie Tuadles, and Freddie Hubalde. Much of what remained of those beloved teams became combined in Ginebra, which attracted a massive following of both Crispanatics and Toyota lifers.

Jaworski ran the team as if in a time warp. While the rest of the league modernized, Ginebra remained proudly mired in the seventies. Practice consisted of stretching and then a scrimmage to 200 points. They played run-and-gun basketball and their strategy boiled down to playing with more passion than their opponents. Jaworski recruited wily defensive specialists like the rotund Loyzaga brothers, Chito and Joey, who looked more like the Mario Brothers than basketball players; he cultivated enforcers like Wilmer Ong and Rudy "the Destroyer" Distrito, who recently did time in a Nevada prison for a cuckoldry manslaughter; and he showcased dazzling scorers like Vince Hizon and Noli "the Tank" Locsin, a chunky, undersized power forward who could hang in midair and spin shots off the board as well as the most agile guards. Ginebra's legion of fans saw in the team a condensed history of Philippine basketball. They saw themselves in Ginebra's style of play, which elevated street-corner basketball to the level of PBA champions. So in 1998, when Jaworski finally left the PBA and the Gin-Kings caught up with other teams' training techniques and coaching philosophies, the fans remained loyal. Jaworski's aura would be forever linked with Ginebra.

A few days before Alaska was to play Ginebra, Cone devoted the first hour of morning practice to a core conditioning workout, exactly the kind of training the cigarette-smoking, beer-guzzling athletes of the Crispa-Toyota generation rarely considered worth their time. In today's PBA, however, every team used plyometric drills and core-strengthening exercises. The methods might still lag behind NBA techniques, but they were nevertheless more forward-looking than Jaworski's "roll the balls out" approach. Cone scheduled these workouts throughout the season, and he was careful to always leave a few days between the grueling sessions and the next game to allow his players time to recuperate.

That morning, the players walked into the gym and groaned when they saw the floor divided into seven stations, each containing some combination of medicine balls, twenty-five-pound plates, yoga mats, giant rubber exercise balls, and a pair of platforms attached via bungee cords to harness and garter belt contraptions. The court looked like a cross between a medieval torture den and Plato's Retreat. Two players set themselves up at each station, where one performed a designated exercise while the other assisted. After two minutes they reversed roles, and after both players finished they rotated to the next drill. At the first station, directly under the basket, Nic Belasco watched Roe bend over at the waist while holding a twenty-five-pound plate to his chest, then swivel his torso from side to side. It seemed like the kind of low-tech, brute strength technique Rocky Balboa might use. Fifteen feet down the baseline from them, Aaron Aban's task resembled a children's game, albeit a sweaty one that inspired lots of grunting. Starting from a prone position, Aaron was doing sit-ups while holding a seven-pound medicine ball over his head. Once he sat up, he tossed the ball against the wall, let it bounce back to him, then repeated.

Things got kinky near the free throw line. There, Sonny Thoss was on his back, holding a small medicine ball pressed between his ankles. Keeping his legs straight, Sonny lifted them until they were perpendicular to the floor, then lifted his derriere off the mat and clenched for a beat before starting again. John Ferriols was supposed to be spotting Sonny, but instead he was positioning his crotch inches away from Rensy Bajar's face, which kept rising and falling as part of a drill that required Mike Cortez to stand behind Rensy, who was kneeling, and push him forward. Rensy was breaking the fall by doing a push-up that bounced him back up to the original position. At least, that was how Alaska's trainers intended the exercise to be performed. In actuality, Rensy spent half of his two minutes facedown on the floor, laughing at John's carnal groaning.

Closer to half-court two VertiMax platforms were set up and the scene looked like something out of a bondage convention. Poch Juinio was standing on the platform, harnessed into a belt with four bungee cords—two on each hip—tethering him to the device. The coaches arranged plastic cones between Poch's legs, and his job was to jump from one foot to the other over the cones. The cords provided roughly the same amount of resistance as another player grabbing Poch's waist and trying to hold him down, and the exercise was meant to test his balance, leaping ability, and endurance. Poch, however, had just turned thirty-four and had almost no muscle tone. His body had natural bulk and old-man strength, both of which he used expertly to outposition younger, fitter players in games, but all of Poch's know-how was useless on the VertiMax. He breezed through the first twenty seconds of the drill. Then his form started to break down. With each jump, his upper body bent forward a little more, until he was nearly doubled over. For the rest of the two minutes he ceased "jumping," in a literal sense of the word, and instead stepped gingerly from one foot to the other, sometimes losing his balance and kicking a cone across the gym. When the whistle blew, Poch hobbled off the platform, his face ashen and his hair plastered to his forehead. With his hands on his knees, he uttered "Shit *na malagkit!*"—sticky shit—between gasps.

Poch's partner, Eddie Laure, was his near-perfect athletic foil. Lean and nimble, Eddie possessed boundless energy and a wingspan that would impress the engineers at Boeing. When his turn came to do the VertiMax hop, Eddie bounced effortlessly back and forth, waving his fingers in a jazz hands flourish.* But in terms of athletic exhibition and sheer performance, Eddie's joyful demonstration was nothing compared to what Willie Miller was doing on the other platform. The bungee cords were attached to his thighs using makeshift garter belts. Before he strapped himself in, Willie had pulled his socks to his knees, tucked a long-sleeve thermal undershirt into his shorts, and hiked the waistline up to his sternum. The look revealed his bulbous thighs, which looked thicker than some men's midsections and supplied the horsepower for his astonishing quickness. Once the bungee cords were snapped onto his thighs, Willie began marching, bringing a knee to his chest with every step. He pumped his legs like a cartoon robot set to move on overdrive, but his upper body remained placid and so controlled that he managed to whistle a tune during his two minute sprint.

---

* Besides his springiness and length, which are pretty standard traits for basketball players, Laure's flexibility could probably earn him a contortionist's role in Cirque du Soleil. When he stretched in the locker room before games, Eddie would sit in a natural split and lean forward until his chest reached the ground. Once, while standing under an eight-foot-tall overhang, Eddie, who's about six-foot-three, began swinging his right leg back and forth to loosen his hip. His foot moved up and down a pendulum arc like the passenger car in a carnival ride. After five or six swings there was a sudden thud, and everyone in the room turned to see what had happened. Eddie had kicked the ceiling and left a dark rubber smudge behind.

The other players dropped their medicine balls to laugh and cheer for Willie, the player expected to lead them to victory against Ginebra and in the playoffs, grinning and whistling on the VertiMax with a self-inflicted wedgie.

Was this good or bad for the team? Willie sometimes acted like the high school smart-aleck who goofed off because class was too easy, while his less academically gifted partners-in-crime struggled to make grades. After the VertiMax routine, I asked Cone if he wanted Willie to act more serious. "A lot of coaches have done that," he said. "They try to battle him. Make him conform. Tell him, 'This is the kind of player you should be.' You're just gonna butt heads with him and you're gonna lose him eventually. The key with Willie is learning to accept him for what he is."

Yes, Willie could be a distraction, but Cone could rarely find reasons to discipline him because the clowning hardly ever affected his play. "You watch him do the core stuff," Cone continued. "He does it better than anybody. He's so instinctive. When I'm doing the plays on the blackboard, he knows exactly what I'm doing before anybody else, by far. He sees the game extremely well."

Inside Alaska's locker room, the team tried to prepare for the Ginebra tiebreaker like it was any other game. Willie was dribbling in front of a mirror. Roe's head had disappeared behind the jeans and shirt hanging in his cubby, where he was plugged into an iPod and thumbing through a John Maxwell leadership book. Eddie was practicing his human pretzel act in a corner. The assistant coaches were huddled around a bucket of french fries, rehashing stories from the biggest games of their careers and comparing Nealy to old-time imports like Byron "Snake" Jones, Cyrus Mann, and Lew Massey. The sound of athletic tape being ripped from rolls and wrapped around ankles filled the room, along with fumes from the rubbing alcohol being kneaded into players' backs and thighs. Rubbing alcohol was the PBA's cure-all; it was used as a massage oil, hand sanitizer, and short-notice shower. Alaska went through seven half-liter bottles per week, and much of that was used on game days, when the air inside the locker room could be downright noxious. Early in the season, before I developed a tolerance for the chemical haze, I would feel woozy after twenty minutes in the room.

Cone stood up to review the Rod Nealy scheme. "Stop him early," the coach warned. "He's had some huge, just gigantic first quarters: 21, 24, 26 points. Get the ball out of his hands. Don't let him do that to us." While Cone illustrated the backcourt chaser on a dry-erase board, I noticed Willie staring at me. He raised his eyebrows twice and pointed with his lips at the table next to me. If I stretched, I could reach a bunch of bananas resting on the far end of the table. I pointed to the bananas and Willie smiled. He made a target with his hands, like he was waiting for a chest pass. I looked at Cone, who was fully engrossed in the whiteboard, and shook my head. Willie nodded to reassure me; his smile grew wider. He held his hands out again and mouthed "Ba-na-na" to me. I tore off a fruit and shovel-passed it across the room. Just before Willie could catch it, John Ferriols snatched the banana out of midair. All three of us started snickering until we felt eyes on us. It was Roe, glowering in disgust.

The shame turned everyone serious. This was the most important game of the season, and we were playing catch with bananas. The automatic semifinal berth at stake against Ginebra could make the difference between a championship and a playoff flame-out. A handful of teams had won titles after surviving the play-in phase of the PBA playoffs, but many more ran out of steam in the semis or finals. A loss tonight would put the Aces in a hole they might not be able to climb out of, and Roe wasn't about to let Willie, John, or me forget that.

Cone reminded the team that the Ginebra crowd would make them feel like they were playing against the entire nation: "The only guys that want us, Alaska, to win tonight are in this room. There's gonna be a time-out when the crowd's just going crazy, and you need to sit down, relax, and focus on what you need to do to win this game. Composure, fellas. Let's do two minutes." Alaska always observed this suspended moment of silence before games. Cone wanted his players to visualize executing the game plan they learned in practice. This time, the players seemed more grave than usual. Roe threw a towel over his head and sat motionless in his cubby. Jeff Cariaso leaned forward and rested his head against his interlocked hands. Rey Hugnatan buried his head in the nook of his elbow and fiddled with the braided, three-inch rat tail trailing down the back of his neck. Even Willie, knowing that a win was crucial, acted serious. Well, he tried. For the first minute, Willie seemed meditative. He leaned back and kept his eyes closed. Eventually, however, a grin crept across his face. He opened his eyes and looked around the room. The rest of the team was still in its preparatory trance. He turned to me and pumped his hydraulic eyebrows. Eventually, I covered my face with my shirt to muzzle any giggles that might escape. Willie was ready to get on the court, not just to compete and win, but to perform, to feel thousands of eyes focused on him.

"Hee-neh-bra! Hee-neh-bra!" The fans' hymn to Jaworski filled the tunnel where the Alaska players lined up before taking the court. The overflow crowd of close to 20,000 was thin at courtside, where ushers enforced assigned seating. The upper regions of Araneta Coliseum, however, were given over to general admission tickets, where people filled seats on a first-come, first-served basis and thousands squeezed into the concrete staircases between rows. Clusters of Ginebra fans clogged the passages leading from the arena's peripheral hallway to the stands. The coliseum was a pickpocket's dream and a fire marshal's worst nightmare. All through the arena, people waved pro-Ginebra and anti-Alaska banners—slapdash slogans painted on white sheets—and swung towels given out by Ginebra employees. It was gin versus milk;

the grit, pluck, and populism of Ginebra, a drink that can get you stumbling, slurring drunk for less than a dollar, against the wholesome striving and family values of Alaska, which came in boxes illustrated with the face of a cherubic blond boy who looked like a long-lost cousin of Macaulay Culkin. The organizations were natural rivals, and Jaworski's legend ensured that the Aces would be playing in front of a raucous Gin-King crowd.

A sliver of Alaska supporters sitting behind the basket closest to the Aces' bench put up token resistance, matching the Ginebra chant with *"Ee-skwa-ter! Ee-skwa-ter!"* Calling the lumpen Gin-King fans squatters—slum dwellers who lived in improvised shacks—was insensitive and not necessarily accurate. But the Alaska die-hards, led by Hector the aging ladyboy and his mildly disabled sidekick who punctuated the rallying cry by thrusting his wooden crutch into the air, hailed from the same rungs of society as the Ginebra *masa*, so their off-color retort wasn't mistaken for elitism. Besides, hardly anyone could hear Hector and his band of misfits, since they were outnumbered almost two hundred to one. Even though I was with the undermanned Alaska posse, I found the Ginebra crowd intoxicating. The chant made my hair stand on end, and I remembered Chito Loyzaga describing the way players became addicted to it. Once you heard the booming voice of 20,000 people cajoling you to victory, how could you play without it? But I also recalled what Nic Belasco told me about playing against the crowd—when you hear that chant, you want to beat Ginebra even more just to shut them up.

Alaska had beaten Ginebra twice already, but when this third match began the Aces looked rattled. Early in the game Willie penetrated and found Sonny Thoss alone in front of the rim. All season Sonny had finished these plays with two-handed dunks, yet this time he tried to finger-roll the ball. It clunked off the back of the rim. Sonny was able to grab his own rebound and salvage the play with a layup, but the mishap was a sign of the Aces' hesitant play. Ginebra was steamrolling them. A few possessions later Sonny caught a pass in the low post, faced up to the basket and saw his defender playing two steps off him. He rose for a simple seven-foot jumper and badly short-armed the shot, which dropped into Ginebra hands without touching the rim. Sonny wasn't the only player having a hard time finding his range. All of Alaska's outside shots were short. The team scored on a few offensive rebounds, but they mostly relied on Roe's willpower to put points on the board. A few times in the first quarter Roe caught outlet passes or took defensive rebounds, then dropped his shoulder and plowed through the whole Ginebra defense to flip in lefty half hooks. It was an unsightly rendition of basketball gridiron, but it was Alaska's only way of staying close.

One of the Ginebra players doing the most first-quarter damage was Johnny Abarrientos, the thirty-six-year-old point guard beloved within the Alaska organization for leading the Aces to the 1996 grand slam. To Cone, the assistant coaches, and their loved ones, Abarrientos was literally family—a perennial guest at birthday parties, a sponsor at their weddings, and a godfather to their children. When Abarrientos poked a crossover out of Willie's hands and cruised downcourt for a layup, Bong Hawkins's teenage daughter, sitting a few seats away from me, covered her eyes and said, "Oh crap! My *ninong!*" Her godfather was abusing his former team.

Cone's plan to contain Rod Nealy had run into a major hiccup. Keeping the ball out of Nealy's hands was turning out to be much easier said than done. The backcourt chaser had been effective. Whenever Nealy saw a double team coming, he passed the ball to an open teammate. From there, Nic or Rey was supposed to deny any passes back to him. In theory, they would do this by keeping a hand in the passing lane between Nealy and the ball and shadowing the import's every move. The problem, however, was that Nealy was too shifty for Alaska's defenders, whose feet seemed tangled as they tried to follow his barrage of jab steps and head-and-body fakes. Once he had them off balance, he'd pop out, receive the ball, and create scoring opportunities for himself and other Ginebra players. By the end of the first quarter Nealy's penetrations and Alaska's ensuing defensive rotations had created openings for a trio of Ginebra three-pointers and a nine-point lead for the Gin Kings.

Nealy also had a knack for turning Alaska's best defensive possessions into disheartening failures. Early in the second quarter, Rey guarded Nealy so tight that his hand was momentarily caught inside Nealy's jersey. The Ginebra import just shrugged Rey off, caught a pass near half-court, dribbled twice toward the key, then crossed over into a step-back three-pointer that splashed through the net. Meanwhile, Cone was substituting new players after almost every dead ball, trying to find someone on his bench who could hit a shot. He came up empty. The Aces were en route to missing their first twenty-five outside shots. The team's only baskets came from Roe, who saved the team from a near shutout in the second quarter with his steady mix of push shots in the lane and assists to teammates cutting along the baseline for layups.

But Roe's point production couldn't keep pace with the entire Ginebra team, especially Nealy. Near the end of the second quarter Jeff Cariaso tried to foul the import on a fast break. He wrapped both arms around Nealy to prevent him from attempting a shot, but all it took for Nealy to break free was a simple jump to the hoop. Jeff tumbled away like a rag doll, and Nealy got the score and the foul. Nealy converted another and-one on his team's next possession, this time wresting an offensive rebound from three Alaska players before head-faking them into the rafters. Just as Eddie Laure landed on Nealy's back, the import launched through the knot of defenders and scored. Nealy's bonus free throw put Alaska in a seventeen-point hole.

Alaska called time-out and Cone earned a technical foul for chasing a referee onto the court to argue that a hand-check foul the ref neglected to call led to a Ginebra steal. A thunderous "Hee-neh-bra" chorus welcomed Cone as he stomped back to the bench. The tiny island of

Alaska fans were cowed into silence, with one exception. Nic's wife, a beauty queen and model who represented the Philippines in the 2003 Miss World pageant, cocked back a half-full water bottle and sent it skidding across the hardwood. In a country where the shy, modest woman is a gender ideal, and *mahinhin*, which translates loosely as "demure," is among the highest compliments a woman can receive, the sight of Miss Philippines winging debris at the court meant that Jaworski's spirit was very much alive inside the Araneta Coliseum. Nobody, not even a woman chosen to embody Philippine femininity, could avoid the Big J's hotheaded legacy.

The Aces didn't score from the perimeter until midway through the third quarter. The shot that broke the seal was a Nic Belasco baseline jumper from sixteen feet. A minute later Eddie Laure connected on a three-pointer. Shots began to fall, and with each make a little energy returned to the browbeaten Aces. By the end of the third quarter they were chasing the ball out of Nealy's hands and recovering to Ginebra's shooters with more vigor than they had all game. Ginebra's lead shrunk to seven points. Somehow, Alaska was in the game.

The Aces kept surging in the final period, but Ginebra never folded. Roe began to pull ahead in his duel with Nealy, knocking the ball away from him with an uppercut swipe and forcing Nealy to give up his fifth foul. On the ensuing possession, Roe drove into Ginebra's zone, absorbed a foul and scored. His three-point play cut the lead to four. Minutes later Willie's three-pointer from the left wing, his first of the game, brought Alaska within three points. The teams traded baskets, with Roe cutting the lead to one, then Nealy engineering a basket to push Ginebra's margin back to three. With about three minutes to play, Alaska finally got a stop when Ginebra's Ronald Tubid lofted a reckless eighteen-foot runner from the baseline that soared clear over the rim. Willie responded with a jump shot that pushed Alaska ahead 93-92.

The Alaska bench celebrated Willie's go-ahead shot like it was a playoff buzzer-beater. The comeback was complete. They were still jumping up and down when Nealy swished a three-pointer over Roe's fingertips. The Aces had spent most of the game clawing back from that seventeen-point deficit, only to have Nealy coolly erase their short-lived lead. The bench sunk back into their seats. Alaska might have given up after Nealy's three if it weren't for Mike Cortez. He caught a pass on the next trip downcourt, shot-faked a defender into flying past, then reclaimed the lead with his own triple. With Alaska up a point and less than two minutes to play, Mike intercepted a pass to the wing. Mike and Willie ran a two-on-one fast break, shuffling the ball back and forth and then dishing to Roe, who trailed the play and finished with a two-handed dunk that put Alaska up three with about 90 seconds left to play.

To seal the win, Alaska needed a stop. Ginebra ran a play to get Nealy the ball in the low post. Roe, Nic, and Sonny swarmed him with their arms high above their heads. Nealy managed to wheel into the paint and attempt a floater, and this time the ball struck backboard and nothing else. The miss seemed like his first of the game. After an Alaska timeout, the Aces worked the ball around the perimeter until the ball landed again in Mike's hands. His second three-ball in less than a minute gave Alaska a six-point lead. The crowd fell silent except for Alaska's pocket of fans, who filled the void with a new take on Ginebra's mantra: *"U-wi na! U-wi na!"* Go home.

Alaska owner Fred Uytengsu followed his euphoric players into the locker room after the win. When the boss stepped inside, all the players' hooting and hugging ceased. They sat down and watched the breakfast magnate, tan and impeccably coiffed with a neat pompadour. "I think that's one of the greatest comebacks I've seen us do," he said. "We didn't give up. If we play like this the rest of the conference, we've got big things in store for us." As Uytengsu turned to leave the locker room, the players all chanted, "Bo-nus! Bo-nus!" The owner grinned, flashed his empty wallet, and walked out. Alaska was in the semis.

13

Skirts Versus Squirts

With two weeks to rest and prepare while the league's lower ranked teams contended for the remaining semifinal berths, Cone gave Alaska three days off, and the players scattered across the nation to relax and visit family in the provinces or unwind at hot springs and surfing resorts. Jeff Cariaso, still playing more than thirty minutes per game in his thirteenth PBA season, started his playoff ice-bath regimen. During the regular season, generous five-day buffers between games were the norm. Once the semifinals began, Alaska would play Wednesday, Friday, and Sunday every week until they won the championship or lost trying. In recent years Jeff, bearing down on his thirty-fifth birthday, readied his body for the playoffs and recuperated after games with a dip in ice water. Every day, he would submerge his body from the neck down in a frigid bathtub and emerge twenty minutes later, blue but refreshed.

I also took a trip, although not really a vacation, during this respite from Alaska's day-to-day grind. I flew to Cebu, the regional hub of the Visayan islands south of Manila. Cebu City had a reputation for being the Philippines' most feverish basketball madhouse. The city was a regional gateway to the universe of elite college and professional basketball, so hoops talent from the Visayas and Mindanao bottlenecked there. Players proved themselves in Cebu City before making the leap to Manila. Of the many pro players who followed this path, two of the greatest were Ramon Fernandez and Abet Guidaben, dominant centers from the Toyota-Crispa days. Another was Alaska assistant coach Jojo Lastimosa, who grew up in northern Mindanao but began his career in Cebu with Mama's Love, a cosmetics company-owned semipro team that played under various skin care-related names like the Lotion Makers. But I wasn't headed to Cebu to learn about the city's proud basketball tradition. I was searching for something I'd heard rumors about; a twisted, outlandish take on hoops.

The whispers started with a drunken Peace Corps volunteer at a karaoke parlor. The American lived in a fishing town north of Cebu City, where he advised the local government on coastal resource management; that is, he encouraged anglers not to fish by dropping dynamite and cyanide into the water, but rather to preserve coral reefs and promote them as ecotourism destinations. He was visiting Manila for an annual meeting with Peace Corps administrators, and I met him with some volunteers who I previously helped conduct writing workshops in southeastern Luzon. Someone in the group mentioned my interest in basketball, and the Cebu volunteer peeled his eyes away from the Bon Jovi lyrics scrolling across the karaoke screen. "Come to Cebu," he said. "We've got midgets playing against transvestites at the town fiestas." He shared this tip in the jovial manner appropriate to our surroundings of Red Horse "Extra Strong" beer and synthesized monster ballads. Then, however, he seemed to reconsider as his voice turned grim. "Seriously," he continued, "that game is intense."

The mere existence of a "skirts versus squirts" basketball game was not that outrageous. I had already watched a provincial Miss Gay pageant;* in fact, I was selected from the crowd to present a bouquet to the winner of the national outfit competition. These events seemed in tune with other beloved rituals of mass humiliation like *Wowowee,* so grafting a strain of demented humor onto basketball seemed within reason. No one in the PBA hoops establishment had heard of Cebu's midget-transvestite five-on-five, but it was all over the Internet in jittery handheld YouTube chronicles and on the home page of Aksyon Radyo, the Cebu-based talk and public affairs AM station that organized and promoted the exhibitions. Before long I was chatting online with Dexter Ligan, one of Aksyon's on-air hosts. By the end of our conversation, I had finalized my plans to visit Cebu and witness a scintillating cement-court encounter. Little people versus ladyboys! The misunderstood against the maligned! This is where amazing happens.

A few weeks later I was crammed into the passenger seat of Dexter's sputtering, fire engine red Volkswagen Beetle, with his wife Margie riding in the backseat. Dexter and Margie filled me in on the basics of the *Unano-Bading* Showdown† as we rambled past the Cebu provincial capital's Romanesque facade on the way to an evening game in Lapu-Lapu, a small city on nearby Mactan Island. Dexter, the station's earnest, mustachioed anchorman and play-by-play announcer for the *Unano-Bading* games, proudly noted that the midget-gay basketball sensation was hardly confined to Cebu City or even the whole of Cebu province. Adopting the model of a traveling carnival, Aksyon Radyo had taken the game all over the Visayas, from Leyte, site of MacArthur's landing in WWII, to Siquijor, an island reputedly overrun by witches, and most provinces in between. The station charged flat rates on a sliding scale from about $400 to $1000, depending on the amount of travel

---

* I remember noting, with amateur anthropological pride, that Miss Gay 2006 of Barangay Masaguitsit, Lobo, Batangas, was crowned underneath the backboard of the town basketball court.

† In Tagalog, this was roughly equivalent to calling the game the "Midget-Homo Showdown."

required, to bring the game to a town near you. From there, the local sponsors, usually municipal governments or Catholic parishes, would set ticket prices and use the profits however they saw fit. The game had already broken into Mindanao with games as far away as Cagayan de Oro and Surigao City, and Dexter said the organizers had further plans of conquering audiences in Manila and Filipino migrant communities across the globe.

The game's origins, according to Dexter, were altruistic. Carlo Dugaduga, the station manager of Aksyon Radyo and Ligan's coannouncer, came up with the idea as a livelihood project for midgets who couldn't find regular work. The first games featured midget-on-midget action, and although spectators seemed impressed with the diminutive players' ability to execute reverse layups and shoot three-pointers using regulation-size balls and baskets, the novelty wore off fast. By the third and fourth quarters the spectacle of exhausted little people summoning the strength to hurl air balls lost its charm. Then Dugaduga had a eureka moment that is to midget sports entertainment what Benjamin Franklin's kite experiment was to electricity. To keep the show from dragging, Dugaduga added drag queens to the mix. The formula was a hit; as Dexter said, "We found that this format was much funnier." Margie chimed in from the back: "People really enjoy the halflings!"

The cross-dressing players were brought in as stock villains, to be the Washington Generals to the midgets' Harlem Globetrotters. For most people, community service means writing a check to the Red Cross or creating a mentoring program for troubled youth; for Dugaduga, it meant recruiting people who, due to physical disabilities or their sexual orientations, had been relegated to the margins of Philippine society, then convincing them to let hundreds of people mock them in a basketball-themed freak show. Although my instinct was to condemn Dugaduga's Mother Teresa by way of P. T. Barnum scheme, I have to admit that it had been successful. Depending on how long they had been with the troupe, the performers earned between eight and twenty dollars for each game. It sounds like a paltry sum, but in a country where almost half the population lives on less than two dollars a day, fifteen bucks is nothing to sneeze at. For many of the midgets, it was their only opportunity to contribute income to the families who supported them. Allan Castro, the shortest midget and the Showdown's brightest success story, had been discovered during a game and cast in a local TV sitcom, *Tres Metros,* about the lives of three midgets who were each one meter tall.

For Dexter, this was simply too much inspiration to bear. While the Bug idled at a red light, with missionary spirit pulsing through his veins, he reached into his knapsack and retrieved a pocket version of the Ten Commandments.

"Have you heard of this book, Rafe?" he asked me.

Believe it or not, I had. I even saw the movie. And, although I already knew the Ten Commandments, I accepted the gift, not only to be polite, but also because I thought to myself, What better way to prepare for a two-hour basketball drag show than by brushing up on the central tenets of Judeo-Christian theology?

"Rafe, look on your right," Dexter said as we approached the bridge to Mactan. "That used to be the biggest *shabu*"—Philippine slang for methamphetamines—"factory in the Philippines."

We pulled into a gravel parking lot behind Lapu-Lapu's central basketball court just as the fading sun was giving way to the amber glow of sixty-watt lightbulbs rigged above vendors' carts of fried fish balls and peanuts shot through with garlic and chili peppers. Jeepneys cruising the town plaza had the destination LAPU 2X painted on their sides, shorthand for the city named after Lapu-Lapu, the native chief credited with slaying Ferdinand Magellan in 1521 and temporarily repelling the Spanish conquistadors. Maybe an hour after we arrived, a battered green van rumbled into the parking lot. A dented loudspeaker was lashed to the roof with extension cords and the vehicle's pocked metal shell looked like a soda can that had been crushed and then bent back into shape. It nudged through the dark, crowded streets and settled into a spot next to the court, where seven men dressed in various permutations of miniskirts, booty shorts, baby tees, and halter tops emerged from the back and began unloading midgets, some of whom were too short to climb down from the van.

Welcome to the apocalypse, as imagined by Adam Sandler. Wait, scratch that. Rather, welcome to fiesta in Lapu-Lapu City! The guests at Shangri-La's prissy five-star resort on the other side of Mactan Island had no clue what they were missing.

For three years running, the people of Lapu-Lapu hired Aksyon Radyo to stage the Unano-Bading Showdown. The local population just couldn't get enough of the spectacle, which combined the roundball flair of Rucker Park, the exaggerated schtick of professional wrestling, and the good taste of midget tossing. In the words of Harry Radaza, the city's sports and recreation chief, it all added up to "great family entertainment."

Yet even Radaza didn't expect to see Aksyon Radyo's motley crew roll into town for a third straight year. The staged exhibition always followed the same storyline: The munchkin team, literal underdogs, fell behind the taller RuPaul squad, until the dwarfs surged ahead to claim an improbable comeback victory. Along the way there was taunting and dancing, midgets were lifted and tickled, skirts were pulled down and bras became unstuffed. Having watched this game twice, Radaza assumed the town would be ready for a new set of cheap thrills. Something new and fresh, like a gay talent show. Not so. Once again the people demanded Aksyon Radyo's basketball burlesque, and the local government delivered.

"What can I say? People just love midgets," Radaza offered as an explanation of the game's popularity, and, looking at the hundreds of people lined up to buy tickets, and the dozens of others who had already staked out viewpoints in the branches of surrounding trees and on top of nearby trucks, it was hard to disagree with him.

Elmer Gonzales's pregame routine started in the dark, semiprivacy of the van, where Team Unano's star guard solemnly changed into his yellow Aksyon Radyo uniform. His miniature physique was so impressively muscled that even his angular cheekbones seemed chiseled in the weight room. In his final act before taking the court, Gonzales meticulously polished his kids' size sneakers with an old rag, scrubbing every smudge like he was preparing for the biggest game of his life.

Outside the car, leaning with his back against a tire, Ran-ran Genio was far less stoic. He was the dwarf team's Mister Personality, and he felt particularly outgoing that night because Lapu-Lapu was his hometown. Cousins approached and greeted him by pinching his potbelly, which was large enough to weigh down Yao Ming. He high-fived them and smiled at the attention, flashing a wide grin and a sparkling, faux-diamond stud in his left ear. But even though Genio's disposition was all sunshine, his story was dark.

"Is it true, where you come from, the people will respect you even if you're like us?" he asked me in Tagalog. My country wasn't perfect, I said, but disabled people probably have more opportunities there. Genio, it turned out, had performed in a litany of bizarre spectacles that blurred the distinction between so-called "family entertainment" and human rights violations. He played one-on-one against a man who had been electrocuted and lost both arms at the elbows. He played one-on-two against a pair of smaller midgets. He competed in backward foot-races against drunks pulled from the crowd. And he boxed another midget who was paid to sucker punch him before the opening bell and then bite his ear in homage to Mike Tyson. Thankfully, Genio's opponent did not chew as forcefully as Iron Mike.

While Genio recounted his entertainment career, he was interrupted by a child, maybe nine years old, who darted from a crowd to poke his shoulder and then vanish back into the mob. Genio said the boy was probably dared to touch him, to see if he was a real person. And that, along with the money, was one of the reasons Genio played in these games: to show people, especially kids who didn't know better, that they needn't be afraid of little people. Philippine folklore was full of stories about *duwende*, impish gnomes with magic powers, and *tiyanak*, vicious changelings that assumed children's bodies to lure their human prey. The Aksyon Radyo exhibitions gave Ran-ran an opportunity to demonstrate that he wasn't some kind of mystical troll but in fact a basketball-crazy Filipino like most of his countrymen.

The transvestites played under stage names like Beyoncé and Mother Nature and walked the well-trodden ground of gay entertainers in Philippine society. For decades male diva impersonators, showbiz reporters, and Miss Gay hopefuls have been vamping and prancing to please their audiences. While the drag queen dream team vogued for a group of local men who acted repulsed but couldn't stop staring, I thought of Danton Remoto, the gay rights activist and English professor. Remoto once explained for me the niche Filipino homosexuals occupied: "In a society like this—very hierarchical and patriarchal—gays were traditionally seen as like women, and therefore inferior. In short, being inferior, they can serve you, which means either food or entertainment."

Samantha was the prettiest man on the team. With full lips, soft, almond eyes, and a small red scar on his chest, he confirmed Remoto's analysis. Samantha told me that the Unano-Bading game was one of the few places where he felt accepted while wearing a silver bikini top and denim miniskirt. Who cared if the people in the crowd laughed and jeered? All he wanted was to put on a good show and make people happy.

Like any basketball game, the Unano-Bading Showdown began with a jump ball. And from the moment that Castro, the shortest midget, waddled into the circle at center court and measured eye-to-knee against Samantha, the crowd let out an ecstatic howl that wouldn't subside for ten minutes.

To no one's surprise and everyone's delight, Samantha won the tip and sent the ball to Beyoncé, who looked like a bodybuilder under his halter top. The drag queens stampeded up and down the court, slapping the ball rather than dribbling it and chucking spastic overhead heaves at the rim. Sometimes they shot five or ten times in one possession and hit nothing but backboard. With each miss, the crowd laughed harder, until people were writhing on the sidelines in fits of hysteria.

The midgets looked like a real basketball team. Genio dribbled around Mother Nature and then passed to Gonzales, who drove the lane. He was headed for a finger roll until Beyoncé scooped him off the ground and shook Gonzales until he dropped the ball. Mother Nature collected it and scored an easy layup, then ran up the sideline taunting the crowd with cartwheels that exposed the manly bulge beneath his ruffled miniskirt. Mother Nature continued the victory celebration by singling out an unfortunate man in the front row and forcing a triumphant lap-dance on him, and the fan reacted like he'd been set on fire. Again, the crowd let out a delirious *"Eeeeeee!"* loud enough to move the Earth off its axis.

Beyoncé seemed poised to score when he caught the ball a few feet from the basket. That is, until the midget defense arrived. Because of Beyoncé's height advantage, they made no attempt to disrupt his shot. Instead, three midgets grabbed hold of their opponent's frilly skirt. Beyoncé jumped and his hips went up but the skirt stayed down. When he realized his G-string was exposed, he dropped the ball and fell to the ground, covering his junk while the midgets stormed off to score. At this point some unwitting grandfather in my row had seen too much. Still chuckling and shaking his head, the old man covered his face with a washcloth and rested his head in his daughter's lap.

Nothing got the crowd more worked up, however, than the midgets' actual basketball talent. Watching Castro, whose tiny hands looked like marshmallows, hoist the ball from his waist and through the hoop seemed like the human equivalent of an ant lifting fifty times its body weight. When Genio sank a shot from the foul line, teenage boys grabbed each other by the shoulders and pointed to the basket. The younger kids reenacted the shot the same way awestruck PBA fans once mimicked Billy Ray Bates's spectacular dunks.

After the game (as expected, the midgets won) Dugaduga approached me. "I'm interested in bringing Unano-Bading to the States," he said. "Do you think we can find a sponsor?"

Could he see the horror spread through my eyes? I could only imagine the mob of activists and do-gooders waiting to crucify Dexter and Dugaduga if they took their show to the United States. The truth was that I had almost as much trouble watching the game as the man with the towel over his face. During the first five minutes, while the 1,500 onlookers shrieked to high heavens, the air of mass hysteria mingled with the event's absurdity to suck me into the enjoyable mayhem. Soon thereafter, however, a lump of doom formed in my throat. This comedic take on basketball hit the same unfunny note—desperate people pulling each other's pants down—over and over again. Yet everyone around me remained doubled over in laughter, and Dexter, the guy who had invited me to church with his family and given me a Ten Commandments booklet, was riling up the unruly masses. I had been living in the Philippines for two years already, but I never felt more American, or more outraged for that matter. I loved Philippine basketball and its excesses, but the Unano-Bading Showdown was too much. It was wrong. Yet somehow the performers didn't feel demeaned and fans enjoyed themselves with no apparent malice. I couldn't understand it. Later that night, when I lay down to sleep in a grungy Cebu City pension house, I heard the howling Lapu-Lapu crowd. I felt guilty. I couldn't rest. The best I could do was accept that there was no intended cruelty behind Aksyon Radyo's spectacle.

Back in Manila, I sought out Remoto to help me reconcile what I saw in Cebu with the country and basketball tradition that I loved. He revealed his own inner struggle over amusements like the Unano-Bading game. "One half of me would be laughing and laughing, and the other half would say, 'They've consigned us again to the carnival!'" Remoto told me. "The side of me that's a westernized gay rights activist, who went to Rutgers and who studied in the U.K., says, 'Oh no, fucking hell!' and the other half says, 'Uy! How funny!' These are gay men who dress up female and play basketball, which is a man's game in the Philippines. It's so postmodern. There are layers and layers of references and subreferences. We're the first po-mo in the world without even meaning it!" Maybe so, but if the Unano-Bading showdown was somehow avant-garde, I was looking forward to banishing it from my mind and focusing on something old-fashioned, like Alaska's goal of winning a PBA championship.

14

Powers that Be

side from the occasional Cebu flashback, I was eager to see how Alaska would respond to the greater stresses of the playoffs. I'm afraid, however, that somewhere in my subconscious I will always carry the image of Elmer Gonzales's petite body playing dead while receiving overenthusiastic mouth-to-mouth resuscitation and gratuitous dry humping from a chubby transvestite.

When practice resumed after the break, the Aces seemed focused. So did the coaches. And the trainers. Even the ball boys seemed intent on finding the extra gear that championship teams ride to titles. There was one problem, however. The team had no specific adversary to prepare for. It would be another week before Ginebra and San Miguel wrapped up their quarterfinal series, and a few days after that Alaska would face one of them in the semifinals. The coaches, especially Cone and Joel Banal, seemed elated to have this respite from the usual formula of scouting and game-planning. Their eyes lit up and they spoke faster, like they had been liberated from mundane practicalities like deciding whether to double-team an import or have Roe guard him one-on-one. Instead, they returned to teaching pure basketball—honing Alaska's press break, tinkering with rotations in Banal's match-up zone, and rehearsing every imaginable permutation of Cone's triangle offense.

For the players these drills were the hoops equivalent of homework. Someday the team would be better off for having spent an extra hour perfecting their box-out positions and listening to Cone and Banal recite treatises on the importance of basketball possession-by-possession. In the playoffs, Cone reminded his players, one turnover could cost them a series. However, when the coach unveiled lines like, "You want to treat each possession as its own, singular possession," the players shot furtive glances at each other, gestured for ball boys to bring them Gatorade, and stared longingly at the wall clock. The coaches, unfazed by their tuned-out audience, continued in their strategic ecstasy.

In one such moment, Cone stopped a five-on-five scrimmage to share some observations on the NBA's pinnacle of staid execution, the San Antonio Spurs. That week, the Spurs had swept the Cleveland Cavaliers in the Finals and made the league's best player, Lebron James, look ordinary. "That's precision, fellas," Cone said. "Think about that word: precision. The Spurs knew exactly what they wanted to do, exactly where on the floor they wanted to push Lebron, and they executed it on every possession. Precision." Banal piped in: "Another word for precision is accuracy," and he repeated Cone's speech almost word for word while substituting "accuracy" for "precision."

Even Roe, a player who prided himself in taking practice seriously and paying attention to his coaches' instructions, started to lose his patience. He rolled his eyes and made the "Yap, yap, yap" sign with one hand. Dale Singson, who was standing next to Roe, noticed and placed a palm on the small of his back as if to say, "I know, big guy. Hang in there."

Throughout the season, I had enjoyed Cone and Banal's tag-team seminars. Cone always had the first and last word, and he spoke with urgency. *Guys, if we don't push San Miguel's big men out of the low post, we're going to lose! We can't give them position. So big guys, when their guards run off screens on the baseline, don't help too much. They're not looking for the guards. They want you to step away and help, because when you do, their bigs will retake the post."* In the middle of Cone's instructions, Banal would chime in to reinforce the plan, sometimes restating it in pure Tagalog for the local players who might not be as attentive in English. Finally, before relinquishing the spotlight to Cone, Coach Joel would toss in some spiritual guidance. Banal regularly shared his reflective, meditative side with the team. He was Alaska's roundball Confucius; his best aphorisms—equal parts sage insight and mumbo jumbo—sounded like they were pulled out of basketball-themed fortune cookies. "Winning to me is not selfishness," Banal told the team. "Winning is like the fulfillment of a man."

That was a good line, but he couldn't stop there. Banal, feeling righteous, told the players to consider the sport their "earthly master" and to honor him with victory: "Please your earthly master as unto the Lord. If you please your earthly master, you're also pleasing the Lord. And we please them by winning." The players, not so easily stricken by whimsy, formed a bewildered column of furrowed brows. Mike Cortez turned to Roe and mouthed, *Huh?* Roe just shrugged.

Normally, I appreciated Coach Joel's musings. He had the warm, even canter of a hypnotist, and his conviction was infectious. Hearing him talk about basketball reminded me of watching Bob Ross, the serene, afroed landscape painter who discussed "happy trees" on public television. Not to mention, I could be equally guilty of sporadic, maudlin ruminations on basketball as the meaning of life; that Banal had the aplomb to share his ideas with twenty macho ballplayers was brave and refreshing. But even my tolerance for hoops gibberish wore thin during the first week of preplayoff practice. Cone and Banal's instruction and inspiration, repeated over and over again, became ambient noise not much different from the rain that pounded the gym's metal roof like thousands of tiny mallets.

One afternoon while the coaches held class on one end of the court,

I kept busy by dribbling a ball in low figure-eights through my legs. I heard Roe hiss at me and felt ashamed. I had been around the game long enough to know that handling the ball—even the quiet patter of my low dribble—while a coach talked was taboo. I expected Roe, who could be a Boy Scout when it came to basketball etiquette, to set me straight. Instead, he wanted the ball. He caught it and started shooting around on the far end of the court, while Cone lectured on the other side. If dribbling was a taboo, this was outright defiance. I chased Roe's rebounds and passed to him while he launched baseline jumpers. The coaches didn't seem to mind our breach of protocol. Perhaps they understood how antsy the players were feeling, or maybe they knew better than to pick a fight with their import this late in the season, especially a player like Roe, who always came prepared for games and ran himself ragged on the court. "I wanna tell him to put that clipboard down," Roe said after banking a shot from the left wing. "This week has been the hardest since I got out here. I'm ready to go home, and not to Makati, I mean Seattle. My mental fatigue—" his voice trailed off. "I wish we just had a game."

When the players weren't listening to their newly verbose coaches during the run-up to the semifinals, they devoted their time to defense. All season long the Aces had been known as a stout defensive team that relied on classic man-to-man principles—stay between your man and the basket; play defense with your feet, not your hands; deny passes to the post; away from the ball, always be able to see the ball and your man. But Cone saw room for improvement. He thought the team owed its stopper reputation to its collection of gritty individual defenders. Starters like Roe, Nic Belasco and Jeff Cariaso were among the league's best all-around defenders at their positions, and certain reserves brought specialty skills to the floor. Eddie Laure could smother perimeter players with his go-go gadget arms and manic pursuit of the ball. John Ferriols was scarcely a hair taller than six-foot-three, but he had the heft and experience to outwork most big men for low-post position. Even when he got beat, John had quick hands and could strip the ball from an opponent who was going up for a shot.

These lockdown defenders provided a safety net that masked their teammates' missed rotations. That wasn't good enough for Cone. Covering up for one player's lapses meant leaving someone else open. Smart teams like Ginebra and San Miguel would find those open men and either score or draw fouls. Cone wanted the Aces' opponents to feel like there were no soft spots to attack. In practice, he focused on getting the players to stay in a low defensive stance for entire possessions. During drills, all the Aces could squat in a mean, alert position with their weight on the balls of the feet, their knees bent, and their arms open wide to deflect passes. Too often, they looked different in games—straight and relaxed, like they were waiting at a bus stop. Their tendency was to wait until an offensive player caught the ball, then crouch and get ready to guard him. But by then it was too late; the Alaska defender had already ceded the advantage.

Cone's solution was to require his players to pound the floor with both palms and shout *"Defense!"* at the beginning of each possession. The court slap went mainstream in the nineties thanks to a gnat-like Duke University point guard named Steve Wojciechowski. The *Washington Times* called him the "most reviled 6.6-point scorer in NCAA basketball history," and although the emphatic gesture reeked of Wojo's loathsome scrappiness, it was nevertheless an effective way to force players into defensive position. "The best players on our team don't stay low on defense, and we follow their example," Cone said with the sound of a court slap still reverberating through the gym. "Don't just be the top scorers. Lead us on defense too."

Although he addressed the entire team, everyone in the gym understood he was speaking to Willie Miller. Each Alaska defender was guilty of sloughing off from time to time, but Willie was the Aces' most habitual offender. Thanks to his athletic gifts, which led Willie to believe he could always recover after falling a step behind, and his happy-go-lucky nature, the team's star guard frequently got caught dozing on defense. In a couple late season games, including Alaska's second loss to Red Bull, Willie played straight-legged defense and couldn't catch up to his man. He had to hack opposing guards to prevent them from dribbling past him and he ended up benched with foul trouble during crucial stretches of the game.

Now, Cone prevailed upon his top local scorer to change his ways. But rather than yell at Willie as he would most other players, Cone decided to protect Willie's famously brittle confidence by delivering this coded reprimand. Throughout his career, Willie had been a riddle to coaches. Telling him to do something was often the worst way to get him to do it. Cone believed direct criticism would drive Willie into his shell; not only would the mercurial star not respond to defensive instructions, but Willie's brilliant offense might also subside. Unlike past coaches who butted heads with Willie, Cone tried to influence him obliquely. "Down the stretch, you're better off running a play for another player, and telling him in private to pass to Willie," Cone told me after practice. "If you make the play straight for Willie, he'll make a turnover or do something silly. If you give it to somebody else, who then gives it to him, then he'll make a fabulous play for you. I don't know why it works that way. Rather than banging your head against a wall trying to change him, you work within that." So far, Cone's approach had been successful; Alaska won a bye to the semifinals, and Willie, who was logging some of the best scoring and assist numbers of his career, was a front-runner for the MVP award.

A few days later, Alaska's worst nightmare became Ginebra's reality. The San Miguel Beermen—the team the Aces avoided by beating the Gin-Kings in the tiebreaker—eliminated Ginebra in a close best-of-three quarterfinal. The mood inside the Alaska players' lounge was muted the day after San Miguel clinched the series. The team finally had an opponent, which meant the coaches' nebulous training sessions would give way to more concrete preparations. Earlier in the week this might have been cause for celebration. Now that the moment had arrived, the team was grim. The Aces were hoping to play Ginebra, a team they had beaten three times already. They felt like they had the Gin-Kings figured out. San Miguel was another story. The Beermen—their nonthreatening moniker notwithstanding—were scary.

"Eight games—that's no joke," Jeff Cariaso told me, regarding San Miguel's mid-season winning streak. He had sensed that Alaska would play the Beermen, although he seemed unenthusiastic now that the prediction came true: "When they got matched up with Ginebra, I said, 'We're gonna have to play these fools.' I would rather have played Ginebra, because at least with them you know who you need to stop—Nealy. San Miguel is full of surprises. Every time they're in a must-win game, they win."

Jeff was referring to the Beermen's playoff run, during which they had survived four win-or-go-home elimination games and ended three other teams' seasons. San Miguel would not be an easy out, but that was just one reason for Alaska to worry. The Beermen had a stingy defense much like Alaska's. With a beefy, veteran front line that included two-time MVP Danny Ildefonso, San Miguel may have been the only PBA team capable of outmuscling the Aces on the boards. The Beermen possessed a cast of rugged perimeter defenders who would be champing at the bit to limit Willie's output, plus a handful of offensive wild cards who could take over any game. The catalog of potential threats included Willy Wilson and Brandon Cablay, two former Aces who would be eager to punish the team that traded them; Chris Calaguio, a three-point specialist enjoying a career year; and L.A. Tenorio, a twenty-two-year-old point guard rocket whose speed and limitless energy seemed tailor-made to expose Willie's sins of nonchalance.

Then there was Galen Young, the San Miguel import who rescued the team from its 0-6 tailspin at the beginning of the conference. Until he arrived in Manila, a string of import-related fiascos nearly ruined the Beermen's season. Their first choice, Kelly Whitney, was sent home for being too tall before he got a chance to play. With only three days between Whitney's failed measurement and San Miguel's first game, the team scrambled to find a warm foreign body to field as an import. They came up with Vidal Massiah, who, despite his Atlantic 10 Conference credentials and dramatic name, was no savior. In his second and final PBA game, Massiah scored no points. Next came Paul McMillan, a husky forward with a permanently sour look on his face. McMillan was a competent rebounder and inside scorer—he even put up a 41-point game against Talk 'N Text—but he didn't have the all-around game needed to revive San Miguel's local talent and save the season.*

A month into the season, the Beermen brought in Young. The team figured they had finally hired a surefire import. The thirty-one-year-old forward had already proven himself in the PBA—in 2004 he played for Alaska—and the team knew he was in shape because he flew to Manila weeks after leading the Yakama Sun Kings to the CBA championship. Yet in Young's first game, a blowout loss to Alaska, the jet-lagged import made four of twenty-three shots and was booed for most of the

---

* I will always have a soft spot for Paul McMillan and his sour puss. Throughout his 41-point explosion, McMillan dutifully poured in seven-foot bank shots while shrugging, slouching, grimacing, and looking generally homesick. It had to be among the most ho-hum monster scoring games in basketball history, and his dolorous body language became a running joke between me and Ravi, my fellow Boracay import. The gag became legendary the following week, when Ravi was driving me home after a pickup game. We passed Chili's and spotted McMillan standing outside the entrance. Ravi stuck his head out the window and screamed, "P-Mac! You're my idol, bro!" True to form, McMillan acknowledged us with a lethargic wave.

second half. His performance was such a dud that there was talk around the league of San Miguel's plan to drop Young and hire their fifth import of the season. As Young grew familiar with his teammates, however, the wins began to pile up. He was different from the archetypal PBA import, whose idea of an assist was a pass to himself off the backboard for a dunk. Young loved to stand at the top of the key and pick apart defenses with his passing. He didn't know his personnel in San Miguel's first loss to Alaska, so he didn't know how to set them up. Once he figured them out, the Beermen steamrolled through the rest of their schedule.

Young played the same role for the Beermen as Roe did for the Aces, but their styles were slightly different. Young's game had more slickness and finesse; Roe relied on strength and hustle. Yet both players acted as the lubricant that made their teams run smoothly. That wasn't all the two imports had in common. They were old friends from the international hoops circuit, admirers of one another's games, and teammates on a 2006 Yakama squad. Recently, they had both signed to play for the Australian league's Townsville Crocodiles in the coming season. The rival imports would be teammates in a few months. On top of all that, Young had also unveiled a silver mohawk for the playoffs. Although the style made Young look like Wesley Snipes's psychotic villain in *Demolition Man*, it also gave the Beermen a certain rally-cap charm. They could care less about Alaska's long-awaited championship; San Miguel had pulled off a laudable mid-conference turnaround, and now they were out to complete their own storybook season.

Alaska had other reasons to feel apprehensive about San Miguel. The Beermen were the PBA's most storied franchise, the local answer to the New York Yankees. Of the league's ten teams, San Miguel was the sole remaining pioneer franchise that joined the PBA in 1975. Their power ful owner, onetime Marcos crony Eduardo "Danding" Cojuangco, was chairman of the San Miguel Corporation, the Philippines' largest food and beverage company. San Miguel controlled three PBA teams—the others were the Purefoods Tender Juicy Giants and Barangay Ginebra Kings—but the flagship Beermen were reputedly closest to Cojuangco's heart. No other team had won as many championships, and San Miguel was the only active team other than Alaska to have pulled off a grand slam, when they captured all three conference titles in 1989.[*] As such, there was a feeling among teams outside Cojuangco's umbrella that the Beermen, thanks to their owner's wealth and influence and the team's tradition and history, were the league's favorite sons.

If Alaska felt like they took on the entire Philippines when they faced Ginebra, then playing against San Miguel felt like taking on the basketball powers-that-be. In a country where the will of the people often lost to the will of the powerful, taking on the hoops establishment felt like Alaska's ultimate test. As soon as the match-up was announced, Cone began telling the players to expect bad calls from the referees. He was especially concerned because Alaska owner Fred Uytengsu was leaving that week to take his family on an African safari. Without his presence behind the bench, Cone worried that the one-sided officiating could become more brazen. Only Uytengsu had the stature to make a stink in the press and cajole the commissioner into giving Alaska a fair

---

[*] The sweetness of this historic achievement was dulled considerably by the fact that San Miguel's third title coincided with a coup attempt on President Corazon Aquino's government. In a weeklong rebellion that began the day after San Miguel took a 2-0 lead in their best-of-seven series, an alliance of disgruntled armed forces leaders and pro-Marcos soldiers seized military bases and airfields and occupied nearly two dozen high-rise office and condominium buildings in the Makati business district. They attacked the Malacañang Palace—the Philippine White House—with air force planes and helicopters, until larger progovernment forces quelled the insurrection. The PBA Finals resumed after the coup, but for once, the shaken nation's attention was not focused on basketball.

shake. Meanwhile, Boss Danding Cojuangco was expected to be sitting behind the Beermen during every game.

The perceived favoritism benefiting Cojuangco's teams was especially strong heading into the semifinals, just weeks after San Miguel obtained forward Enrico Villanueva in a lopsided trade with Red Bull. San Miguel gave up aging big man Rommel Adducul for Villanueva, who was then considered one of the league's bright young stars. On its own, that would have been an unfair swap, but Red Bull then turned around and dealt Adducul to Purefoods for Don Camaso, a player so low on the PBA totem pole that he was supposedly slated to be an import in the same Boracay tournament where I dropped my pants until Purefoods activated him from their reserve roster. Purefoods, of course, was San Miguel's sister franchise, so the three-team swap smacked of collusion. Translated into NBA terms, an exasperated Cone compared Red Bull's decision to give up Villanueva for the eventual prize of Camaso to "Dwight Howard being traded for Ronnie Turiaf."

There was no proof of malfeasance in the Villanueva trade, but most PBA observers believed that Red Bull was "selling players." Teams with lower operating budgets were often suspected of trading their best players to big-spending teams for benchwarmers and large under-the-table cash payments. The scuttlebutt around the league priced Villanueva's bounty at almost half a million dollars, money Red Bull might use to cover operating expenses, pad employees' Christmas bonuses, or develop more young stars to sell. Another well-known but officially unacknowledged act of PBA subterfuge was laundering players. League rules stipulated that teams owned by the same individual or corporation could not trade directly with each other. This gave cash-strapped teams an incentive to act as trade conduits for sister teams. For example, if Purefoods and Ginebra wanted to shuffle their line-up, a team like Red Bull or Air 21 might facilitate the deal in exchange for token deadweight players, future draft picks, and untold cash considerations.

For Red Bull, it helped to have a coach like Yeng Guiao, whose approach to nurturing basketball talent reminded me of slash and burn agriculture. The raging mentor had a sterling track record of turning other teams' castaways into borderline stars. Once he gave them a taste of his acid tongue, they became inspired—some might say intimidated—to play their absolute best. Few players, however, could endure Guiao's badgering for long. After a couple seasons they would stop responding, but by then Guiao had squeezed every drop of talent from them and maximized their trade value for Red Bull to make another deal. Once again, Guiao's methods sounded wicked, but his results were unquestionable. As the season went on, I found myself admiring Guiao's style. There was something exhilarating about watching him take players who other teams considered deadweight, then plug them into his system and beat the same teams that traded them. Guiao was one of the league's last practitioners of Jaworski-style coaching, where toughness and passion mattered more than strategy and talent. His Red Bull teams proved that there wasn't just one way to win basketball games.

What amazed me about the PBA's gentlemanly frauds was that they were open secrets, existing not only as locker room gossip but fodder for the press. Yet no honest effort was made to stop teams from selling or laundering players, probably because most of the league's franchises had benefited from these kinds of deals in recent years, and trades were approved by a majority vote of team representatives. Only Alaska and the Santa Lucia Realtors objected publicly to the Villanueva swap. Team managers Joaqui Trillo of Alaska and Buddy Encarnado of Santa Lucia condemned the deal in the *Philippine Daily Inquirer*. "Let's call an apple an apple," Encarnado told reporters. "We all know our basketball, we've been here for a long time. How can that trade be fair? We will never resort to selling our players." Trillo added: "This is too much already. I don't know where the league is going. We may be stupid, but we're not dumb." Mixed in with this avalanche of botched idioms was a scathing critique of how unscrupulous trades were corrupting the league.

From what I could tell, the PBA trade rules existed in a parallel legal universe, along with regulations on Fil-foreign players and maximum salaries. The rulebook didn't matter because the real-life test of any transaction was the ability to get away with it. If no one stopped teams from hiring players of questionable Filipino heritage, from paying franchises to accept their washed-up talent, or from rewarding stars with bonuses worth orders of magnitude more than their contracts guaranteed, then these practices were considered acceptable. In that case, why even have rules? Why not allow teams to conduct business however they pleased, since that was what they did anyway? When I asked Cone to reflect on this charade, he said years in the league had dulled his frustration.

"When I heard about the trade, I was surprised at myself that I wasn't angry," he said, holding back a fateful chuckle. "I've gotten numb to it all." He showed a flash of indignation but recognized that it was fruitless to take on the whole PBA: "The shortsightedness of it all is typical of our league and typical of our culture. You power up your team in the short run and destroy the league in the long run. No one has the wherewithal to say flat out: 'This is wrong.' If I say it, it becomes sour grapes. I'm an arrogant American. So we just deal with it. Other teams are going to have certain advantages, and it's my job to win in spite of them. If you get punched enough, you get beat up enough, you don't feel the punches anymore." One thing was for sure: even though Alaska had fresher legs and a better record, beating San Miguel was going to be an uphill battle.

After all of Alaska's apprehension over the Beermen, the Aces went out and claimed a relatively painless 2-0 lead in the semifinals. Alaska outclassed San Miguel in seven of the first eight quarters the teams played, with the lone exception coming in the fourth quarter of game one, when the Beermen clawed out of a double-digit hole with help from the referees, who saddled the Aces with eleven fouls in the period. Desp sputtering down the stretch, Alaska held on for a 100-99 win sealed by one of Roe's jump hooks. In game two the Aces jumped to an early lead and never looked back in a twenty-five-point blowout. The team they had dreaded was beginning to look like a pushover.

In practice Cone tried to curb his team's emerging overconfidence. Yes, Alaska was halfway to the finals, but taking two more games from a team that was undefeated in must-win situations would be no cakewalk. The coach's principal concern heading into game three was Young. San Miguel's import looked sharp through the first two games. He was matching Roe's scoring numbers, beating Nic Belasco and Rey Hugnatan off the dribble, and manhandling the Aces' big men in the paint. Worst of all, Young was averaging close to 10 assists per game. His pinpoint passes—the "sweet pass," as Cone called it—energized his teammates and sparked his own confidence to take over games. While watching a series of possessions late in the fourth quarter of game one, Cone couldn't help but marvel at Young's ability to dominate a close contest. Time after time Young caught the ball at the top of the key, surveyed the court, and then charged toward the basket, where he'd score or create contact with his defender to draw a foul. "Man, Galen just puts the ball on the floor and it's go, go, go, and the refs bail him out every time," Cone said. "You can't do anything about it."

The coaches didn't want to send a chaser at Young, as they'd done against Ginebra's Rod Nealy, because it would only open up another cutter for Young's passes. They decided to give Nic and Rey a consistent approach to guarding the import; that way, at least, they wouldn't feel marooned twenty-two feet away from the basket, wondering which way Young would go and how to stay in front of him. The plan was to always shade Young toward the baseline. Then when he picked up his dribble, the passing lanes would be limited to one side of the court. If he got to the middle, his options multiplied and he became more deadly. Cone expected Young to beat Alaska's defense and score from the baseline a ⌐ times, but he could live with that. "He's gonna put up some big numbers," Cone warned, "but while he's putting up those numbers the rest of their guys aren't going to get involved."

Midway through this symposium there was a quiet commotion on one side of the room, apparently caused by Poch Juinio's silent-but-deadly gastrointestinal combustion. Willie Miller, who had been resting his head in Poch's lap, bolted upright and pulled his shirt over his nose. Before long half the team was peering out at Cone's video from behind towels, washcloths, T-shirts—anything they could use to dull the fumes. A couple stifled guffaws emerged from behind their impromptu masks, and the players' smiling eyes betrayed the laughter they were struggling to restrain. They managed to remain composed, but Poch's inadvertent distraction deep-sixed Cone's atmosphere of playoff intensity.

During Cone's scouting sessions, the coach entered a basketball fugue state. His focus on explaining the game plan was unbreakable. To an attentive audience, this made him a powerful communicator. But once the players became distracted, Cone tended to be so deeply enmeshed in the cross screens and lag passes flashing through his mind that he wouldn't notice the chaos around him. After Poch farted, the levity in the room overtook Cone's fascination with guarding Galen Young. Oblivious, Cone moved on to the next urgent hoops concern—counteracting a move Young used to snatch offensive rebounds when his teammates shot free throws. The video showed Nic start to box out Young, who slid his hand underneath Nic's armpit and then back-stroked him out of position. So far in the series, Young had used the trick to steal at least three extra possessions for San Miguel, and sooner or later it could cost Alaska a game. While Cone discussed techniques Nic could use to counter Young's move, Willie was busy demonstrating to Poch, Eddie Laure, and Rensy Bajar that he could jam a paper Gatorade cup onto his chin and look like King Tut.

"We won those games, fellas," Cone said, "but we can really prove on our game plan."

That set Roe off. "That's why I hope these guys will pay attention and actually improve instead of making the same fucking mistakes over and over again because y'all are in here playing," the import said, directing his frustration at Willie's side of the room. "Pay some fucking attention." An awkward silence followed. With Alaska two wins away from the finals, Roe had chosen an odd time to call out a vital teammate, but he could no longer hold back his disgust. "Let them run around playing for forty-five minutes and let me sit around and rest. Shit."

Scouting ended right there. Cone sent the players into the gym to warm up for practice. On the way out the door, Nic put his arm around Poch, whose gas played catalyst to Willie's antics and Roe's outburst. "You guys fart too much." Inside the gym, Willie covered his eyebrows with a pair of Band-Aids. Giggling, he said, "They don't want me to laugh! Willie-boy needs to laugh."

Games three and four were a near mirror image of the first two, with San Miguel outplaying the Aces throughout except for one crucial quarter. Facing an insurmountable deficit had they lost game three, the Beermen won by ten points to narrow Alaska's lead. After the game, Roe, whose lefty hook shot had been short all night, admitted he was tired. "I caught myself not running the court like three times," he told Nic. "I couldn't move, man. Just couldn't get up and down." San Miguel continued to best Alaska's levels of energy and aggression in game four and seemed poised to tie the series. The Beermen led 68-60 after three quarters, and the Aces' comeback hopes looked weak with Roe resting as the final period began. That's when Mike Cortez, whose performance had ·een uneven since returning from knee surgery, displayed the form that ·ᵈ Cone to call the preinjury Mike Alaska's best player. Over the first ʳ minutes of the quarter, Mike scored or assisted on nearly every ʰ basket during a 19-10 spurt that gave the Aces a one-point advantage. San Miguel couldn't keep him from driving into the lane, where he rebounded his own miss and scored a putback, dished to Rey for a running one-hander, kicked a pass to Eddie for a game-tying three-pointer, and sank two or three of his own picturesque teardrops. That momentum sparked Alaska to a game four win and a three games to one series lead.

When the Aces arrived at practice the next day, they didn't carry themselves like a team that had just seized command of the series. They ambled into the gym on rubbery legs, groaning about Charley horses and tweaked ankles, and they talked as if needing just one more win to make the finals was a burden. In fact, the 3-1 margin was weighing on the players' minds; it was the same situation the team found itself in the previous year against Purefoods. Alaska lost three games in a row and blew that series. Cone chided the players for losing their edge. "We've gotten loose, fellas," the coach said. "Not everyone is taping [their ankles]. That's bad news when you're playing every other day and a sprain could mean you're out for two or three games.* That could cost the whole series, and it shows me you've stopped taking this seriously. We had a lot of fear coming into this series. We thought we weren't ready for this team. Fear can be healthy, fellas. We lost our fear and that caused us to be sloppy."

Prior to game five, Joel Banal's words of inspiration hearkened back to the Philippines' agricultural heritage: "When a fruit is ready for harvest and it's hanging off the tree, don't let it fall off that tree, because then it's too late. It's rotten already. You climb that tree and get it." Perhaps he should have chosen a less flowery metaphor to urge the team to close out the series, because game five was a disaster. San Miguel scored on its first seven possessions. Alaska's out-of-sync offense produced few scoring opportunities; instead, the hesitant players shov

---

* This was another indirect swipe at Willie, who had neglected to have his knee taped before practice—a mandatory precaution—and suffered a mild

passes back and forth like a game of hot potato before attempting last-ditch heaves as the shot clock ran down. Trailing by sixteen points at halftime, several Alaska players had already been charged with three or four personals. In the fourth quarter, with the Aces down more than twenty, the drubbing took on grave implications when Young drew a foul and tumbled into Jeff Cariaso's knee. Alaska's trainers had to help Jeff off the floor, and his severe limp suggested he wouldn't return for game six. When the final buzzer sounded, Alaska still led the series, but the Aces shuffled off the court looking like the 126-108 pasting had broken their will.

No one spoke inside the locker room. Cone stood alone in the showers, the water off, holding the wall with one hand and staring down at the grimy tile floor. He either didn't want to speak to the team or didn't know what to say to them. The players didn't change into street clothes; they just sat in front of their cubbies, heads down, watching drops of sweat pool at their feet. The ball boys handed out spaghetti and implored the players and coaches to eat. The food mostly got pushed around plates and left behind. In two days Alaska would have to return to the arena and defeat the team that just routed them. The pressure would be on the Aces, who had plenty of reasons—San Miguel favoritism, the fear of choking, their mounting fatigue—to want to avoid a game seven. "If it's game seven, San Miguel will win," Mang Tom told me earlier that day, and that likelihood hung in the players' minds.

There was also a feeling that despite leading the series, Alaska's play-off run was close to derailing. After game five Jeff knew his season was over. "That's not how this conference is supposed to end," he told me, away from the rest of the team. "Fuck! We're not even in [the finals] t. When I walked off I thought, damn, this don't feel right. You can when it's hurt but you can still play on it, and this one felt different." ouldn't break the news—a partial ligament tear—to his team- ntil the next day, but they already sensed that they had lost their ff's on-court production wouldn't be that hard to replace;

Mike Cortez was gaining strength and could step in at guard, while rangy swingmen like Eddie Laure and Aaron Aban could compensate for some of Jeff's tough defense. But Jeff was the team's compass. Playing on championship teams had given him a sense of the moment; in close games it was often Jeff who found a way to get to the free throw line or leaked out for an easy layup when Alaska needed it most. And Jeff was everyone's confidante: Roe complained to him about Willie's childishness; Willie trusted him enough to take him seriously; and Cone relied on Jeff for honest reports on tensions among the players. Of course, Jeff would remain with the team in practice and on the bench, but without him on the court, it was unclear who could hold Alaska together.

Nothing worried the team more than Willie. He had averaged only 11 points for the series, and that number was skewed upward by the 19 points he scored—mostly in garbage time—in the game five blowout. Night after night the confidence seemed to be draining out of Alaska's star guard. San Miguel was trapping him every time he caught the ball, stripping it away when he tried to dribble through double teams, and deflecting it when he passed out of them. On the rare occasions that Willie received the ball with room to shoot, he hesitated. Instead of taking shots he had made all season, he held the ball and waited to pass to a big man in the low post. He seemed flustered and committed errors I'd never seen him make. During game four he had a chance to go one-on-one against San Miguel's Willy Wilson. He rocked forward on his pivot foot to push back Wilson, who had been playing him chest-to-chest. He faked a drive, then rocked Wilson back again, then tried another fake. Earlier in the season Willie would have blown by Wilson but now his game seemed to have developed a stutter. The fakes creat hardly any space, but Willie, desperate to score, tried to shoot any He reconsidered in midair, double-pumped the ball, and forced to Eddie Laure. Wilson deflected it, and even though Eddie man recover the loose ball, there wasn't enough time remaining or clock to attempt a decent shot. Willie's indecisive play was a sure sign that San Miguel's pressure had gotten into his head.

Finally, Cone stepped out of the shower room. He hardly had anything to say. The loss was so bad there weren't any lessons to take home. "That can't happen on Sunday, guys. Nothing worthwhile has ever been gotten easily. I don't want everybody moping around here. Let's get dressed and get out of here."

The players changed without speaking. They left full plates of spaghetti lined up on the floor in front of their lockers. On my way out the door I passed the showers. Willie was there, alone. When he saw me pass he flashed a wide smile, grabbed an overhead pipe and began humping air. His swinging dong splattered soap suds on the wall, and I had to duck to avoid the spray. This time, however, Willie's nakedness seemed more melancholy than outrageous, like he was trying to convince himself that he was still Willie "the Thriller" Miller, the PBA's most irrepressible and unstoppable combo guard. But it would take more than exhibitionist hijinks to assure anyone that the same-old-Willie was back. He needed to prove it on the court.

So far in the series, the officiating had been respectable. The San Miguel highway robbery that Alaska expected hadn't occurred. More fouls were called against the Aces than the Beermen,* but the imbalance was no greater than earlier in the playoffs, when a frustrated sports columnist, Ronnie Nathanielsz, suggested that "the PBA is indeed a San Miguel league." Alaska's 3-2 lead seemed enough proof that the referees

---

Many of the games were called close on both sides, with the teams whistled for many as seventy-four fouls combined. Of those seventy-some violations, only ten more would go against Alaska than the Beermen. Cone believed that perfect fifty-fifty split on fouls gave San Miguel an edge when the referees at many, because Alaska shot poorly from the free throw line, largely due percent average.

hadn't prevented the Aces from winning, but instead just ratcheted up the degree of difficulty.

The pattern held through most of game six. Neither team was at its best, with San Miguel maintaining a slim lead over Alaska after each of the first three quarters. At practice the day before, Roe had played with the energy and determination of an import trying to prove himself on his first day with the team. He missed only one or two shots during several lengthy scrimmages. The succession of dunks, mid-range bank shots, and coast-to-coast drives made it clear that despite Jeff's injury, Willie's struggles, and his own homesickness, Roe was ready to beat San Miguel on his own, if necessary. That aggression carried over to the game. Roe attacked every defender San Miguel threw at him. He abused lighter defenders like Wilson and Wesley Gonzales in the low post and drove past slower big men like Dorian Peña and Danny Ildefonso. Roe's 22 first-half points allowed Alaska to go into halftime trailing San Miguel by just two points, 49-47.

In the second half every time a five- or seven-point Alaska run seemed to tip the momentum in the Aces' favor, the referees conjured ways to keep San Miguel ahead. When Mike Cortez chased down the rebound off an errant San Miguel jumper, Rico Villanueva raked him across the arm and the ball bounced out of bounds. There was no foul call; instead, a turnover was charged to Mike. A few possessions later Roe deflected an inbound pass intended for Galen Young. The ball glanced off Young's hand and sailed out of bounds. The officials saw Roe's deflection but not Young's, and the Beermen retained possession. Phantom push and over-the-back fouls salvaged San Miguel's unsuccessful offensive drives by giving the Beermen free throws and extra possessions. San Miguel wasn't playing a poor game. Without help from the referees, they probably would have held a slight lead over the Aces. But throughout the second half, whenever a play didn't work out for the Beermen, the referees gave them a do-over.

At the time I was incensed, but after the game I realized that to feel something rare for a foreigner in the Philippines. Unfortunately, that emotion was utter helplessness. As an outsider in Manila, I always had an escape route. If a coup attempt stirred up the restive public and I sensed danger, or if local officials harassed me for bribes, I could ride my American passport back to a comparatively safer, more equitable society. But since I had attached myself to purely Filipino endeavors like Alaska and the PBA, I couldn't bail at the first whiff of unfairness. I had to choke down the plume of bile rising in my chest and swallow my frustration. After some of the whistles in game six, I started to understand why Filipino basketball fans historically felt so comfortable targeting referees for coin and battery attacks; I sensed why public opinion had been strangely supportive of Robert Jaworski and Big Boy Reynoso after they mauled those officials back in 1971; I sympathized with the vengeful Ginebra crowds who milled around parking lots, waiting until the early morning for a chance to confront the referees. Filipinos were used to getting cheated. Their government did it to them, in various manners and degrees of severity, every day; before that, *our government* did the cheating. People in the Philippines almost certainly would never get a chance to hurl debris at corrupt politicians. They probably wouldn't even get meaningful opportunities to confront public officials in more civilized ways. But given the chance to lash out at crookedness in basketball, they let loose a fury so intense that it seemed like more than a response to shameless refereeing. It felt like a battle cry against a power structure built to serve its leaders and not its people. In game six, while watching what looked like an attempt to fix a basketball game, I felt a fraction of that mass pathos. I could read hundreds of Asian Development Bank and Transparency International reports about corruption in the Philippines and I still wouldn't feel the depth of the country's problems as I had during game six. I was watching something happen that I knew was wrong, and I knew I was powerless to stop it.

With ten seconds left in the game it looked like I was about to re-

ceive a final lesson in Philippine fatalism. With San Miguel leading by
a point, Brandon Cablay crossed over against Willie, drove to the basket, and banked home a runner. There was hardly any contact on the
play, yet Willie was whistled for a foul, and Cablay sank his foul shot to
give the Beermen a four-point lead. Alaska called time-out, then scored
a quick two points to cut the deficit in half. With 3.6 seconds to play,
Alaska fouled Wesley Gonzales, who made one of two free throws to
extend San Miguel's lead to three. Alaska needed a three-pointer to
stave off game seven. Because Mike Cortez had committed his sixth
and final foul to stop the clock and send Gonzales to the line, Cone
wasn't sure who should take the last shot. He summoned Eddie Laure,
then, just before sending the team onto the floor, he changed his mind.
"No!" Cone shouted. "Dale, you inbound the ball." Dale hadn't played
all night, and his job was to inbound the ball for Alaska's Hail Mary.
Dale found Nic Belasco at the three-point line. Three San Miguel
defenders surrounded Nic before he could even turn and face the basket. His only play was to shovel the ball to Dale, who had stepped in
bounds almost thirty feet from the hoop. The twenty-eight-foot prayer
was Dale's first shot of the game; the buzzer sounded just as the ball
reached the rim, rattled around, and fell through the basket. The score
was 92-all. Dale—the erstwhile washout whom Roe once angrily referred to as the PBA's "scraps," who was playing as a ringer in Cebu City
corporate tourneys when Alaska hired him—had just saved the Aces'
season.

It would take two overtimes to settle the game. In the first, Alaska
took a two-point lead thanks to a late three-pointer by Willie, but Young
tied the score on a pair of free throws. Alaska battled back in the second
overtime and seized another two-point advantage, thanks to a pair of
slow-motion drives by John Ferriols and two clutch free throws from
Rey Hugnatan. Down two with twenty-four seconds to play, L.A. Tenorio dashed through the lane and released a floater while gliding i-

John, who stood still with his arms up and then collapsed backward from the contact. When I heard the whistle, I was certain a blocking call would go against John and Tenorio, who made the shot, would receive a free throw to win the game for San Miguel. Instead, the referee waved off the basket and pointed in the other direction. Charging. Given the way the referees had called the game, this was the one ending to game six that no one foresaw. Who knows what the ref was thinking when he made the deciding call in favor of Alaska. The Aces won 113-109. It was like fate intervened and told the powers-that-be they could wait. This was Alaska's year.

"I've never seen refs as obvious as in the last two games," Jeff told me after the win. "But the way we won, with John taking the charge from Tenorio and actually getting that call—it's like poetic justice." It was, and for the time being it restored my faith in the basketball universe.

15

The Gift of Basketball

t turned out that the Beermen's relentless double teams weren't the only thing bothering Willie Miller in the semifinals. After the San Miguel series, I asked Willie's teammates if they expected him to bounce back in the finals, and although all the players remained confident in him, they kept alluding to "the problem with Willie's contract." Cone told me what happened. Due to a managerial mix-up, Willie's contract, which was supposed to expire at the end of the season, had actually expired on July first, between games five and six of the semis. Cone himself didn't know about the situation until about a week before the contract was up, when the team and Willie had to negotiate. They settled on a temporary fix that preserved all the details of Willie's old deal and extended it an extra month. By August, the finals would be over and they would have time to discuss a proper extension. "From an organizational standpoint, we dropped the ball," Cone admitted. "We should have seen that a long time ago."

On a practical level, the oversight didn't make a huge difference. Willie was already earning a maximum salary worth about $90,000 pe year, not including performance bonuses for won games, individ statistics, and playoff success.* According to league rules, he couldn't sign for any more than he was already earning, and Alaska was sure to offer him a multiyear contract at the same max level after the season. Still, it sent a discouraging message—we'll keep paying you until the end of the playoffs, and see if we still want you after that—to the team's most psychically fragile individual, who also happened to be, aside from Roe, its top scorer and most talented player. Of course, Willie played the good soldier and denied feeling any anxiety over his unresolved contract, but it was hard to believe that a player whom coaches were afraid to criticize directly wouldn't take this slight personally. In the semifinals, when San Miguel made taking Willie out of the game their top priority, this compounded the dilemma by giving Willie a reason to doubt himself and his future with the team. He had just played the six worst games of his season, and now Alaska management was telling him they'd prefer to wait until after the postseason to discuss his extension. It was like opening up a black hole of insecurity in Willie's mind and then covering it with a Band-Aid.

Willie's contract woes stirred his teammates' sense of worker solidarity. Many of them had also experienced uncomfortable negotiations with Alaska's front office, which was known among players as one of the league's most frugal. Of course, the Alaska Milk Corporation had an unassailable excuse for the way it handled the Aces—the salaries they paid were as high as the league allowed. But viewed in the funhouse mirror of behind-the-scenes PBA transactions, a maximum deal like Willie's might be considered a pay cut by stars on teams with more free-spending owners and more creative accountants. Whenever team manager Joaqui Trillo was confronted with his franchise's tight-pocketed reputation, he was quick to counter that in 2001 Alaska signed Kenneth

---

Every Alaska player, for example, received an extra month of salary for reaching the semifinals and then the finals. The team's championship bonus was two months of pay.

Duremdes, a former MVP, to the most expensive contract in league history.* This was true, and Alaska willingly signed worthy players to maximum deals; they just wouldn't sweeten the pot with under-the-table benefits or extravagant performance incentives. In another league this principled stand might be considered honorable although not extraordinary; only in the topsy-turvy PBA, where the prevailing ethics permitted a certain amount of graft, could a pledge to obey the rules be interpreted as miserly.

Aside from the moral principle of wanting to do the right thing, Alaska's outwardly scrupulous management of the team stemmed from the company's wholesome corporate image. Alaska sold milk; having clean-cut players and a franchise that played by the rules was a non-negotiable aspect of the brand. I sat down with Fred Uytengsu, who ran the family-owned company and team, to hear the full corporate spiel. Dressed in a painstakingly coordinated dark suit accented with a mauve shirt and burgundy tie, he talked about the challenge of managing a PBA franchise without cutting corners: "There are other things that we want to do. Set a good example, not just in youth and role model situations but as a company. Being a good corporate citizen. Honoring the salary cap. I know some teams are violating the salary cap. It's just obvious. You look at some teams when they've got ten-deep star players, all making max money. Yeah, it's a little bit frustrating when you see the odds stacked against you, and then they have the audacity to say: 'Oh no, we're all under the salary cap.' Bullshit."†

----

* Alaska traded Duremdes to Santa Lucia in 2003, shortly before injuries, age, and weight gain reduced Duremdes to a bench player. By the time Roe arrived in 2007, "Captain Marbel," as Duremdes was known, was still cashing checks worth more than $10,000 per month, and his contract, which was signed before th league lowered max salaries, had become a battered souvenir of out-of-cont spending in the PBA's recent past.

† Franchises that spent so freely on their rosters justified the expense of c so by comparing their team budgets to the amount it would cost to pu

Alaska's players weren't so invested in the corporate image; they were mostly concerned with earning as much as possible during their limited playing years. Besides, the salary cap didn't serve a moral purpose. It was instituted to protect megalomaniacal team owners from spending irresponsibly and hurting not just the league, but also their principal businesses. At the same time, however, the cap did create a level playing field of team-building guidelines, and when franchises ignored the spending limits it threatened the league's competitive balance. The trick for Alaska, Uytengsu explained, was to find players who might not be thrilled about earning less than players on other teams, but who nevertheless were too prideful to let that interfere with the goal of winning. "Before we trade for a particular player, we try to see if he has the capacity to understand and finally live up to our belief system," Uytengsu told me. "It may not be there right away because he was spoiled with another team, and maybe we can break that down, we can break into his inner core and have him really understand. Take Jeffrey [Cariaso], for example. I'm sure he could go and get special favors at other teams. But he's a good person in his heart, and he knows what's right and what's wrong. So we have a player like him, who then can talk to other players who might think: 'I got shafted, man. I don't get that extra perk I got before. I don't get the free car.' I haven't been promised a side contract.' It's worked with some players and it hasn't with others, so we're not perfect in doing this, but we are firm. We're gonna win with pride and integrity or we're not gonna win at all."

Uytengsu delivers a bravura speech. Maybe the Alaska ethos didn't always convince players, but it definitely rubbed off on me. The idea

---

print and television advertising equal to all the free ink and airtime their PBA teams received. For even the most gilded lineups, the ad costs would be almost ~uble the basketball expenditures.

~eam manager Joaqui Trillo, point man for Alaska's contract negotiations, told me about a player who asked what kind of perks came with their offer. ~ response: "Maybe we can give you a few cases of milk?"

that Alaska went against the grain with its straitlaced approach had me pulling for the team to defeat higher-profile franchises like Ginebra, San Miguel, and Talk 'N Text. I wasn't inspired by the honor and integrity of it all as much as the simple underdog narrative: Here was a team trying to do more with less. A squad whose own import, in a moment of frustration, compared his supporting cast to the league's detritus. Yet here they were, poised to win a title.

On the other hand, there was an undeniable expediency to Alaska's value system. The franchise paid lower salaries than competing teams, then explained to the players that earning less would make them better men. It also made the Alaska Milk Corporation wealthier. Alaska officials were always quick to wax poetic about the team's family atmosphere, which was relatively unique among PBA teams. Homegrown players and Fil-Ams forged actual friendships; Cone's relationships with veterans were marked by mutual trust and respect; the players' families spent time with each other away from games and official team functions. All of it was true. The Aces were a tight-knit group. But in the right situation—an aging player, a can't-miss trade—Alaska's familial bonds took a backseat to the business of professional basketball. "Players will be surprised when we make some of the deals we make," Uytengsu admitted. "They just have to understand that the life of a professional basketball player is that you can be traded." Again, he's correct, but for the players who drank the company Kool-Aid and accepted off-the-books pay cuts to be part of this basketball family, it was understandable that they might feel hoodwinked and betrayed. Willie's contract snafu wasn't so severe, but it reawakened the players' dormant perception that Alaska didn't always repay in kind the loyalty and sacrifice it asked of its athletes.

A new accoutrement appeared in the Alaska lounge the week before t Finals began. To accompany Manila's rainy season and the head c caused by its daily swings from stifling morning humidity t afternoon downpours, the trainers placed a plastic bucket filled with eucalyptus oil next to the couches where the players sat. This was the hydrogen bomb of cold remedies. Each whiff of the pungent sludge—I initially thought it was some variant of high-viscosity turpentine—blasted the players' sinuses clear, and judging by the woozy expression left on their faces afterward, also erased a cluster of brain cells. When Jeff and Poch Juinio arrived for practice, they went straight for the eucalyptus. Poch buried his face in the bucket like he was bobbing for an apple, huffed the fumes and emerged coughing and snorting. His nose had turned red, almost purple, and his eyes were watery. Poch passed the container to Jeff, who sniffed cautiously then turned his head to the side, his face scrunched like he'd just been maced.

The redolent goo appeared to have helped eradicate the players' bad memories from the difficult San Miguel series. After surviving the Beermen, Alaska's players and coaching staff thought the team they would face for the championship, the Talk 'N Text Phone Pals, would be a comparative walk in the park. The Phone Pals were a young team with scant finals experience, especially compared to Alaska's multititled veterans like Jeff, Poch, and Nic Belasco. Their import, J. J. Sullinger, had been the subject of replacement rumors when Talk 'N Text suffered an early season slump. The brash, twenty-four-year-old reinforcement's penchant for shooting step-back, fadeaway three-pointers after ten seconds of shake-and-bake dribbling was considered harmful to the Phone Pals' chances; that is, until he started sinking these supposedly low-percentage shots at a high rate and the team surged up the standings. Alaska planned to concede the highlight reel to Sullinger while riding Roe's steady scoring, rebounding, ballhandling, and defense to the championship.

'he maturity gap between Sullinger and Roe was so large that the title seemed ‑ned for the more experienced import. I remember seeing Sullinger at a Ma‑ ‑ghtclub late in the season. He wore a pink polo shirt with the collar popped

For a little extra motivation, several Alaska players and coaches held personal grudges against Talk 'N Text. The telecom franchise first brought Roe to the Philippines in 2001, but they sent him home before the season began because they deemed him too small. Alaska assistant Joel Banal was head coach of the Phone Pals for almost four seasons until early 2006 and led the team to a string of semifinals and finals, but was dismissed for failing to deliver a championship. Months after Talk 'N Text fired Banal, they traded Willie to Alaska. At various points in their careers, Roe, Willie, and Banal had been spurned by Phone Pals owner Manuel V. Pangilinan, and they considered the chance to deny him a title fitting payback.

Pangilinan, the same tycoon who bankrolled the Ateneo team and liked to be called "M.V.P.," also spared no expense on his professional team. If San Miguel owner Danding Cojuangco was the PBA's staid mogul, its Steinbrenneresque boss of bosses, then M.V.P. was the league's Mark Cuban, its Young Turk hell-bent on accumulating championship bling for the chairman's boardroom. During off-seasons Pangilinan sent the Phone Pals around the world on training tours, exposing the team to techniques used by the coaching vanguard of the United States, Serbia, and Australia. Since 2000 the team had shuffled through coaches at the rate of almost one per year, and the Talk 'N Text roster was in perpetual flux, with Pangilinan acquiring as many top-flight stars as possible. The boss's performance incentives were fodder for such leg-

---

and matching pink sunglasses, and he was bouncing around the dance floor in frat-boy glee. This was hardly unexpected, since he was just a year removed from the Big Ten bacchanalia of Ohio State University. In contrast, when Roe hit the town, he tended to play the sidelines, observing the revelry from behind the anonymity of a custom-made fedora. There was nothing wrong with Sullinger's frolicking; he was having the kind of life experiences expected of a twenty-something traveling the world. But based on their behavior on and off the court, Roe seemed the calmer, more serious man. The one who had no time for vivaciousness. The one who was focused solely on the finals.

endary gossip that at the pre-finals press conference, journalists hec-
tored Talk 'N Text coaches and players for hints about their promised
championship bonus and never bothered to ask Cone what goodies
awaited the Aces. Alaska's philosophy—long-term continuity* and
lower bonuses to keep winning itself the primary goal—couldn't have
been more different.

Talk 'N Text and Alaska also played different styles of basketball.
The Aces were a defensive-minded, half-court team that won by out-
rebounding and outworking their opponents while counting on a touch
of offensive dazzle from Willie, Roe, and Mike Cortez. Cone loved to
point out that the triangle was "an equal opportunity offense" that relied on court spacing, sharp player movement, and precise passing. The
Phone Pals had a slew of gifted scorers, starting with Sullinger but also
including two second-year swingmen, Mark "Macmac" Cardona and
Anthony Washington. Both had breakout seasons that year, especially
Cardona, who led all nonimports in scoring. The team based its offense
on isolating these players and giving them space to break down opponents and score via difficult, often spectacular one-on-one moves. The
Phone Pals played pressure defense with an eye toward creating steals
and easy points, not necessarily getting stops. They were quick and athletic, but did not have the team defensive mind-set that they were going
to get low, stay in front of their men, and challenge every shot. Cone
believed that if the Alaska guards could avoid turning the ball over, the
Aces could score easily against Talk 'N Text's half-court defense.

I sensed a mild, slightly haughty disapproval in the way Cone talked
about Talk 'N Text, as if they weren't quite worthy of being Alaska's
final test. The coach had a puritan streak when it came to proper team
basketball. He was a hoops aesthete, and in his mind there was nothing

---

* Cone and his triangle offense had been with the team for more than fifteen
years, and many of the players had spent the bulk of their PBA careers with
Alaska.

subjective about hardwood beauty. It was Willie curling over a baseline screen and catching the ball for an open six-footer; it was Jeff sliding his feet to cut off an offensive player's drive; and it was not Macmac Cardona blindly charging into the lane to shoot a running one-hander over four defenders. With its deep pockets and star-studded roster, Talk 'N Text just seemed gauche. Cone didn't see how a team full of scorers could defeat the Aces. Roe more or less shared this sentiment. "They don't play defense like San Miguel, and I don't think they've been in too many dogfights—real tough dogfights—like we have," he told me before the Finals. "To be honest, I think we could really just dominate Talk 'N Text."

Only Banal, who had firsthand knowledge of the Phone Pals and Pangilinan's largesse, foresaw another struggle. "It's a professional league," was his cryptic response when I asked him about Talk 'N Text's aggressive style. "They're properly motivated, if you know what I mean."

A few days before the finals, I headed to Roe's apartment. I found him sorting through a stack of thirty or so bootleg DVDs he bought that afternoon. At the beginning of the season, when I accompanied him on similar shopping sprees, Roe had seemed buoyant, delighting in the endless selection of plastic-wrapped discs, from the World War II miniseries *Band of Brothers* to Michael Jackson concert recordings. He envisioned collecting enough to start a small-scale Netflix in the Pacific Northwest and reminisced about an earlier PBA tour, when he hired a seamstress to make hundreds of retro NFL jerseys, which he took home to Seattle and sold out of his trunk. Now, however, he poked through the heap with disgust, wondering aloud if any of the films were worth lugging back to the States. The thrill had long since gone from Roe's hoops sojourn. He had logged many more minutes on his couch, splitting time between CNN and pirated versions of *Transformers* and *D Hard* than he had on the court. During the last two weeks of the seas

Roe took on the weary, hard-headed attitude of Bruce Willis's character in the movie, a hostage to a career that kept him alone, on the road, and toiling against long odds for most of the past decade. The Finals were Roe's last stand, and they meant more to him than just another check on his hoops to-do list. More than the wealth he'd accumulated over the years, a title would validate his choice to leave friends and family behind and spend almost a third of his years chasing an orange ball around the globe.

"All season, all the sacrifices everybody has to make, this is the last time we have to sacrifice," he told me, glancing up from the DVDs. "I've been away from home for—God damn—eleven months now. That's my sacrifice right there. And I'm not even gonna have a month's break before I have to go play again. The ultimate satisfaction will be winning the championship. Then I can go to the next team and be like, shit, I didn't even get a rest but at least I won."

And now that Roe had built up this season into a culmination of his life's work, he saw Willie, the man whose help Roe needed most to complete the quest, faltering. The guard's dreadful showing in the semifinals shook Roe's confidence in the teammate he once trusted as his number two scorer. Roe flashed a touch of sympathy for Willie, considering the hostile double-teams San Miguel unleashed on him and Alaska's careless handling of his contract. "You know, there's so much going on with Willie right now, I don't know whether to blame him, or what," Roe said when I first asked about Willie.

But as Roe kept talking, his mood darkened. His duty as an import—playing all but two or three minutes of every game and leading the team in nearly every statistical category—was more demanding than anything expected of his teammates, and he wasn't permitted the luxury of excuses. Willie had been a scorer since he first picked up a basketball. There was no doubt he'd seen hundreds of double teams and traps. By now he should know how to pass out of them, run the offense, and look scoring opportunities by moving without the ball instead of catching it at the wing and going one-on-two. "Damn," Roe said. "How long you been playing basketball in the PBA? This is the first time a team ever ran something against you?" Whatever trust he had in Willie was vanishing, and Roe seemed ready to try and win the next series single-handedly, if need be: "He gets out there and does some good things and he does some bonehead things. So that's why I picked up my scoring, because right now I don't know what I'm gonna get from Willie."

In the last games of the semifinals I noticed Roe freezing Willie out of the Alaska offense—purposely passing to other players, even when Willie was open, to keep him from getting the ball. When I asked about it, Roe snickered. "Yeah, you already know," he admitted. "Fucking right. I'm going where I'm comfortable right now, man, 'cause I don't know what to expect from Willie. It's all about winning." Most irksome, however, was the coaching staff, who kept handing out warm fuzzies to Willie when, according to Roe, what the slumping guard really needed was a kick in the ass: "I get so mad with Tim for not saying nothing to him because everybody's afraid of him going into his shell. I'd rather him go into his shell and sit on the bench and cry instead of being in the game, fucking up and losing for us. Because of Willie going into his shell, I'm going into a rampage. So you pick your poison."

In practice the next day, while the players broke into groups of three and practiced free throws, I asked Cone about the tension between his top two players. The coaching staff had warned him that Roe was starting to give up on Willie, but Cone didn't want to hear it. "I don't look for those things," he said. "I don't think they're good games to play, and I don't think there's a whole lot you can do. You can't force a guy to trust somebody else. So, if he's losing his trust, it doesn't hurt us to start our offense on the other side. But I think Roe's smart enough that when push comes to shove and Willie's playing well, then he will pass to him." Against Talk 'N Text, Cone expected much of the frustration the Aces felt against San Miguel to melt away. The defensive scheme that reduced Willie to a bumbling turnover machine was in the past, and Cone w talking about his star's comeback as if it were a foregone conclusion. "Willie will have a big series," he said, his eye on a grandmotherly fan hugging Willie for a photograph on the opposite side of the gym. "The team that we're playing now is not the defensive team that San Miguel was, and they're not nearly as disciplined, where they'll recognize Willie every time and trap him. Their guards will be able to deny him but once he gets the ball it's over."

Cone was right about Willie and Roe. Willie returned to form against Talk 'N Text, averaging 24 points through the first four games, with many of his baskets assisted by Roe, who, like the willing passer he had been all season, kicked the ball out for Willie's three-point bombs and bounced passes through the lane to the slashing guard. Roe's scoring and rebounding were steady as ever—he averaged 25 points and 15 boards. Both players won the expected accolades, with Roe hoisting a Best Import plaque that misspelled his name "Roselle Ellis" and Willie accepting the league's Most Valuable Player trophy for the second time in his career. The stage seemed set for Alaska's fairy-tale ending. There was only one problem: Alaska wasn't winning.

The series was tied at two games apiece, and Alaska was fortunate not to be behind 3-1. Only in game one did Alaska actually outplay Talk 'N Text. The Phone Pals won games two and three convincingly and were close to vanquishing the Aces for a third consecutive time when Cone engineered a fourth quarter comeback by springing traps on Talk 'N Text's ballhandlers after time-outs. The surprise maneuver led to two steals that Alaska converted for layups on the way to a comeback win. But the game five outlook was bleak. Before the series, Cone worried that the team wasn't taking Talk 'N Text seriously; to them, beating San Miguel was the real test and the Phone Pals were a formality. According to Cone's script, losing game two should have jolted the team from its semifinal honeymoon, but it didn't. Alaska lost game three in the same fashion, struggling to keep pace with Talk 'N Text's frenzied, up-tempo style, and the Aces were only able to salvage the fourth game through Cone's trickery. By then the Aces' blasé confidence had dissolved into panic—the team had let its guard down, and the Phone Pals turned out to be tougher than any opponent they'd faced all season.

The main source of Alaska's dismay was Macmac Cardona. The gangly, six-foot-one shooting guard with a floppy, rust-dyed burr of hair didn't cut an imposing figure on the court. Yet Cardona's demeanor—a scowl affixed to his face with his lips curled in an eternal snarl—set the twenty-five-year-old scorer apart. Like a pit bull, he seemed hardwired to attack. While he was a competent three-point shooter, Cardona's weapon of choice was the drive. Every time he received the ball, he lunged toward the basket and kept defenders perpetually on their heels. The entire league knew that Cardona always dribbled to his right; they also knew that when they forced him left, he would inevitably spin back to his right to shoot. It made no difference. His one-dimensional offense was unstoppable thanks to the one-handed floaters he managed to loft through the air and into the hoop from almost any spot on the floor. These shots earned him the nickname "Captain Hook," but the handle was a misnomer. Cardona's shot wasn't a classic hook, a half hook, or even a baby hook. It was something unto itself, one of those singular inventions of Philippine street corners, where styles of play were learned ad hoc and "fundamentally sound" meant any shooting form that resulted in made baskets. Against Alaska, Cardona's one-hander took on multiple forms: running teardrops in the lane, spinning jump hooks, even twenty-foot set shots. Most of them found their mark. Cone shuffled through his roster of perimeter defenders—Willie, Mike, Dale Singson, Eddie Laure, Aaron Aban—and not one of them consistently bothered Cardona.

In game two, desperate to stop a Cardona-sparked Talk 'N Text run, Cone assigned his last-resort defender—Roe. Taller, stronger, and just as quick as Cardona, Roe should have been overkill, like squirre hunting with a bazooka. When Cardona caught the ball nineteen feet from the hoop on the right wing, he saw Roe and appeared to growl at the import. Cardona's fight or flight response had only one setting. He drove right and Roe cut him off. He drove left and got nowhere. He dribbled in place for a second, openly contemplating his next move, then launched a one-handed jumper from a step inside the three-point line. All net. After the basket, Cone turned away from the court, smirked and shook his head. How was Roe supposed to stop a shot that didn't exist?

I was a secret admirer of Cardona's game. Even though he was the prime mover behind Alaska's potential demise, he was a unique talent not unlike Willie, whose eccentric basketball style was a leitmotif evoking the essence of Philippine basketball. If Willie's freestyle combinations of wheeling pivots and spin shots embodied creativity, Cardona, with his full-throttle hoopward blitzes, was the avatar of desire. I had pulled off only a handful of truly artistic moves as a player—my first spin in traffic,* an alley-oop pass I threw on the run from half-court, a Willie-esque layup I converted over my shoulder while absorbing a violent push—and I remembered them more vividly than any single game a team of mine won. Players like Cardona and Willie, who conjured these transcendent moments every time they took the court, helped me connect with the Philippine game in an elemental way.

Although Cardona's game was inspirational, his on-court persona was repellent. His exaggerated aggression had a put-on quality that left fans feeling put off. He had the heart of an attack dog and the presence of a Chihuahua. Except for the Talk 'N Text faithful, Cardona was the

---

* I was twelve years old, playing at the tiny Carmine Street Recreation Center gym in Greenwich Village. The referee called a travel after my shot fell through the hoop, and fifty-some parents watching on the sideline groaned in unison. After the game the ref apologized. He just wasn't expecting a kid shaped like me I was a chubby one) to make a move like that.

PBA's preeminent heel, the player people bought tickets to cheer against. Not even his remarkable path to the PBA could endear him to fans. When he was a toddler, his mother left to work as a domestic servant in Greece. As a child, he was shuttled between different extended family members' homes and spent much of his time selling cigarettes and newspapers to mourners at wakes outside a Mandaluyong City church. His mother escaped Greece on a ship manned by Filipino seamen and sneaked into the United States, where she settled in the Los Angeles area, married a Filipino-American, and petitioned to have Cardona join her once she gained legal status. He attended Carson High School in California, the same school where Mike Cortez had been a star point guard. Cardona never made the varsity at Carson; instead, he played in public parks and worked at a Jack in the Box. He dropped out in eleventh grade and returned to Manila, where he earned a high school equivalency degree and joined the De La Salle University basketball team as a walk-on in 2001. Among his teammates at the basketball powerhouse was Mike Cortez, the player Cardona supposedly didn't belong on the court with in Carson. Six years later Cardona was playing against Mike in the PBA Finals. It's the kind of rags-to-riches story that would have Horatio Alger creaming in his knickers, but to his legion of haters, Cardona's journey was no reason to cheer for such a foul-humored player.

Cone was less concerned with Cardona than with tempo. Alaska's pre-finals swagger was predicated on forcing Talk 'N Text to play deliberate basketball so the Aces could capitalize on their grinding defense and patient half-court execution. So far in the series, the opposite had occurred. The Phone Pals were making the Aces play *their* game, pressuring and pushing the ball with abandon, galloping up and down the court in search of steals and layups. "The thing that gets me is that they just seem to be able to imprint their will on us," Cone told me in practice. "When you're used to playing up and down, you're much mor comfortable. We can't get them to play our tempo, and it's very uncomfortable for us. And, honestly? I don't want to use him as an excuse, but that's where we miss Jeffrey." A few minutes later Jeff, sitting with his leg strapped into a clunky knee brace that extended from his calf to his upper thigh, picked up the ball he'd been dribbling and pounded it against the floor with two hands.

"I feel so out of shape already," he moaned. He wasn't talking to anyone in particular, but I was nearest to him, so I scooted down the bench to listen. It had been a week since his injury, and Jeff wouldn't be able to run for several more weeks. "I've been waiting three years to get this team back to the finals," he said. "I never thought I'd miss a championship because of an injury." Every game, he'd sit in uniform on Alaska's bench and watch, the brace poking out from below his shorts. Late at night he'd light up Cone's cell phone with text messages describing how painful it was to see the team struggle, knowing that he was Alaska's missing link. Jeff was the team's strongest perimeter defender. No one was going to completely shut Cardona down, but Jeff would have contained him better than any other player on the Aces' roster. The team's composure came from Jeff, and Alaska's inability to control tempo through the first four games stemmed from his absence.

As usual, the Alaska locker room reeked of rubbing alcohol before game five. This evening, however, an anticipatory air cut through the chemical funk. Boss Fred Uytengsu had just returned from his African safari and planned to address the team prior to tip-off. While the players stretched, Cone gathered with his coaching staff in the vestibule connecting Alaska's lockers with the Araneta Coliseum's main hallway.

"Maybe Fred is going to make an announcement," Jojo Lastimosa said. He was floating the possibility that Uytengsu would tell the players about their championship bonus—rumored to be a vacation in California or Australia.

Cone dismissed the notion: "No chance. It's way too early for that."
Cone knew that Uytengsu disapproved of using cash bonuses or team
trips to motivate athletes.*

But the coaches had heard the players' whispers that their Talk 'N
Text counterparts received game bonuses several times larger than the
ones Alaska paid. Even when the Phone Pals lost, they supposedly took
home more cash than the Aces. The staff suspected Talk 'N Text was
trying to drive a wedge between Alaska's players and management. Each
indulgent baksheesh sent a message: *Your team doesn't treat you as well.
Why should you play so hard for them?*

"It's the perfect time for an announcement," Jojo parried. "Game
five. We need to win."

When Uytengsu finally spoke, there was no mention of bonuses. He
held up a book of Vince Lombardi quotes and read a selection of the
NFL coach's sayings:

"Winning isn't everything. It's the only thing."

"Winning is not a sometime thing. It's an all the time thing."

After the gridiron psalms, Uytengsu told the team he missed them
while he was away. "It was killing me not to be able to support you
guys," he said, channeling his inner Tom Landry. "I woke up this morning excited as hell. I take a lot of pride in this organization, because we
play by the rules; we do it by the book. We're decent human beings.
Guys, you are great men. Tonight, you are going to beat the little men."

---

* When I spoke privately with Uytengsu, he was adamant about his desire to
field teams that didn't need any incentive aside from competitive glory. "You
can't just throw money at a situation," he told me. "If you wave more money in
front of a player, that's not going to make him win. Sure, you might get a good
game out of him, but that's really not going to make the difference in the long
term. I tell these guys, especially as we approach big games: 'The papers are going
to write this about you tomorrow. This is the clip that you're going to put in your
diary, that you're going to show your grandchild, together with your championship ring. That's the stuff that's golden.'"

The team knelt for Jeff's pregame prayer. He blessed them, and the Aces charged onto the court.

Perhaps Uytengsu should have taken Jojo's suggestion to offer a more tangible reward. For whatever reason, the Aces came out flat in game five and played what they all agreed afterward was the team's worst half of the season. Throughout the first two quarters they allowed Harvey Carey, the Phone Pals' rugged hustle specialist, to beat them to offensive rebounds. Alaska's guards watched Cardona drive around them, then chanced feeble jabs at the ball from behind. It was classic matador defense, scorned by coaches the world over, and not surprisingly, it had little effect on Cardona, who scored eight quick points. The Alaska crowd tried to pick up the slack by haranguing Cardona with chants of *"Buwaya!"*—Tagalog for "crocodile" and basketball slang for "ball hog," which likened Cardona's affinity for shooting to the reptile's insatiable appetite—and waving long red balloons with the message GO BACK TO HIGH SCHOOL, MAC CARDONA printed in white letters.

Midway through the second quarter Roe had a look on his face that was half disbelief and half frustration with a dash of homicidal wrath. He was resting for the first time that night, and he didn't like what he saw. He watched Dale Singson lunge into the lane to challenge three long-armed Talk 'N Text defenders. Dale sidestepped and sent up a one-handed runner, but the defense had a bead on the shot and swatted it into the crowd. Roe's eyes bulged. He alternated between mouthing silent obscenities to no one in particular and biting his lower lip. He balled his fists, rocked back and forth, and looked to the upper decks for some kind of assistance, but none would come. All the Alaska guards played with Dale's death wish, chucking blind shots at the rim. Meanwhile, Sonny Thoss and Nic Belasco played like they had traded their high-tops for cement clogs. They stood motionless on offense, gazing at the guards' reckless forays to the hoop and fumbling the few passes intended for them. The Phone Pals blitzed Alaska's defense with a barrage of layups and three-pointers. Roe struggled to keep his team in the game. He scored with several short floaters in the paint, but too often Willie and Mike committed turnovers before they could pass to Roe.

Alaska's debacle continued until the halftime buzzer. Just before the second quarter ended, Talk 'N Text point guard Donbel Belano snagged a long rebound, slalomed from coast-to-coast through Alaska's indifferent defense, stopped at the three-point line and rolled in a shot that sent Alaska into the locker room down nine points. Roe was livid. He felt his last best chance at an international championship slipping away. With his basketball career flashing before his eyes, he was ready to express his anger with more than a grimace.

Inside the locker room, he walked past his cubby and lay down on a massage table. His teammates filed in and sat around him. With all heads bowed in silence, Roe began talking about the game to blow off steam. The coaching staff followed the players in, and by the time they entered the room, Roe's rage was free-flowing. With his hands folded behind his head and his legs crossed, he spoke: "You got in the game for eight minutes and you ain't do shit! If I'm gonna be out there busting my ass, you best believe you better go out there and bust your ass. You ain't gonna ride me to death. Fuck that! I'm talking to everybody collectively now, but in a minute I'm starting to get personal."

Cone, equally furious with the team, thought Roe's invectives were some kind of fiery pep talk. Not quite. The coach tried to transition from Roe's tirade into his own halftime oratory. He walked to Roe, gently squeezed his thigh and said, "I got it now, Roe."

Roe bolted upright, looked down into Cone's face and shouted, "Fuck that! You ain't got shit!" He accused the coaches of twiddling their thumbs on the sideline instead of challenging the players. "You guys just stand there collecting a check," he screamed. "What are you guys here for? You don't say nothing! When a guy comes out the game, tell him what he did wrong or tell him what he needs to do. Don't just be sitting there. That's what the goddamn fans are for."

"Fuck you Roe!" Cone shouted, defending his staff, and from there the two faced off in an obscenity-riddled, two minute tête-à-tête as the Filipino players and assistant coaches, most of whom adhered to cultural values of saving face and eschewing confrontation, watched in horror. Here were Alaska's two most vital cogs—the import and head coach—on the verge of attacking each other. Eventually, Cone backed down. The coaches stormed out of the locker room. Roe continued his rampage. To him, Cone's retreat was yet another sign of cowardice. "Yeah, get the fuck out of here," he yelled as they left the room. "Run, you pussies."

Outside, the coaches huddled to discuss their response; this wasn't the halftime game plan Cone expected to concoct. Even though Cone agreed with Roe's analysis of the game, the coach couldn't allow a player to challenge him. "He painted me into a corner where I have to come out swinging," he told the assistants. "If I don't, I could lose whatever respect I have with the rest of the players."

Finally, Cone burst into the room and heaved a six-by-three-foot dry-erase board in the general direction of John Ferriols, who deflected the airborne slab with a kick. The floor was now his, with even Roe watching to see what Cone would do next. He berated the team for their listless play and told Roe he was wrong to disrespect his coaches and teammates. Cone told Roe he was thinking of sitting him for the rest of the series, and the suggestion drew guffaws from the import. Cone stared at him. Fury was boiling behind his eyes. Then he told Roe he wasn't going to sacrifice the title to make an example out of him and dismissed the team for the second half.

The Aces actually responded to the halftime eruption and seized a late fourth quarter lead. Up four with three minutes to play, Alaska submitted one of its finest defensive possessions of the season. They scrambled and harassed the Phone Pals all over the court, until the only shot Talk 'N Text could manage was a rushed three-pointer. Yancy de Ocampo, the Phone Pals' six-foot-eight center, forced a turnaround from about twenty-four feet with the shot clock down to its last five seconds. When I saw the shot go up, I held my breath. I thought the Aces had the game. Talk 'N Text was panicking. One more Alaska bucket could break them, and to win this game would soothe many of the egos Roe had mauled at halftime. Then chance intervened. De Ocampo's shot, an air ball, dropped into Anthony Washington's hands like a perfect lob pass, and Washington was fouled while flipping in a reverse layup. Washington's free throw cut Alaska's lead to one. The Phone Pals seized the momentum and carried it to a three-point win, 107-104. Alaska was down three games to two and would need two straight wins to become champions.

After the game, no one spoke inside the locker room. The white board that Cone hurled earlier had been reassembled with duct tape and now wobbled precariously in the corner. Cone broke the apocalyptic silence: "I'm not so sure what to say. We can come out and quit on the season. I'm not going to say I have a lot of hope right now."

The following afternoon in practice the mood hadn't lifted. Cone stalked into the players' lounge like a pallbearer and announced that he wasn't ready to talk to the team. Instead, he'd meet privately with Roe and a few others; everyone else could shoot around. Willie arrived an hour late and spoke to no one. For once, he wasn't feuding with Roe, but with Cone. Willie had disappeared in game five, scoring six points on six shots, and Cone criticized him in the postgame press conference. "We didn't get a whole lot from Willie," Cone told reporters. "He has to be careful he doesn't get satisfied with that MVP award. Being MVP means showing up every night." It was precisely the kind of direct confrontation Roe had demanded, and Willie, just as Cone predicted, withdrew. He came to practice late so the whole team would know he was upset. He put on his practice uniform but didn't bother to lace up his sneakers. A half hour later he was back in street clothes, lying prone on the bleachers with his arm covering his face. First Poch, then Jeff, sat down next to Willie to coax him out of his forlorn mood. Even Roe reached out to him. He slapped the despondent guard on the foot and smiled, but Willie's sole response was a solemn nod.

Cone was no longer upset about the game five altercation, but he continued to feign anger toward Roe and the team to create tension, which he hoped would stir the players from the complacent muck they'd been mired in all series. "If you're feeling bad, frankly, guys, I could give a shit," he told the team before game six. "This isn't about rubbing each other on the shoulder and making us feel good, because if we lose, we're not gonna like each other anyway. All I care about is are you ready to come out and win this game."

The Aces didn't look ready. Cardona scored on his patented spinning hook the first play, and a couple minutes into the game Talk 'N Text already led 10-2. Alaska couldn't get a stop. Cone tried three defenders on Cardona, including Roe, whom the Talk 'N Text guard lit up with a three-pointer and another one-hander. By the end of the first quarter the Phone Pals had put 34 points on the board and led Alaska by twelve. Cardona was on pace to score 60 points.

John Ferriols hit a jumper from the high post to open the second quarter. On defense, Willie stripped Cardona and rocketed down court to score an and-one layup. Alaska pulled within a point after Willie canned two free throws, Roe scored a putback, and Rey Hugnatan scored on a drive. The Phone Pals had yet to score. Roe shoveled a pass to John beneath the basket, who banked a layup to give the Aces their first lead. This was it—the moment. I no longer felt like I was watching a live basketball game, but the inspirational montage in a movie when the team comes together. The Aces kept scoring—off fast breaks, in the post, off the triangle offense. Cardona tried to stop Alaska's run with a three-pointer. Air ball. Somewhere, I heard "Eye of the Tiger," but I wasn't sure if it was playing in my mind or a nearby karaoke stall. Talk

'N Text didn't put up a point for the first seven and a half minutes of the quarter. When Sullinger finally made a free throw, Alaska had opened the period on a 22-point scoring spree. The Aces carried the momentum into halftime, with Willie whirling and sidestepping past Cardona to score an and-one on the quarter's final play. Alaska never looked back in game six. Willie emerged from his shell to score a career-high 37 points. Maybe Roe was right, and Cone should have been direct in his criticism of Willie all along. Or perhaps Cone played his hand perfectly, using his nuclear option motivational ploy when the team needed it most.

Due to a scheduling conflict, the final game would not be played at the Araneta Coliseum,* the PBA's usual venue, but at a shabbier facility in southern Metro Manila called the Cuneta Astrodome. The Astrodome was the PBA's home for most of the nineties, but since the Araneta's 1999 renovation, the league scheduled only a handful of games each season at Cuneta. A crumbling, turquoise eyesore overlooking Manila Bay, the Astrodome underscored the state of decay on Roxas Boulevard, an eight-lane coastal highway that was once home to glamorous, Copacabana-style nightclubs but more recently had developed a reputation for neon-clad sex fortresses† and its proximity to Smokey Mountain, the infamous, now-closed landfill that was home to tens of thousands of slum-dwelling scavengers.

The walk along Libertad Street from the commuter train station to the Astrodome was a minigallery of Metro Manila street life. The

---

* The Quezon City arena had been booked for the weekend summit of an international Evangelist group.

† One such girlie bar was the Firehouse, reportedly a favored haunt of Ramzi Yousef, architect of the 1993 World Trade Center bombing, who brought his bomb-building, lady-loving act to the Philippines in 1994 before being captured, the following year, in Pakistan.

steady march of jeepneys and motorcycle-sidecar taxis choked the air with exhaust, while adolescent boys in tattered shorts and T-shirts darted through traffic to sell single cigarettes ("One stick!") and individually wrapped mints. Every variety of two-bit entrepreneur—key-cutters, watch repairmen, notaries public—seemed represented along Libertad's sidewalks. Outside the curiously named "New Harlem Restaurant," home of Chinese cuisine, voracious construction workers crowded around food stands to buy fried fish balls and sticks of barbecued entrails. Larger flocks assembled in Libertad's open-air canteens around the glow of television sets tuned to the pregame coverage of Alaska and Talk 'N Text's game seven. Side streets inevitably led to basketball hoops and games of three-on-three. Outside the Astrodome a homeless family slept facedown on sheets of cardboard in a shady alcove that was once the entrance to a now-mothballed telegraph office. I slipped into the arena through a back entrance and headed for Alaska's locker room.

Walking through the Cuneta hallways, I passed bathrooms marked HE and SHE. The reminder NO SPITTING ON THE FLOOR was stenciled on a massive cement buttress. The walls were painted in Easter egg pastels, as if the building's architects noticed how imposing the concrete structure felt and decided to lighten the mood with a Pepto-Bismol–inspired veneer. I noticed fewer upper-class families in the Astrodome crowd; instead, the narrow seats were packed to the rafters with spindly young men in their twenties and thirties, the kind of guys who would probably be playing in the street on any other clear July evening. Washcloths wiped the grit from a day's work off their faces and they inched forward in their seats as the arena's clock wound down to gametime. Whereas the Araneta Coliseum had Starbucks, Wendy's, and Taco Bell franchises, Cuneta's only concessions were a couple hot dog stands and hawkers roaming the crowd with wire baskets stuffed with bags of chips and soda cans.

In the locker room, Cone chose to avoid the standard game seven clichés. He told the team to play Alaska basketball—man-to-man defense and the triangle offense, with an emphasis on rebounding. "Don't be afraid to make mistakes," were his final words of advice. "Go out and win the game. Take chances." Once the players left to begin their warm-ups, Cone turned to Banal. "There's not a whole lot you can control," Cone told his top lieutenant. "It's either going to happen or it's not."

Alaska appeared tired in the first half. They didn't play poorly, but Talk 'N Text beat them to a lot of rebounds, and the extra possessions helped the Phone Pals grab an early lead. I got the feeling that game six had been the Aces' last hurrah. Then, toward the end of the half, Roe was fouled on a drive, and he and Cardona jawed at each other while Roe headed to the free throw line. The teams separated the players, but Roe walked to the Talk 'N Text bench and started taunting the entire team, including Pangilinan, who was seated behind them. The referees called a technical foul on Roe, and when Cardona made the penalty free throw he started nodding maniacally while the entire Alaska crowd booed him. Talk 'N Text held an eight-point halftime lead, but Roe's confrontation reenergized the Aces.

At halftime Roe was once again on the warpath, but this time he wasn't fuming at his own team but at Cardona and the Phone Pals. "You know they're front runners," Roe said, stomping his feet in the center of the locker room. "This is our half. We fittin' to fuck these little kids. They wanna talk shit and get hype? We 'bout to fuck them like little kids." I'm pretty sure Roe's Tagalog-speaking teammates had trouble following this diatribe, since even I was a little bewildered by his choice of words. It didn't matter, because the message was clear. Roe was going to channel all the anger he poured into his game five tirade into winning the championship. He wouldn't let the Aces lose.

Throughout the second half, Roe posted up on the left side of the key and scored on a steady stream of lefty jump hooks. Talk 'N Text seemed afraid to double team him and open the passing lanes, so Roe just kept lofting shots over Sullinger and Washington. In the last minute, Willie crossed over at the top of the key, barreled to the rim and flipped in a finger roll to give Alaska a two-point lead. On the next play, Willie stripped Cardona, walked the ball upcourt and found Roe, ready one last time on the block. His final hook gave Alaska a 98-94 lead with forty-four seconds to play. The players on the Alaska bench rose to their feet, then grabbed each other's arms and shook. *It's really happening!* The Aces needed a stop to put some distance between themselves and the Phone Pals. Talk 'N Text gave the ball to Sullinger, and the import wheeled through the lane, where he bounced off the chests of Roe and John Ferriols. His runner fell way short of the rim, and Alaska secured the rebound.

Down four with thirty seconds to play, Talk 'N Text started fouling to get the ball back. Alaska's expectant bench players were already jumping up and down and Jojo Lastimosa's daughters were weeping tears of joy three seats away from me. The Phone Pals fouled Willie, who coolly stepped to the free throw line. After missing his first shot, Willie glared at the rim and licked his lips. The look of intensity was unnatural on him, like a caricature of determination. His second shot bounced in and out, and Talk 'N Text rushed downcourt and scored on a putback. Next they fouled Rey Hugnatan with fifteen seconds left, and he too flubbed both free throws. The choke was on. The Phone Pals sensed an opening, and I was afraid the basketball gods would punish Alaska for leaving the game in the hands of fate. Jojo's daughters' tears skipped from joy to dread. After a time out, Cardona received the ball and drove on the right side of the court. The defense collapsed around him and he passed to Belano in the corner. Belano's go-ahead three-pointer rattled around the rim, sunk halfway down and popped out. Rey rebounded the ball and was fouled again with a second left and the Aces leading, 98-96. Rey managed to hit one out of two free throws, but Alaska's five misses in the final minute meant a buzzer-beating three could tie the game. Coming out of a time out, Sullinger caught the ball thirty feet away from the basket and elevated for a shot. It was on target and the game appeared destined for overtime. But Sullinger's prayer struck the back of the rim and ricocheted high into the air and away from the basket.

Alaska clinched the title. It was the team's first since 2003, so the wait for a championship hadn't been unbearably long in Chicago Cubs terms, but given how low the franchise sunk after 2003, their turn-around was remarkable. The Astrodome public address system blared Kool and the Gang's "Celebration" while the Aces stormed the court and mobbed Roe and Willie. Most of the crowd followed suit, and before long an impromptu hugging orgy took over the hardwood. There was no champagne, so the giddy players sprayed one another with cans of San Miguel Beer. Uytengsu was in the middle of it, high-fiving and embracing fans and complete strangers. Willie, carrying his two young children, couldn't hug anyone, so he let fans rub his bald pate. Roe stood arm in arm with a portly fan who rolled up his sleeve to expose a shoulder tattooed with the Aces' logo. The festive air was punctured somewhat by pickpockets, who fleeced Uytengsu and several of the players' wives of cell phones, wallets, and digital cameras. It didn't matter, as the victory party continued, moving away from Cuneta's urban griminess to the plush confines of the Hard Rock Café, where the players and Uytengsu sang "We Are the Champions" on stage and drank until dawn.

A few days later Jeff hosted a going away party for Roe. The entire team was there, reliving game seven, laughing at the hard-boiled face Willie made prior to missing his second free throw, and planning for their upcoming trip to California and—where else?—Disneyland. Before dinner, the players, coaches, and their families formed a circle in the living room around Joel Banal, who said grace: "Dear Lord, we thank you for the gift of family, the gift of friends, the gift of basketball. Amen." When I have a family, this will be our Thanksgiving Day grace.

Deep into the night, the players sat on Jeff's deck, arguing over con-

trol of the stereo—Nic wanted New Edition; Poch preferred Fergie—
and watching the distant city lights. The Filipino players brought cases
of San Miguel Pale Pilsen and Light, while Roe chipped in a couple
bottles of Hennessy and Grand Marnier. It was a cross-cultural love fest
that would have seemed impossible a week earlier, capped by Roe and
Willie posing together for a picture. They stood side by side, holding a
roasted pig head in front of them, each player grinning with a crispy ear
between his teeth.

On my way home from Jeff's house, I stopped for a nightcap at Countryside Restaurant, an institution in the Quezon City booze and barbecue
scene. The place wasn't much, just a heap of meat and a grill next to
some aluminum picnic tables and a counter set up along the street.
There was no music, just the buzz of cars speeding past from time to
time. My bottle of Red Horse beer and two skewers of pork intestine
arrived, and I nodded to the chef, who grinned and yelled, "Alaska,
man!" In recent weeks, more and more people had been recognizing me
for my affiliation with the Aces. It was the Mang Tom effect: casual PBA
fans watched games and noticed the people sitting behind the benches.
Because I was a particularly novel hanger-on—tall, foreign, always
scrawling in a spiral notebook—spectators were curious about me. Was
I an injured player? A fourth-tier assistant coach? Poch Juinio liked to
propagate the fiction that I was Tim Cone's son, which led to countless
awkward encounters where self-styled experts asked me to relay triangle
offense advice to my dad. One day, Leo, the longtime employee responsible for washing the players' uniforms, called me "Raffy Boy, the lucky
charm of Alaska." The label stuck, and as the team went deeper and
deeper into the playoffs, I embraced the role.

When Cone agreed to let me spend the season with the Aces, I never
seriously considered the possibility that they'd win the championship.

After their nineties dynasty dissolved, Alaska lost its team identity and spent years as one of the PBA's middling, lackluster franchises. I just wanted to see the league from the inside. But once the Aces reached the semifinals and finals, I found myself rubbing my hands together, crossing my fingers, making the sign of the cross, doing anything I could to give the team a karmic boost. I'm sure my superstitions accomplished nothing, but it didn't matter. I couldn't help feeling like part of the team. I wasn't, but it was the closest I'll ever get to being with a championship franchise. Or a last place squad, for that matter. Now that the Aces had reached the promised land, I dreaded leaving them. Life without Cone's coaching schemes, Roe's weary determination, Jeff's dignified leadership, or Banal's basketball mysticism would lack meaning; and without Poch's silent-but-deadlies, Mang Tom's molested backside, and the constant fear of being flashed by Willie, it definitely wouldn't be as much fun.

My mind drifted to the hundreds of Filipinos I'd met who had somehow been drawn into basketball's orbit: The teenagers practicing Willie Miller jukes and spins in their flip-flops. The beauty queens crowned on their *barangay* basketball courts. Elmer Gonzales, the Cebuano midget who buffed his playing sneakers like they were his most prized possession. Freddie Webb, the PBA legend and former senator who devoted his government career to peppering the archipelago with roofed, cement-floor courts, because when he was young, "Every day I'd come home from school, look up at the sky and ask God, 'Please don't let it rain because I want to play basketball.'" The writer Krip Yuson, who recited his basketball verse, "Larry Bird Smells the Flowers" and "No More Jordan," when I met him at an outdoor coffee shop. And Recah Trinidad, a grizzled boxing scribe with a taste for goat meat and brandy, who took me to his "clubhouse"—a shed skirting a swamp behind his home—and said: "How could you think of Filipino life without basketball? It's not only a pastime; it's a passion. There is no other game." They came from disparate nooks of Philippine society; I came from thousands of miles away. Yet I understood their passion as well and as deeply as anything I've ever known, because the love for basketball that so many Filipinos felt was no different from my own; it was a love that anyone who ever scored a reverse layup in traffic, or stayed in front of a great ballhandler's crossover, or threaded the needle on a pass could understand.

Somewhere in the night—behind Countryside, heading down the hill into the Marikina Valley, I heard the faint, steady thump of a ball being dribbled. I closed my eyes, sipped the beer, and chewed a chunk of intestine. The food and the footwear were different here, but the soul of the game was the same.

ABOUT THE AUTHOR

Rafe Bartholomew is a freelance writer and former editor at *Harper's Magazine*. He received his master's degree from Northwestern University's Medill School of Journalism before traveling to the Philippines as a U.S. Fulbright scholar in 2005, when he first studied basketball's role in the country. His articles have been featured in *The New York Times*, *Seattle Weekly*, *Detroit Free Press*, and Slate, among other publications. His work has been featured twice in the *Best American Sports Writing* series and he's received multiple sports feature awards from the Society of Professional Journalists. In October 2008, he returned to New York City after three years in Manila.

Printed in the United States
by Baker & Taylor Publisher Services